CALIFORNIA'S
BEST TRIPS

33 AMAZING ROAD TRIPS

Amy Balfour, Brett Atkinson, Andrew Bender, Alison
Bing, Cristian Bonetto, Celeste Brash, Jade Bremner,
Bailey Freeman, Michael Grosberg, Ashley Harrell,
Mark Johanson, Andrea Schulte-Peevers,
Wendy Yanagihara

SYMBOLS IN THIS BOOK

✓ Top Tips	📖 History & Culture	📷 Essential Photo
🔗 Link Your Trips	👨‍👩‍👧 Family	🏃 Walking Tour
⭕ Tips from Locals	🍷 Food & Drink	🍴 Eating
↪ Trip Detour	🌳 Outdoors	🛏 Sleeping

📞 Telephone Number	@ Internet Access	📖 English-Language Menu
🕐 Opening Hours	📶 Wi-Fi Access	👪 Family-Friendly
P Parking	✈ Vegetarian Selection	🐾 Pet-Friendly
⊖ Nonsmoking		
❄ Air-Conditioning	🏊 Swimming Pool	

MAP LEGEND

Routes
━━ Trip Route
━━ Trip Detour
━━ Linked Trip
━━ Walk Route
━━ Tollway
━━ Freeway
━━ Primary
━━ Secondary
━━ Tertiary
━━ Lane
━━ Unsealed Road
▨▨ Plaza/Mall
⫶⫶⫶ Steps
)⸱(Tunnel
═══ Pedestrian Overpass
--- Walk Track/Path

Boundaries
--- International
--- State/Province
⌐⌐⌐ Cliff

Hydrography
〜 River/Creek
〜 Intermittent River
⌇ Swamp/Mangrove
⌇ Canal
◯ Water
◯ Dry/Salt/ Intermittent Lake
◯ Glacier

Route Markers
⟨97⟩ US National Hwy
⟨5⟩ US Interstate Hwy
⟨44⟩ State Hwy

Trips
1 Trip Numbers
9 Trip Stop
🐿 Walking tour
↪ Trip Detour

Population
✪ Capital (National)
◉ Capital (State/Province)
● City/Large Town
○ Town/Village

Areas
▨ Beach
✛✛✛ Cemetery (Christian)
××× Cemetery (Other)
▨ Park
▨ Forest
▨ Reservation
▨ Urban Area
⊙▨▨ Sportsground

Transport
✈ Airport
B BART station
T Boston T station
⟨⟩ Cable Car/ Funicular
M Metro/Muni station
P Parking
S Subway station
⟨⟩ Train/Railway
⟨⟩ Tram
U Underground station

2

Note: Not all symbols displayed above appear on the maps in this book

---

CONTENTS

Northern California
p72

Central California
p174

Southern California
p288

Contents cont.

ROAD TRIP ESSENTIALS

Classic Trips

Look out for the Classic Trips stamp
on our favorite routes in this book.

WELCOME TO
CALIFORNIA

California dreamin'? Enough already.
Grab your car keys, slip on your sunglasses
and hit the gas.

Incredible landscapes. Sensational food. And
glimpses of the future in the making on the
USA's creative coast. Already live in California?
Rest assured there are scenic routes,
swimming holes and a gold mine of mom-and-
pop restaurants to be discovered.

California's road trips swoop from the breezy,
wildlife-rich Pacific coast, to the towering
redwoods of Big Sur and the north, to off-the-
beaten-track deserts and gold rush towns,
to big-name national parks such as Yosemite
and Death Valley, and through the vine-strewn
valleys of celebrated wine countries, starting
with Sonoma and Napa.

From backcountry lanes to beachside
highways, we've got something for you. And if
you've only got time for one trip, make it one
of our nine Classic Trips, which take you to the
very best of California. Turn the page for more.

Highway 101 along the Pacific Coast

CALIFORNIA HIGHLIGHTS

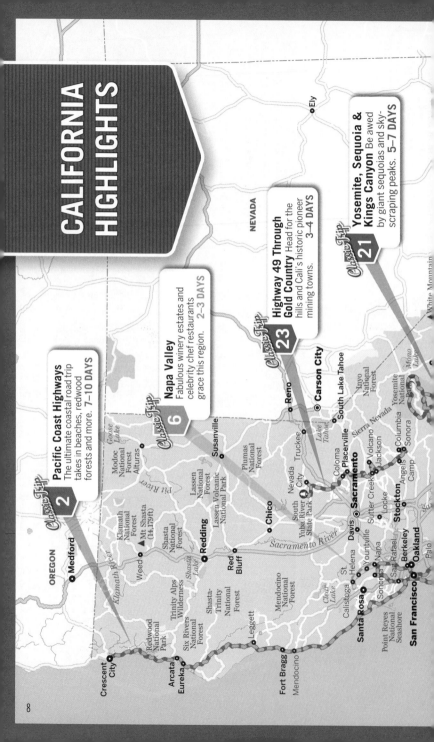

Classic Trip

2 Pacific Coast Highways
The ultimate coastal road trip takes in beaches, redwood forests and more. **7–10 DAYS**

Classic Trip

6 Napa Valley
Fabulous winery estates and celebrity chef restaurants grace this region. **2–3 DAYS**

Classic Trip

23 Highway 49 Through Gold Country
Head for the hills and Cali's historic pioneer mining towns. **3–4 DAYS**

Classic Trip

21 Yosemite, Sequoia & Kings Canyon
Be awed by giant sequoias and sky-scraping peaks. **5–7 DAYS**

8

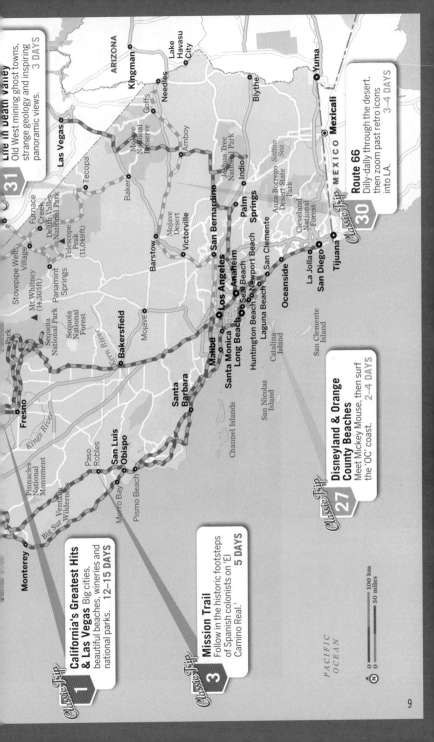

Life in Death Valley
Old West mining ghost towns, strange geology and inspiring panoramic views. **3 DAYS**

31

ARIZONA

Kingman

Lake Havasu City

Las Vegas

Needles

Goffs

Mojave National Preserve

Furnace Creek

Stovepipe Wells Village

Death Valley National Park

Tecopa

Baker

Amboy

Blythe

Telescope Peak (11,049ft)

Panamint Springs

Mojave Desert

Victorville

Barstow

Joshua Tree National Park

Indio

Palm Springs

▲ Mt Whitney (14,505ft)

Sequoia National Park

Sequoia National Forest

Bakersfield

Kern River

Mojave

San Bernardino

Anza-Borrego Desert State Park

Salton Sea

Classic Trip **Route 66**

30
Dilly-dally through the desert, then zoom past retro icons into LA. **3–4 DAYS**

MEXICO Mexicali

Yuma

... Park

Fresno

Kings River

Pinnacles National Monument

Paso Robles

San Luis Obispo

Santa Barbara

Malibu

Santa Monica

Los Angeles

Anaheim

Seal Beach

Long Beach

Newport Beach

Huntington Beach

Laguna Beach

San Clemente

Oceanside

Cleveland National Forest

La Jolla

San Diego

Tijuana

San Clemente Island

Catalina Island

San Nicolas Island

Channel Islands

Monterey

Big Sur

Ventana Wilderness

Morro Bay

Pismo Beach

Classic Trip **Disneyland & Orange County Beaches**
Meet Mickey Mouse, then surf the 'OC' coast. **2–4 DAYS**

27

Classic Trip **California's Greatest Hits & Las Vegas** Big cities, beautiful beaches, wineries and national parks. **12–15 DAYS**

1

Classic Trip **Mission Trail**
Follow in the historic footsteps of Spanish colonists on 'El Camino Real.' **5 DAYS**

3

PACIFIC OCEAN

0 — 100 km
0 — 50 miles

Ⓝ

9

California's best sights and experiences, and the road trips that will take you there.

CALIFORNIA
HIGHLIGHTS

Redwoods

Ditch the cell phone and hug a tree, dude. California's towering giants grow along much of the coast, from Big Sur north to the Oregon border. It's possible to cruise past the trees – or even drive right through them at old-fashioned tourist traps – but nothing compares to the awe you'll feel while walking underneath these ancient ones. Explore Redwood National and State Parks on **Trip 12: Northern Redwood Coast**.

Trips

Redwoods National Park

Palm Springs Aerial Tramway

Golden Gate Bridge

From San Francisco's iconic bridge, pedestrians and cyclists can watch cargo ships navigate the pylons and admire 360-degree views of the rugged Marin Headlands, downtown skyscrapers and tiny Alcatraz Island. Drive across this impressive 20th-century engineering feat on **Trip 2: Pacific Coast Highways**.

Trips

Palm Springs

This chic desert oasis has drawn trendsetters since the early days of Hollywood and the Rat Pack. Today, indie-music's elite swarm annually to Coachella. Live like an A-lister: lounge by your hotel pool with cocktails, soak in hot-spring spas or hike trails through desert canyons and mountain forests atop the headspinning aerial tramway on **Trip 32: Palm Springs & Joshua Tree Oases**.

Trips

Disneyland

Beloved cartoon characters still waltz arm-in-arm down Main Street, USA, and fireworks explode over Sleeping Beauty's Castle. New *Star Wars*–themed attractions bring the force to you. If you're a kid or young-at-heart, this might really be 'the Happiest Place on Earth.' Make a date with Mickey on **Trip 27: Disneyland & Orange County Beaches**.

Trips

Glacier Point Yosemite National Park

BEST SCENIC ROUTES

Pacific Coast Highway (PCH) Cruise oceanfront Hwy 1 in Orange County. **Trips** 2 27

Avenue of the Giants Wind past the world's biggest redwood trees. **Trips** 2 11

Kings Canyon Scenic Byway Descend into California's deepest river canyon. **Trips** 1 21

Ebbetts Pass Scenic Byway Climb over the Sierra Nevada from Gold Country to Lake Tahoe. **Trip** 24

Eastern Sierra Scenic Byway Traces the rugged backside of the Sierra Nevada mountains **Trip** 22

Yosemite National Park

Everything is enormous in Yosemite, whether it's thunderous waterfalls, a hulking granite dome or a grove of soaring giant sequoias. Conservationist John Muir dubbed the place a temple. For your own sublime views, perch at Glacier Point under a full moon or along high-elevation Tioga Rd on **Trip 21: Yosemite, Sequoia & Kings Canyon National Parks**.

Trips 1 21

Big Sur Bixby Bridge above Rainbow Canyon

Big Sur

Hidden by redwood forests, the bohemian Big Sur coast keeps its secrets for those who will savor them: hidden hot springs, waterfalls and beaches where the sand is tinged purple or where gigantic chunks of jade have been found. Don't forget to look skyward to catch sight of endangered California condors soaring above craggy sea cliffs on **Trip 15: Big Sur**.

Trips

BEST SMALL TOWNS

Bolinas A not-so-secret coastal hamlet in Marin County. **Trip** 4

Calistoga For Napa Valley's blue-jeans-and-boots crowd and hot-springs lovers. **Trips** 1 6

Avila Beach Sunny beach boardwalk and a creaky fishing pier. **Trip** 18

Nevada City Atmospheric Old West mining town newly reenergized. **Trip** 23

Arcata Bohemian counter-culture behind the Redwood Curtain. **Trips** 2 12 13

15

Monterey Monterey Bay Aquarium

Santa Monica Pacific Park's Ferris wheel on Santa Monica Pier

Lake Tahoe

The Sierra Nevada mountains flank this four-season playground. In summer, clear blue waters invite splashing, kayaking and boating, while mountain bikers careen and hikers stride on trails through pine forests. In winter, ski Olympic-worthy runs or snowshoe under the moon then retreat to your cozy lakefront cottage to toast s'mores by the fire pit. **Trip 20: Lake Tahoe Loop** is adventure ready.

Trip

Monterey

Forget Hollywood visions of sun-soaked beaches. Instead imagine John Steinbeck and his novels of American realism set on this rugged peninsula. To meet local wildlife, hop aboard a whale-watching cruise in the bay or step inside Cannery Row's renowned aquarium. Then poke around the West Coast's oldest continuously operating lighthouse on **Trip 17: Around Monterey & Carmel**.

Trips

Santa Monica

Route 66 ends at California's quintessential golden beach. Learn to surf, ride a solar-powered Ferris wheel, catch jaw-dropping sunsets from an old-school pier, amaze the kids at the aquarium's tidal touch pools or just dip your toes in the water and relax. Experience it all on **Trip 1: California's Greatest Hits & Las Vegas**.

Trips 1 2 29 30

17

Joshua Tree National Park

Whimsical-looking Joshua trees define this park, where the Colorado and Mojave deserts converge. This is one of California's top places to rock climb, but even kids can scramble around the larger-than-life boulders. Hikers seek fan-palm oases fed by springs and streams. See spring wildflowers on **Trip 32: Palm Springs & Joshua Tree Oases**.

Trips

Sonoma County

Amid the sun-dappled vineyards and pastoral ranchlands of 'Slow-noma,' the uniqueness of *terroir* is valued more than a winery's fine-art collection. In this down-to-earth wine region, which is also known for making fine artisanal food, craft beer and spirits, you might taste new vintages straight from the barrel. Who cares if it's not even noon yet? Conventions need not apply on **Trip 7: Sonoma Valley**.

Trips

(left) **Joshua Tree National Park** Bouldering;
(below) **Sonoma County** Vineyard with an oak tree

San Diego's Beaches

Cruise past impossibly white sands on Coronado's Silver Strand, then stop for cotton candy and a roller-coaster ride at Mission Beach. La Jolla sits pretty atop rocky bluffs, a whisper's breath from the sea, while beyond stretches an eclectic line-up of North County beach towns. Whatever you've been dreaming about for your SoCal beach vacation, find it on **Trip 28: Fun on the San Diego Coast**.

Trips

BEST ROADSIDE ODDITIES

Trees of Mystery Animatronic Paul Bunyan in the redwoods. **Trip** 12

Solvang Where windmills collide with Danish village kitsch. **Trips** 3 19

Elmer's Place Folk-art 'bottle trees' on Route 66. **Trip** 30

World's Biggest Dinosaurs Concrete behemoths outside Palm Springs. **Trip** 1

Mirage Volcano Erupting nightly on the Las Vegas Strip. **Trip** 1

19

IF YOU LIKE...

Death Valley Zabriskie Point (Trip 31)

Beaches

With more than 1100 miles of Pacific coastline, California is a beach lover's dream. Northern beaches are all about crashing waves, rocky tidepools and solitary strolls along the continent's edge. If you're dreaming of golden strands lapped by frothy surf and bronzed bods hanging out in lifeguard huts, head to SoCal.

27 Disneyland & Orange County Beaches Over 40 miles of surf, sand and sun in the OC.

28 Fun on the San Diego Coast Take your pick of ritzy or bohemian beach towns.

18 Around San Luis Obispo Steal away to the Central Coast's laidback beaches.

12 Northern Redwood Coast Walk rocky headlands past tidepools and barking sea lions.

History

Gold mining is the usual reason given for the madcap course of California's history. Yet Native American tribes, Spanish missionaries and conquistadors, Mexican ranchers, and later waves of immigration to the Golden State have all left important traces too.

23 Highway 49 Through Gold Country Follow the footsteps of 19th-century gold seekers, bordello keepers and outlaws.

3 Mission Trail Trace the path of Spanish colonialists and Catholic priests through 'Alta California.'

31 Life in Death Valley Where the dreams of miners and pioneers are just ghosts today.

30 Route 66 Watch tumbleweeds roll along on the USA's 'Mother Road.'

Food & Wine

In California, star chefs' menus show off ingredients sourced from local farmers, fishers, ranchers and artisan food makers. As for wine? Although Napa Valley is the most famous, California's other wine regions more than hold their own.

5 Bay Area Culinary Tour Sample farmers markets and the sources of California's cuisine.

7 Sonoma Valley Napa's rustic-chic country cousin is a patchwork of pastoral farms and vineyards.

19 Santa Barbara Wine Country Where the hit movie *Sideways* romped, find seriously sophisticated vintages.

23 Highway 49 & Gold Country Sip Zinfandel in the Sierra Nevada foothills and explore the farms of Apple Hill.

Ebbetts Pass Mosquito Lakes in summertime (Trip 24)

Family Trips

The Golden State thrills pint-sized travelers. Just keep them covered in sunblock! Southern California's theme parks are something special, but sunny beaches, cool mountains and lakes, and natural wonders are also top contenders for family fun.

27 Disneyland & Orange County Beaches Families are all smiles at Disneyland. Afterwards cruise coastal Hwy 1.

21 Yosemite, Sequoia & Kings Canyon National Parks Giant sequoia trees and huge waterfalls amaze the kids.

20 Lake Tahoe Loop Drive around the 'Big Blue' for swimming, ziplines and skiing.

28 Fun on the San Diego Coast Tour the zoo's wild safari park, then treat tots to Legoland.

Parks & Wildlife

California's national and state parks protect an astonishing diversity of life zones, from misty redwood forests to snowy mountain peaks to marine sanctuaries where migratory whales breach.

21 Yosemite, Sequoia & Kings Canyon National Parks Don't miss the Sierra Nevada's prime-time parks, with wildflower meadows, vistas and wildlife galore.

12 Northern Redwood Coast See sandy beaches and calm lagoons where migratory birds flock, plus the tallest trees on earth.

14 Volcanic Legacy Byway Find alpine lakes, volcanic peaks, hot-spring 'hells' and more.

32 Palm Springs & Joshua Tree Oases Clamber through a wonderland of rocks and flowering desert gardens.

Backwoods Byways

Far from coastal California's bumper-to-bumper freeways, these scenic backroads and country highways let you finally lose the crowds – and maybe yourself – in cinematic landscapes of jagged peaks, rushing rivers and placid lakes.

13 Trinity Scenic Byway Watch for bald eagles (or Bigfoot!) as you dangle a fishing pole in lakes.

22 Eastern Sierra Scenic Byway Explore real Wild West landscapes, from Mt Whitney to the ghost town of Bodie.

24 Ebbetts Pass Scenic Byway Take this rugged route over the Sierra Nevada to Lake Tahoe.

25 Feather River Scenic Byway Wind through a peaceful river canyon up unto the 'Lost Sierra.'

NEED ^{TO} KNOW

CURRENCY
US dollars ($)

LANGUAGE
English

VISAS
Generally not required for citizens of Visa Waiver Program (VWP) countries with ESTA approval (apply online at least 72 hours in advance).

FUEL
Gas stations are everywhere, except in national parks and sparsely populated areas. Expect to pay around $3 per US gallon.

RENTAL CARS
Car Rental Express (www.carrentalexpress.com)

Enterprise (www.enterprise.com)

Simply Rent-a-Car (www.simplyrac.com)

Super Cheap! Car Rental (www.supercheapcar.com)

IMPORTANT NUMBERS
American Automobile Association (AAA; ☏800-922-8228)

Emergencies (☏911)

Highway conditions (☏800-427-7623)

Climate

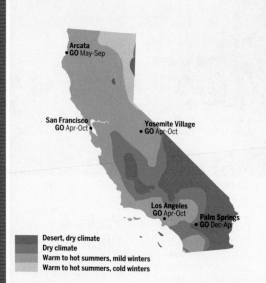

Arcata
● GO May-Sep

San Francisco
GO Apr-Oct ●

Yosemite Village
● GO Apr-Oct

Los Angeles
GO Apr-Oct ●

Palm Springs
● GO Dec-Apr

■ Desert, dry climate
■ Dry climate
■ Warm to hot summers, mild winters
■ Warm to hot summers, cold winters

When to Go

High Season (Jun–Aug)
» Accommodations prices up 50% to 100% on average.

» Major holidays are even busier and more expensive.

» Summer is low season in the desert, where temperatures exceed 100°F (38°C).

Shoulder (Apr–May & Sep–Oct)
» Crowds and prices drop, especially on the coast and in the mountains.

» Mild temperatures and sunny, cloudless days.

» Typically wetter in spring, drier in autumn.

Low Season (Nov–Mar)
» Accommodations rates lowest along the coast.

» Chilly temperatures, frequent rainstorms and heavy snow in the mountains.

» Winter is peak season in SoCal's desert regions and at ski resorts.

Your Daily Budget

Budget: Less than $100
» Hostel dorm beds: $32–62

» Take-out meal: $8–12

Midrange: $100–200
» Two-star motel or hotel double room: $100–150

» Rental car per day, excluding insurance and gas: $35–87

Top End: More than $200
» Three-star hotel or beach resort room: $195–300

» Three-course meal in top restaurant: $75–100

Eating

Roadside diners and cafes Cheap and simple.

Beach shacks Casual burgers, shakes and seafood.

National, state and theme parks Mostly so-so, overpriced cafeteria-style or deli picnic fare.

Eating price indicators represent the average cost of a main course at dinner:

$	less than $15
$$	$15–25
$$$	more than $25

Sleeping

Motels and hotels Ubiquitous along well-trafficked highways and in busy tourist areas.

Camping and cabins Ranges from rustic campsites to luxury 'glamping' resorts.

B&Bs Quaint, romantic inns in urban and rural areas.

Hostels Cheap and basic; almost exclusively in cities.

Sleeping price indicators represent the average cost of a double room with private bathroom during high season:

$	less than $150
$$	$150–250
$$$	more than $250

Arriving in California

Los Angeles International Airport (LAX) Taxis to most destinations ($30 to $50) take 30 minutes to one hour. Door-to-door shuttles ($12 to $29) operate 24 hours. FlyAway bus runs to downtown LA ($9.75). Free airport shuttles to LAX City Bus Center and Metro Rail station.

San Francisco International Airport (SFO) Taxis into the city ($48 to $68) take 25 to 50 minutes. Door-to-door shuttles ($19 to $23) operate 24 hours. BART trains to downtown San Francisco ($9.65, 30 minutes) leave the airport between 6:34am and 10:09pm daily.

Cell Phones

The only foreign phones that will work in the USA are GSM multiband models. Network coverage is often spotty in remote and rural areas.

Internet Access

Wi-fi (free or fee-based) is available at most lodgings, coffee shops and public libraries.

Money

ATMs are widely available. Credit cards are accepted almost universally and are usually required for reservations.

Tipping

Tipping is expected, not optional. Standard tipping is 18% to 20% in restaurants, 15% for taxi drivers, $1 minimum per drink in bars, and $2 per bag for porters.

Useful Websites

California Travel & Tourism Commission (www.visitcalifornia.com) Multilingual trip-planning guides.

Lonely Planet (www.lonelyplanet.com/usa/california) Destination info, hotel bookings, travelers forums and more.

Sunset (www.sunset.com/travel/california) Local and insider travel tips.

Opening Hours

Businesses, restaurants and shops may close earlier and on additional days during the off-season (usually winter, except summer in the deserts).

Bars 5pm to 2am daily

Business hours (general) 9am to 5pm Monday to Friday

Restaurants 7:30am to 10:30am, 11:30am to 2:30pm, 5pm to 9pm daily, some later Friday and Saturday

Shops 10am to 6pm Monday to Saturday, noon to 5pm Sunday (malls open later)

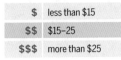

For more, see Road Trip Essentials (p360).

CITY GUIDE

SAN FRANCISCO

Ride the clanging cable cars up unbelievably steep hills, snake down Lombard St's famous hairpin turns, cruise through Golden Gate Park and drive across the arching Golden Gate Bridge. Then get lost in the creatively offbeat neighborhoods of California's capital of weird.

San Francisco Coit Tower and downtown at sunset

Getting Around

Avoid driving downtown. Cable cars are slow and scenic (single-ride $8). MUNI streetcars and buses are faster but infrequent after 9pm (fares $2.50 to $3). BART (tickets from $2.10) runs high-speed Bay Area trains. Taxis cost $2.75 per mile; meters start at $3.50.

Parking

Street parking is scarce. Meters take coins, credit cards and pay-by-phone or SFMTA parking cards. Overnight hotel parking can be as high as $62 per night; downtown parking garages start at $2.25 per hour or from $18 per day.

Where to Eat

The Ferry Building, Mission District and South of Market (SoMa) are foodie faves. Don't miss the city's farmers markets.

Where to Stay

The Marina is near the family-friendly waterfront and Fisherman's Wharf. Union Square and SoMa are most expensive, but conveniently located for walking.

Useful Websites

San Francisco Travel (www.sanfrancisco.travel) Destination info, events calendar and accommodations bookings.

SF Station (www.sfstation.com) Nightlife, restaurants, shopping, events and the arts.

Lonely Planet (www.lonelyplanet.com/usa/san-francisco) Travel tips, travelers' forums and hotel and hostel bookings.

Trips Through San Francisco

1 2 3 4 5

For more, check out our city and country guides. www.lonelyplanet.com

TOP EXPERIENCES

➡ Golden Gate Bridge

Sunny days suit most cities just fine, but San Francisco saves its most dramatic Golden Gate Bridge views for when fog swirls around the towers, and romantics and photographers rejoice.

➡ Cruise to Alcatraz

No prisoner is known to have escaped alive from the USA's most notorious jail – but after you enter D-Block solitary, the swim through riptides might seem worth a shot.

➡ Ferry Building Feasts

Global food trends start in San Francisco. To see what's next on the menu, head to the Ferry Building, the city's monument to local, sustainable food.

➡ Golden Gate Park

Join San Franciscans doing what comes naturally: roller-discoing, drum-circling, sniffing orchids, petting sea stars and strolling toward the Pacific.

➡ Ride a Cable Car

Carnival rides can't compare to cable cars, San Francisco's vintage public transit. Regulars grip the leather hand-straps, lean back, and ride downhill slides like surfers.

➡ Mission District Murals

See garage doors, billboards and storefronts transformed into more than 500 visual portrayals of community pride, social commentary and political dissent. Balmy Alley has some of the oldest murals.

➡ Climb Coit Tower

Wild parrots might mock your progress up Telegraph Hill, but they can't expect to keep panoramic scenery like this to themselves.

LOS ANGELES

Yes, the City of Angels is the land of starstruck dreams and Hollywood magic. And the stereotypes often hold some truth: celebrity worship, Botoxed blondes and endless traffic. But it's also California's most ethnically diverse city, with new immigrants arriving daily, infusing LA's ever-evolving arts, music and food scenes.

Getting Around

Freeway traffic jams are endless, but worst during extended morning and afternoon rush hours. LA's Metro operates slower buses and speedier subway and light-rail trains (fares $1.75), with limited night services. DASH minibuses (single-ride 50¢) zip around downtown. Santa Monica's Big Blue Bus (fare $1.25) connects West LA. Taxis cost $2.70 per mile; meters start at $2.85.

Parking

Street parking is limited. Meters take coins and credit and debit cards. Valet parking is ubiquitous, typically $5 to $10 plus tip. Overnight hotel parking averages $30 to $50.

Los Angeles Hollywood Boulevard

TOP EXPERIENCES

➡ Do Downtown

Rub shoulders with fashionistas, sip cocktails in sleek lounges, sample global cuisine and get a dose of arts and culture in glam-yet-gritty DTLA.

➡ Experience Venice

Mingle with snake charmers, tarot readers, body builders and skaters on the boardwalk, not far south of Santa Monica's beautiful beach and pier. Murals and cool architecture too.

➡ See Stars in Hollywood

Traipse along the Hollywood Walk of Fame past historic theaters, then hit the bars and clubs for a night of tabloid-worthy debauchery.

➡ Getty Center at Sunset

Feel your spirits soar on a hilltop in West LA, surrounded by fantastic art, architecture, views and gardens.

Where to Eat

Food trucks and pop-up kitchens are a local obsession. Downtown LA cooks up a global mix, with Little Tokyo, Chinatown, Thai Town, Koreatown and Latin-flavored East LA nearby. Trend-setting eateries pop up in Hollywood, Santa Monica and Venice.

Where to Stay

For beach life, escape to Santa Monica or Venice. Long Beach is convenient to Disneyland and Orange County. Party people adore Hollywood and West Hollywood (WeHo). Culture vultures head to Downtown LA.

Useful Websites

LA Inc (www.discoverlosangeles.com) City's official tourism website for trip planning.

LA Weekly (www.laweekly.com) Arts, entertainment, dining and an events calendar.

Trips Through Los Angeles

`1` `2` `3` `29` `30`

San Diego Downtown in the morning

SAN DIEGO

San Diego shamelessly promotes itself as 'America's Finest City.' Smug? Maybe, but it's easy to see why. The weather is idyllic, with coastal high temperatures hovering around 72°F/22°C year-round. Wander Balboa Park's museums and gardens, laze on the beaches and then party in the Gaslamp Quarter after dark.

Getting Around

Driving is how most people get around. MTS operates a metro-area network of buses, trolleys and trains (one-way $2.50, day pass $6, plus $2 one-time card fee). Taxi meters start at $2.80, plus $3 per mile.

Parking

Street parking is crowded. Meters take coins and credit cards, some accept cell-phone payments. Valet parking, public lots and garages downtown cost from $10. Overnight hotel parking runs $13 to $50.

Where to Eat

Hit the Gaslamp Quarter for creative cuisine, Hillcrest for casual and international fusion eats, and beach towns for seafood and craft beer. Mexican food and the city's famous fish tacos are everywhere.

Where to Stay

Boutique and luxury hotels are in the Gaslamp Quarter and around downtown. Old Town has chain hotels and motels, as does Mission Valley inland. Beach towns near kid-friendly attractions have the biggest range of lodgings, from Coronado north to Carlsbad.

Useful Websites

San Diego.org (www.sandiego.org) City's official tourism site for trip planning and events.

San Diego Reader (www.sandiegoreader.com) Nightlife, arts, entertainment and an events calendar.

Trips Through San Diego 2 3 28

Las Vegas Bellagio Hotel water fountains

LAS VEGAS

Las Vegas rises from the desert like an oasis of indulgence. If you're behind the wheel and a Sin City first-timer, arrive after dark. As you approach the city, pull over and admire the neon glow from afar. Then cruise Las Vegas Blvd (aka the Strip).

Getting Around

Traffic jams on the Strip and the I-15 Fwy are common. Buses run 24/7 between the Strip and downtown (24-hour pass $8). Fast monorail trains (single-ride $5, 24-hour pass $13) make limited stops, mostly by the Strip. Taxi meters start at $3.50, plus $2.76 per mile.

Parking

Free self-parking and valet parking at casino hotels is rapidly disappearing downtown and on the Strip. Rates vary wildly. Street parking downtown is metered; meters accept credit and debit cards, coins and payment from a smartphone app.

Where to Eat

Casino hotels have the full gamut of dining options, from all-you-can-eat buffets to celebrity chefs' restaurants. Downtown, head to Fremont East and the Container Park to find local eateries. West of the Strip, Chinatown has scores of Asian kitchens.

Where to Stay

The Strip has the biggest range of casino hotels, from budget to luxury. Downtown has cheaper casino digs, sketchy motels and hostels. More casinos and chain motels and hotels are found just east and west of the Strip.

Useful Websites

Las Vegas Convention and Visitors Authority (www.lasvegas.com) Official tourist information site.

Las Vegas Weekly (www.lasvegasweekly.com) Nightlife, arts, dining, entertainment and an events calendar.

Trips Through Las Vegas 1

CALIFORNIA
BY REGION

The amazing thing about driving California's highways and byways is that sights get more dramatic with every winding mile – trees get bigger, mountain peaks higher and beaches more idyllic. It's enough for a lifetime of road trips.

Northern California
p73

San Francisco is the launchpad for leisurely drives around coastal Marin County and NorCal's bucolic Wine Country, or more rugged adventures further north in the realm of ancient redwood groves, peaked volcanoes and sparkling mountain lakes.

Taste Napa Valley wine on Trip 6

See redwood trees on Trip 12

Central California
p175

Explore the craggy shores of the state's gorgeous Central Coast, stretched between San Francisco and Los Angeles, and bordered by beaches, lighthouses and vineyards. Or dart inland to the majestic Sierra Nevada, with its national parks, high-elevation passes, whitewater rivers and historical gold-mining country.

Get wild in Big Sur on Trip `15`

Discover Yosemite National Park on Trip `21`

Southern California p289

SoCal is a place of extremes, where you can motor from the lowest and hottest place on the continent to hot-springs oases in the desert outside LA. Or just kick back on the coast, where surfers, bronzed beach beauties and kids all cavort.

Hit the OC's beaches on Trip `27`

Drive into Death Valley on Trip `31`

What is a Classic Trip?

All the trips in this book show you the best of California, but we've chosen nine as our all-time favorites. These are our Classic Trips – the ones that lead you to the best of the iconic sights, the top activities and the unique California experiences. Turn the page to see our cross-regional Classic Trips, and look out for more Classic Trips on the following pages:

Left: Riding along Route 66
Above: Balboa Park Bell Tower, San Diego

33

Classic Trip

California's Greatest Hits & Las Vegas

This epic road trip hits the all-time greats of the Golden State plus a slew of fascinating spots along the way, ultimately stopping in glitzy Las Vegas, Nevada.

1

TRIP HIGHLIGHTS

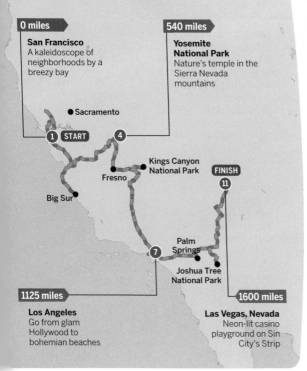

0 miles

San Francisco
A kaleidoscope of neighborhoods by a breezy bay

● Sacramento

1 START

4

Kings Canyon National Park

● Fresno

Big Sur

540 miles

Yosemite National Park
Nature's temple in the Sierra Nevada mountains

FINISH
11

7

Palm Springs

Joshua Tree National Park

1125 miles

Los Angeles
Go from glam Hollywood to bohemian beaches

1600 miles

Las Vegas, Nevada
Neon-lit casino playground on Sin City's Strip

12–15 DAYS
1600 MILES / 2575KM

GREAT FOR...

BEST TIME TO GO

June to September for sunny days and snow-free mountain roads.

ESSENTIAL PHOTO

Waterfalls and iconic peaks from Tunnel View in Yosemite Valley.

BEST FOR FOOD & DRINK

Napa Valley wineries and star chefs' tables.

California's Greatest Hits & Las Vegas

California is big, so seeing its most famous places all in one trip could mean resigning yourself to driving boring multilane freeways for hours on end. But forget that. Instead, this super-sized drive connects the dots on scenic state highways and local back roads, with a minimum of mind-numbing empty miles between San Francisco, Yosemite National Park, Los Angeles and Las Vegas.

TRIP HIGHLIGHT

① San Francisco

In two action-packed days, explore **Golden Gate Park** (https://goldengatepark. com; btwn Stanyan St & Great Hwy; **P**; 5, 7, 18, 21, 28, 29, 33, 44, N), spy on sea lions lolling around **Pier 39** (415-623-4734; www.pier39.com; cnr Beach St & the Embarcadero; 24hr; ; 47, Powell-Mason, E, F) at Fisherman's Wharf and saunter (p170) through the streets of busy **Chinatown** to the Italian sidewalk cafes of **North Beach**. Feast on an overstuffed burrito in the **Mission District** after wandering its mural-splashed alleys. Queue up at Powell and Market

Sts for a ride on a bell-clanging cable car (fare $8) and then cruise to the infamous prison island of **Alcatraz** (Alcatraz Cruises 415-981-7625; www. alcatrazcruises.com; tours adult/child 5-11yr day $39.90/24.40, night $47.30/28, behind the scenes $92.30, over 12yr only; call center 8am-7pm, ferries depart Pier 33 half-hourly 8:45am-3:50pm; night tours 5:55pm & 6:30pm;) out in the bay. Book Alcatraz tickets online at least two weeks ahead. At the foot of Market St, indulge your inner epicurean at the food stalls of the **Ferry Building** (415-983-8000; www.ferrybuilding marketplace.com; cnr Market St & the Embarcadero; 10am-7pm Mon-Fri, 8am-6pm Sat, 11am-5pm Sun; ; 2, 6,

9, 14, 21, 31, Embarcadero, Embarcadero), and stop by its **farmers market** (415-291-3276; www.cuesa. org; street food $3-12; 10am-2pm Tue & Thu, from 8am Sat;) year-round to wallow in the bounty of California-grown prod-uce and gourmet prepared foods. Inside the historic **Castro Theatre**

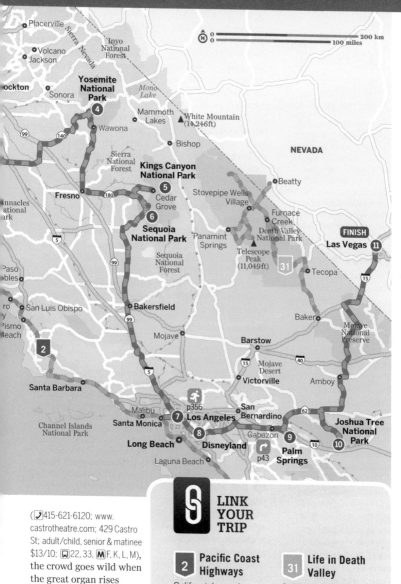

CALIFORNIA'S CLASSIC TRIPS **1** CALIFORNIA'S GREATEST HITS & LAS VEGAS

(☏415-621-6120; www.
castrotheatre.com; 429 Castro
St; adult/child, senior & matinee
$13/10; ☐22, 33, Ⓜ F, K, L, M),
the crowd goes wild when
the great organ rises
from the floor and pumps
out show tunes until the
movie starts, and the
sumptuous chandelier
complements a repertory
of silver-screen classics.

LINK YOUR TRIP

2 Pacific Coast Highways

California's most
famous driving route
hugs the Pacific
Ocean from Mexico to
Oregon. Join up in San
Francisco, Big Sur or LA.

31 Life in Death Valley

California's biggest,
wildest and most road-
trip-worthy national
park is just over two
hours' drive west of Las
Vegas, Nevada.

✕ 🛏 p46, p61, p73, p93

The Drive » Without traffic jams, it's an hour's drive from San Francisco to Napa, the nexus of Wine Country. Take Hwy 101 north over the soaring Golden Gate Bridge, stopping at the Vista Point on the far side of the bridge, and into Marin County. Zigzag northeast on Hwys 37, 121, 12 and 29 to reach downtown Napa.

- - - - - - - - - - - - - - - -

❷ Napa Valley

The Napa Valley is famous for regal cabernet sauvignon, château-like wineries and fabulous food. The city of Napa anchors the valley, but the real work happens up-valley. Scenic towns along Hwy 29 include St Helena, Yountville and Calistoga – the last more famous for its natural hot-springs water than its wine.

Start by the river in downtown Napa, where the **Oxbow Public Market** (📞707-226-6529; www. oxbowpublicmarket.com; 610 & 644 1st St; items from $3; ⊙7:30am-9:30pm; 🛜 ♿) showcases all things culinary – produce stalls, kitchen shops, and everywhere something to taste – with emphasis on seasonal eating and sustainability. Come hungry.

A dozen miles north of Napa, tour buses flock to the corporate-owned winery **Robert Mondavi** (📞707-226-1395; www.

robertmondaviwinery.com; 7801 Hwy 29, Oakville; tasting/ tour from $25/30; ⊙10am-5pm; 🅿 ♿); if you know nothing about wine and can cope with crowds, the worthwhile tours provide excellent insight into winemaking. Driving back down-valley, follow the bucolic Silverado Trail, which passes several other landmark, over-the-top wineries, including **Robert Sinskey Vineyards** (📞707-944-9090; www.robertsinskey.com; 6320 Silverado Trail; bar tastings $40, seated food & wine pairings $70-175; ⊙10am-4:30pm; 🅿), where a dramatic hilltop tasting room resembles a small cathedral.

The Drive » From Napa, it's a four-hour drive of nearly 200 miles to the dramatic Big Sur coast. Head south over the Carquinez Bridge to Berkeley, then sail over the Bay Bridge into San Francisco, taking Hwy 101 south toward Silicon Valley. Detour on Hwy 17 over the mountains to Santa Cruz, then join Hwy 1 south past Monterey and Carmel-by-the-Sea.

- - - - - - - - - - - - - - - -

❸ Big Sur

Highway 1 along Big Sur coast may be the most famous stretch of highway in the entire state. The road twists and turns a thousand feet above the vast blue Pacific, hugging the skirts of mile-high sea cliffs, above which California condors fly.

In the 1950s and '60s, Big Sur – so named by Spanish settlers who referred to the wilder-

ness as *el país grande del sur* (the big country to the south) – became a bohemian retreat for artists and writers, including Henry Miller and the Beat Generation. Today it attracts new-age mystics, hippies and city slickers seeking to unplug on this emerald-green edge of the continent.

All along Hwy 1 in Big Sur's **state parks** (www. parks.ca.gov; parking fee $10, valid for same-day admission to all other parks), you'll find hiking trails through forests of redwoods (incidentally, the tallest trees on earth) and to magical waterfalls – don't miss McWay Falls, which picturesquely tumbles onto an ocean beach.

✕ 🛏 p46, p184

The Drive » It's about a five-hour, 220-mile trip from Big Sur to Yosemite Valley. Backtrack north on coastal Hwy 1 past Monterey, then veer inland through California's agricultural valleys, taking Hwy 152 east past San Luis Reservoir and crossing I-5, then continuing east toward Hwy 99. Outside Merced, join Hwy 140 – an all-weather highway normally open year-round – to Yosemite National Park.

- - - - - - - - - - - - - - - -

TRIP HIGHLIGHT

❹ Yosemite National Park

With wild rock formations, astonishing waterfalls, vast swaths of granite and humbling Sierra Nevada peaks, **Yosemite National Park** (📞209-372-0200; www.

nps.gov/yose; 9035 Village
Dr; ⊙9am-5pm) is no less
than perfect. On your
way in, stop at **Tunnel
View** to drink in views
of the Yosemite Valley,
with iconic Half Dome
and plunging Bridalveil
Fall in the distance. Go
deeper into the valley to
see triple-decker **Yosemite Falls** up close, or to
hike the **Mist Trail**, which
climbs a rocky staircase
beside mighty **Vernal and
Nevada Falls**. Drive up to
Glacier Point to catch a
brilliant sunset.

The next day, detour
along high-elevation
Tioga Rd (closed in
winter and spring)
to wildflower-strewn
Tuolumne Meadows,
encircled by skyscraping
peaks and granite domes.
Picnic beside sparkling
Tenaya Lake and pull
over at roadside **Olm-
sted Point** for panoramic
views over the rooftop of
the Sierra Nevada. Then
backtrack down to the
valley and take Hwy 41
south, exiting the park
near the **Mariposa Grove**
(⊙8am-8pm summer, hours
vary rest of year) of giant
sequoia trees.

The Drive ›› It's a straight
shot south on Hwy 41 from
Yosemite's south entrance to
Fresno, then head east on Hwy
180, which eventually winds
uphill and gains over 6000ft in
elevation to enter Kings Canyon
National Park. The 120-mile trip
to Grant Grove Village takes
about 2½ hours, without traffic.

---

❺ Kings Canyon National Park

From giant sequoia
crowns down into one of
the USA's deepest can-
yons, the twisting scenic
drive in **Kings Canyon
National Park** (☏559-
565-3341; www.nps.gov/seki;
7-day entry per car $35; Ⓟ ⚐)
is an eye-popping, jaw-
dropping revelation.

At the northern end of
the Generals Hwy, take
a walk in **General Grant
Grove** (N Grove Trail; Ⓟ ⚐),
encompassing the world's
second-largest living tree,
then wash off all that
sweat with a dip down
the road at **Hume Lake**.
Get back on the **Kings**

Canyon Scenic Byway
(Hwy 180; closed in
winter and spring), which
makes a precipitous de-
scent, and make sure you
pull over to survey the
canyon depths and lofty
Sierra Nevada peaks from
Junction View.

At the bottom of the
canyon, cruise past Cedar
Grove Village. Admire
striking canyon views
from verdant **Zumwalt
Meadow**, a wildlife-
watching hot spot with a
boardwalk nature trail. At
truthfully named **Road's
End** (⊙ usually 7am-3:30pm
late May-late Sep), cool off
by the sandy Kings River
beach or make an 8-mile
round-trip hike to **Mist**

🗨 LOCAL KNOWLEDGE: HIKING HALF DOME

Just hold on, don't forget to breathe and – whatever
you do – don't look down. A pinnacle so popular
that hikers need a permit to scale it, Half Dome lives
on as Yosemite Valley's must-reach-it obsession
for millions. It's a day hike longer than an average
work day, an elevation gain equivalent to almost 480
flights of stairs, and a final stretch of near-vertical
steps that melts even the strongest legs and arms to
masses of quivering jelly.

Reaching the top can only be done when the
fixed cables are up, usually from late May until
mid-October. To stem lengthy lines (and increasingly
dangerous conditions) on the vertiginous cables,
the park now requires that all day and overnight
backpackers obtain an advance permit. Half Dome
permits go on sale by a preseason lottery in March,
with a limited number available via another daily
lottery two days in advance during the hiking
season. Permit regulations and prices are subject to
change; check the park website (www.nps.gov/yose/
planyourvisit/hdpermits.htm) for current details.

Classic Trip

WHY THIS IS A CLASSIC TRIP
AMY C BALFOUR, WRITER

This jam-packed journey sweeps in the best of California – beaches, mountains, deserts, wineries, big trees and even bigger cities. It even includes the glitzy charms of Las Vegas, a casino-loving city a short hop away in Nevada and a favorite weekend getaway for Californians. The Sierra Nevada mountains are best visited in summer; spring brings wildflower blooms to the deserts.

Above: Hollywood Boulevard, Los Angeles
Left: Tuolumne Meadow, Yosemite National Park
Right: Giant sequoia trees in Sequoia National Park

Falls, which roars in late spring and early summer.

The Drive » It's only a 60-mile drive from Cedar Grove to the Giant Forest in Sequoia National Park, but it can take nearly two hours, thanks to hairpin turns and gawking drivers. Backtrack along the Kings Canyon Scenic Byway (Hwy 180) to Grant Grove, then wind south on the Generals Hwy through the sun-dappled forests of the Giant Sequoia National Monument.

- - - - - - - - - - - - - - - - - -

⑥ Sequoia National Park

Big trees, deep caves and high granite domes are all on the agenda for this day-long tour of Sequoia National Park. Arriving in the Giant Forest, let yourself be dwarfed by the majestic **General Sherman Tree**. Learn more about giant sequoias at the **Giant Forest Museum** (☎559-565-3341; www.nps. gov/seki; 47050 Generals Hwy; ⊙9am-4:30pm winter, to 6pm summer; P). Snap a photo of your car driving through the **Tunnel Log**, or better yet, leave your car behind and hop on the park shuttle for a wildflower walk around **Crescent Meadow** and to climb the puff-and-pant stairway up **Moro Rock**, granting bird's-eye canyon and peak views.

Picnic by the river at the Lodgepole Market Center, then get back in the car and make your way to the chilly underground wonderland of **Crystal Cave**

(www.recreation.gov; Crystal Cave Rd, off Generals Hwy; tours adult/child/youth from $16/5/8; ☻late May-late Sep; P), where you can marvel at delicate marble formations while easing through eerie passageways. You must book tour tickets online in advance. Before sunset, take the dizzyingly steep drive down the Generals Hwy into the **Foothills** area, stopping at riverside swimming holes.

The Drive ≫ After a few days in the wilderness, get ready to zoom down to California's biggest city. The fastest route to Los Angeles takes at least 3½ hours to cover 200 miles. Follow Hwy 198 west of Three Rivers to Hwy 65 south through the valley. In Bakersfield, join Hwy 99 south to I-5, which streams south toward LA.

- - - - - - - - - - - - - - - - - -

 TRIP HIGHLIGHT

❼ Los Angeles

Make a pilgrimage to **Hollywood**, with its pink-starred sidewalks, blingy nightclubs and restored movie palaces. Long ago, the TV and movie biz (locals just call it 'the Industry') decamped over the hills to the San Fernando Valley. Peek behind the scenes on a **Warner Bros Studio Tour** (☎818-972-8687; www.wbstudiotour.com; 3400 Warner Blvd, Burbank; tours adult/child 8-12yr from $69/59; ☻8:30am-3:30pm year-round, extended hours Jun-Aug; 🚌155, 222, 501 stop about 400yd from tour center), or get a thrill along with screaming tweens at **Universal Studios Hollywood** (☎800-864-8377; www.universalstudioshollywood.com; 100 Universal City Plaza, Universal City; 1-/2-day from $109/149, child under 3yr free; ☻daily, hours vary; P 🚹; M B Line to Universal City).

Downtown LA (p356) is a historical, multilayered and fascinating city within a city, known for its landmark architecture. Wander through the old town of **El Pueblo** (☎213-485-6855; www.elpueblo.lacity.org; Olvera St; ☻tours 10am, 11am & noon Tue-Sat; 🚹; M B/D/L Lines

to Union Station), then be awed by the museum of art **Broad** (☎213-232-6200; www.thebroad.org; 221 S Grand Ave; ☻11am-5pm Tue & Wed, 11am-8pm Thu & Fri, 10am-8pm Sat, 10am-6pm Sun; P 🚹; M B/D Lines to Civic Center/Grand Park), which is free but requires reservation, before partying at the entertainment complex **LA Live** (☎213-763-5483; www.lalive.com; 800 W Olympic Blvd; P 🚹; M A/E Lines to Pico) and worshipping at the star-spangled altar of the **Grammy Museum** (☎213-765-6800; www.grammymuseum.org; 800 W Olympic Blvd; adult/child $15/13; ☻10:30am-6:30pm Sun, Mon, Wed & Thu, 10am-8pm Fri & Sat; P 🚹; M A/E Lines to Pico).

Hitting LA's sunny beaches is also a must-do – and pretty darn fun. In laid-back **Santa Monica** and hipper **Venice**, you can mix with the surf rats, skate punks, muscled bodybuilders, yogis and street performers along a stretch of sublime coastline cradling the city.

🍴 🛏 p46, p72

The Drive ≫ It's a tedious 25-mile trip south on I-5 between Downtown LA and Anaheim. The drive can take well over an hour, especially in rush-hour traffic. As you approach Anaheim, follow the freeway signs and take exit 110b for Disneyland Dr.

- - - - - - - - - - - - - - - - - -

❽ Disneyland

When Walt Disney opened Disneyland on July 17, 1955, he declared it the

---

✓ **TOP TIP:**
SAFE DRIVING
IN ALL WEATHER

If you plan on driving this route in winter, be prepared for snow in the Sierra Nevada; carry tire chains in your car. During summer, the deserts can be dangerously hot; avoid overheating your car by not running the air-conditioning and by traveling in the cooler morning and late-afternoon hours.

'Happiest Place on Earth.' More than 65 years later, it's hard to argue with the ear-to-ear grins on the faces of kiddos, grandparents, honeymooners and everyone else here in Anaheim.

If you've only got one day to spend at **Disneyland** (☏714-781-4636; www.disneyland.com; 1313 Harbor Blvd; 1-day pass adult $104-149, child 3-9yr $96-141, 2-day pass adult/child 3-9yr $225/210; ⏱open daily, seasonal hours vary), buy tickets online in advance and arrive early. Stroll **Main Street USA** toward Sleeping Beauty Castle. Enter **Tomorrowland** to ride Space Mountain. In **Fantasyland** don't miss the classic 'It's a Small World' ride or racing downhill on the Matterhorn Bobsleds. Grab a FASTPASS for the **Indiana Jones Adventure** or the **Pirates of the Caribbean** before lunching in **New Orleans Square**. Plummet down Splash Mountain, then visit the Haunted Mansion before the **Fantasmic!** show and fireworks begin. In the new **Galaxy's Edge** area, which celebrates the best of the *Star Wars* movie franchise, the thrilling Millennium Falcon: Smugglers Run hurtles you into hyperspace.

The Drive » A few different routes from Anaheim to Palm Springs all eventually funnel onto I-10 eastbound from Los Angeles. It's a trip of almost 100 miles, which should take less than three hours without traffic jams. Watch

DETOUR: WORLD'S BIGGEST DINOSAURS

Start: ❾ **Palm Springs**

West of Palm Springs, you may do a double take when you see the **World's Biggest Dinosaurs** (☏951-922-8700; www.cabazondinosaurs.com; 50770 Seminole Dr, Cabazon; adult/child $13/11; ⏱9am-6pm Mon-Fri, to 7pm Sat & Sun; Ⓟ👶). Claude K Bell, a sculptor for Knott's Berry Farm, spent over a decade crafting these concrete behemoths, now owned by Christian creationists who contend that God created the original dinosaurs in one day, along with the other animals, as part of his 'intelligent design.' In the gift shop you'll find the sort of dino-swag you might find at science museums.

for the towering wind turbines on the hillsides as you shoot through San Gorgonio Pass. Take Hwy 111 south to downtown Palm Springs.

- - - - - - - - - - - - - - - - - -

❾ Palm Springs

In the 1950s and '60s, Palm Springs was the swinging getaway of Sinatra, Elvis and dozens of other stars. Now a new generation has fallen for the city's mid-century modern charms: steel-and-glass bungalows designed by famous architects, boutique hotels with vintage decor and kidney-shaped pools, and hip bars serving perfect martinis.

North of downtown 'PS,' ride the revolving **Palm Springs Aerial Tramway** (☏760-325-1391; www.pstramway.com; 1 Tram Way; adult/child $27/17, parking $8; ⏱1st tram up 10am Mon-Fri, 8am Sat & Sun, last tram up 8pm, last tram down 9:45pm daily, varies seasonally; Ⓟ👶), which climbs 6000ft vertically in under 15 minutes. It's 30°F to 40°F (up to 22°C) cooler as you step out into pine forest at the top, so bring warm clothing – the ride up from the desert floor is said to be the equivalent (in temperature) of driving from Mexico to Canada.

Down-valley in Rancho Mirage, **Sunnylands** (☏760-202-2222; www.sunnylands.org; 37977 Bob Hope Dr; visitor center & gardens free; ⏱house tours Wed-Sun, birding tours 8:45am Thu & Sat, visitor center & gardens 8:30am-4pm Wed-Sun mid-Sep–early Jun; Ⓟ) was the glamorous modern estate of the Annenberg family. Explore the magnificent desert gardens or book ahead for tours of the stunning house with its art collection.

🍴 🛏 p47, p347

ROMAN_SLAVIK / GETTY IMAGES ©

The Drive » North of Palm Springs, take I-10 west to Hwy 62, which winds northeast to the high desert around Joshua Tree. The 35-mile trip goes by quickly; it should take you less than an hour to reach the park's west entrance. Fuel up first in the town of Joshua Tree – there's no gas, food or water inside the park.

- - - - - - - - - - - - - - - - -

⑩ Joshua Tree National Park

Taking a page from a Dr Seuss book, whimsical-looking Joshua trees (actually tree-sized yuccas) symbolize this **national park** (☎760-367-5500; www.nps.gov/jotr; 7-day pass per car $30; P 🐾) at the convergence of the Colorado and Mojave Deserts. Allegedly, it was Mormon settlers who named the trees because the branches stretching toward heaven reminded them of the biblical prophet pointing the way to the promised land.

Rock climbers know 'JTree' as the best place to climb in California, but kids and the young at heart also welcome the chance to scramble up, down and around the giant boulders. Hikers seek hidden, shady, desert-fan-palm oases fed by natural springs and small streams. Book ahead for fascinating guided tours

of **Keys Ranch** (☎reservations 877-444-6777; www.nps.gov/jotr; tours adult/child 6-11yr $10/5, plus park admission; ⊙tours Oct-May; 🐾), built by a 20th-century desert homesteader.

Scenic drives worth taking inside the park include the side road to panoramic **Keys View** and the **Pinto Basin Rd**, which winds down to Cottonwood Spring, letting you watch nature transition from the high Mojave Desert to the low Colorado Desert. A bird's-eye view of the park is your reward at the end of the steep **Ryan Mountain Trail**, which is 3 miles round-trip.

✕ 🛏 p47, p347

The Drive » It's a gloriously scenic back-road adventure to Las Vegas, three hours and nearly 200 miles away. From Twentynine Palms, Amboy Rd barrels east then north, opening up desert panoramas. At Amboy, head east on Route 66 and north on Kelbaker Rd across I-40 into the Mojave National Preserve. North of the preserve, join I-15 northbound to Las Vegas.

- - - - - - - - - - - - - - - - -

TRIP HIGHLIGHT

⑪ Las Vegas, Nevada

Vegas is the ultimate escape. It's the only place in the world where you can spend the night partying in ancient Rome, wake up in Egypt, brunch under the Eiffel Tower, watch an erupting volcano at sunset and get married

in a pink Cadillac at midnight.

Double down with the high rollers, pick up some tacky souvenirs and sip a neon 3ft-high margarita as you stroll along the **Strip**. Traipse through mini versions of New York, Paris and Venice before riding the **High Roller** (☎702-322-0593; www.caesars.com/linq/high-roller; 3545 S Las Vegas Blvd,

Joshua Tree National Park

LINQ Promenade; adult/child $25/10, after 5pm $37/20; ⊙11:30am-2am; P 🚻; 🚌Deuce, 🚌Harrah's/Linq), the world's tallest Ferris wheel (for now). After dark, go glam at ultra-modern casino resorts Cosmopolitan and Wynn.

Do you like old-school casinos, vintage neon signs and dive bars more than celebrity chefs and clubbing? No problem.

Head downtown to historic 'Glitter Gulch' along the **Fremont Street Experience** (📞702-678-5600; www.vegasexperience.com; Fremont St Mall; ⊙24hr, shows hourly dusk-midnight or 1am; P 🚻; 🚌Deuce, SDX), a pedestrian-only zone with the **Slotzilla zip-line canopy** (📞844-947-8342; www.vegasexperience.com/slotzilla-zip-line; lower/upper line $29/49; ⊙1pm-1am

Sun-Thu, to 2am Fri & Sat; 🚻), near the **Mob Museum** (📞702-229-2734; www.themobmuseum.org; 300 Stewart Ave; adult/student/under 10yr $30/17/free; ⊙9am-9pm; P; 🚌Deuce). Afterward, mingle with locals at hip hangouts in the **Fremont East** entertainment district.

🍴 🛏 p47

Eating & Sleeping

San Francisco ①

✕ La Taqueria — Mexican $

(☏415-285-7117; www.facebook.com/lataqsf; 2889 Mission St; burritos $3-11; ◷11am-8:45pm Mon-Sat, to 7:45pm Sun; ☏; ⬚12, 14, 48, 49, Ⓑ24th St Mission) SF's definitive burrito has no saffron rice, spinach tortilla or mango salsa – just perfectly grilled meats, slow-cooked beans and tomatillo or mesquite salsa in a flour tortilla. You'll pay extra to skip the beans at James Beard Award–winning La Taqueria, because they add more meat. For total burrito bliss, add spicy pickles and *crema* (sour cream). Worth the wait.

✕ City View — Dim Sum $

(☏415-398-2838; www.cityviewdimsum.com; 662 Commercial St; dishes $3-8; ◷11am-2:30pm Mon-Fri, from 10am Sat & Sun; ⬚; ⬚1, 8, 10, 12, 30, 45, ⬚California) Take a seat in the sunny dining room and make way for carts loaded with delicate shrimp and leek dumplings, garlicky Chinese broccoli, tangy spareribs, coconut-dusted custard tarts and other tantalizing traditional dim sum. Arrive before the midday lunch rush to nab prime seating near the kitchen for first dibs on passing carts.

⬚ Hotel del Sol — Motel $

(☏415-921-5520; www.jdvhotels.com; 3100 Webster St; d $99-210; ⓅⓈⓄ☏Ⓧ☏; ⬚22, 28, 30, 43) Cartoons come to life in this 1950s motor lodge redone in eye-popping beach-ball colors, with a palm-lined courtyard and heated outdoor pool – a rare treat in San Francisco. Kids aren't an afterthought but are honored guests treated to afternoon cookies, board games, a movie library and hammocks. The quiet Marina District location is near restaurants, parks and Fort Mason; parking costs $30 per night.

⬚ Hotel Bohème — Boutique Hotel $$

(☏415-433-9111; www.hotelboheme.com; 444 Columbus Ave; d $185-295; ⓈⓄ☏; ⬚10, 12, 30, 41, 45, ⓂT) Eclectic, historic and unabashedly romantic, this quintessential North Beach boutique hotel has jazz-era color schemes, wrought-iron beds, paper-umbrella lamps, Beat poetry and original artwork. The vintage rooms are smallish with teensy bathrooms, some face noisy Columbus Ave (quieter rooms are in the back) and there's no elevator – but novels practically write themselves here, with City Lights and legendary bars as handy inspiration.

Big Sur ③

✕ Big Sur Roadhouse — Californian $

(☏831-667-2370; www.glenoaksbigsur.com/big-sur-roadhouse; 47080 Hwy 1; snacks & mains $8-16; ◷8am-2:30pm; ☏⬚) This modern roadhouse glows with color-splashed artwork and an outdoor fire pit. At riverside tables, tuck into upscale bar food such as spicy wings, pork sliders and gourmet burgers, with craft beer on tap. It's also a top spot for coffee and cake.

⬚ Ripplewood Resort — Cabin $$

(☏831-667-2242; www.ripplewoodresort.com; 47047 Hwy 1; cabins $110-275; Ⓟ☏☏) North of Pfeiffer Big Sur State Park, Ripplewood supports fiscal equality by charging the same rates year-round. Most of the throwback Americana-style cabins have kitchens and sometimes even wood-burning fireplaces. Quiet riverside cabins are surrounded by redwoods, but roadside cabins can be noisy. There's a small general store and a popular cafe which serves breakfast and lunch (8am to 2pm). Wi-fi is available in the cafe only.

Los Angeles ⑦

✕ Connie & Ted's — Seafood $$$

(☏323-848-2722; www.connieandteds.com; 8171 Santa Monica Blvd, West Hollywood; mains $15-46; ◷4-10pm Mon & Tue, 11:30am-10pm Wed & Thu, 11:30am-11pm Fri, 10am-11pm Sat, 10am-

10pm Sun; P; Metro Lines 4, 218) Acclaimed chef Michael Cimarusti is behind this buzzing, homely take on the New England seafood shack. Freshness and sustainability underscore the offerings, with up to a dozen oyster varieties at the raw bar, as well as superb, authentic renditions of northeast classics such as lobster rolls (served cold with mayo or hot with drawn butter), clam cakes, chowder and steamers.

Palihotel   Boutique Hotel $$

(323-272-4588; www.pali-hotel.com; 7950 Melrose Ave, Mid-City; r from $234; P ❄ 🛜; Metro Lines 10, 217, 218, 780, DASH Fairfax Route) Within walking distance of trendy Fairfax boutiques, the wood-paneled Palihotel offers that rarest of LA commodities: boutique digs at mere-mortal prices. Flouncy settees and woven rugs set a homely feel in the lobby, with rooms a snug, smart combo of cushy beds, books, architect lamps and velvety Chesterfield sofas. Some rooms come with their own terrace. Overnight self-parking is $25.

Palm Springs ⑨

✗ Farm   French $$

(760-322-2724; www.farmpalmsprings. com; 6 La Plaza; breakfast & lunch mains $7-18, dinner prix-fixe $56; ⏱8am-2pm daily, 6-9pm Fri & Sat; ❄ 🛜 🌿 🐾) Farm is so fantastically Provençal, you expect to see lavender fields pop up in the desert. Greet the day with fluffy crêpes or omelets, tuck into a salad or sandwich for lunch or book ahead for the three-course prix-fixe surprise dinner. It's in the heart of Palm Springs, yet secluded thanks to its country-style courtyard.

🛏 Arrive Hotel   Hotel $$

(760-227-7037; www.arrivehotels.com; 1551 N Palm Canyon Dr; studios $190-390; P ☺ ❄ 🛜 🐕 🐾) Rusted steel, wood and concrete are the main design ingredients of this high-octane lair where the bar doubles as reception. The 32 spacious, phone-less rooms, some with enclosed patio, tick such hipster boxes as rain shower, Apple TV and fancy bath products. At weekends the pool, bar and restaurant turn into a lively party zone for both guests and locals. No resort fee.

Joshua Tree ⑩

✗ Crossroads Cafe   American $

(760-366-5414; www.crossroadscafejtree. com; 61715 29 Palms Hwy/Hwy 62, Joshua Tree; mains $8-17; ⏱7am-9pm; ❄ 🛜 🌿 🐾) Before hitting the trail, rocks or road, fuel up at this JT institution with a carb-loaded breakfast, garden salad or fresh sandwiches that make both omnivores (burgers, Reuben) and vegans ('Fake Philly' with seitan) happy. Also a chill spot to unwind with a cold one at the end of the day.

🛏 Harmony Motel   Motel $

(760-401-1309, 760-367-3351; www. harmonymotel.com; 71161 29 Palms Hwy/Hwy 62, Twentynine Palms; d $90-95; P ❄ 🛜 🏊) This immaculately kept 1950s motel, run by the charming Ash, was where U2 stayed while working on the *Joshua Tree* album. It has a small pool and seven large, cheerfully painted and handsomely decorated rooms (some with kitchenette) set around a tidy desert garden with serene views. Free coffee and tea are available in the communal guest kitchen.

Las Vegas, Nevada ⑪

✗ Wicked Spoon Buffet   Buffet $$$

(877-893-2001; www.cosmopolitanlasvegas. com; Chelsea Tower, 2708 S Las Vegas Blvd, Cosmopolitan; brunch/dinner from $29/42; ⏱8am-9pm Sun-Thu, 8am-10pm Fri & Sat; P ❄ 🐾; Deuce) Wicked Spoon gives casino buffets a contemporary feel, with freshly prepared temptations served on individual plates to encourage portion control. The spread has all the expected meat, sushi, seafood and desserts, but with upgrades – think roasted bone marrow and a gelato bar. Add unlimited champagne, mimosas or Bloody Marys for $17.

🛏 Cosmopolitan   Casino Hotel $$

(702-698-7000; www.cosmopolitanlasvegas. com; 3708 S Las Vegas Blvd; d weekday/weekend from $105/138; P ❄ @ 🛜 🏊 🐾; Deuce) With at least eight distinctively different and equally stylish room types to choose from, Cosmo's digs are the hippest on the Strip. Ranging from oversized to decadent, about 2200 of its 2900 or so rooms have balconies, many sport sunken Japanese tubs and all feature plush furnishings and design quirks you'll delight in uncovering.

Pacific Coast Highways

Our top pick for classic California dreamin' snakes along the Pacific coast for more than 1000 miles. Uncover beaches, seafood shacks and piers for catching sunsets over boundless ocean horizons.

TRIP HIGHLIGHTS

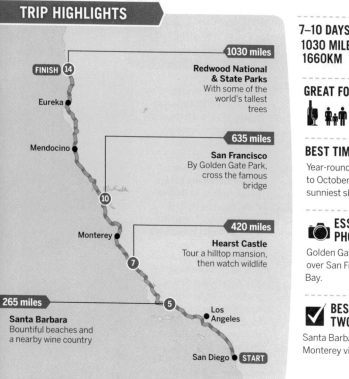

1030 miles
Redwood National & State Parks
With some of the world's tallest trees

635 miles
San Francisco
By Golden Gate Park, cross the famous bridge

420 miles
Hearst Castle
Tour a hilltop mansion, then watch wildlife

265 miles
Santa Barbara
Bountiful beaches and a nearby wine country

7–10 DAYS
1030 MILES / 1660KM

GREAT FOR...

BEST TIME TO GO
Year-round, but July to October for the sunniest skies.

 ESSENTIAL PHOTO
Golden Gate Bridge over San Francisco Bay.

 BEST TWO DAYS
Santa Barbara north to Monterey via Big Sur.

San Francisco Golden Gate Bridge

49

Classic Trip

2 Pacific Coast Highways

Escape from California's tangled, traffic-jammed freeways for a breezy cruise in the slow lane. Once you get rolling, you'll never want to leave those ocean views behind. Officially, only the short, sun-loving stretch of Hwy 1 through Orange and Los Angeles Counties can legally call itself Pacific Coast Highway (PCH). But never mind those technicalities, because equally bewitching ribbons of Hwy 1 and Hwy 101 await all along this route.

❶ San Diego

At the bottom of the state map, the pretty peninsular beach town of **Coronado** is connected to the San Diego mainland via the white-sand beaches of the **Silver Strand**. If you've seen Marilyn Monroe cavort in *Some Like It Hot,* you'll recognize the dapper **Hotel del Coronado** (☑619-435-6611, tours 619-522-8100; www. hoteldel.com; 1500 Orange Ave; tours $40; ⊙tours 10am daily plus 2pm Sat & Sun; ℗), which has hosted US presidents, celebrities and royalty, including the Prince of Wales who gave up his throne to marry a Coronado divorcée.

Wander the turreted palace's labyrinthine corridors, then quaff tropical cocktails at ocean-view Babcock & Story Bar.

Hold tight driving over the 2.1-mile-long **San Diego–Coronado Bridge**. Detour inland to **Balboa Park**. Head west, then south to Point Loma's **Cabrillo National Monument** (☑619-557-5450; www.nps. gov/cabr; 1800 Cabrillo Memorial Dr; per car/walk-in/motorcycle $20/10/15; ⊙9am-5pm, tide pools to 4:30pm, bayside trail to 4pm; ℗🚶) for captivating bay panoramas from the 19th-century lighthouse and monument to the West Coast's first Spanish explorers. Roll north of **Mission Beach** and the

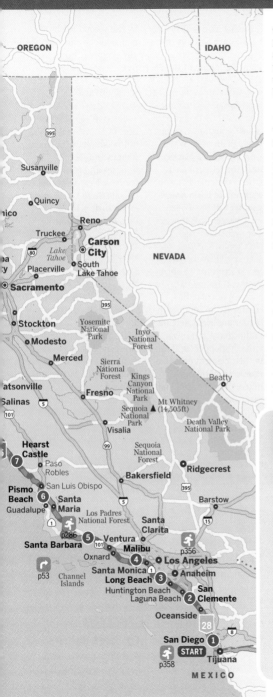

old-fashioned amusement park at **Pacific Beach**, and suddenly you're in hoity-toity **La Jolla**, beyond which lie North County's beach towns.

✕ ⊨ p60, p72

The Drive ≫ It's a 70-mile trip from La Jolla north along coastal roads then I-5 into Orange County (aka the 'OC'), passing Camp Pendleton Marine Corps Base and recently shuttered – but still decommissioning – San Onofre Nuclear Generating Station. Exit at San Clemente and follow Avenida del Mar downhill to the beach.

❷ San Clemente

In off-the-beaten-path spots such as beautiful San Clemente, sloping steeply toward the sea, the Orange County coast feels like a trip back to the beach culture of yesteryear. Home to living

LINK YOUR TRIP

15 **Big Sur**
Get lost on the rugged Big Sur coast, stretched between Hearst Castle and the painterly scenery of Carmel-by-the-Sea on the Monterey Peninsula.

28 **Fun on the San Diego Coast**
Start your California coastal road trip slowly with an extra couple of days in sunny San Diego.

Classic Trip

surfing legends and top-notch surfboard companies, this may be the last place in the OC where you can authentically live the surf lifestyle. Ride your own board or swim at the city's main beach beside San Clemente Pier. A fast detour inland, the community's **Surfing Heritage & Culture Center** (☎949-388-0313; www.surfingheritage.org; 110 Calle Iglesia; suggested donation $5; ⏰11am-5pm Tue-Sun; P) exhibits surfboards ridden by the greats, from Duke Kahanamoku to Kelly Slater. Head back toward the pier for the California sunset of your dreams.

The Drive ⟫ Slingshot north on I-5, exiting onto Hwy 1 near Dana Point. Speed by the wealthy artists colony of Laguna Beach, wild Crystal Cove State Park, Newport Beach's yacht harbor and 'Surf City USA', Huntington Beach. Turn west off Hwy 1 near Naples toward Long Beach, about 45 miles from San Clemente.

❸ Long Beach

In Long Beach, the biggest stars are the **Queen Mary** (☎877-342-0738; www.queenmary.com; 1126 Queens Hwy; tours adult/child from $30/20 Mon-Thu, $40/30 Fri-Sun, $10 daily after 6pm; ⏰tours 10am-6pm or later; P 🚻; 🚌Passport line C, ⛴AquaBus, AquaLink), a grand (and

allegedly haunted) British ocean liner permanently moored here, and the giant **Aquarium of the Pacific** (☎tickets 562-590-3100; www.aquariumofpacific.org; 100 Aquarium Way; adult/senior/child $35/32/25; ⏰9am-6pm; P 🚻), a high-tech romp through an underwater world in which sharks dart and jellyfish float. Often overlooked, the **Museum of Latin American Art** (☎562-437-1689; www.molaa.org; 628 Alamitos Ave; adult/senior & student/child Wed-Sat $10/7/free, Sun free; ⏰11am-5pm Wed & Fri-Sun, 11am-9pm Thu; P) shows off influential, contemporary Latinx creators from south of the border and right here in California. A mile away, vintage shoppers will be in their element on **Retro Row**, several blocks of mid-century fashion and furnishings.

The Drive ⟫ Wind slowly around the ruggedly scenic Palos Verdes Peninsula. Follow Hwy 1 north past the South Bay's prime-time beaches. Curving around LAX airport and Marina del Rey, Hwy 1 continues north to Venice, Santa Monica and all the way to Malibu, almost 60 miles from Long Beach.

❹ Malibu

Leaving traffic-jammed LA behind, Hwy 1 breezes northwest of Santa Monica to Malibu. You'll feel like a movie star walking around on the public beaches, fronting gated compounds owned

by Hollywood celebs. One mansion you can actually explore inside – for free – is the **Getty Villa** (☎310-430-7300; www.getty.edu; 17985 Pacific Coast Hwy, Pacific Palisades; ⏰10am-5pm Wed-Mon; P 🚻; 🚌Metro Line 534 to Coastline Dr), a hilltop showcase of Greek, Roman and Etruscan antiquities and manicured gardens. Next to Malibu Lagoon State Beach, west of the surfers by Malibu Pier, **Adamson House** (☎310-456-8432; www.adamsonhouse.org; 23200 Pacific Coast Hwy; adult/child $7/2; ⏰tours 11am-3pm Wed-Sat, last tour 2pm; P; 🚌Metro Line 534) is a Spanish-Moorish villa lavishly decorated with locally made hand-painted tiles. Motoring further west along the coast, where the Santa Monica Mountains plunge into the sea, take time out for a frolic on Malibu's mega-popular beaches such as sandy Point Dume, Zuma or Leo Carrillo.

🍴 p60

The Drive ⟫ Hwy 1 crosses into Ventura County, winding alongside the ocean and windy Point Mugu. In Oxnard join Hwy 101 northbound. Motor past Ventura, a jumping-off point for boat trips to Channel Islands National Park, to Santa Barbara, just over 90 miles from Malibu Pier.

TRIP HIGHLIGHT

❺ Santa Barbara

Seaside Santa Barbara has almost perfect

weather and a string of idyllic beaches, where surfers, kite flyers and dog walkers mingle. Admire the city's iconic Spanish Colonial Revival–style architecture along **State St** downtown or from the **county courthouse** (☏805-962-6464; www.sbcourthouse.org; 1100 Anacapa St; ⏰8am-5pm Mon-Fri, 10am-5pm Sat & Sun), its tower rising above the red-tiled rooftops. Gaze south toward the busy harborfront and **Stearns Wharf** (www.stearnswharf. org; ⏰8am-10pm; P 🚻) or north to the historic Spanish **Mission Santa Barbara** (☏805-682-4713; www.santabarbaramission. org; 2201 Laguna St; adult/child 5-17yr $12/7; ⏰9am-4:15pm Sep-Jun, to 5:15pm Jul & Aug; P). Santa Barbara's balmy climate is also perfect for growing grapes – its **wine country**, made famous by the 2004 movie *Sideways*, is a 45-minute drive northwest along Hwy 154. Hit wine-tasting rooms in **Los Olivos**, then take Foxen Canyon Rd north past more wineries to rejoin Hwy 101.

✕ 🛏 p60, p72, p217, p319

The Drive ›› Keep following fast Hwy 101 northbound or detour west onto slow Hwy 1, which squiggles along the coastline past Guadalupe, gateway to North America's largest sand dunes. Both highways meet up again in Pismo Beach, 100 miles northwest of Santa Barbara.

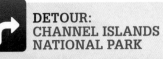

DETOUR: CHANNEL ISLANDS NATIONAL PARK

Start: ➍ **Malibu**

Imagine hiking, kayaking, scuba diving, camping and whale-watching, and doing it all amid a raw, end-of-the-world landscape. Rich in unique flora and fauna, tide pools and kelp forests, the islands of this national park are home to nearly 150 plant and animal species found nowhere else in the world, earning them the nickname 'California's Galápagos.' Anacapa and Santa Cruz, the most popular islands, are within an hour's boat ride of Ventura Harbor, off Hwy 101 almost 40 miles northwest of Malibu on the way to Santa Barbara. Reservations are essential for weekends, holidays and summer trips. Before you shove off from the mainland, stop by the park's **visitor center** (Robert J Lagomarsino Visitor Center; ☏805-658-5730; www.nps.gov/chis; 1901 Spinnaker Dr, Ventura; ⏰8:30am-5pm; 🚻) for educational natural history exhibits, a free 25-minute nature film and family-friendly activities.

➏ Pismo Beach

A classic California beach town, Pismo Beach has a long, lazy stretch of sand for swimming, surfing and strolling onto the pier at sunset. After digging into bowls of clam chowder and baskets of fried seafood at surf-casual cafes, check out the retro family fun at the bowling alley, billiards halls and bars uphill from the beach, or dash 10 miles up Hwy 101 to San Luis Obispo's vintage **Sunset Drive-In** (☏805-544-4475; www.facebook.com/sunset-drivein; 255 Elks Lane; adult/child 5-11yr $10/4; 🚻), where you can put your feet up on the dash and munch on bottomless bags of popcorn while watching Hollywood blockbuster double-features.

✕ p60, p209

The Drive ›› Follow Hwy 101 north past San Luis Obispo, exiting onto Hwy 1 west to landmark Morro Rock in Morro Bay. North of Cayucos, Hwy 1 rolls through bucolic pasture lands, only swinging back to the coast at Cambria. Ten miles further north stands Hearst Castle, about 60 miles from Pismo Beach.

TRIP HIGHLIGHT

➐ Hearst Castle

Hilltop **Hearst Castle** (☏reservations 800-444-4445; www.hearstcastle.org; 750 Hearst Castle Rd; tours adult/child 5-12yr from $25/12; ⏰from 9am, last tour departs 4pm; P 🚻) is California's most famous monument to wealth and ambition. William Randolph Hearst,

Classic Trip

BILL PERRY / SHUTTERSTOCK ©

HARUN OZMEN / SHUTTERSTOCK ©

WHY THIS IS A CLASSIC TRIP
AMY C BALFOUR, WRITER

Rock-'em-sock-'em scenery never stops on this coastal adventure, from the gorgeous sun-kissed beaches of Southern California to soaring coastal redwoods in foggy Northern California. My travels on this route have ranged from joyous romps to reflective sojourns – and the landscape has somehow matched my mood every time. Laguna Beach, Malibu, Big Sur, north of Santa Cruz, and Jenner to Mendocino and Westport are reliable crowd-pleasers.

Above: Santa Barbara
Left: The Queen Mary
Right: Promenade at Santa Cruz beach

FRANK FELL MEDIA / SHUTTERSTOCK ©

the early-20th-century newspaper magnate, entertained Hollywood stars and royalty at this fantasy estate furnished with European antiques, accented by shimmering pools and surrounded by flowering gardens. Try to make tour reservations in advance, especially for living-history evening programs during the Christmas holiday season and in spring.

About 4.5 miles further north along Hwy 1, park at the signposted vista point and amble the boardwalk to view the **elephant seal colony** that breeds, molts, sleeps, plays and fights on the beach. Seals haul out year-round, but the winter birthing and mating season peaks on Valentine's Day. Nearby, **Piedras Blancas Light Station** (☎805-927-7361; www.piedrasblancas.org; Hwy 1, San Simeon; tours adult/child 6-17yr $10/5; ☼tours 9:45am Mon, Tue & Thu-Sat mid-Jun–Aug, 9:45am Tue, Thu & Sat Sep–mid-Jun) is an outstandingly scenic spot.

✗ p60

The Drive » Fill your car's gas tank before plunging north into the redwood forests of the remote Big Sur coast, where precipitous cliffs dominate the seascape, and tourist services are few and far between. Hwy 1 keeps curving north to the Monterey Peninsula, approximately a three-hour, 95-mile trip from Hearst Castle.

Classic Trip

⑧ Monterey

As Big Sur loosens its condor's talons on the coastal highway, Hwy 1 rolls gently downhill toward Monterey Bay. The fishing community of Monterey is the heart of Nobel Prize–winning writer John Steinbeck's country, and although **Cannery Row** today is touristy claptrap, it's worth strolling down to step inside the mesmerizing **Monterey Bay Aquarium** (☑info 831-648-4800, tickets 866-963-9645; www.montereybayaquarium.org; 886 Cannery Row; adult/child 3-12yr/13-17yr \$50/30/40, tours \$15; ◷9:30am-6pm May-Aug, 10am-5pm Sep-Apr; 🚻), inhabiting a converted sardine cannery on the shores of a national marine sanctuary. All kinds of aquatic denizens swim in the giant tanks, from sea stars to pot-bellied seahorses and comical sea otters.

✗ 🛏 p61, p201

The Drive » It's a relatively quick 45-mile trip north to Santa Cruz. Hwy 1 traces the crescent shoreline of Monterey Bay, passing Elkhorn Slough wildlife refuge near Moss Landing boat harbor, Watsonville's strawberry and artichoke farms, and a string of tiny beach towns in Santa Cruz County.

---

⑨ Santa Cruz

Here, the flower power of the 1960s lives on, and bumper stickers on surfboard-laden woodies shout 'Keep Santa Cruz weird.' Next to the ocean, **Santa Cruz Beach Boardwalk** (☑831-423-5590; www.beachboardwalk.com; 400 Beach St; boardwalk free, per ride \$4-7, all-day pass \$40-50; ◷daily late May-Aug, most weekends Sep-Apr, weather permitting; 🅿 🚻) has a glorious old-school Americana vibe and a 1911 Looff carousel. Its fun-for-all atmosphere is punctuated by squeals from nervous nellies on the stomach-turning Giant Dipper, a 1920s wooden roller coaster that's a national historic landmark, as seen in the vampire cult-classic movie *The Lost Boys*.

Visit Santa Cruz' **Museum of Art & History** (MAH; ☑831-429-1964; www.santacruzmah.org; McPherson Center, 705 Front St; adult/child 12-17yr \$10/8, 1st Fri of each month free; ◷10am-6pm Sun-Thu, to 8pm Fri, to 3pm Sat; 🚻) for regular special exhibitions and excellent permanent displays on the city's history and culture. Interesting one-off exhibitions have included the history of both skateboarding and tattooing in the city. Adjacent, there's good eating and drinking at **Abbott Square Market** (www.abbottsquaremarket.com; 725 Front Street; mains \$8-15; ◷7am–10pm Sun-Thu, to midnight Fri-Sat; 🍴 🚻).

✗ 🛏 p61, p193

The Drive » It's a blissful 75-mile coastal run from Santa Cruz up to San Francisco past Pescadero, Half Moon Bay and Pacifica, where Hwy 1 passes through the tunnels at Devil's Slide. Merge with heavy freeway traffic in Daly City, staying on Hwy 1 north through the city into Golden Gate Park.

TRIP HIGHLIGHT

⑩ San Francisco

Gridlock may shock your system after hundreds of lazy miles of wide-open, rolling coast. But don't despair. Hwy 1 runs straight through the city's biggest, most breathable greenspace: **Golden Gate Park** (https://goldengatepark.com; btwn Stanyan St & Great Hwy; 🅿 🚻; 🚌5, 7, 18, 21, 28, 29, 33, 44, Ⓜ N). You could easily spend all day in the

---

TROUBLE-FREE ROAD-TRIPPING

In coastal areas, thick fog may impede driving – slow down, and if it's too soupy, get off the road. Along coastal cliffs, watch out for falling rocks and mudslides that could damage or disable your car if struck. For current highway conditions, including road closures (which aren't uncommon during the rainy winter season) and construction updates, call ☑800-427-7623 or visit www.dot.ca.gov.

conservatory of flowers, arboretum and botanic gardens, or perusing the **California Academy of Sciences** (☎415-379-8000; www.calacademy.org; 55 Music Concourse Dr; adult/student/child $36.50/31.25/28; ☺9:30am-5pm Mon-Sat, from 11am Sun; Ⓟ 🖈; 🚍5, 6, 7, 21, 31, 33, 44, ⓂN) and the fine arts **de Young Museum** (☎415-750-3600; http://deyoung.famsf.org; 50 Hagiwara Tea Garden Dr; adult/child $15/free, 1st Tue of month free, $2 discount with Bay Area public transit ticket; ☺9:30am-5:15pm Tue-Sun; 🚍5, 7, 44, ⓂN). Then follow Hwy 1 north over the **Golden Gate Bridge** (☎toll information 877-229-8655; www.goldengatebridge.org/visitors; Hwy 101; northbound free, southbound $5-8; 🚍28, all Golden Gate Transit buses). Guarding the entry to San Francisco Bay, this iconic bridge is named after the strait it spans, not for its 'International Orange' paint job. Park in the lots on the bridge's south or north side, then traipse out onto the pedestrian walkway for a photo.

🍴 🛏 p46, p61, p73, p93

The Drive » Past Sausalito, leave Hwy 101 in Marin City for slow-moving, twisted Hwy 1 along the Marin County coast, passing nearby Point Reyes. Over the next 100 miles from Bodega Bay to Mendocino, revel in a remarkably uninterrupted stretch of coastal highway. More than halfway along, watch for the lighthouse road turnoff north of Point Arena town.

DETOUR: POINT REYES

Start: ⑩ San Francisco

A rough-hewn beauty, **Point Reyes National Seashore** (☎415-654-5100; www.nps.gov/pore; Ⓟ) lures marine mammals and birds, as well as scores of shipwrecks. It was here that Sir Francis Drake repaired his ship the *Golden Hind* in 1579 and, while he was at it, claimed the indigenous land for England. Follow Sir Francis Drake Blvd to the point's edge-of-the-world **lighthouse** (☎415-669-1534; www.nps.gov/pore/planyourvisit/lighthouse.htm; ☺10am-4:30pm Fri-Mon, first gallery 2:30-4pm Fri-Mon, weather permitting; Ⓟ), whipped by ferocious winds, where you can observe migrating whales in winter. The lighthouse, which reopened in 2019 after a multi-million-dollar renovation, sits below the headlands and is reached via 300 descending steps. You'll find it about 20 miles west of Point Reyes Station off Hwy 1 along Marin County's coast.

⑪ Around Point Arena

The fishing fleets of Bodega Bay and the seal colony at Jenner's harbor are the last things you'll see before Hwy 1 dives into California's great rural northlands. The road twists and turns past the Sonoma Coast's state parks packed with hiking trails, sand dunes and beaches, as well as underwater marine reserves, rhododendron groves and a 19th-century Russian fur-trading fort. At **Sea Ranch**, don't let exclusive-looking vacation homes prevent you from following public-access trailhead signs and staircases down to empty beaches and across ocean bluffs. Further north, guarding an unbelievably windy point since 1908, **Point Arena Lighthouse** (☎707-882-2809; www.pointarenalighthouse.com; 45500 Lighthouse Rd; adult/child $8/1; ☺10am-3:30pm mid-Sep–mid-May, to 4:30pm mid-May–mid-Sep) is the only lighthouse in California you can actually climb to the top. Check in at the museum, then ascend the 115ft tower to inspect the Fresnel lens, and panoramas of the sea and the jagged San Andreas Fault below.

🛏 p61

The Drive » It's an hour-long, 35-mile drive north along Hwy 1 from the Point Arena Lighthouse turnoff to Mendocino, crossing the Navarro, Little and Big Rivers. Feel free to stop and stretch at wind-tossed state beaches, parklands crisscrossed by hiking

trails and tiny coastal towns along the way.

12 Mendocino & Fort Bragg

Looking more like Cape Cod than California, the quaint maritime town of **Mendocino** has white picket fences surrounding New England–style cottages with blooming gardens and redwood-built water towers. This yesteryear timber town and shipping port with dramatic headlands jutting into the Pacific was 'discovered' by artists and bohemians in the 1950s and has served as a scenic backdrop in more than 50 movies. Once you've browsed the cute shops and art galleries selling everything from driftwood carvings to homemade fruit jams – the town is nicknamed 'Spendocino' – escape north to workaday **Fort Bragg**, with its simple fishing harbor and brewpub. Stop first for a short hike on the ecological staircase and pygmy forest trail at oceanfront **Jug Handle State Natural Reserve** (707-937-5804; www.parks.ca.gov; Hwy 1, Caspar; sunrise-sunset).

The Drive >> About 25 miles north of Mendocino, Westport is the last hamlet along this rugged stretch of Hwy 1. After 28 miles, rejoin Hwy 101 northbound at Leggett for another 90 miles to Eureka, detouring along the Avenue of the Giants and, if you have more time to spare, to the Lost Coast.

13 Eureka

Highway 101 trundles alongside **Humboldt Bay National Wildlife Refuge** (707-733-5406; www.fws.gov/refuge/humboldt_bay; 1020 Ranch Rd, Loleta; 8am-5pm), a major stopover for migratory birds on the Pacific Flyway. Next comes the sleepy railroad town of Eureka. As you wander downtown, check out the ornate **Carson Mansion** (www.ingomar.org; 143 M St, Ingomar Club), built in the 1880s by a timber baron and adorned with dizzying Victorian turrets, towers, gables and gingerbread details. **Blue Ox Millworks & Historic Park** (707-444-3437; www.blueoxmill.com; 1 X St; adult/child 6-12yr $12/7; 9am-5pm Mon-Fri year-round, plus 9am-4pm Sat Apr-Nov;) still creates Victorian detailing by hand using traditional carpentry and 19th-century equipment. Back by Eureka's harborfront, climb aboard the blue-and-white 1910 **Madaket** (Madaket Cruises; 707-445-1910; www.humboldtbay maritimemuseum.com; 1st St; narrated cruises adult/child $22/18; 1pm, 2:30pm & 4pm Wed-Sat, 1pm & 2:30pm Sun-Tue mid-May–mid-Oct), docked at the foot of C St. Sunset cocktail cruises are served

/ SHUTTERSTOCK ©

from California's smallest licensed bar.

✗ 🛏 p61, p153

The Drive >> Follow Hwy 101 north past the Rastafarian-hippie college town of Arcata and turnoffs for Trinidad State Beach and Patrick's Point State Park. Hwy 101 drops out of the trees beside marshy Humboldt Lagoons State Park, rolling north toward Orick, just over 40 miles from Eureka.

Redwood National Park

TRIP HIGHLIGHT

⑭ Redwood National & State Parks

At last, you'll reach **Redwood National Park** (☏707-464-6101, 707-465-7335; www.nps.gov/redw; Hwy 101). Get oriented to the tallest trees on earth at the coastal **Thomas H Kuchel Visitor Center** (☏707-465-7765; www.

nps.gov/redw; Hwy 101; ⏱9am-5pm Apr-Oct, to 4pm Nov-Mar), just south of the tiny town of Orick. Then commune with the coastal giants on their own mossy turf inside **Lady Bird Johnson Grove** or the majestic **Tall Trees Grove** (free drive-and-hike permit required). For more untouched redwood forests, wind along the 10-mile **Newton B Drury**

Scenic Parkway in **Prairie Creek Redwoods State Park** (☏707-488-2039; www.parks.ca.gov; Prairie Creek Rd; ⏱9am-5pm Apr-Oct, to 4pm Nov-Mar), passing grassy meadows where Roosevelt elk roam. Then follow Hwy 101 all the way north to **Crescent City**, the last pit stop before the Oregon border.

Eating & Sleeping

San Diego ❶

🛏 Pearl Hotel
Boutique Hotel $$

(📞619-226-6100; www.thepearlsd.com;
1410 Rosecrans St, Point Loma; r $169-290;
🅿❄🛜🏊) This 1959 gem was showing its
age, which is why the new owners have given
it a big-bucks face-lift while preserving its
mid-century-modern bone structure. New
rooms are tasteful and modern with light tones,
hardwoods and beachy design touches. Abodes
wrap around a heated peanut-size swimming
pool where guests and locals mingle during
'dive-in movies' on Wednesday nights.
The restaurant has a big local following too, as
much for its modern American cuisine as its
potent cocktails. On-site parking is very limited.

Malibu ❹

🍴 Neptune's Net
Seafood $$

(📞310-457-3095; www.neptunesnet.com; 42505
Pacific Coast Hwy; mains $10.50-21; ⏱10:30am-
8pm Mon-Thu, 10:30am-9pm Fri, 10am-8pm
Sat & Sun Apr-Oct; 10:30am-7pm Mon-Thu,
10:30am-9pm Fri, 10am-7pm Sat & Sun Nov-Mar;
🚗🐕) Not far past the Malibu line in Ventura
County, the 1950s vintage Neptune's Net is part
restaurant, part biker bar. Whether you arrive
by rad chopper or Range Rover, everyone can
enjoy the beer-and-seafood (fried, grilled etc)
hospitality on inviting wooden porches.

Santa Barbara ❺

🍴 Santa Barbara
Shellfish Company
Seafood $$

(📞805-966-6676; www.shellfishco.com; 230
Stearns Wharf; dishes $4-24; ⏱11am-9pm;
🚗🐕) 'From sea to skillet to plate' sums up this
end-of-the-wharf seafood shack that's more of a
buzzing counter joint than a sit-down restaurant.

Chase away the seagulls as you chow down on
garlic-baked clams, crab cakes and coconut-
fried shrimp at wooden picnic tables outside.
Awesome lobster bisque, ocean views and the
same location for almost 40 years.

🛏 El Capitan
Canyon
Cabin, Campground $$$

(📞reservations 866-352-2729; www.
elcapitancanyon.com; 11560 Calle Real; safari
tents $180, yurts $235, cabins $255-795;
🅿🐕🛜🏊) Inland from El Capitán State
Beach, this 'glamping' resort is for those who
hate to wake up with dirt under their nails. No
cars are allowed up-canyon during peak season,
making this woodsy resort more peaceful.
Safari tents are rustic and share bathrooms,
while creek-side cabins are more deluxe, some
with kitchenette; all have an outdoor fire pit.

Pismo Beach ❻

🍴 Cracked Crab
Seafood $$

(📞805-773-2722; www.crackedcrab.com; 751
Price St; mains $16-61; ⏱11am-9pm Sun-Thu,
11am-10pm Fri & Sat; 🐕) Fresh seafood and
regional wines are staples at this super-casual
family-owned grill. When the famous Big Bucket
– a messy bonanza of crab, clams, shrimp and
mussels accompanied by Cajun sausage, red
potatoes and cob corn – gets dumped on your
butcher-paper-covered table, make sure you're
wearing one of those silly-looking plastic bibs.
No reservations, but the wait is worth it.

Hearst Castle ❼

🍴 Truck at Sebastian's
Food Truck $

(📞805-927-3307; 442 SLO-San Simeon Rd;
snacks $9-15; ⏱11am-5pm) Now operating
as a food truck adjoined to the Hearst Ranch
Winery's spacious new tasting room. Try the
pork tacos or Cubano sandwich.

Monterey 8

✕ Alta Bakery & Cafe   Cafe $

(📞831-920-1018; www.altamonterey.com; 502 Munras Ave; snacks & mains $8-12; ⏰7am-4pm; 🅿️♿) In the restored **Cooper-Molera Adobe** (📞831-223-0172; www.coopermolera. org; 525 Polk St; ⏰11am-4pm Tue-Sat, to 2:30pm Sun), Alta Bakery & Cafe's excellent baking is showcased with brunch options including orange marmalade and ricotta on sourdough, while daily donut, strudel and muffin specials are always worth trying. There's kombucha on tap and organic and fair-trade coffee, and interesting historical photos in the main dining area. In warmer weather, adjourn to the lovely gardens.

Santa Cruz 9

✕ Bad Animal   Bistro $$

(📞831-900-5031; www.badanimalbooks.com; 101 Cedar St; shared plates & mains $12-23; ⏰5-10pm Wed-Sat, 11am-2pm & 5-9pm Sun; 🥢) A thoroughly modern menu – including contemporary interpretations of French flavors and natural and organic wines – complements this brilliant bookstore showcasing Santa Cruz' bohemian and counterculture roots. Try the mussel cassoulet or yuzu-tinged steak tartare for dinner, or enjoy a leisurely Sunday brunch with the duck hash. Make time to also explore the overflowing bookshelves.

San Francisco 10

✕ Greens   Vegetarian, Californian $$

(📞415-771-6222; www.facebook.com/ greensrestaurant; 2 Marina Blvd, Bldg A, Fort Mason Center; mains $18-28; ⏰5:30-9pm Mon, 11:30am-2:30pm & 5:30-9pm Tue-Thu, 11:30am-2:30pm & 5-9pm Fri, 10:30am-2:30pm & 5-9pm Sat & Sun; 🥢♿; 🚌22, 28, 30, 43, 47, 49) Career carnivores won't realize there's zero meat in the hearty black-bean chili or the other flavor-packed vegetarian dishes – all made using ingredients from a Zen farm in Marin. The on-site cafe serves to-go lunches, and light bites are served on reclaimed-redwood-stump

tables – but book ahead for stellar weekend brunches with breathtaking Golden Gate Bridge views in the window-lined dining room.

🛏 Argonaut Hotel   Boutique Hotel $$$

(📞415-345-5519, 415-563-0800; www. argonauthotel.com; 495 Jefferson St; d $269-474; 🅿️♿❄️🛜🐾; 🚌19, 47, 49, 🚋Powell-Hyde) Originally built as a cannery in 1908, Fisherman's Wharf's top hotel remains a waterfront character, with exposed-brick walls, century-old beams, and nautical decor. Guest rooms are fit for a first mate, with shiplap walls, plush navy-blue furnishings and ultracomfy beds with compass bedheads. All rooms are shipshape, but some are so tiny and dark, you might feel like a stowaway. Parking runs $65.

Around Point Arena 11

🛏 Mar Vista Cottages   Cabin $$$

(📞707-884-3522; www.marvistamendocino. com; 35101 Hwy 1, Anchor Bay; cottages $195-320; ♿🛜🐾) These elegantly renovated 1930s fishing cabins offer a simple, stylish seaside escape with a vanguard commitment to sustainability. The harmonious environment is the result of pitch-perfect details: linens are line-dried over lavender, guests browse the organic vegetable garden to harvest their own dinner and chickens cluck around the grounds laying the next morning's breakfast. It requires two-night stays.

Eureka 13

🛏 Inn at 2nd & C   Historic Hotel $$

(📞707-444-3344; www.theinnat2ndandc.com; 139 2nd St; r/ste from $129/199; 🛜🐾) Formerly the Eagle House Inn, this glorious Victorian hotel has been tastefully restored to combine Victorian-era decor with every possible modern amenity. The magnificent turn-of-the-century ballroom is used for everything from theater performances to special events. There is also a yoga studio. Breakfast, tea and complimentary cocktails are additional perks. Although the hotel is nonsmoking, the owners have thoughtfully designated an outside secluded area for smokers (with a bay view, no less!).

Classic Trip

Mission Trail

Follow the path of early Spanish colonists from San Diego to Sonoma, embracing the most intriguing of California's original missions, with atmospheric inns and eateries along the way.

3

TRIP HIGHLIGHTS

570 miles

San Francisco
Take time out in the buzzing Mission District

FINISH
Sonoma

7

6

475 miles

San Juan Bautista
A ghostly, earthquake-rattled, old mission town

San Luis
Obispo

225 miles

Santa Barbara
Spanish colonial outpost by the sea

4 Ventura

Los
Angeles

2

San Diego

START

San Juan Capistrano
Justifiably nicknamed 'the Jewel of the Missions'

70 miles

5 DAYS
620 MILES / 998KM

- - - - -

GREAT FOR...

📖

- - - - -

BEST TIME TO GO
April to October for sunny skies.

- - - - -

📷 ESSENTIAL PHOTO
Swallows returning to Mission San Juan Capistrano in March.

- - - - -

✓ BEST FOR FOODIES
San Francisco's Mission District.

3 Mission Trail

Established over the course of more than 50 years, a chain of 21 missions stretches along El Camino Real (the Royal Road), first forged by Spanish conquistador Gaspar de Portolá and Franciscan priest Junípero Serra in the late 18th century. Each mission was a day's ride on horseback from the next, but today you can drive the entire route in less than a week.

❶ San Diego

In the spring of 1769, a forlorn lot of about 100 Spanish soldiers and missionaries straggled ashore at San Diego Bay. After sailing for weeks up the coast from Baja California, many were sick and over half had died. They were soon joined by Padre Junípero Serra, who had traveled from Baja California by land. Serra spearheaded the establishment that year of **Mission Basilica San Diego de Alcalá** (☎619-281-8449; www.missionsandiego.org; 10818 San Diego Mission Rd; tours adult/child/under 5yr $5/2/free; ⏰9am-4:30pm; Ⓟ), the oldest in California's chain of missions.

West atop Presidio Hill, the **Junípero Serra Museum** (☎619-232-6203; www.sandiegohistory.org; 2727 Presidio Dr; entry by donation, suggested $5; ⏰10am-4pm Sat & Sun Oct-Apr, 10am-5pm Fri-Mon May-Sep; Ⓟ) recounts Native American struggles with mission life. Where the colonists' original military fort and church once stood, this 1920s Spanish Colonial Revival building echoes early mission architecture.

Nearby, **Old Town San Diego State Historic Park** (☎619-220-5422; www.parks.ca.gov; 4002 Wallace St; ⏰visitor center & museums 10am-5pm May-Sep, 10am-4.30pm Oct-Apr; Ⓟ ⏹) preserves buildings from the Spanish, Mexican and early American periods, with an old-fashioned plaza surrounded by shops and cafes.

✗ 🍴 p60, p70

The Drive » El Camino Real, which is marked throughout California by freestanding bronze mission bells erected in the 1920s, follows I-5 north from San Diego. After more than 60 miles, exit onto Hwy 74 (Ortega

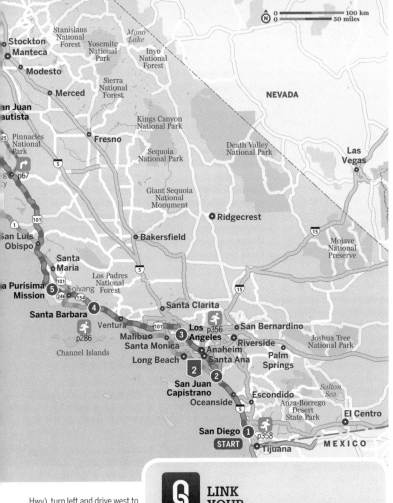

Hwy), turn left and drive west to
Mission San Juan Capistrano.

- - - - - - - - - - - - - - - - - -

TRIP HIGHLIGHT

② San Juan Capistrano

Archaeologists, engineers
and restoration artists
have done an exquisite job
of keeping alive **Mission
San Juan Capistrano**

LINK YOUR TRIP

② Pacific Coast Highways

California's mission
trail intersects with the
classic coastal route at
San Diego, Los Angeles,
Santa Barbara and San
Francisco.

⑦ Sonoma Valley

Where this trip
ends at Sonoma Plaza,
you can start exploring
Northern California's
rustic-chic Wine Country.

Classic Trip

(📞949-234-1300; www.missionsjc.com; 26801 Ortega Hwy; adult/child $10/7; ⏰9am-5pm; ♿). Built around a series of 18th-century arcades, the mission complex encloses bubbling fountains and flowery gardens. The Serra Chapel, where the padre first celebrated mass in 1783, is considered California's oldest building, and even the mighty San Andreas Fault hasn't been able to topple it yet. Every year on March 19, the Festival of the Swallows celebrates the birds' return from their Argentine sojourn to make their nests in the mission's walls. One block west, by the train depot, the tree-shaded **Los Rios Historic District** collects quaint cottages and adobes housing cafes and gift shops.

✖️ p70

The Drive » Get back on I-5 north for the often traffic-jammed 50-mile drive to downtown Los Angeles. Take the Alameda St/Union Station exit, turn right onto Main St and look for metered street parking or pay-parking lots.

- - - - - - - - - - - - - - - -

❸ Los Angeles

A few dozen Spanish colonists founded the 'City of Angels' in 1781, near the site of today's **El Pueblo de Los Ángeles Historical**

Monument (📞213-485-6855; www.elpueblo.lacity.org; Olvera St; ⏰tours 10am, 11am & noon Tue-Sat; ♿; Ⓜ️B/D/L Lines to Union Station). Peek inside 19th-century historical buildings like the Avila Adobe and 'La Placita' plaza church and jostle down crowded block-long Olvera St, an open-air marketplace lined with Mexican food vendors and *folklorico* shops, then unwind in front of the wrought-iron bandstand, where mariachis often play on sunny weekend afternoons. Nearby, **LA Plaza** (La Plaza de Cultura y Artes; 📞213-542-6200; www.lapca.org; 501 N Main St; ⏰noon-5pm Mon & Wed-Fri, 10am-5pm Sat & Sun; ♿; Ⓜ️B/D/L Lines to Union Station) vibrantly chronicles the Mexican American experience in LA.

✖️ 🛏️ p46, p70

The Drive » Follow Hwy 101 north of Downtown LA past Hollywood and west through the suburban San Fernando Valley all the way to the Pacific coast. Northwest of Ventura, another SoCal mission town with beautiful beaches, lies Santa Barbara, about 100 miles from LA.

- - - - - - - - - - - - - - - -

TRIP HIGHLIGHT

❹ Santa Barbara

After a magnitude 6.3 earthquake hit Santa Barbara in 1925, downtown's **State St** was entirely rebuilt in Spanish Colonial Revival style, with whitewashed adobe walls and red-tile roofs. Head north to hillside **Old**

Mission Santa Barbara (📞805-682-4713; www.santabarbaramission.org; 2201 Laguna St; adult/child 5-17yr $12/7; ⏰9am-4:15pm Sep-Jun, to 5:15pm Jul & Aug; 🅿️), another victim of historical quakes. From the front of its imposing Doric facade, itself a homage to an ancient Roman chapel, you can look up at the unique twin bell towers. Founded in 1786 on the feast day of St Barbara, the mission has been continuously occupied by Franciscan priests, having escaped Mexico's enforced policy of secularization that destroyed most of California's other missions. Artwork by Chumash tribespeople adorns the chapel. Look for a centuries-old cemetery out back.

✖️ 🛏️ p60, p70, p217, p319

The Drive » El Camino Real follows Hwy 101 north. For a more scenic route, take winding Hwy 154 up into the mountains and Wine Country. Turn left onto Hwy 246 (Mission Dr) toward the Danish village of Solvang, which has a pretty little mission, then keep driving west along Hwy 246 almost to Lompoc. It's a 50-mile trip from Mission Santa Barbara.

- - - - - - - - - - - - - - - -

❺ La Purísima Mission

Drive through the hills outside Lompoc, past vineyards and commercial flower fields, to **La Purísima Mission State Historic Park** (📞805-733-

3713; www.lapurisimamission.org; 2295 Purísima Rd; per car $6; ⏱ park 9am-5pm, visitor center 10am-4pm Tue-Sun year-round, 11am-3pm Mon Jul & Aug; P ♿). Resurrected by the Civilian Conservation Corps (CCC) during the Depression era, almost a dozen buildings have been restored to their original 1820s appearance. Amble past Spanish soldiers' living quarters, a weaving room and a blacksmith's shop, all beside grassy fields where cows, horses and goats graze.

The Drive >> Follow scenic, rural Hwy 1 north to Pismo Beach, then rejoin Hwy 101 north to San Luis Obispo, a peaceful mission town that's a convenient place to break your journey. The next day, follow Hwy 101 north for 140 more miles past Salinas to Hwy 156, connecting east to San Juan Bautista.

TRIP HIGHLIGHT

❻ San Juan Bautista

Unknowingly built atop the San Andreas Fault, **Mission San Juan Bautista** (☎831-623-4528; www.oldmissionsjb.org; 406 2nd St; adult/child 5-17yr $4/2; ⏱9:30am-4:30pm; P ♿) has the largest church among California's historical missions. The original chapel was toppled by the 1906 San Francisco earthquake. Scenes from Alfred Hitchcock's 1960s film *Vertigo* were shot here, although the climactic bell tower was just a special-effects prop. The old Spanish plaza oppo-

site the mission anchors **San Juan Bautista State Historic Park** (☎831-623-4881; www.parks.ca.gov; 2nd St, btwn Mariposa & Washington Sts; museum adult/child $3/free; ⏱10am-4:30pm; P). A short walk away, dusty downtown San Juan Bautista is crowded with Mexican restaurants and antiques shops.

The Drive >> Backtrack west on Hwy 156 to Hwy 101, which speeds north past Gilroy's garlic farms to San Jose, then curves alongside San Francisco Bay and Silicon Valley. After almost 90 miles, you'll arrive in San Francisco: exit at Duboce Ave, turn left on Guerrero St, then right on 16th St to arrive at Mission San Francisco de Asís.

TRIP HIGHLIGHT

❼ San Francisco

Time seems to stand still at **Mission San Francisco**

de Asís (☎415-621-8203; www.missiondolores.org; 3321 16th St; adult/child $7/5; ⏱9am-4:30pm May-Oct, to 4pm Nov-Apr; 🚌22, 33, Ⓑ16th St Mission, Ⓜ J), also known as Mission Dolores. With its gold-leafed altar and redwood beams decorated with Native American art-work, this is the only intact original mission chapel in California, its adobe walls having stood firm in the 1906 earthquake. Today it's overshadowed by the ornate 1913 basilica, where stained-glass windows commemorate the 21 original California missions. The graveyard out back, where Kim Novak wandered in a daze in Hitchcock's *Vertigo,* is where 5000 Ohlone and Miwok who died in measles epidemics are

---

DETOUR: PINNACLES NATIONAL PARK

Start: ❺ **La Purísima Mission**

Named for the towering spires that rise abruptly out of the chaparral-covered hills, this **park** (☎831-389-4486; www.nps.gov/pinn; 5000 Hwy 146, Paicines; weekly pass per car $30; ⏱park 24hr, east visitor center 9:30am-5pm, west visitor center 9am-4:30pm; P ♿) is a study in geological drama, with its craggy monoliths, sheer-walled canyons and ancient volcanic remnants. Besides hiking and rock climbing, the park's biggest attractions are its endangered California condors and talus caves where bats live. It's best visited during spring or fall; summer's heat is too extreme. Camping is available near the east entrance off Hwy 25 between San Juan Bautista and King City, accessed via Hwy 101 north of San Luis Obispo.

Classic Trip

WHY THIS IS A CLASSIC TRIP

AMY C BALFOUR, WRITER

California's original road trip connects a string of Spanish colonial missions, beautified by sunny cloisters, adobe buildings and pleasingly frescoed chapels. Striking in their reverent simplicity, the missions are direct links to the earliest days of the modern state. The most moving of them thoughtfully spotlight the glories as well as the tragedies stemming from their creation. Serene San Juan Capistrano should not be missed.

Above: Historical Old Town, San Diego
Left: Interior of Mission San Juan Bautista
Right: Church of the Mission San Francisco de Asís

memorialized, surrounded by the graves of early Mexican and European settlers. In the surrounding Mission District, a gentrifying neighborhood once best known for its colorful murals, Mexican taquerias mix with California farm-to-table kitchens.

✕ ☞ p46, p61, p71, p93

The Drive ❯❯ Hwy 101 rolls up and down San Francisco's famous hills, from the Mission District to the Marina and the Presidio, finally exiting the city via the Golden Gate Bridge. North of the mission town of San Rafael, follow Hwy 37 east to Hwy 121 north, then take Hwy 12 north into downtown Sonoma, over a 40-mile drive from San Francisco.

------

⑧ Sonoma

The Wine Country town of Sonoma is not only the site of the last Spanish mission established in California. It also happens to be the place where American settlers attempted to declare independence from Mexico in 1846. Mission San Francisco Solano is now part of **Sonoma State Historic Park** (📞707-938-9560; www.parks.ca.gov; 363 3rd St W; adult/child $3/2; ⏰10am-5pm; P), which preserves military barracks and a mid-19th-century Mexican general's home. Its petite adobe chapel, dating from 1841, is also the finish line for El Camino Real.

✕ ☞ p71, p113

Eating & Sleeping

San Diego ❶

✖ El Agave   Mexican $$$

(☎619-220-0692; www.elagave.com; 2304 San Diego Ave; dishes from $12, dinner mains $22-39; ⊙11am-10pm; ℗) Candlelight flickers in this romantic 2nd-floor, white-tablecloth, high-end place catering to cognoscenti. The mole is superb (there are seven types to choose from), and there are a whopping 2000 tequilas covering just about every bit of wall space and in racks overhead – enough that it calls itself a 'tequila museum.'

☷ Cosmopolitan Hotel   B&B $$

(☎619-297-1874; ww.oldtowncosmopolitan.com; 2660 Calhoun St; r $119-210; ⊙ front desk 9am-9pm; ℗☺☎) Right in Old Town State Park, this creaky, 10-room hotel has been restored to its 1870 glory and has oodles of charm, antique furnishings and is possibly haunted (!). There's a restaurant downstairs for lunch and dinner, with regular live music and afternoon tea. Breakfast is a simple affair centered on coffee and scones. Free wi-fi and free parking.

San Juan Capistrano ❷

✖ Ramos House Café   Californian $$

(☎949-443-1342; www.ramoshouse.com; 31752 Los Rios St; weekday mains $16-21, weekend brunch $35; ⊙8:30am-3pm Thu-Tue) The best spot for breakfast or lunch in Los Rios Historic District, this Old West–flavored, wood-built house from 1881 (with brick patio) does organically raised comfort food flavored with herbs grown on-site: banana-nutella *pain perdu* (French toast), apple-cinnamon beignets, basil-cured salmon lox, huevos rancheros and duck mac and cheese. Breads are baked in-house daily.

Los Angeles ❸

✖ Grand Central Market   Market

(www.grandcentralmarket.com; 317 S Broadway; ⊙8am-10pm; ☎; Ⓜ B/D Lines to Pershing Sq) Designed by prolific architect John Parkinson and once home to an office occupied by Frank Lloyd Wright, LA's beaux-arts market hall has been satisfying appetites since 1917 and today is Downtown LA's gourmet mecca. Lose yourself in its bustle of neon signs, stalls and counters, peddling everything from fresh produce and nuts to sizzling Thai street food, hipster breakfasts, modern deli classics, artisanal pasta and specialty coffee.

Santa Barbara ❹

✖ Bouchon   Californian $$$

(☎805-730-1160; www.bouchonsantabarbara. com; 9 W Victoria St; mains $26-36; ⊙5-9pm) The perfect, unhurried follow-up to a day in the wine country is to feast on the bright, flavorful California cooking at pretty Bouchon (meaning 'wine cork'). A seasonally changing menu spotlights locally grown farm produce and ranched meats that marry beautifully with almost three dozen regional wines available by the glass. Lovebirds, book a table on the candlelit patio.

☷ Spanish Garden Inn   Boutique Hotel $$$

(☎805-564-4700; www.spanishgardeninn.com; 915 Garden St; r from $489; ℗☺✳@☎☒) At this cloistered yet central Spanish-style inn, casual elegance, first-rate service and a romantic central courtyard will have you feeling like the don or doña of your own private villa. Rooms front a balcony or patio; beds are draped in luxurious linens; and bathrooms come with oversized tubs. Chill by the small outdoor pool, or unwind with a massage in your room.

San Francisco ❼

✕ Pancho Villa   Mexican $

(☎415-864-8840; www.sfpanchovilla.com; 3071 16th St; burritos $5-10; ☺10am-midnight; ☝; ☐14, 22, 33, 49, Ⓑ16th St Mission) The hero of the downtrodden and burrito deprived, Pancho Villa supplies tinfoil-wrapped burritos the girth of your forearm and lets you add ammunition at the fresh, heaping salsa bar. The line moves fast going in and, as you leave, the door is held open for you and your newly acquired Pancho's paunch. Stick around for serenades by roving mariachis.

☐ Inn San Francisco   B&B $$

(☎415-641-0188; www.innsf.com; 943 S Van Ness Ave; r $175-400, with shared bath $155-215, cottages $370-495; Ⓟ ☺ @ ☎ ☕; ☐14, 49) An elegant 1872 Italianate-Victorian mansion has become a stately Mission District inn, impeccably maintained and packed with antiques. All rooms have fresh-cut flowers and sumptuous mattresses with feather beds; some have Jacuzzis. The freestanding garden cottage sleeps four adults and two children. Outside there's an English garden and a redwood hot tub open 24 hours – a rarity in SF.

Sonoma ❽

✕ Cafe La Haye   Californian $$$

(☎707-935-5994; www.cafelahaye.com; 140 E Napa St; mains $26-42; ☺5:30-9pm Tue-Sat) Warm feelings are mutual between farmers and chefs, regulars and visitors at cozy La Haye, which champions produce sourced within 60 miles. Neighboring farmers earn co-star credits on seasonal favorites, including sherry-basted Wolfe Ranch quail with sourdough stuffing and hearty chopped salads with George's farm eggs and Humboldt Fog goat's cheese. Save room for simple, sensational desserts such as yuzu-citrus cheesecake.

☐ El Dorado Hotel   Boutique Hotel $$$

(☎707-996-3030; www.eldoradosonoma.com; 405 1st St W; d Sun-Thu $225-330, Fri & Sat $385-500; Ⓟ ☺ ❄ ☎ ☒) Stylish stays in a local landmark right on Sonoma Plaza. The original 1843 adobe building has been thoughtfully remodeled with smart guest rooms that are eco-conscious, compact and comfortable, with high-end linens and private balconies overlooking the plaza or the fig-shaded courtyard. Enjoy the solar-heated saltwater pool, free bikes, tasty farm-to-table restaurant, and famous ice cream drizzled with Sonoma olive oil.

Northern California Trips

San Francisco is the anchor of California's most diverse region. From exploring the rugged beaches of the Lost Coast and floating down the tranquil Russian River, to poking around (and through) the redwoods and surmounting volcano summits, there's no shortage of natural places to explore and scenic roads to drive in Northern California.

Then there's the wine and food. Napa Valley is world-famous for top-drawer cabernet sauvignon, chardonnay and sparkling wines, but you can sip equally impressive vintages in Sonoma Valley, the nearby Russian River, Dry Creek and Alexander Valleys, plus the bucolic Anderson Valley near Mendocino. Then soak in some hot springs, where conversations start with, 'Hey, dude!' and end hours later.

McArthur-Burney Falls

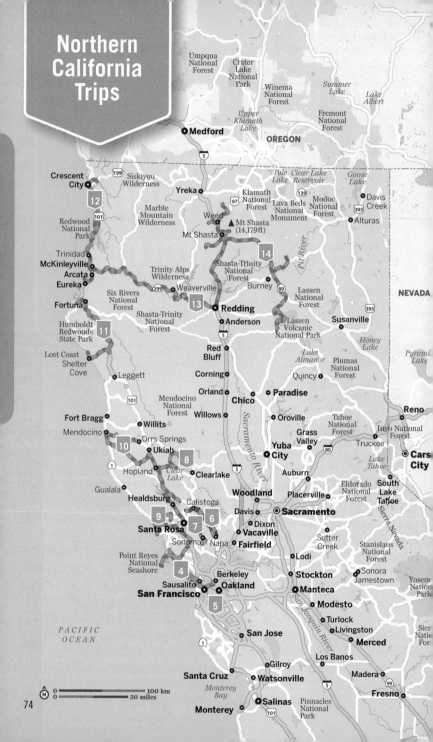

Northern California Trips

Medford

OREGON

Umpqua National Forest

Crater Lake National Park

Winema National Forest

Upper Klamath Lake

Summer Lake

Lake Albert

Fremont National Forest

Crescent City
12

199 Siskiyou Wilderness

Tule Lake

Clear Lake Reservoir

Goose Lake

Davis Creek

Yreka

Klamath National Forest

97

139

Modoc National Forest

Alturas

Redwood National Park
101

Marble Mountain Wilderness

Weed

▲ Mt Shasta (14,179ft)

Lava Beds National Monument

Trinidad
McKinleyville
Arcata
Eureka

Mt Shasta

Shasta-Trinity National Forest

14

NEVADA

Trinity Alps Wilderness

299

Weaverville

Burney

Lassen National Forest

89

395

Fortuna

Six Rivers National Forest

Shasta-Trinity National Forest

13

Redding

Anderson

Lassen Volcanic National Park

Susanville

Honey Lake

Pyrami Lake

Humboldt Redwoods State Park
11

5

Red Bluff

Lake Almanor

Plumas National Forest

Lost Coast Shelter Cove

Leggett

Corning

Quincy

Mendocino National Forest

Orland

Chico

Paradise

101

Willows

Oroville

Reno

Fort Bragg

Willits

Sacramento River

Tahoe National Forest

Inyo National Forest

Mendocino

10

Orrs Springs

Grass Valley

Truckee

80

Cars City

Hopland

Ukiah
8

Yuba City

Lake Tahoe

Gualala

Clear Lake

Clearlake

5

Auburn

Eldorado National Forest

South Lake Tahoe

Healdsburg

Calistoga

Woodland

Placerville

9

Sierra Nevada

6

Davis

⊙ **Sacramento**

7

Santa Rosa

Sonoma

Napa

Dixon
Vacaville

Sutter Creek

Stanislaus National Forest

Sonora
Jamestown

Point Reyes National Seashore

4

Fairfield

Lodi

Berkeley

Stockton

Yosem Nation Park

Sausalito

Oakland

Manteca

San Francisco

5

Modesto

San Jose

Turlock
Livingston

Sier Natio For

Merced

PACIFIC OCEAN

1

Los Banos

Madera

99

Santa Cruz

Gilroy

Watsonville

5

Fresno

Monterey Bay

Salinas

Pinnacles National Park

Monterey

101

0   100 km
0   50 miles

74

DON'T MISS

Wine Tasting

Napa has the most famous names, but rustic-chic wineries in Sonoma County and beyond will charm you on Trips

Conzelman Rd

Gawk at million-dollar views of San Francisco and the Pacific while exploring the hilly Marin Headlands on Trip **4**

Lost Coast

Lose yourself amid black-sand beaches and abandoned lighthouses on a wild, windy stretch of shoreline that time forgot on Trip **11**

Tall Trees Grove

Deep inside Redwood National Park, this ancient forest casts a spell over the lucky few who find it on Trip **12**

McArthur-Burney Falls

Between volcanic Mt Shasta and Mt Lassen, be mesmerized by an ethereal 129ft-high waterfall fed by natural springs on Trip **14**

Marin County

Follow coastal highways and country backroads to drink in stunning vistas from 19th-century lighthouses, dizzying ocean lookouts and the top of Mt Tamalpais.

4

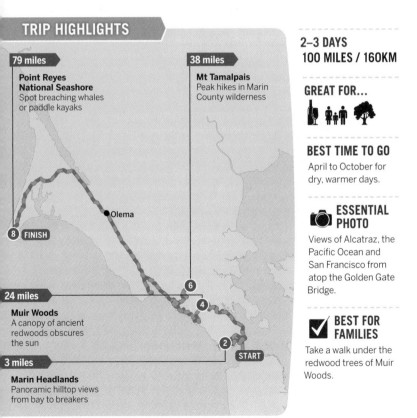

79 miles

Point Reyes National Seashore
Spot breaching whales or paddle kayaks

38 miles

Mt Tamalpais
Peak hikes in Marin County wilderness

8 FINISH

●Olema

24 miles

Muir Woods
A canopy of ancient redwoods obscures the sun

6

4

2

START

3 miles

Marin Headlands
Panoramic hilltop views from bay to breakers

2–3 DAYS
100 MILES / 160KM

GREAT FOR...

BEST TIME TO GO
April to October for dry, warmer days.

ESSENTIAL PHOTO
Views of Alcatraz, the Pacific Ocean and San Francisco from atop the Golden Gate Bridge.

BEST FOR FAMILIES
Take a walk under the redwood trees of Muir Woods.

4 Marin County

Leave behind the heady hills of cosmopolitan San Francisco by driving north across the wind-tunneling passageway of the Golden Gate Bridge. From there, the scenery turns untamed, and Marin County's undulating hills, redwood forests and crashing coastline prove a welcome respite from urban living. Finish up with exhilarating, end-of-the-world views at wild Point Reyes, jutting 10 miles out into the Pacific.

❶ Golden Gate Bridge

Other suspension bridges impress with engineering, but none can touch the **Golden Gate Bridge** (📞toll information 877-229-8655; www.goldengatebridge.org/visitors; Hwy 101; northbound free, southbound $5-8; 🚌28, all Golden Gate Transit buses) for showmanship, with its soaring art-deco design. On sunny days it transfixes crowds with its radiant glow – thanks to a couple dozen daredevil painters, who reapply about 1000 gallons of

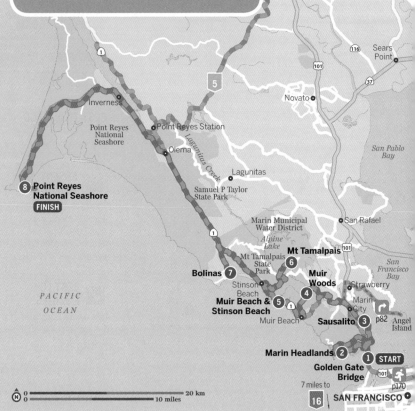

'International Orange' paint weekly. When afternoon fog rolls in, the bridge performs its disappearing act: now you see it, now you don't and, abracadabra, it's sawn in half.

There's no toll to pay when driving north-bound over the turret-topped bridge, which first opened in 1937. On the Marin side of the span, pull into the parking lot and stroll around the **Vista Point** area. Sashay out onto the iconic bridge to spy on cargo ships threading through its pylons. Memorize the 360-degree views of the rugged Marin Headlands, downtown skyscrapers and the speck that is **Alcatraz**.

LINK YOUR TRIP

5 Bay Area Culinary Tour

From Point Reyes Station, drive meandering Point Reyes–Petaluma Rd northeast past green pastures for 19 miles to Petaluma.

16 Along Highway 1 to Santa Cruz

Wind south from San Francisco along Hwy 1 for more lighthouses, organic farms and your pick of sandy cove beaches.

The Drive ›› Immediately north of the bridge and the Vista Point turnoff, take the Alexander Ave exit and take a left on Bunker Rd before swinging back under the highway and through the Barry–Baker Tunnel (also referred to as the Five-Minute Tunnel, because its single lane of traffic changes direction every five minutes). From there, it's 3.5 miles to Point Bonita Lighthouse.

- - - - - - - - - - - - - - - - - - -

TRIP HIGHLIGHT

② Marin Headlands

Near echoey WWII battery tunnels, bird-watchers should stop to hike up **Hawk Hill** (www. nps.gov/goga/learn/nature/hawk-hill.htm; Conzelman Rd;). Thousands of migrating birds of prey soar here from late summer to early fall, straddling a windy ridge with views of Rodeo Lagoon all the way to Alcatraz.

Stay west on Conzelman Rd until it ends in about 2 miles, then bear left towards the bay. The third lighthouse built on the West Coast, **Point Bonita Lighthouse** (☏415-331-1540; www.nps.gov/goga/pobo.htm; ⊙12:30-3:30pm Sun & Mon, hours may vary;) was completed in 1855, but after complaints about its ridgetop performance in fog, it was scooted down to the promontory in 1877. Two afternoons a week you can traverse a steep half-mile trail and cross through a dark rock tunnel – carved out with hand tools only – and

over suspension bridges to inspect the beacon.

Continue north along the oceanview bluffs of Field Rd, joining west-bound Bunker Rd after passing the **visitor center** (☏415-331-1540; www.nps.gov/goga/marin-headlands.htm; Bunker Rd, Fort Barry; ⊙9:30am-4:30pm Wed-Mon). At the end of the road, picnic-worthy **Rodeo Beach** (www.parksconservancy.org/visit/park-sites/rodeo-beach.html; off Bunker Rd; P) awaits with breezy Pacific panoramas and hiking trails.

🛏 p84

The Drive ›› Turn around and take Bunker Rd eastbound (signed San Francisco). Pass back through the timed one-way tunnel and continue straight ahead onto Murray Circle. Down by the waterfront, turn left onto Center Rd. The 5-mile drive takes 15 minutes or less.

- - - - - - - - - - - - - - - - - - -

③ Sausalito

Just under the north tower of the Golden Gate Bridge, at East Fort Baker, families should stop by the **Bay Area Discovery Museum** (☏415-339-3900; https://bayareadiscoverymuseum.org; 557 McReynolds Rd; $16, first Wed of every other month free; ⊙9am-4pm Tue-Fri, to 5pm Sat & Sun; P ♿), an excellent hands-on activity museum with exhibits including an oversized kitchen sink called Wobbleland and a large playground area with a shipwreck.

Follow East Rd as it curves alongside Richardson Bay, then take three quick rights onto Alexander Ave, 2nd St and Bridgeway Blvd. Perfectly arranged on a secure little harbor on the bay, Sausalito's pretty houses tumble neatly down a green hillside into a well-heeled downtown with stunning bay views.

Northwest of downtown, you can poke around Sausalito's picturesque houseboat docks off Bridgeway Blvd between Gate 5 and Gate 6½ Rds. Structures range from psychedelic mural-splashed castles to dilapidated salt-sprayed shacks and three-story floating mansions.

✕ p84

The Drive » Follow Bridgeway Blvd onto Hwy 101 north for less than a mile to the Hwy 1 exit. Ascend a mostly residential section of two-lane Hwy 1 and after 3 miles, follow signs to Muir Woods via the Panoramic Hwy. Parking must be booked online in advance.

- - - - - - - - - - - - - - - - - - -

TRIP HIGHLIGHT

④ Muir Woods

The old-growth redwoods at **Muir Woods National Monument** (☎415-561-2850; www.nps.gov/muwo; 1 Muir Woods Rd, Mill Valley; adult/child $15/free; ☻8am-8pm mid-Mar–mid-Sep, to 7pm mid-Sep–early Oct, to 6pm Feb–mid-Mar & early Oct-early Nov, to 5pm early Nov-Jan; P) are the

closest redwood stand to San Francisco. Logging plans were halted when power couple William Kent (a congressman and naturalist) and Elizabeth Thatcher Kent (a women's rights activist) bought a section of Redwood Creek, and in 1907 donated 295 acres to the federal government. President Theodore Roosevelt made the site a national monument in 1908, the name honoring John Muir, naturalist and founder of environmental organization the Sierra Club.

Muir Woods can get crowded, especially on weekends. But even at busy times, a short hike will take you to quieter trails with huge trees and stunning vistas. Near the entrance, a bustling cafe serves sandwiches, soups, baked goods and hot drinks.

The Drive » Head southwest on Muir Woods Rd (signed Muir Beach/Stinson Beach) and rejoin Hwy 1/Shoreline Hwy, a spectacularly scenic and curvy Pacific Ocean byway that winds north. It's about 3 miles downhill from Muir Woods to the turnoff for Muir Beach.

- - - - - - - - - - - - - - - - - - -

⑤ Muir Beach & Stinson Beach

The turnoff from Hwy 1 for **Muir Beach** (www.nps.gov/goga/planyourvisit/muirbeach.htm; off Pacific Way; P) is marked by the north coast's longest row of mailboxes at mile marker

5.7, just before the Pelican Inn. Another mile northwest along Hwy 1, there are superb coastal views at **Muir Beach Overlook**, where WWII scouts kept watch from the surrounding concrete lookouts for invading Japanese ships.

Over the next 5 miles, Hwy 1 twists and makes hairpin turns atop ocean cliffs – both the road and the seascapes unfurling below will make you gasp. The highway eases as it rolls gently downhill to the town of **Stinson Beach**, a three-block strip of densely packed art galleries, shops, eater-

Stinson Beach

ies and inns. A block west of Hwy 1, the three-mile long beach itself is often blanketed with fog, but when the sun is shining, it's covered with surfers, families and picnickers.

✗ ⊨ p84

The Drive ⟫ In town, turn onto the Panoramic Hwy for Mt Tamalpais. It's a curvy 3.5-mile drive uphill to the state park's headquarters at Pantoll Station.

TRIP HIGHLIGHT

❻ Mt Tamalpais

Standing guard over Marin County, majestic 'Mt Tam' affords breathtaking 360-degree views of ocean, bay and hills rolling into the distance. The rich, natural beauty of the mountain is inspiring – the 6300-acre **state park** (☎415-388-2070; www.parks.ca.gov/mttamalpais; per car $8; ⊙7am-sunset; Ⓟ) is home to deer, foxes, bobcats and many miles of hiking and cycling trails.

Mt Tam was a sacred place to the coastal Miwok people for thousands of years before the arrival of European and American settlers. By the late 19th century, San Franciscans were escaping the bustle of the city with all-day outings on the mountain, and from 1896 to 1930, the 'world's crookedest railroad' (281 turns) connected Mill Valley to the summit (2571ft).

Turn left at Pantoll Station onto Pantoll Rd, then after almost 1.5 miles, turn right onto Ridgecrest Blvd, which climbs another 3 miles to a parking lot below **East Peak** summit. Follow the short but steep hiking trail uphill to a fire lookout with commanding ocean-to-bay views.

The Drive ⟫ Backtrack downhill to Stinson Beach, turning right onto Hwy 1 northbound. Trace the eastern shore of Bolinas Lagoon, where waterfowl prowl during low tide and harbor seals often haul out. Take the first left after the lagoon then go left on Olema–Bolinas Rd, continuing on Wharf Rd into central Bolinas. The 15-mile drive takes just over half an hour.

- - - - - - - - - - - - - - - - - - -

❼ Bolinas

Don't look for any signs directing you here. Residents from this famously private town tore the road sign down so many times that state highway officials finally gave in and stopped replacing

it years ago. Known as 'Jugville' during the gold rush days, this sleepy beachside community is home to writers, musicians and fisherfolk. Stroll along the sand from access points along Wharf Rd or Brighton Ave.

Hikers veer off Olema–Bolinas Rd onto Mesa Rd and follow it northwest nearly 5 miles to road's end at Palomarin Trailhead, the tromping-off point for lovely coastal day hikes. On a sunny day, hightail it out to **Bass Lake**, a popular

freshwater swimming spot reached by way of a 3-mile hike skirting the coast. Another 2.5 miles of walking brings you to majestic **Alamere Falls**, a waterfall that tumbles 50ft off a cliff to the beach below.

✗ p85

The Drive ≫ Return to Hwy 1 and continue 9 miles northwest through Olema Valley. Just past the stop sign in Olema, turn left onto Bear Valley Rd and follow the brown Point Reyes National Seashore signs to the Bear Valley Visitor Center.

DETOUR: ANGEL ISLAND

Start: ❸ Sausalito (p79)

Inland from Hwy 101, just over 8 miles northeast of Sausalito, is the well-to-do town of Tiburon (Spanish for 'shark'). There you can catch a **ferry** (☏415-435-2131; http://angelislandferry.com; 21 Main St; round-trip adult/child/bicycle $15/13/1) to **Angel Island State Park** (☏415-435-5390; www.parks.ca.gov/AngelIsland) and its historical sites, hiking and cycling trails, campgrounds and beaches in the middle of the bay.

Angel Island's varied history – it was a hunting and fishing ground for the Miwok people, a military base, an immigration station, a WWII Japanese internment camp and a Nike missile site – has left it with evocative old forts and bunkers to explore. You can get back to nature on 13 miles of hiking trails, including up Mt Livermore (788ft), granting panoramic views when it's not foggy, or by cycling the 6-mile perimeter loop road.

Nicknamed the 'Ellis Island of the West,' the **Angel Island Immigration Station** (USIS; ☏415-435-5537; www.aiisf.org/visit; adult/child $5/3, incl tour $7/5, cash only; ⊙11am-3pm Wed-Sun) operated from 1910 to 1940. It was primarily a screening and detention center for Chinese immigrants, who were at that time restricted from entering the US. Tours of the haunting site are given three times daily. It's a 1-mile walk, bicycle ride or shuttle trip (round-trip $6) from Ayala Cove's dock.

The best times to visit Angel Island are on summer weekends, when more of the historical buildings and sites are open, and when spring wildflowers bloom. Bring your own food, or grab sandwiches, salads, drinks and snacks from **Angel Island Café** (http://angelisland.com; mains $6-15; ⊙10am-3pm Mon-Fri, to 4pm Sat & Sun May-Sep, hours vary Oct-Apr; 🐾🍴) near the ferry dock. For more information on bike rentals, shuttles and tram tours, visit http://angelisland.com.

Q LOCAL KNOWLEDGE: WILDLIFE WATCHING

Want to see marine wildlife in Marin County? The following are a few choice spots:

In the Marin Headlands, sea lions, seals and other injured, sick and orphaned marine creatures are rehabilitated at the **Marine Mammal Center** (📞415-289-7325; www.marinemammalcenter.org; 2000 Bunker Rd; by donation, tour adult/child $10/5; ⏰10am-4pm; P) before being returned to the wild.

In Bolinas, stroll along Wharf Rd to spot great blue herons, great egrets and snowy egrets, who build nests on the western shore of **Bolinas Lagoon** in springtime. Outside town, drop by **Palomarin Field Station** (📞415-868-0655; www.pointblue.org; 999 Mesa Rd; ⏰dawn-dusk; P) to watch bird-banding demonstrations most mornings.

At Point Reyes National Seashore, you can spot whales from **Point Reyes Lighthouse** (📞415-669-1534; www.nps.gov/pore/planyourvisit/lighthouse.htm; end of Sir Francis Drake Blvd; ⏰10am-4:30pm Fri-Mon, first gallery 2:30-4pm Fri-Mon, weather permitting; P), where barking sea lions laze on the shore. At nearby **Chimney Rock**, a seasonal colony of elephant seals breeds and gives birth between December and March. Hike out toward windy **Tomales Point** to observe free-ranging herds of tule elk.

TRIP HIGHLIGHT

8 Point Reyes National Seashore

A national park that covers much of the peninsula, wind-blown **Point Reyes National Seashore** (📞415-654-5100; www.nps.gov/pore; P) shelters free-ranging elk, scores of marine mammals and all manner of raptors and wild cats. Beginning across the street from the **Bear Valley Visitor Center** (📞415-464-5100; www.nps.gov/pore; 1 Bear Valley Rd, Point Reyes Station; ⏰10am-5pm Mon-Fri, 9am-5pm Sat & Sun), the short, paved **Earthquake Trail** reaches a 16ft gap between the two halves of

a once-connected fence line, a testimonial to the power of the magnitude 7.8 earthquake that rocked SF in 1906.

Follow Bear Valley Rd north to Sir Francis Drake Blvd. Raptors perch on fence posts of historical cattle ranches, and the road bumps over rolling hills as it twists for almost 20 miles out to the lighthouse. Initially, the road parallels **Tomales Bay**, a thin channel that teems with harbor seals. In Point Reyes Station, **Blue Waters Kayaking** (📞415-669-2600; www.bluewaters kayaking.com; 11401 Shoreline Hwy; rentals/tours from $70/78; ⏰usually 9am-5pm, last rental 3pm) offers bay

tours or you can rent a kayak and paddle the secluded beaches and rocky crevices on your own.

At the very end of Sir Francis Drake Blvd, **Point Reyes Lighthouse** (📞415-669-1534; www.nps.gov/pore/planyourvisit/lighthouse.htm; end of Sir Francis Drake Blvd; ⏰10am-4:30pm Fri-Mon, first gallery 2:30-4pm Fri-Mon, weather permitting; P) endures ferocious winds at the base of more than 300 stairs. This is one of the best whale-watching spots along the coast, as gray whales pass during their winter migration. During busy times, visitors must park and take a shuttle bus ($7) from Drakes Beach.

🛏 p85

Eating & Sleeping

Marin Headlands ➋

🛏 Cavallo Point   Lodge $$$
(📞415-339-4700; www.cavallopoint.com; 601 Murray Circle; r from $400; P 😊 @ 🎤 🐾 🛁)
Spread over 45 acres of the Bay Area's most scenic parkland, Cavallo Point lodge flaunts an eco-conscious focus with a full-service spa, restaurant and bar, and easy access to outdoor activities. Choose from richly renovated rooms in the landmark Fort Baker officers' quarters or contemporary, stylish 'green' accommodations with exquisite bay views (including a turret of the Golden Gate Bridge).

🛏 HI Marin Headlands   Hostel $
(📞415-331-2777; www.hiusa.org; Fort Barry, Bldg 941; dm $33-41, r with shared bath $85-150; ⏲ reception 7:30am-10:30pm; P 😊 @ 🎤)
Wake up to grazing deer and dew on the ground at this spartan 1907 military compound snuggled in the woods. It has comfortable beds, two well-stocked kitchens and a yoga room; guests can also gather round a fireplace, shoot pool and play foosball and ping-pong. Coin-op laundry machines and basic ingredients for DIY breakfasts are included in the price.

Sausalito ➌

🍴 Avatar's   Indian $$
(📞415-332-8083; www.facebook.com/avatarsrestaurant; 2656 Bridgeway Blvd; mains $13-19; ⏲11am-3pm & 5-9:30pm Mon-Sat; 🍴)
Boasting a cuisine of 'ethnic confusions,' the Indian-fusion dishes here incorporate Mexican, Italian and Caribbean ingredients and will bowl you over with flavor and creativity. Think Punjabi enchiladas with curried sweet potato, or spinach fettuccine with mild-curry tomato sauce. All diets (vegan, gluten-free etc) are graciously accommodated. It sounds weird, but it's all amazing.

🍴 Poggio Trattoria   Italian $$
(📞415-332-7771; www.poggiotrattoria.com; 777 Bridgeway Blvd; mains $16-38; ⏲6:30am-9pm Sun-Thu, to 10pm Fri & Sat) A classic Northern Italian restaurant specializing in handmade pastas, wood-fired pizzas and tasty salad grown in the owner's spring-fed garden. It's all served up in a swanky, old-world dining room or on the lively outdoor patio. Service is flawless. *Bollito misto* (a rich, meaty Northern Italian stew) graces the menu each winter.

Muir Beach & Stinson Beach ➎

🍴 Parkside   Cafe $$
(📞415-868-1272; www.parksidecafe.com; 43 Arenal Ave; restaurant mains $16-30, snack bar $4-9; ⏲7:30am-9pm, coffee bar from 6am; 🍴)
Famous for its hearty breakfasts and lunches, this cozy eatery next to the **beach** (🍴lifeguard tower 415-868-0942; www.nps.gov/goga/stbe.htm; off Hwy 1; ⏲ from 9am, closing time varies seasonally; P) serves wood-fired pizzas and an array of fresh seasonal seafood at dinner, when reservations are recommended. The bakery cranks out decadent and delicious Gruyère levain bread and pastries, luring families, beachgoers, hikers and cyclists.

🍴 Pelican Inn   Pub Food $$$
(📞415-383-6000; www.pelicaninn.com; 10 Pacific Way; dinner mains $15-38; ⏲8-11am Sat & Sun, 11:30am-3pm & 5:30-9pm Sun-Fri, to 9:30pm Sat) The oh-so-English Pelican Inn lures in visitors almost as much as the beach itself. Hikers, cyclists and families come for pub lunches inside its dark, timbered restaurant and cozy bar, perfect for a pint, bangers-and-mash and a game of darts. Enjoy the lawn in sunshine or warm up beside the open fire when it's colder.

🛏 Sandpiper Lodging   Cabin $$
(📞415-868-1632; www.sandpiperstinsonbeach.com; 1 Marine Way; r $145-180, cabins $220-250, cottage $350; P 😊 🎤) Just off Hwy 1 and a quick stroll to the beach, Sandpiper's rooms, cabins and cottage are all comfortable and truly adorable. All have a gas fireplace and kitchenette, and are ensconced in a lush garden and picnic area. Two-night minimum stay on weekends and holidays between April and October. Bright and friendly management.

Bolinas 7

✖ Eleven Wharf   Pizza $$

(☎415-868-1133; www.11wharfroad.com; 11 Wharf
Rd; pizzas $14-17; ⊙5-9pm Thu-Mon; 🎅) This chic,
sister-owned 'backyard-to-table' restaurant offers
freshly shucked oysters, delicious Neapolitan-style
pizza (topped with fresh local produce) and a mostly
natural wine list. Save space for the *fior di latte*
gelato made with local water-buffalo milk.

✖ Bolinas People's Store   Market $

(☎415-868-1433; 14 Wharf Rd; ⊙8:30am-6:30pm;
🐾) A little co-op grocery store behind the
community center, the People's Store serves fair-
trade coffee and sells organic produce, fresh soup
and excellent tamales. Eat at tables in the shady
courtyard.

Point Reyes Station

✖ Side Street Kitchen   Rotisserie $$

(☎415-663-0303; www.sidestreet-prs.com; 60
4th St; $14-23; ⊙11am-5pm Sat-Wed; 🐾) Order
at the counter for quick bites that are as good as
what you'd get after a long wait in a restaurant.
The specialty here is slow-cooked local meat and
chicken but everything – from the crispy brussels
sprouts to the apple fritters – is divine. Great for
takeout sandwiches too. Bring your dog to the
outdoor patio.

Point Reyes
National Seashore 8

🛏 Cottages at
Point Reyes Seashore   Cottage $$

(☎415-669-7250; www.cottagespointreyes.
com; 13275 Sir Francis Drake Blvd; r $159-249;
🅿️😊🎅🐾🎅) Tucked into the woods, this family-
friendly place offers contemporary kitchenette
rooms in A-frame structures, plus a tennis court,
hot tub, croquet, horseshoe pitches, barbecue grills
and a saltwater pool. There's also a large garden and
private nature trail.

🛏 HI Point Reyes   Hostel $

(☎415-663-8811; www.hiusa.org/pointreyes; 1390
Limantour Spit Rd; dm $35-39, r with shared bath
$105-130; ⊙reception 7:30-10:30am & 4:30-10pm;
🅿️😊@) Just off Limantour Rd, this rustic hostel
has bunkhouses with warm and cozy front rooms,
big-view windows and outdoor areas with hill vistas.
A newer ecofriendly building has four private rooms
(two-night minimum stay on weekends) and a
modern kitchen. It's in a beautiful secluded valley
2 miles from the ocean and surrounded by lovely
hiking trails.

Bay Area Culinary Tour

Combining country and city, this drive is a deeply satisfying taste of California's good earth, ending at revolutionary chef Alice Waters' touchstone restaurant Chez Panisse.

5

TRIP HIGHLIGHTS

0 miles

Sebastopol
Meet the next generation of artisanal taste makers

START 1

●Petaluma

●Marshall

Point Reyes National Seashore ●

3

Stinson Beach

FINISH
●Berkeley

6

●Oakland

Point Reyes Station
Bread, cheese and more Marin County goodies

42 miles

San Francisco
Visit the gourmet nucleus of the Bay Area

145 miles

**2–3 DAYS
160 MILES / 255KM**

GREAT FOR...

BEST TIME TO GO
Late summer or early fall, when farms deliver their tastiest bounty.

ESSENTIAL PHOTO
The lighthouse, bluffs and endless horizon at Point Reyes National Seashore.

☑ **BEST PICNIC**
Briny oysters, local bread and cheeses, and Heidrun sparkling mead at Hog Island Oyster Company.

int Reyes Lighthouse

5

Bay Area Culinary Tour

Making a delicious loop around the Bay Area, you'll wander through the aisles of celebrated farmers markets and drop in on artisanal food and drink producers, from Hog Island oyster farm to Cowgirl Creamery and more. A hike at Point Reyes National Seashore will work up a healthy appetite. You'll need it on this straight-from-the-source trip to foodie heaven.

TRIP HIGHLIGHT

❶ Sebastopol

This western Sonoma farm town was founded in the 19th century, when apples were its main cash crop. Swing by in August for the **Gravenstein Apple Fair** (www.gravensteinapplefair.com; 500 Ragle Rd, Ragle Ranch Park; ⏱Aug; 👪), a lively weekend celebration of local food, wines and brews, accompanied by live music and more. In late summer and early autumn, you can pick your own apples at

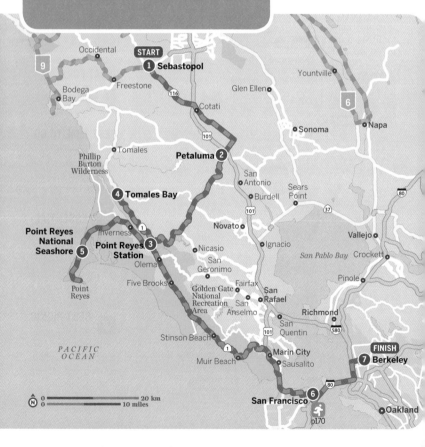

orchards on the outskirts of town along Sonoma County's **Farm Trails** (www.farmtrails.org).

But Sebastopol is about so much more than apples these days. Just look at the **Barlow** (☑707-824-5600; www.thebarlow.net; cnr Sebastopol Ave & Morris St; ⊙hours vary; P ⊞), a former apple processing plant that has been repurposed into a 12-acre village of food producers, artists, winemakers, coffee roasters and spirits distillers who showcase West County's culinary and artistic diversity. Wander shed to shed, sample everything from microbrewed beer to nitrogen flash-frozen ice cream, and meet

LINK YOUR TRIP

6 Napa Valley

Cruise 26 miles east from Petaluma to Napa, the gateway to America's most famous wine region, home to several of California's best restaurants.

9 Russian River & the Bohemian Highway

Starting in Sebastopol, revel in the country charms of 'Slownoma,' stopping at orchards, vineyards and Freestone's famous bakery.

artisanal makers in their workshops.

The Drive » Follow Hwy 116 south out of town for 8 miles to Cotati. Keep going across Hwy 101 (the speedier but more boring route to Petaluma) and turn right onto Old Redwood Hwy. After 3 miles, go left on pastoral Old Adobe Rd for 6 miles, turning left just past Petaluma Adobe State Historic Park.

❷ Petaluma

'The world's egg basket' – as the agrarian town of Petaluma has long been known – is home to countless chicken farms that sell fresh eggs and dairy products. Across Hwy 101 and west of downtown, the **Petaluma Creamery** (☑707-762-9038; www.springhillcheese.com; 711 Western Ave; items $3-9; ⊙8am-5pm; ⊅ ⊞) has been in business for more than a century. Stop by to sample organic cheeses or for a scoop of lavender or Meyer-lemon ice cream from the small specialty foods market and cafe.

More recently, Petaluma has earned a reputation for its densely foggy and wind-whipped appellation, which winegrowers have dubbed 'the Petaluma Gap.' As wineries such as **Keller Estate** (☑707-765-2117; www.kellerestate.com; 5875 Lakeville Hwy, Petaluma; tour & tasting $25-40; ⊙tour/tastings 11:30am, 1pm, 2:30pm Fri-Mon) have become more

prominent, the region's chardonnays, pinot noirs and syrahs have gained recognition for their elegance and complexity.

The Drive » From downtown Petaluma, take D St southwest to Red Hill Rd and follow Point Reyes–Petaluma Rd toward the coast, turning left onto Hwy 1 for Point Reyes Station. It's a relaxing 19-mile country drive; stop en route for Camembert or Brie at the Marin French Cheese factory store.

TRIP HIGHLIGHT

❸ Point Reyes Station

Surrounded by dairies and ranches, Point Reyes Station became a hub for artists in the 1960s. Today it offers a collection of art galleries, boutique shops and excellent food. The tour of the town's edibles begins by fighting your way through the spandex-clad crowd of weekend cyclists to grab a crusty loaf of fire-baked Brickmaiden Bread at **Bovine Bakery** (☑415-663-9420; www.bovinebakeryptreyes.com; 11315 Hwy 1; most items $2-6; ⊙6:30am-5pm Mon-Fri, 7am-5pm Sat, 7am-4pm Sun; ⊅). Next, step down the block to the restored barn that houses one of California's most sought-after cheesemakers, Cowgirl Creamery & Cantina (p93). In spring the must-buy is its St Pat's, a smooth, mellow round wrapped in wild nettle leaves. Otherwise, the Mt Tam (available year-round) is pretty damn good, and there's a gourmet deli for picking up picnic supplies. Heading north out of town, **Heidrun Meadery** (☎415-663-9122; www.heidrunmeadery.com; 11925 Hwy 1; tasting $15, incl tour $35; ⊙11am-4pm Mon & Wed-Fri, to 5pm Sat & Sun) pours tasting sips of sparkling mead, made from aromatic small-batch honey in the style of French champagne.

✕ p93

The Drive ›› Follow Hwy 1 north out of the tiny village of Point Reyes Station. Cruise for 9 miles along the east side of tranquil Tomales Bay, which flows many miles out into the Pacific. Just before the turnoff for rural Marshall–Petaluma Rd, look for the sign for bayfront Hog Island Oyster Company on your left.

❹ Tomales Bay

Only 10 minutes north of Point Reyes Station, you'll find the salty turnout for the **Hog Island Oyster Company** (☎415-663-9218; www.hogislandoysters.com; 20215 Hwy 1, Marshall; dozen oysters $14-36, picnic per person $5; ⊙ shop 9am-5pm daily, picnic area from 10:30am, cafe & bar 11am-5pm Fri-Mon). There's not much to see: just some picnic tables and BBQ grills, an outdoor cafe and a small window vending the famously silky oysters and a few other picnic provisions. While you can buy oysters to go (by the pound), for a

fee you can nab a picnic table, borrow shucking tools and take a lesson on how to crack open the oysters yourself. Lunch at the waterfront farm is unforgettable – and very popular, so reserve ahead for a picnic table or for a seat at the communal tables.

✕ ⊨ p93

The Drive ›› Backtrack 10 miles south on Hwy 1 through Point Reyes Station. Turn right onto Sir Francis Drake Blvd, following the signs for Point Reyes National Seashore, just on the other side of Tomales Bay.

❺ Point Reyes National Seashore

For another perfect picnic spot, look down the coast to **Point Reyes National Seashore** (☎415-654-5100; www.nps.gov/pore; P). The windswept peninsula's rough-hewn beauty lures marine mammals and migratory birds. The 110 sq miles of pristine ocean beaches also offer excellent hiking and camping opportunities. For an awe-inspiring view, follow Sir Francis Drake Blvd beside Tomales Bay all the way out toward the **Point Reyes Lighthouse** (☎415-669-1534; www.nps.gov/pore/planyourvisit/lighthouse.htm; end of Sir Francis Drake Blvd; ⊙10am-4:30pm Fri-Mon, first gallery 2:30-4pm Fri-Mon, weather permitting; P). Follow the signs and turn left before the lighthouse

to find the trailhead for the 1.6-mile round-trip hike to **Chimney Rock**, where wildflowers bloom in spring.

The Drive ›› Leaving the park, trace the eucalyptus-lined curves of Hwy 1 south toward Stinson Beach and past one stunning Pacific view after another. If you don't stop, you'll be back across the Golden Gate Bridge in about an hour and a half. From the bridge, follow Hwy 101 through the city to Broadway, then go east to the waterfront piers.

TRIP HIGHLIGHT

❻ San Francisco

From the center of the Golden Gate Bridge, it's

MICHAEL LEE /GETTY IMAGES ©

Ferry Plaza Farmers Market

possible to view the clock tower of the city's **Ferry Building** (📞415-983-8000; www.ferrybuildingmarketplace.com; cnr Market St & the Embarcadero; ⏰10am-7pm Mon-Fri, 8am-6pm Sat, 11am-5pm Sun; 🚻; 🚃2, 6, 9, 14, 21, 31, MEmbarcadero, BEmbarcadero), a transit hub turned gourmet emporium, where foodies happily miss their ferries slurping Hog Island oysters and bubbly. Star chefs are frequently spotted at the thrice-weekly **Ferry Plaza Farmers Market** (📞415-291-3276; www.cuesa.org; cnr Market St & the Embarcadero; street food $3-12; ⏰10am-2pm Tue & Thu,

from 8am Sat; 🚲 🚻; 🚃2, 6, 9, 14, 21, 31, MEmbarcadero, BEmbarcadero) that wraps around the building year-round. The largest market is on Saturday, when dozens of family farmers and artisanal food and flower vendors show up. From dry-farmed tomatoes to organic kimchi, the bounty may seem like an embarrassment of riches. If your trip doesn't coincide with a market day, never fear: dozens of local purveyors await indoors at the **Ferry Building Marketplace**. Take a taste of McEvoy Ranch and Stonehouse olive oils, fresh-baked

loaves from Acme Bread Company and Humphry Slocombe ice cream.

🍴 🛏 p93

The Drive » It's a straight shot over the San Francisco–Oakland Bay Bridge and into Berkeley via I-80 eastbound. Exit at University Ave and follow it east to Shattuck Ave, then go north of downtown Berkeley to the 'Gourmet Ghetto.'

- - - - - - - - - - - - - - - - -

7 Berkeley

San Francisco might host a handful of banner dining rooms, but California's food revolution got started across the bay, in Berkeley. You may spot the inventor of California

CHEZ PANISSE PROTÉGÉS

Operating a restaurant for 45 years, lauded chef Alice Waters has seen a whole lot of people come through the kitchen. Of her alumni in San Francisco, try Michael Tusk, who offers elegant, seasonally inspired Californian cuisine at **Quince** (🖉415-775-8500; www.quincerestaurant.com; 470 Pacific Ave; 10-course tasting menu $298, wine pairing $275, abbreviated menu $195; ⏲5:30-9pm Mon-Thu, 5-9:30pm Fri & Sat; 🚃3, 10) and more rustic Italian fare at **Cotogna** (🖉415-775-8508; www.cotognasf.com; 490 Pacific Ave; mains $19-38; ⏲11:30am-10:30pm Mon-Thu, to 11pm Fri & Sat, 5-9:30pm Sun; 🍴; 🚃10, 12), or Gayle Pirie, who operates **Foreign Cinema** (🖉415-648-7600; www.foreigncinema.com; 2534 Mission St; mains $28-36; ⏲5:30-10pm Sun-Wed, to 11pm Thu-Sat, brunch 11am-2:30pm Sat & Sun; 🚃12, 14, 33, 48, 49, Ⓑ24th St Mission), a gourmet movie house in the Mission District.

More casual eateries by other Waters' protégés are found across the bay in Oakland. Tuck into grilled herby lamb and spiced king-trumpet-mushroom kebabs at Russell Moore's **The Kebabery**; and Alison Barakat serves what may be the Bay Area's best fried-chicken sandwich at **Bakesale Betty** (🖉510-985-1213; 5098 Telegraph Ave; sandwiches $10; ⏲11am-2pm Tue-Sat; 🚃AC Transit 6).

cuisine, famed chef Alice Waters, in her element and in raptures at the **North Berkeley Farmers Market** (🖉510-548-3333; www.ecologycenter. org; Shattuck Ave, at Rose St; ⏲3-7pm Thu; 🍴; 🚃AC Transit 79), run by the Ecology Center. It's in the so-called 'Gourmet Ghetto' – a neighborhood that marries the progressive 1960s ideals of Berkeley with haute-dining sensibility. The neighborhood's anchor, and an appropriate final stop, is Chez Panisse (p93), Alice Waters' influential restaurant. It's unpretentious, and every mind-altering, soul-sanctifying bite of the food is emblematic of the chef's revolutionary food principles. The kitchen is even open so diners can peek behind the scenes.

🍴 p93

Eating & Sleeping

Point Reyes Station ③

✘ Cowgirl Creamery & Cantina   Deli $

(☎415-663-9335; www.cowgirlcreamery.
com; 80 4th St; deli items $3-12; ◷10am-5pm
Wed-Sun; ♪) Perhaps the best cheeses
made in Northern California, Marin, and
probably beyond. The milk is local and organic,
with vegetarian rennet in soft cheeses.The
cheesemaking facility is in an indoor deli and
marketplace in an old barn that also sells farm-
fresh picnic items, organic produce and some
local clothing and crafts.

Tomales Bay ④

✘ Nick's Cove   Californian $$$

(☎415-663-1033; www.nickscove.com; 23240
Hwy 1, Marshall; mains $16-38; ◷11am-8pm
Mon-Thu (to 9pm in summer), to 9pm Fri-Sun)
At this vintage 1930s roadhouse perched over
Tomales Bay, trophy heads are mounted on
knotty-pine walls and there's a roaring fireplace.
Book a window table at sunset while you sup on
impeccable seafood, wood-fired meats and local
oysters – all sustainably farmed. Reservations
are strongly recommended. It's about a
20-minute drive north of Point Reyes Station.

⌂ Dancing Coyote
Beach Cottages   Cottage $$$

(☎415-669-7200; www.dancingcoyotebeach.
com; 12794 Sir Francis Drake Blvd; cottages
$200-325; P ⊖ 🛜😼) Serene and
comfortable, these four modern cottages back
right onto Tomales Bay, with skylights and
decks extending the views in all directions.
Full kitchens contain locally sourced breakfast
foods, and fireplaces are stocked with firewood
for foggy nights.

San Francisco ⑥

✘ Hog Island
Oyster Company   Seafood $$

(☎415-391-7117; www.hogislandoysters.com; 1
Ferry Bldg, cnr Market St & the Embarcadero; 6

oysters $19-21; ◷11am-9pm; 🚌2, 6, 9, 14, 21,
31, Ⓜ Embarcadero, Ⓑ Embarcadero) Slurp the
bounty of the North Bay with East Bay views
at this local, sustainable oyster bar. Get them
raw, grilled with chipotle-bourbon butter, or
Rockefeller (cooked with spinach, Pernod and
cream). Not the cheapest oysters in town, but
consistently the best, with excellent local wines –
hence the waits for seating. Stop by Hog Island's
farmers-market stall 8am to 2pm Saturday.

⌂ Orchard
Garden Hotel   Boutique Hotel $$

(☎415-393-9917; www.theorchardgardenhotel.
com; 466 Bush St; d $278-389; P ⊖ ❄ @ 🛜;
🚌2, 3, 30, 45, Ⓑ Montgomery) San Francisco's
original LEED-certified, all-green-practices
hotel uses sustainably grown wood, chemical-
free cleaning products and recycled fabrics in
its soothingly quiet rooms. Don't think you'll
be trading comfort for conscience: rooms have
unexpectedly luxe touches, like high-end down
pillows, Egyptian-cotton sheets and organic
bath products. Toast sunsets with a cocktail on
the rooftop terrace. Book directly for deals, free
breakfast and parking.

Berkeley ⑦

✘ Chez Panisse   Californian $$$

(☎cafe 510-548-5049, restaurant 510-548-
5525; www.chezpanisse.com; 1517 Shattuck Ave;
cafe dinner mains $23-35, restaurant prix-fixe
dinner $75-125; ◷cafe 11:30am-2:45pm &
5-10:30pm Mon-Thu, 11:30am-3pm & 5-11pm
Fri & Sat, restaurant seatings 5:30pm & 8pm
Mon-Sat; ♪; 🚌AC Transit 7) Foodies come
to worship here at the church of Alice Waters,
inventor of California cuisine. Panisse is located
in a lovely arts-and-crafts house in Berkeley's
'Gourmet Ghetto.' Pull out all the stops with a
prix-fixe meal downstairs or go less expensive
and a tad less formal in the upstairs cafe.
Reservations accepted one month ahead.

Napa Valley

California's wine-and-dine landmark has been winning global prizes for half a century – see why in sun-dappled vineyard tastings and starlit gourmet feasts. Napa keeps cooking and pouring out joy.

6

TRIP HIGHLIGHTS

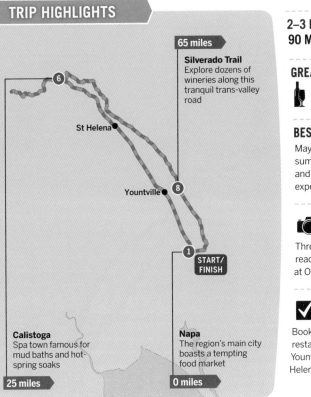

65 miles

Silverado Trail
Explore dozens of wineries along this tranquil trans-valley road

St Helena

Yountville **8**

1 START/FINISH

Calistoga
Spa town famous for mud baths and hot-spring soaks

25 miles

Napa
The region's main city boasts a tempting food market

0 miles

2–3 DAYS
90 MILES / 145KM

GREAT FOR...
🍷

BEST TIME TO GO
May for the lull before summer; September and October to experience 'the crush.'

📷 **ESSENTIAL PHOTO**
Three...two...one! Get ready for an eruption at Old Faithful Geyser.

✅ **BEST FOR FOODIES**
Book a star chef's restaurant table in tiny Yountville or historic St Helena.

6 Napa Valley

Wining and dining is a glorious way of life in Napa today – grapes have grown here since the gold rush. Right off Hwy 29, organic family wineries are daring to make wines besides classic cabernets, and indie winemakers have opened up shop on Napa's revitalized 1st St. Traveling through this lush valley, you'll notice Napa's commitment to sustainability and local character. Between feasts, you'll spot sous-chefs weeding organic kitchen gardens to seed farm-to-table menus. The signs are clear: you've arrived right on time for Napa's renaissance.

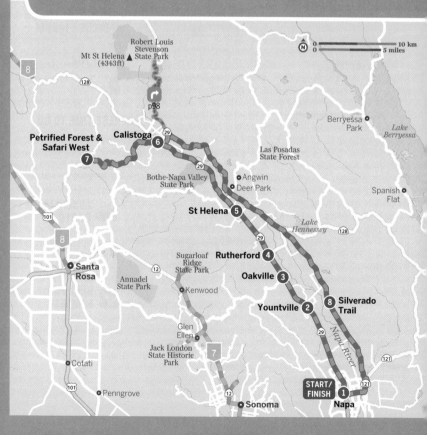

TRIP HIGHLIGHT

1 Napa

Your first stop in Napa may be the only one you need. This is where Napans come to unwind at laid-back downtown tasting rooms, historic music halls, and local gourmet Oxbow Public Market (p105). Napa's newly revitalized 1st St is lined with indie wine-tasting rooms and world-class, California-casual bistros.

The new **Napa Valley Vine Trail** (www.vinetrail.org) connecting downtown Napa to Yountville provides a welcome respite from Hwy 29 traffic, and Napa's riverbank parks help manage seasonal floods with sustainable design. Lately downtown Napa has raised its profile with the star-studded **Napa Valley Film Festival** (www.napavalleyfilmfest.org; passes from $125; ☉Nov) and breakout-hit **BottleRock Music Festival** (www.bottlerocknapavalley.com; 575 3rd St, Napa Valley Expo; ☉end of May). Between events, Napa remains the sweet spot where wine flows and conversation meanders.

✕ ⇤ p104

The Drive » From Napa, Yountville is 9 miles north on Hwy 29, a divided four-lane road surrounded by vineyards and framed by low hills.

---

2 Yountville

Planets and Michelin stars are aligned over Yountville, a tiny Western stagecoach stop that's been transformed into a global dining destination. Sounds like an urban legend – until you take a stroll down Yountville's quiet, tree-lined Washington St. Say hey to interns weeding **French Laundry Gardens** (6639 Washington St; ☉morning-sunset), chocolatiers pouring out new creations at **Kollar Chocolates** (www.kollarchocolates.com; 6525 Washington St, Marketplace at the Yountville Estate; ☉10am-5:30pm; 🚸), and trainee sommeliers grabbing lunch at Tacos Garcia (p104). You've just met the talents behind Yountville's gourmet landmarks, including the legendary (but reservation-only) **French Laundry** (☎707-944-2380; www.thomaskeller.com/tfl; 6640 Washington St; prix-fixe dinner from $350; ☉seatings 5-9pm daily, 11am-12:30pm Fri-Sun).

✕ ⇤ p104

The Drive » Go north to Oakville via 4 miles of vineyard vistas on Hwy 29, which narrows to two lanes just outside Yountville. Tracks for the Napa Valley Wine Train line the west side of the road.

---

3 Oakville

Except for the famous **Oakville Grocery** (☎707-944-8802; www.oakvillegrocery.com; 7856 Hwy 29; sandwiches $10-14, pizzas $15-16; ☉7am-5pm Sun-Thu, to 6pm Fri & Sat; 🚸) and its next-door **wine-history museum**, you could drive through Oakville and never know you'd missed it. But when wine aficionados look at this green valley, they see red – thanks in no small part to **Robert Mondavi** (☎888-766-6328, 707-226-1395; www.robertmondaviwinery.com; 7801 Hwy 29, Oakville; tasting/tour from $25/30; ☉10am-5pm; P 🚸), the visionary vintner who knew back in the 1960s that Napa was capable of more than jug wine. His marketing savvy launched Napa's premium reds to cult status, including his own Opus One Meritage (Napa red blend).

The Drive » Pass gilded signs of name-brand mega-wineries as you continue 2 miles north on Hwy 29 to Rutherford.

LINK YOUR TRIP

7 Sonoma Valley

For lower-key wine tasting and early California historical sites, head to Sonoma Valley via Hwy 12/121.

8 Healdsburg & Around

From Calistoga, take Hwy 128 northwest less than 20 miles to more wineries in Alexander and Dry Creek Valleys.

Classic Trip

④ Rutherford

Hard to believe it looking at these lush vineyards, but Napa Valley's most famous patch of cab country was once covered in wheat. Local farmers saw grape opportunity in this rich bottom land, and the rest is history in a bottle. Trailblazing winemaker Mike **Grgich** (☎707-963-2784; www.grgich.com; 1829 St Helena Hwy, Rutherford; tasting $40; ⏰9:30am-4:30pm; [P]) put Napa chardonnay on the map in 1976 with his historic win in a French wine competition, dubbed the 'Judgment of Paris.'

Exit Hwy 29 onto backroads off Rutherford Rd, and you'll find idiosyncratic organic winemaking flourishing in the heart of mega-brand cab country. Meandering paths wind through fruit-bearing orchards at **Frog's Leap** (☎707-963-4704; www.frogsleap.com; 8815 Conn Creek Rd, Rutherford; tasting & tour $35-55; ⏰by appointment 10am-4pm; [P] 🚻🐾) winery, where merlot and sauvignon blanc are produced in an 1884 barn.

✖ p104

The Drive ⟩⟩ St Helena is another 4 miles north on Hwy 29, though you may be slowing to a crawl before reaching downtown.

⑤ St Helena

Even people with places to go can't resist downtown St Helena, which looks like a Western movie set. Three blocks of Main St are a designated national historic site, covering 160 years of California history, including one of the oldest cinemas in America still in operation. Up the street, the 1889 Greystone Cellars château is home to the **Culinary Institute of America**.

This area was native Wappo land until it was claimed by Spain, then Mexico – more specifically, the property of Dona Maria Ygnacia Soberanes. She gave her daughter Isadora **Bale Grist Mill** (☎707-963-2236; 3369 St Helena Hwy; adult/child $5/2; ⏰10am-4pm Sat & Sun; 🚻), still grinding flour today, and prime vineyards to her daughter Caroline, who married a German winemaker named Charles Krug. Together they founded the first commercial winery in Napa in 1858.

Today if you're thirsty, you're in luck: there's more than an acre of winegrapes per resident in St Helena. So raise a toast to the women who put that wine in your glass, and their hearts

DETOUR:
ROBERT LOUIS STEVENSON STATE PARK

Start: ⑥ **Calistoga**

Eight miles north of Calistoga via curving Hwy 29, the extinct volcanic cone of Mt St Helena marks a dramatic end to Napa Valley at **Robert Louis Stevenson State Park** (☎707-942-4575; www.parks.ca.gov; 3801 Hwy 29; ⏰sunrise-sunset; [P]). It's a strenuous 5-mile climb to the park's 4343ft summit, but what a view – 200 miles on a clear day. For a shorter hike with views over valley vineyards, take **Table Rock Trail** (2.2 miles one-way) from the parking-area trailhead. Check conditions before setting out.

The park also includes the old **Silverado Mine** site where writer Robert Louis Stevenson and artist Fanny Osbourne honeymooned in 1880 in an abandoned bunkhouse. Broke, sick and cold, they miraculously survived – and stayed married. He became famous as the author of *Treasure Island*, *Silverado Squatters*, and *Dr Jekyll and Mr Hyde*, with Fanny as his editor. Robert never recovered his health and died young.

CALISTOGA SPAS

Bubbling with mineral hot springs, Calistoga is famous as the best place in the West to wallow in the mud. Sliding into a tub full of warm, silky, squishy volcanic mud is uniquely relaxing – prepare for deep muscle relaxation, accompanied by rather rude squelching sounds.

Calistoga mud is a blend of volcanic ash, peat and hot mineral springwater. Brochures promise glowing skin and a range of health benefits, including 'detoxifying', but lifted spirits and soothed muscles are reasons enough to wallow.

Mud-bath packages ($95 to $110) take 60 to 90 minutes. You start semi-submerged in hot mud, then soak in hot mineral water – a steam bath and blanket-wrap typically follow. A massage increases the cost (from $140), and may not be strictly necessary once your muscles relax. Baths are usually solo, though some offer couples' options. Variations include thin, painted-on clay-mud wraps called 'fango' baths, good for those uncomfortable sitting in mud. Reservations are essential.

Indian Springs (☎844-378-3635; www.indianspringscalistoga.com; 1712 Lincoln Ave; mud bath $110; ☺by appointment 8:15am-7pm) The original Calistoga resort has kept up with the times, filling modern concrete tubs with locally sourced volcanic mud and a vast outdoor pool with hot natural springwater.

Spa Solage (☎707-266-0825; www.aubergeresorts.com/solage; 755 Silverado Trail; treatments from $110; ☺by appointment 8am-8pm; 👶💃) Serene top-end spa, with paint-on mud treatments and private tubs. Hang out afterwards wrapped in blankets in zero-gravity chairs, or dip into separate-gender, clothing-optional mineral pools.

Mount View Spa (☎707-942-1500; www.mountviewhotel.com; 1457 Lincoln Ave; mud bath per person 25/45min single $75/95, couple $50/65; ☺by appointment 8:30am-7pm) Historic spa-hotel with lighter, mineral-rich mud that's easier to wash off; couples' mud baths and CBD-infused baths available.

Calistoga Spa Hot Springs (☎707-942-6269, 866-822-5772; www.calistogaspa.com; 1006 Washington St; mud bath $105; ☺by appointment 9am-4pm Mon-Thu, to 7pm Fri-Sun; 👶) Traditional mud baths and massage at a motel complex with two huge swimming pools, where you can invite one friend to join you (surcharge $25).

into building this charming town.

✕ 🛏 p105

The Drive » Trees break up the vineyard views as you head 8 miles northwest on Hwy 29 to Calistoga.

---

6 Calistoga

With soothing natural hot springs, bubbling volcanic mud pools and a spurting geyser, the settlement of Nilektsonoma was renowned across Talahalusi (Napa Valley) by the Wappo people for some 8000 years. Then in 1859, legendary speculator Sam Brennan talked bankers into backing his scheme to transform Nilektsonoma into Calistoga, California's signature spa resort. But California cowboys preferred dirt, and by 1873 Sam cut his losses in Calistoga and left town. Only a few Brannan cottages remain from his original resort.

Some 150 years later, Brannan's dream seems to have come true. Local hills dotted with defunct silver and mercury mines are reclaimed as parkland, including **Bothe-Napa** (☎707-942-4575; www.parks.ca.gov; 3801 St Helena Hwy; parking $8; ☺8am-sunset; 👶) and Robert Louis Stevenson State

NAPA VALLEY VINE TRAIL

CITY OF NAPA

PREMIER PARTNERS
NAPA VALLEY VINTNERS • VISIT NAPA VALLEY

SHELTER PARTNER GASSER FOUNDATION

WHY THIS IS A CLASSIC TRIP
ALISON BING, WRITER

Napa Valley is America's fanciest stretch of farmland, with million-dollar steel sculptures in sun-drenched fields and marble bars in architect-designed barns. You'll recognize the scene from glossy magazines – but spend a day in Napa, and you'll also notice 150-plus years of hard work. No matter how early you rise, vineyard workers are already pruning grapes; even after fine-dining restaurants close, taqueros keep pulling *carne asada* off the grill. This calls for a toast: to vigilant firefighters, who protect this wondrous 30-mile stretch of dreams and dirt from increasingly regular wildfires'.

Above: Napa Valley Vine Trail
Left: Infinity pool in Calistoga
Right: Napa Valley Wine Train

Park (p98). Calistoga's extraordinary geology is a featured attraction at the Petrified Forest (p101) and **Old Faithful Geyser** (☎707-942-6463; www. oldfaithfulgeyser.com; 1299 Tubbs Lane, between Hwy 128 & Hwy 29; adult/child/under 4yr $15/9/free; ☺8:30am-7pm, shorter hours Oct-Feb; P ☺) and its spring water still appears on store shelves today. Meanwhile at Calistoga's hot-springs spas (p99), brochures still extol the curative powers of mineral springs and bubbling mud baths. Have some wine at **Sam's Social Club** (☎707-942-4969; www.samssocialclub. com; 1712 Lincoln Ave; dinner mains $17-42; ☺7:30am-9pm Mon-Wed, to 9:30pm Thu-Sun), and go with the volcanic flow.

✕ 🛏 p105

The Drive » Backtrack southeast on Hwy 128 and go 4 miles west on forested, curvy Petrified Forest Rd.

- - - - - - - - - - - - - - -

❼ Petrified Forest & Safari West

Three million years ago, a volcanic eruption at Mt St Helena blew down a stand of redwoods. Their trunks gradually turned to stone, and in 1914, enterprising environmentalist Ollie Bockee preserved this land as an educational attraction. Her vision remains remarkably intact today at the **Petrified Forest**

Classic Trip

(📞707-942-6667; www.
petrifiedforest.org; 4100 Petrified Forest Rd; adult/6-11yr/12-
18yr $12/6/8; ⏰10am-7pm
late May-early Sep, to 6pm
Apr-late May & early Sep-Oct,
to 5pm Nov-Mar; 🅿️👶🐾)
Wildfires struck in 2017,
but the petrified red-
woods were spared and
the living redwoods are
recovering beautifully,
as you can see along two
restored half-mile trails.

Four miles west, where
Petrified Forest Rd curves
right onto Porter Creek,
you may hear some
strange sounds... yes, that
was a rhino. Welcome to
Safari West (📞707-579-
2551; www.safariwest.com;
3115 Porter Creek Rd; adult/
child 4-12yr from $83/45;
⏰tours 9am, 10am, 1pm, 2pm
& 4pm; 🅿️👶), a 400-acre
wildlife preserve where
endangered species
roam free of predators
and poachers. Meet rare
wildlife on a guided two-
hour safari in open-sided
jeeps, plus a 30-minute
hike. Your guide will
point out areas scorched
by wildfires; the owners
heroically saved all 1000
animals. To maximize
quality time among
the giraffes, book a
treehouse-style tent cabin
($310 to $400). Stays
come with continental
breakfast on the deck for
wildlife-watching, plus
optional on-site massages
($100 per hour).

The Drive ≫ Return east via
Petrified Forest Rd and drive
1 mile south on Hwy 29/128,
then 1 mile north on Lincoln Ave
to take lovely, vineyard-lined
Silverado Trail almost 30 miles
southeast to downtown Napa.

- - - - - - - - - - - - - - - -

`TRIP HIGHLIGHT`

⑧ Silverado Trail

Bountiful Silverado Trail
meanders from Calistoga
to Napa, with tempting
pit stops at three dozen
wineries. Just outside
Calistoga, **Joseph Phelps**
(📞800-707-5789; www.
josephphelps.com; 200 Taplin
Rd; ⏰by appointment 10am-
4pm) has been making its
iconic Insignia red blend
sustainably since 1974.
Phelps dares you to make
your own version of Insignia, blending the same six
components winemaker
Ashley Hepworth used for

NAPA VALLEY WINE

Cab is king in Napa. No varietal captures this sun-drenched valley like the fruit of
the cabernet sauvignon vine, and no wine fetches a higher price. But with climate
change, Napa Valley's floor is heating up, so even hardy cabernet grapes can
develop highly concentrated, over-extracted flavors – resulting in fiery tannins,
raisin flavors or syrupy notes. To take the edge off cabs and introduce more subtle
notes, Napa winemakers are increasingly making Napa cab blends called Meritages.

Napa farmers tend to plant prestigious, pricey cabernet, so when they make an
exception and grow another red grape, like merlot, it's because they believe it will be
exceptional. California zinfandel grows extremely well in many of the same sunny
Napa Valley blocks as cabernet – so it's a time-honored specialty at many Napa
wineries. Zin blends are versatile, food-friendly, and often more affordable than
Napa estate-grown zins.

Lately, more unusual varietals and blends are gracing Napa tasting-room shelves.
A new crop of winemakers called 'garagistes' are buying grapes from across
Northern California, and fermenting them in downtown Napa warehouse facilities.
So even in the heart of Napa Valley, tasting rooms are pouring coastal chardonnay,
Russian River sauvignon blanc, white picpoul from the Sierra foothills, and cool-
climate Sonoma pinot noir – and crafty Napa winemakers can turn almost any
grape into a rosé with the right amount of skin contact and early pressing.

LOCAL KNOWLEDGE: GETTING AROUND NAPA VALLEY

Napa Valley is 30 miles long and 5 miles wide at its widest point (the city of Napa), 1 mile at its narrowest (Calistoga). Two roads run north–south: Hwy 29 (St Helena Hwy) and the more scenic Silverado Trail, a mile east. Drive up one, and down the other. Summer and fall weekend traffic crawls, especially on Hwy 29 between downtown Napa and St Helena around 5pm, when wineries close.

Cross-valley roads that link Silverado Trail with Hwy 29 (including Yountville, Oakville and Rutherford Cross Rds) are bucolic and get less traffic. Oakville Grade Rd and rural Trinity Rd (which leads southwest from Oakville on Hwy 29 to Hwy 12 near Glen Ellen in Sonoma Valley) are narrow, curvy and beautiful – but treacherous in rainstorms. Mt Veeder Rd leads through pristine countryside west of Yountville.

Napa Valley Vine Trail (www.vinetrail.org) aims to connect the entire valley via tree-lined bike trails; maps available online. The **Napa Valley Wine Train** (☎707-253-2111, 800-427-4124; www.winetrain.com; 1275 McKinstry St; ticket incl dining from $160) takes you from downtown Napa to St Helena and back in a plush vintage dining car, with meal service included and optional winery stops. Trains depart from **Napa Valley Wine Train Depot** (☎800-427-4124; www.winetrain.com; 1275 McKinstry St, Napa) on McKinstry St near 1st St.

the latest release – and then taste them side by side, or just lounge under California oaks with a panoramic terrace tasting.

If you reserve ahead, a memorable multicourse brunch with sparkling wine awaits on the scenic balcony at **Auberge du Soleil** (☎707-963-1211; www.aubergedusoleil.com; 180 Rutherford Hill Rd, Rutherford; d $1325-4025; ☀✳☎✉). Or follow the convoy of foodies to **Robert Sinskey** (☎707-944-9090; www.robertsinskey.com; 6320 Silverado Trail; bar tasting $40, seated food & wine pairings $70-175; ☺10am-4:30pm; ℗), where close collaboration with chef Maria Sinskey produces Napa's most food-friendly wines and inspired pairings. Sinksey's silky pinot noir and merlot are specifically crafted to harmonize with food. Reserve ahead to enjoy bar tastings of biodynamic, organic wines with small-bite pairings, or bountiful food and wine dining.

One of Napa's most prestigious growing areas is **Stag's Leap** district, east of Yountville. Turn east off Silverado and follow the signs to **Quixote** (☎707-944-2659; www.quixotewinery.com; 6126 Silverado Trail; tasting $45, with tour $65; tour & barrel tasting with food pairings $125; ☺10am-5pm), a gold-leafed onion dome sprouting from a grassy knoll. Reserve ahead to enter the only US building by outlandish Austrian eco-architect Friedensreich Hundertwasser between crayon-colored ceramic pillars – and taste acclaimed, organically farmed Stag's Leap estate cabs and petit syrah.

Eating & Sleeping

Napa ❶

✕ Oenotri   Italian $$

(☏707-252-1022; www.oenotri.com; 1425 1st St; brunch $13-18, dinner mains $19-34; ⊙5:30-9pm Sun-Thu, to 10pm Fri & Sat, brunch 10am-3pm Sat & Sun; 🖊 🚹) Celebrate Napa's Italian farming roots with rustic feasts sourced from chef Tyler Rodde's organic garden. Handmade pasta dishes are generous enough to share – theoretically speaking – and pizzas made with Napa Valley olive oil are wood-fired, for blistered crusts that would make Napa papas proud. Come back for brunch: eggs Benedict on just-baked focaccia and skillet pancakes with caramelized peaches. Bravo.

🛏 Archer   Hotel $$$

(☏707-690-9800; www.archerhotel.com; 1230 1st St; d from $330; P ⊜ ❄ @ 🛜 🏊 🐾) Live like a vintner who's just won double gold at the Archer, downtown Napa's most happening hotel. The vibe is barrel-room chic, all sleek wood panelling and chiseled stone – and guest-room balconies overlook city lights and vineyards beyond. Head to the rooftop to lounge poolside or fireside with a glass of Napa's finest. Spa upstairs, Charlie Palmer steakhouse downstairs: win/win.

Yountville ❷

✕ Tacos Garcia   Tacos $

(☏707-980-4896; 6764 Washington St; tacos $4.50-10; ⊙11am-8pm) Most day-trippers without reservations wait in vain for bar seating at Yountville bistros, but taco aficionados know the deal: follow your nose to Pancha's parking lot, and line up at Napa Valley's best taco truck. Go with juice-dripping *carne asada* (steak), smoky *al pastor* (spice-rubbed pork) or tender *lengua* (tongue) – or during Napa Valley marathons or harvests, double-meat burritos. Cash only.

✕ Mustards Grill   Californian $$$

(☏707-944-2424; www.mustardsgrill.com; 7399 St Helena Hwy; mains $16-48; ⊙11:30am-9pm Mon-Thu, to 10pm Fri, 11am-10pm Sat, to 9pm Sun; 🚹) You could call chef Cindy Palcwyn's cooking California cuisine, but Californians have had another term for it here since 1983: crazy good. No caviar or truffle shavings smother dishes at her landmark roadhouse – her Dungeness crab cakes, Mongolian pork chops, slaws and scene-stealing salads showcase sustainably sourced, California-grown flavors. Leave room for legendary lemon-lime tarts with 'ridiculously tall' brown-sugar meringue.

🛏 Napa Valley Railway Inn   Inn $$

(☏707-944-2000; www.napavalleyrailwayinn. com; 6523 Washington St; d $205-$280; P ⊜ ❄ @ 🛜 🏊) Rest your tired caboose in a converted railroad car. Two trains are parked alongside a covered platform, where guests read and mingle on rocking chairs. Eight snug rail-car guest rooms are comfortable, though not soundproofed – bring earplugs, or you might be awakened by morning hot-air-balloon flights (quite cool, actually). Book the skylit caboose, and enjoy breakfast at on-site Model Bakery.

Rutherford ❹

✕ La Luna Taqueria & Market   Tacos $

(☏707-963-3211; www.lalunamarket.com; 1153 Rutherford Rd; tacos from $2.75; ⊙7am-7pm Mon-Fri, 8am-6pm Sat, to 5pm Sun; P 🚹 🐾) 'Tacos y vinos' says the wine-fridge sign – an excellent pairing suggestion made possible by La Luna for 50 years. Complement generous super-tacos ($4.25) with top-value Napa wines: unoaked Maldonado Farm Worker chardonnay ($20) with crispy fish tacos, and Elouan rosé ($18) with soulful *pollo adobado* (adobo-marinated chicken). One-stop-shop for picnics, camping supplies, and fiestas complete with piñatas.

St Helena ❺

✖ Model Bakery
Bakery $

(☏707-963-8192; www.themodelbakery.com;
1357 Main St; pastries $3-10; ⏰6:30am-5pm
Mon-Sat, from 7am Sun; 🚹) Baked goods are
even better at Model Bakery, where Napa babies
instinctively reach for fluffy cornmeal-dusted
English muffins, and tiny birds hop around the
threshold for crumbs of crusty spelt boules.
For lunch, go with the savory galette of the
day – but leave room for salted-caramel tarts or
accurately named 'chocolate rad' cookies with
top-notch coffee.

✖ Gott's Roadside
American $

(☏707-963-3486; www.gotts.com; 933 Main
St; mains $8-16; ⏰10am-10pm May-Sep, to 9pm
Oct-Apr; 🚹) Welcome to the retro roadside
burger joint you were fantasizing about mid-
cab-tasting. Sprawl on the grassy lawn and feast
on Niman Ranch grass-fed beef burgers oozing
with Point Reyes blue cheese – or enjoy Mary's
free-range fried-chicken sandwiches or massive
Greenleaf Farms Cobb salads. Call ahead, order
online or try **Oxbow Public Market** (☏707-
226-6529; www.oxbowpublicmarket.com; 610
& 644 1st St; items from $3; ⏰7:30am-9:30pm;
🛜🚹).

✖ Charter Oak
Californian $$

(☏707-302-6996; www.thecharteroak.
com; 1050 Charter Oak Ave; mains $20-30;
⏰5-8:30pm Mon-Thu, from 11:30am Fri-Sun;
P❄🍴🚹) The dining-room fireplace isn't
just for looks at Charter Oak: sensational dishes
emerge from the blazing hearth and arrive
tableside still bubbling in enamel cookware.
Each dish showcases a signature seasonal
ingredient or two, often from Charter Oak's
farm – black cod sizzles like gossip atop
vineyard-cover-crop mustard greens, and slow-
smoked short ribs slide drunkenly off the bone
into cabernet-grape saba.

🛏 El Bonita
Motel $

(☏800-541-3284, 707-963-3216; www.
elbonita.com; 195 Main St; d $145-215;
P❄❄@🛜❄❄) Free up funds for
vintage wines by staying at this affordable
vintage motel. Instagrammers pose by original
neon signs, wine-tasters nap poolside under
California oaks, and cyclists recover from

Sugarloaf Ridge rides in the hot tub and sauna.
Rooms are spacious, cheerful and remodeled,
including headboards hand-painted with
California scenes. Request a quieter room in the
back; two-night minimum on weekends.

Calistoga ❻

✖ Buster's Southern BBQ
Barbecue $

(☏707-942-5605; www.busterssouthernbbq.
com; 1207 Foothill Blvd; meals $11-22; ⏰10am-
7pm; 🛜🚹) Make small talk with the sheriff
while you wait for your tri-tip – Buster's is where
all of Napa Valley bonds over barbecue, since
1965. Smoky ribs are served with beer or wine
at sunny outdoor tables, with a side of live jazz
and blues from 2pm to 5pm Sunday. Ya'll come
back for chicken to go for dinner, y'hear?

✖ Lovina
Californian $$

(☏707-942-6500; www.lovinacalistoga.com;
1107 Cedar St; lunch/brunch dishes $10-29,
dinner $20-36; ⏰5:30pm-late Thu, 11:30am-
3pm & 5:30pm-late Fri & Sat, 9:30am-3pm
Sun; 🍴🚹) Lunch in the garden here is a
dream – and nonstop inspiration for chef
Leticia Martinez, who composes produce from
restaurateur Jennifer Bennet's garden into
California sensations like Napa wild-mushroom
risotto, herb-spiked green-goddess salads,
and rich *cioppino* (tomato seafood stew).
For brunch, her Jalisco-style chilaquiles will
'soak up the tannins' (read: fix wine-tasting
hangovers), while veggie-packed omelets will
power you through next week.

🛏 Indian Springs Resort
Resort $$

(☏707-942-4913; www.indianspringscalistoga.
com; 1712 Lincoln Ave; d/cottages from
$229/559; P❄❄🛜❄) The definitive
old-school Calistoga resort, Indian Springs has
vintage bungalows beneath swaying palm trees
strung with hammocks. A grand drive leads to
the historic spa, new Sam's Social Club (p101)
bar/grill, and massive mineral-hot-springs pool.
Bungalows can accommodate families, but
the mellow, upscale 1930s lodge is exclusively
for adults. Serene new 'view rooms' overlook
geothermal ponds and the mountains beyond.

Sonoma Valley

7

A world apart but only an hour from San Francisco, Sonoma Valley is a 17-mile stretch of wild imagination, with pioneering sustainable vineyards and 13,000 acres of parkland heroically reclaimed from wildfires.

TRIP HIGHLIGHTS

17 miles

Glen Ellen
Small town that's big on wineries and tasty food

FINISH

Kenwood

19 miles

Jack London State Historic Park
Find inspiration for your own adventure story in the author's wild backyard

9 miles

Sonoma
Visit California's last mission and first breakaway republic - plus urban farms and wineries galore

START

**2 DAYS
30 MILES / 48KM**

GREAT FOR...

BEST TIME TO GO
Witness 'the crush' in September and October and enjoy warm dry days from May through October.

ESSENTIAL PHOTO
Pause mid-bite for picnic photos in historic Sonoma Plaza.

BEST FOR OUTDOORS
Choose your own adventure at Jack London State Historic Park.

7 Sonoma Valley

Sonoma Valley is an easy groove to fall into. Hwy 12 follows the footsteps of Miwok, Pomo and Wintun people, who called this enchanted place 'Valley of the Moon' – and its charms are undeniable. Historic terraced vineyards and pristine forest parklands survived wildfires and Prohibition amazingly intact, thanks to pioneering conservation efforts and 'communion wine' slyly sold by the trainload. Raise a toast to good times and resilient vines.

❶ Cornerstone Gardens

The giant orange Adirondack chair by the roadside invites you into this Wine Country **garden and design showplace** (☏707-933-3010; www.cornerstone-sonoma.com; 23570 Arnold Dr; ⏰10am-5pm, gardens to 4pm; 🅿 ♿ 🐾), featuring 10 landscape-artist-designed gardens, five kid-friendly experiential education gardens, and local design boutiques. Stop by on-site **Sonoma Valley Visitors Bureau** (www.sonoma valley.com) for free trip

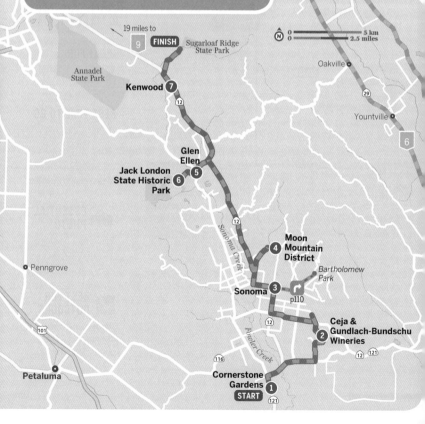

advice and handy tasting-room passes.

The Drive » Go north on Hwy 121 and follow it for 3 miles as it bears east. Turn south on Burndale Rd. Ceja winery is on your right.

❷ Ceja & Gundlach-Bundschu Wineries

Start your tour of Sonoma Valley's historic vineyards at **Ceja** (☎707-255-3954; www.cejavineyards.com; 22989 Burndale Rd; tastings from $20; ☺10am-5pm; **P**), for a taste of true vineyard romance. When Amelia Morán met Pedro Ceja in 1967, they were both picking grapes for Mondavi in Napa. Marriage, kids, and decades of trailblazing later, Amelia is the

LINK YOUR TRIP

6 Napa Valley
Take Hwy 12/121 to Napa's upscale wineries, hot-springs resorts and world-renowned restaurants.

9 Russian River & Bohemian Highway
Head west on Hwy 12 from Kenwood into boho Western Sonoma for Russian River dips, redwood forest rambles, crisp coastal chardonnays and wild, woodsy pinot noirs.

first Mexican-American woman winery president – and her family pours their hearts and 50 years of winemaking savvy into Ceja's signature pinot noir, aged chardonnay and Vino de Casa, a silky blend of Italian arneis and chardonnay (bottles $25 to $60).

From Ceja, go north on Burndale Rd, jog left briefly onto Napa Rd and then right onto Denmark St. That castle just ahead is California's oldest family-run winery, **Gundlach-Bundschu** (☎707-938-5277; www.gunbun.com; 2000 Denmark St; tasting $25-35, incl tour $55-60; ☺11am-5:30pm Sun-Fri, to 7pm Sat Apr-Oct, to 4:30pm Nov-Mar; **P**), where everyone gets a royal welcome at the bar. Six generations of Bundschus have kept the delightful dry Gewürztraminer flowing since 1858, all while innovating sustainable winemaking practices. Follow the country lane to taste their award-winning merlot, and picnic by the water-recycling pond (bottles $20 to $50).

The Drive » Follow Denmark St back to Napa Rd, and go west to Hwy 12. Drive Hwy 12/ Broadway north about 1 mile.

TRIP HIGHLIGHT

❸ Downtown Sonoma

Native Americans once gathered here at the

village of Huichi to trade goods and songs. Spanish missionaries conscripted them to build adobe (☎707-938-1519; www.sonomaparks.org; 114 E Spain St; adult/child $3/2; ☺10am-5pm), but most died of measles and smallpox introduced by the Spanish. Under Mexican rule, land was supposed to revert to Native Californian ownership – but Sonoma's mission vineyards were claimed by ranchers instead.

Then one drunken night in 1846, a motley group of partiers took over the **Sonoma barracks** (☎707-939-9420; www.sonomaparks.org; 20 E Spain St; adult/child $3/2; ☺10am-5pm), staggered over to Mexican **General Vallejo's home** (☎707-938-9559; www.sonomaparks.org; 363 3rd St W; adult/child $3/2; ☺10am-5pm) to confiscate his brandy, and proclaimed a breakaway Bear Flag Republic. After a month, the US military took over Sonoma, Vallejo became a US citizen and Sonoma's first state senator, and the barracks were converted into (what else?) a winery. One ticket covers same-day admission to the mission, barracks, Vallejo's home and **Toscano Hotel** (☎707-938-9560; www.sonomaparks.org; 20 E Spain St; adult/child $3/2; ☺10am-5pm) history museum.

The town's pride and joy remains the **plaza** (www.sonomaplaza.com; btwn

Napa, Spain & 1st Sts) – the largest town square in California, home to a legendary **farmers market** (5:30pm to 8pm Tuesdays, April to October) and ringed with fabulous family-owned bistros, indie boutiques, Victorian inns and dozens of tasting rooms.

Around the corner at **Vella Cheese** (📞707-938-3232; www.vellacheese.com; 315 2nd St E; ⏰9:30am-6pm Mon-Fri, to 5pm Sat; 🚻), parmesan-like Dry Jack has been making spaghetti Western for almost a century. Across the street is **The Patch** (260 2nd St E; ⏰9am-2pm Mon-Sat May-Nov; 🚻), California's oldest community-run urban farm. The

pesticide-free, peak-season produce is yours to select, weigh and purchase on the honor system – drop your cash in the box, and enjoy your picnic with local wine on the plaza.

🍴 🛏 p113

The Drive » From downtown Sonoma, take Hwy 12 about 2 miles north, then turn onto Lomita Ave to climb Moon Mountain toward Hanzell Vineyard.

④ Moon Mountain District

Overlooking downtown Sonoma is an ancient landmark, and the newest local AVA (American

LEBID VOLODYMYR / SHUTTERSTOCK ©

DETOUR: BARTHOLOMEW PARK

Start: ④ Downtown Sonoma

These peaceful woods have seen it all: the 1857 start of California's wine industry under Hungarian count Agoston Haraszthy, devastation by phylloxera and bankruptcy, construction of an 1885 castle for millionaire philanthropist Kate Johnson and her 42 cats, and its 1919 conversion into a home for 'delinquent women' (read: sex workers and addicts) before fires destroyed it. A **winery** (📞707-509-0450; www.bartholomewestate.com; 1000 Vineyard Lane; tasting $25, with vineyard tour $45; ⏰11am-4:30pm; 🅿) rose from the ashes, and despite fires in 2017 and 2019, these certified-organic vineyards are again producing sauvignon blanc, cabernet sauvignon and zinfandel. Picnics are allowed, and the estate's sun-dappled private park is free and open to visitors from 10am to 4:30pm, with a 3-mile trail winding through vineyards, oaks, madrones and redwoods. Pass the windmill and pond to reach an overlook with sweeping views all the way to the San Francisco Bay.

Viticultural Region). Grapes have been grown on Moon Mountain for a century, though its steep slopes and mysterious mists are notoriously tricky. Reserve ahead to visit historic **Hanzell Vineyards** (📞707-996-3860; https://hanzell.com; 18596 Lomita Ave; tasting $45, with farm tour $65; ⏰11am-3pm Tue & Wed, to 4pm Thu & Sun, to 4:30pm Fri, Sat & Mon; 🅿🚻), where Moon Mountain's mists and minerals are captured in exceptional cool-climate chardonnays and pinot noirs. As the morning mists rise, you can see

Wolf House in Jack London State Historic Park

from here clear to San Francisco, 50 miles south.

Head down the mountain to El Molino (p113) for Yucatan-inspired, Sonoma-grown feasts in the warm valley sunshine. Conversation flows among visitors and regulars around outdoor tables, with help from the well-chosen list of sustainable Sonoma- and Moon Mountain–grown wines.

✖ p113

The Drive » Continue 5 miles north on Hwy 12 to reach Glen Ellen.

TRIP HIGHLIGHT

❺ Glen Ellen

You'll know you've arrived at the center of tiny Glen Ellen when you spot gargoyles made of rusted tractor parts grinning at you from the gate of **Chuck Gillet's Cyclops Iron Works** (Brazen Estates; 13623 Arnold Dr). Sonoma lawyer-turned-sculptor Chuck has completely covered his 7ft-high fence with recycled-metal art. 'Private but peek freely,' says the sign next to a garden-shear-eared bat, peering shyly from the ivy. Message received:

invitation accepted, artist respected.

Right across the road, that little cottage is actually a pinot noir powerhouse. **Talisman** (☎707-721-1628; www.talismanwine.com; 13651 Arnold Dr; tasting $30-40; ⊙noon-5pm) founder/winemaker team Scott and Marta Rich worked in major Napa wineries before they jumped the county line, collaborating with legendary Sonoma pinot growers to produce singular, sought-after wines. Tasting fee waived with three-bottle purchase (bottles $30 to $70); call ahead.

✕ 🛏 p113

The Drive » From Glen Ellen, head 1.5 miles west on London Ranch Rd to reach Jack London State Historic Park.

- - - - - - - - - - - - - - - - - -

`TRIP HIGHLIGHT`

❻ Jack London State Historic Park

He wrote the world's longest-running bestseller, *Call of the Wild*, and traveled the world over, but Jack London (1876–1916) claimed his greatest achievement was this 1400-acre preserve he rescued from early settlers' slash-and-burn farming methods. Today it's a **park** (📞707-938-5216; www.jacklondonpark.com; 2400 London Ranch Rd; per car $10, cottage admission $3; ⏰9:30am-5pm; P 🚻), featuring the Beauty Ranch farmstead much as Jack left it. From the farmstead, a short but rugged hiking trail leads past Jack's gravesite to **Wolf House ruins**, Jack's stone-and-redwood lodge that burned down days before completion in 1913.

His widow, fellow writer and free spirit Charmian Kittredge London repurposed Wolf House stones to build the **House of Happy Walls**. Today it's a museum (10am to 5pm) – don't miss Jack's rejection letters in the downstairs bookshop, and Charmian's fabulous flapper dresses in her walk-in wardrobe upstairs. Insightful displays cover Jack's death-defying travels and controversial ideas, including socialism and Darwinism, and address Charmian's strikingly modern writing, outspoken feminism, and challenging role as Jack's editor.

Influenced by his friend, trailblazing Santa Rosa botanist Luther Burbank, Jack also pioneered organic farming and built a **circular piggery** to collect fertilizer. Hike up to the piggery, or take the easy 2-mile loop to **London Lake** for a scenic picnic.

The Drive » Drive 2.5 miles east back to Hwy 12 via Arnold Dr, and hang a right onto Miller Lane to reach Quarryhill Botanical Garden.

- - - - - - - - - - - - - - - - - -

❼ Kenwood Nature Retreats

Take a quick detour off vineyard-lined Hwy 12 into Asian woodlands at **Quarryhill Botanical Garden** (📞707-996-3166; www.quarryhillbg.org; 12841 Hwy 12; adult/child 13-17yr $12/8; ⏰9am-4pm). Over 30 years, founder Jane Davenport Jansen and a dedicated team of conservationists cultivated an artful woodland of Asian magnolias, dogwood, lilies and maples. Today this 25-acre botanical garden is fragrant in spring, colorful in fall, and inspiring year-round.

Further north along Hwy 12, take Adobe Canyon Rd uphill to **Sugarloaf Ridge State Park** (📞707-833-5712; www.sugarloafpark.org; 2605 Adobe Canyon Rd; per car $8; P 🚻) for 25 miles of panoramic hiking and biking. The 2017 fires burned 80% of this 3300-acre park and restoring Sugarloaf has been a mammoth effort, taken on by Sonoma community nonprofits and local volunteers.

Nature is rebounding beautifully. On clear days, **Bald Mountain** views stretch to the Pacific, while **Brushy Peaks Trail** overlooks Napa Valley. Both trails are moderately strenuous; plan on three hours round-trip. For mellower experiences, check online for ecologist-guided forest-bathing walks and weekend stargazing at on-site **Robert Ferguson Observatory**. Check current programs and hiking conditions at the volunteer-run visitor center.

Eating & Sleeping

Downtown Sonoma ❸

✖ Tasca Tasca   Tapas $$

(📞707-996-8272; www.tascatasca.com; 122 W
Napa St; meals $16-26; 🕐11:30am-10pm Sun-Thu,
to 11pm Fri & Sat; ❋) Sea, garden, land: choose
where your next culinary adventure begins, and
this inspired tapas bar menu takes you there.
Select three to seven small plates for a whirlwind
tour that leads from Portuguese goat stew with
potatoes to Dungeness-crab empanadas, ending
with sea-salt chocolate tarts and Sonoma olive-oil
ice cream with 40-year-old madeira. Bravo.

✖ Cafe La Haye   Californian $$$

(📞707-935-5994; www.cafelahaye.com; 140 E
Napa St; mains $26-42; 🕐5:30-9pm Tue-Sat)
Warm feelings are mutual between farmers and
chefs, regulars and visitors at cozy La Haye, which
champions produce sourced within 60 miles.
Neighboring farmers earn co-star credits on
seasonal favorites, including sherry-basted Wolfe
Ranch quail with sourdough stuffing and hearty
chopped salads with George's farm eggs and
Humboldt Fog goat cheese. Save room for simple,
sensational desserts.

⫞ Sonoma Hotel   Historic Hotel $

(📞800-468-6016, 707-996-2996; www.
sonomahotel.com; 110 W Spain St; d $130-298,
ste $195-308; ❄ ❋ 🛜) Welcoming guests since
1872, this classic Western hotel right on Sonoma
Plaza has original features galore: Sonoma-
stone lobby fireplace, wood-paneled halls, in-
room sinks and clawfoot tubs. It was built before
elevators and parking lots, but rooms do have
double-pane glass and A/C to block plaza noise
on summer weekends. Poet Maya Angelou wrote
here; may the scenery inspire you, too.

Moon Mountain District ❹

✖ El Molino Central   Mexican $

(📞707-939-1010; www.elmolinocentral.com;
11 Central Ave; mains $12-16; 🕐9am-9pm;
P 🚲 ♿ ❋) Unforgettable Wine Country meals
combine sustainably homegrown ingredients
and Sonoma's deeply rooted Mexican culinary
traditions at this 1930s roadside diner. Zoraida's

mother's red mole is as profound and tangy as
the finest California zinfandel – get it slathered on
banana-leaf-wrapped tamales or poblano-chicken
enchiladas. *Tatemada birria* (slow-cooked goat)
tacos with slapped-to-order organic stone-ground
tortillas earn California-wide cult followings.

Glen Ellen ❺

✖ Fig Cafe
& Winebar   French, Californian $$

(📞707-938-2130; www.thefigcafe.com; 13690
Arnold Dr; mains $21-27, 3-course meal $39;
🕐dinner from 5pm; ♿) Sondra Bernstein's
earthy California comfort food is as satisfying
as dinner gets. On the seasonal menu, look for
succulent Sonoma duck, fig and arugula salad,
and decadent steak frites with blue-cheese
butter. Service is neighborly – through wildfires
and Covid-19, these folks kept neighbors and staff
fed. No reservations; complimentary corkage.

⫞ Beltane Ranch   Inn $$

(📞707-833-4233; www.beltaneranch.com; 11775
Hwy 12; d $185-375; P ❄ 🛜) African American
millionaire venture capitalist and civil-rights
pioneer Mary Ellen Pleasant built this ranch in
1892 as a country getaway to entertain influential
friends. Beltane remains enchanted – the sunny
yellow gingerbread-trimmed ranch house has
wraparound porches where guests laze away
days amid vineyards, parklands and horses
grazing in pastures. Each suite has a discreet
private entrance, and no phone or TV means zero
distraction from pastoral bliss.

Kenwood ❼

✖ La Cucina at VJB   Italian $

(📞707-833-2300; http://vjbcellars.com/
la-cucina; 60 Shaw Ave; meals $8.50-20;
🕐10am-4pm; P ❋ ♿ ❋) For Sonoma
Valley's most authentic Italian fare, order at the
counter of VJB's Italian-varietal winery. Chef/
VJB co-founder Maria Belmonte makes her *sugo*
(sauce), pesto and mozzarella from scratch – you
may discover new favorites in her *porchetta* with
grilled eggplant, and arugula salads lavished with
ricotta, pistachios and lemon vinaigrette.

Healdsburg & Around

8

For a true taste of California Wine Country, go from Healdsburg's haute cuisine to Clear Lake's hilltop wineries. Unwind in Dry Creek Valley's farmstead wineries, witness nature's comeback in Alexander Valley, then hit the high country.

TRIP HIGHLIGHTS

100 miles

Clear Lake
Loop around Lake County's unfussy grape-growing region

Nice

6

FINISH

Hopland

Kelseyville

25 miles

Dry Creek Valley
Sun yourself on country lanes between vineyards

Geyserville

3   **4**

36 miles

Alexander Valley
Be wowed by hillside estate wineries' views

2

18 miles

Healdsburg
Upmarket Wine Country living and stellar restaurants

Santa Rosa   **START**

**2–3 DAYS
135 MILES / 215KM**

GREAT FOR...

BEST TIME TO GO

April, May, September and October for dry, sunny days that aren't scorching hot.

ESSENTIAL PHOTO

Shimmering Clear Lake from atop Hopland Grade.

BEST FOR FOODIES

Reserve ahead for the meal of a lifetime at SingleThread.

ry Creek Valley Farmhouse and vineyards

8 | Healdsburg & Around

You'll never need to change out of your jeans to get a fabulous meal and inspired wine pairings in this laid-back, sun-blessed corner of Wine Country. But don't let the casual charm fool you: these farmstead wineries are organic pioneers, jaw-dropping natural wonders abound, and Western storefront bistros rack up critical accolades. Shake the dust off your jeans, make yourself comfortable, and let California show you what dreaming is all about.

❶ Santa Rosa

Wine Country's biggest town is classic America-na, with neighbors waving hello from cottage rose gardens. Cheerful mid-century storefronts still beckon visitors into mom-and-pop shops around Old Courthouse Sq, and historic Railroad Sq greets commuters arriving on tracks first laid by local Chinese laborers in the 1870s.

Seems like a vintage comic-strip backdrop, because it is: *Peanuts* creator Charles Schulz

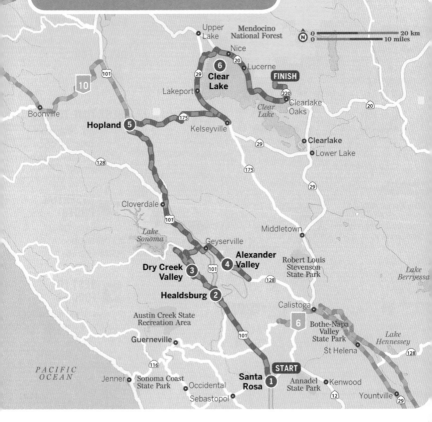

lived, dreamed and doodled here. The **Charles M Schulz Museum** (📞707-579-4452; www.schulzmuseum.org; 2301 Hardies Lane; adult/child $12/5; ☺11am-5pm Mon & Wed-Fri, from 10am Sat & Sun; P ♿) captures his lovable legacy with original drawings of Charlie Brown and company, plus a recreation of his home studio.

Walk around the tree-shaded, mural-lined streets of **SofA, the South of A St Art District**, and you can't help but stop and smell the flowers – many are fragrant heirloom varietals developed just up the street at **Luther Burbank Home & Gardens** (📞707-524-5445; www.lutherburbank.org; 204 Santa Rosa Ave; grounds free, tour adult/child $10/5; ☺gardens 8am-7pm Apr-Dec,

to 5pm Nov-Mar, museum 10am-4pm Tue-Sat, 11am-3pm Sun Apr-Oct). Pioneering horticulturist Luther Burbank (1849–1926) cultivated 800 hybrid plant species over 50 years, aiming for delight, usefulness and sustainability. His backyard experiments with fragrant flowers, spineless cacti and medicinal plants are still growing outside his Greek Revival home.

Today Santa Rosa is so leafy and laid-back, it's hard to believe it survived two earthquakes and wildfires. Destined to be a survivor, the city was named for the patron saint of first responders, and built on land granted in 1841 to one very determined single mom – and Doña María Ygnacia Lopez de Carrillo and her son Julio designed Santa Rosa to be enjoyed by all.

The Drive » Take Hwy 101 north from downtown Santa Rosa for about 14 miles to exit 503 (Healdsburg Ave). Traffic slows to a crawl as you roll over half a mile north to Healdsburg Plaza.

TRIP HIGHLIGHT

❷ Healdsburg

Healdsburg turns on the Western charm, with a sun-dappled central square ringed by Western storefronts, stately Victorian inns and gingerbread-trimmed B&Bs. Downtown stays run around $300 a night – but staying overnight is wise to fully enjoy Healdsburg's

world-class restaurants and 20-plus worthy tasting rooms. Reserve ahead for the meal of a lifetime at SingleThread (p121), inspired Italian pairings at **Idlewild** (www.idlewildwines.com; 132 Plaza St; tastings $20; ☺noon-7pm) and wild pinots at **Lioco** (📞707-395-0148; www.liocowine.com; 125 Matheson St; tastings $20-40; ☺noon-7pm). True to Healdsburg's origins, the best local wines taste of stubborn roots and undeniable romance, with a faint whiff of scandal.

✕ ⊨ p121

The Drive » From Healdsburg Plaza, drive 1 mile north on Healdsburg Ave. Turn west onto Dry Creek Rd, a fast-moving thoroughfare; it's 5.5 miles to Truett Hurst. To reach wineries on West Dry Creek Rd, an undulating country lane with no center stripe (ideal for cyclists), turn onto Lambert Bridge Rd by Dry Creek General Store.

TRIP HIGHLIGHT

❸ Dry Creek Valley

Cross the highway from Healdsburg and head back through time in Dry Creek Valley. The scenery here looks a lot like it did 150 years ago, when **Dry Creek General Store** (📞707-433-4171; www.drycreekgeneralstore1881.com; 3495 Dry Creek Rd; sandwiches $10-14; ☺7am-5pm Sun-Thu, to 5:30pm Fri & Sat) first opened its Western saloon doors. Load up on cowboy picnic provisions – coffee, slow-cooked

LINK YOUR TRIP

6 **Napa Valley**

From Geyserville, head 24 miles southeast on Hwy 128 toward Calistoga, where the showcase wineries and destination restaurants of Napa Valley begin.

10 **Mendocino & Anderson Valley**

Hopland is the jumping-off point for a country drive through Anderson Valley's vineyards and apple orchards to the Pacific Ocean.

brisket, just-baked pie – before making the rounds of Dry Creek's sustainable farmstead wineries.

Picturesque **Preston** (☏707-433-3372; www. prestonvineyards.com; 9282 W Dry Creek Rd; bar tasting/ private tasting/tour $20/30/40; ◷11am-4:30pm; P 🐾) invites you to stay awhile, with bocce courts, fresh-baked bread and cold-pressed organic olive oil to enjoy with your organic sauvignon blanc under walnut trees. Sheep bleat welcome to **Reeve** (☏707-235-6345; www.reevewines. com; 4551 Dry Creek Rd; tastings $35-50; ◷11am-5pm; P), where leisurely pinot pairings with cheese and charcuterie are held on the farmhouse patio. Your new favorite red is served in a shed at **Unti** (☏707-433-5590; www.untivineyards. com; 4202 Dry Creek Rd; tastings $20; ◷ by appointment 10am-4pm; 🐾), where signature sangiovese and radical rosé of mourvedre bring the Mediterranean to the Pacific.

The Drive » Follow Dry Creek Rd north to Canyon Rd, which passes underneath Hwy 101. Hang a right on Geyserville Ave (Hwy 128) into Geyserville.

TRIP HIGHLIGHT

④ Alexander Valley

Welcome to Geyserville, population 862 – but where are the geysers? Wander the town's old wooden boardwalk, and you'll find genuine Wild West character, plus Diavola Pizza (p121) and wine made by Alexander Valley neighbors, but no sign of the geothermal wonders that initially attracted visitors here in 1847.

The hot springs are underground, making Geyserville an early adopter of geothermal power generation. Harnessing 350 fumaroles just uphill from Geyserville, the local power-generating operation now produces 20% of California's renewable energy. The power station is off-limits; to get into hot water, reserve a spot at the vast hilltop swimming pools at **Coppola Winery** (☏707-857-1471; www.francisfordcoppolawinery. com; 300 Via Archimedes; day pass adult/child $35/15; ◷11am-6pm daily Jun-Sep, Fri-Sun May & Oct; 🐾).

Geyserville also invested in a state-of-the-art fire station that has saved the town and rescued the historic vineyards of Alexander Valley. Follow Hwy 128 to **Soda Rock** (☏707-433-3303; www.soda-rockwinery.com; 8015 Hwy 128; tastings $15; ◷11am-5pm) winery's tasting room in the old fire-singed barn, and raise a toast to fire-fighters with signature California zinfandel.

Follow Hwy 128 and turn right onto Chalk Hill Rd, where you'll find resilient Chalk Hill AVA vineyards flourishing at **Sutro** (☏707-509-9695; www.sutrowine.com; 13301 Chalk Hill Rd; vineyard hike with tasting per person $25; ◷ by appointment 11am-4:30pm; P 🐾) and **Carpenter** (☏707-385-8177; www.carpenterwine. com; 14255 Chalk Hill Rd; ◷ by appointment 11am-6pm; P🐾), two indie wineries run by women. Reserve ahead to try velvety Carpenter pinots and mineral-rich Sutro sauvignon blanc, amid rolling hills where nature is staging a glorious comeback.

✕ 🛏 p121

The Drive » Follow Hwy 128 back north through Geyserville and join Hwy 101 northbound. It's

DAVID GREITZER / SHUTTERSTOCK ©

Francis Ford Coppola Winery

a 23-mile trip via Cloverdale to the tiny town of Hopland.

---

⑤ Hopland

You're not out of Wine Country yet: Hopland is the gateway to Mendocino County's wine region. Back in 1866, local fields mostly grew hops for beer – hence the town's name. But after Prohibition decimated their beer business, savvy farmers switched to more profitable crops including grapes and cannabis. Just south of downtown is the 12-acre **Solar Living Center**, a green landmark where solar energy panels were pioneered in 1978, exhibits promote sustainable permaculture farming, and a legal cannabis dispensary showcases locally farmed weed.

Drive up Main St to find a dozen tasting rooms where you can pick up a free map to local wineries. **Brutocao Cellars** (☏800-433-3689; www.brutocaocellars.com; 13500 S Hwy 101; ⊙10am-5pm) has bocce courts, bold red wines and chocolate – a dream combo. Three blocks north, **Graziano Family of Wines** (☏707-744-8466; www.grazianofamily ofwines.com; 13275 S Hwy 101; ⊙10am-5pm) specializes in 'Cal-Ital' wines including primitivo, barbera, dolcetto and sangiovese. Bet you won't miss the hops in Hopland.

🛏 p121

The Drive » Get ready for a stunning yet gut-wrenchingly twisted trip on Hwy 175 east of Hopland. After ascending unnervingly steep Hopland Grade, panoramic views of Clear Lake and Mt Konocti open up below. Eighteen miles from Hopland, turn right to stay on Hwy 175, which joins Hwy 29 south for an easy 5-mile coast into Kelseyville.

LOCAL KNOWLEDGE: HEALDSBURG'S EPIC ORIGIN STORY

Healdsburg seems to have it all, but its history is a real-life telenovela. It begins in 1829 with a forbidden romance, when rebellious teenager Joséfa Carrillo fell for Massachusetts-born sea captain Henry Fitch. California was part of Spanish-controlled Mexico – so to marry Joséfa, Harry became a citizen and converted to Catholicism. But California's governor had a crush on Joséfa, and he blocked the wedding. Joséfa convinced her brothers to help her elope.

Joséfa and Henry's star-crossed affair was California's first major scandal, and it took a lawsuit before the governor recognized the marriage. On a winning streak, Joséfa and Henry applied to homestead a 48,000-acre ranch on leased Wappo land in Sonoma. But Henry died of pneumonia in 1849, leaving Joséfa widowed at age 39, with 11 kids and a not-yet-working ranch.

Joséfa came from a long line of resilient Carillo women – her *ranchera* mother Doña María Ygnacia founded Santa Rosa. So Joséfa made the perilous 700-mile journey north by horse-drawn wagon, only to discover that her mom had died and US prospectors were contesting their land rights. Under US law at the time, women could not own property.

While Joséfa battled in the courts for her property rights, a squatter named George Heald settled on her property refusing to leave for seven years. Turf battles among settlers broke out, dubbed the Healdsburg Wars. When the dust finally settled in the 1870s, the town turned to fighting fires and growing grapes. The pioneering fire department has saved the town many times over, and grapes keep making visitors fall in love with Healdsburg.

TRIP HIGHLIGHT

❻ Clear Lake

With over 100 miles of shoreline, Clear Lake is the largest naturally occurring freshwater lake entirely in California. In summer its warm water blooms with green algae, preventing swimming but creating fabulous habitat for fish and tens of thousands of birds. The 4300ft-tall dormant volcano **Mt Konocti** is reflected in the waters.

What looks like a Western movie set is real-life **Kelseyville**, where family-owned winery tasting rooms bustle alongside vintage soda fountains, general stores and cafes. Four miles northeast of town, **Clear Lake State Park** (☎707-279-4293, 707-279-2267; www.clearlakestatepark. org; 5300 Soda Bay Rd; per car $8; ☉sunrise-sunset) offers hiking trails, fishing, boating and camping on the lake's south shore. Check current conditions at the park; some trails may be closed due to recent wildfires.

Follow Soda Bay Rd back west to Hwy 29, which heads north to Lakeport. Take the Nice-Lucerne Cutoff Rd for a scenic drive on Hwy 20 along the lake's north shore, passing the vintage white-cottage resorts of California's 'Little Switzerland.' About 10 miles east of Lucerne, turn off for a steep climb up High Valley Rd to panoramic **Brassfield Estate** (☎707-998-1895; www.brassfield estate.com; 10915 High Valley Rd, Clearlake Oaks; tastings $15; ☉11am-5pm daily May-Nov, to 4pm Thu-Mon Dec-Apr), where the estate-grown Eruption red is blended from grapes grown on volcanic slopes.

🛏 p121

Eating & Sleeping

Healdsburg ❷

✖ Mateo's Cocina Latina   Fusion $$

(📞707-433-1520; www.mateoscocinalatina.com; 214 Healdsburg Ave; mains $16-30; ⏲3-8pm Mon & Wed-Sat, to 7pm Sun) Stepping up to every plate with all-organic Sonoma ingredients, Michelin-level precision and profound Yucatán flavors, owner/chef/farmer Mateo Granados is rocking Wine Country cuisine. Slow-braised dishes like *pollo alcaparrado* (chicken with olives and capers) and *cochinita pibil* (annatto-marinated pork) are soul-satisfying with made-to-order organic masa tortillas. Reserve ahead; request garden seating.

✖ Single Thread   Californian, Japanese $$$

(📞707-723-4646; www.singlethreadfarms.com; 131 North St; tasting menu per person $330; ⏲dinner from 5:30pm daily, lunch from 11:30am Sat & Sun) Once staff treat you to welcome tea, they usher you to a table seemingly set by a meticulous Pacific tsunami. A mossy log is sprinkled with meadow wildflowers and ceramic dishes of pristine Pacific seafood – all sublime. This edible Sonoma landscape is the first of 11 sensational seasonal courses – a tour de force of nature.

⛺ Madrona Manor   Historic Hotel $$$

(📞707-433-4231; www.madronamanor.com; 1001 Westside Rd; d $295-435; 🅿️ ⊜ ✳️ 🛜 🏊) Live it up at this Victorian hilltop manor like you just invented California sparkling wine. The original 1881 mansion has nine suite-sized rooms with fireplaces, plush king beds and ornate carved furnishings; two have balconies with views across the 8-acre estate. The converted carriage house and schoolhouse offer spacious, cushy accommodations, but star attractions remain the mansion and in-house restaurant – don't skip breakfast.

Alexander Valley ❹

✖ Diavola Pizza   Italian, Californian $$

(📞707-814-0111; www.diavolapizzeria.com; 21021 Geyserville Ave, Geyserville; mains $16-29; ⏲11:30am-9pm; 🖐️) A contender for California's best pizza, Diavola graces perfectly crispy thin-crust, wood-fired pizza with house-cured salumi and sausage. Seasonal oven-roasted beets, Brussels sprouts and broccolini are positively decadent, generously drizzled with Sonoma olive oil, balsamic and parmigiano. Diavola's secret is dedication – when fires raged down the street, Diavola stayed open to make free pizza for firefighters. Anticipate waits; it's worth it.

⛺ Old Crocker Inn   Lodge $$

(📞707-894-4000; www.oldcrockerinn.com; 1126 Old Crocker Inn Rd, Cloverdale; d $165-265; 🅿️ ⊜ ✳️ 🐾) Live large on the historic ranch of Victorian railroad baron Charles Crocker. The Crocker guest room is the lodge's fanciest, with a hand-carved four-poster bed and claw-foot tub – but the most elegant is Canton Cottage, honoring California's Chinese railroad builders. For rustic atmosphere, book Golden Spike cottage, with pine-wood walls, heritage quilts and jetted tub.

Hopland ❺

⛺ Stock Farm   Inn $$

(📞707-744-1977; www.stockfarmhopland. com; 13441 S Hwy 101; ste $185-305; ⊜ 🛜) Modern Californian meets Italian at this very comfortable inn where all of the spacious suites have Jacuzzis, fireplaces and private balconies. The homey taverna and pizzeria in front have big tables for communal dining and fantastic artisanal pizzas, craft beer and wine.

Clear Lake ❻

⛺ Tallman Hotel   Historic Hotel $$

(📞707-275-2245; www.tallmanhotel.com; 9550 Main St, Upper Lake; r $185-265; ⊜ ✳️ 🛜 🏊) The centerpiece may be the smartly renovated historic hotel – tile bathrooms, warm lighting, thick linens – but the rest of the property, including the shady garden, walled-in swimming pool, brick patios and porches, exudes timeless elegance. Some garden rooms come with outdoor Japanese soaking tubs heated by an energy-efficient geothermal-solar system.

Russian River & Bohemian Highway

9

The Bohemian Hwy lets you do what comes naturally. Bark back at seals along the coast, gather good vibes in ancient redwood groves, float down the Russian River in an inner tube, and join Sonoma's freethinkers for sunset toasts.

TRIP HIGHLIGHTS

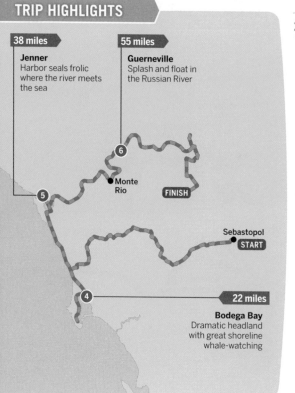

38 miles

Jenner
Harbor seals frolic where the river meets the sea

55 miles

Guerneville
Splash and float in the Russian River

6

●Monte Rio

5

FINISH

Sebastopol
START

4

22 miles

Bodega Bay
Dramatic headland with great shoreline whale-watching

**2 DAYS
75 MILES / 120KM**

GREAT FOR...

BEST TIME TO GO
June to September, for toasty days and refreshing river dips.

 ESSENTIAL PHOTO

Hug a giant redwood in Armstrong Woods.

 BEST FOR WILDLIFE

Gray whales breach at Bodega Head in winter and spring.

Russian River & Bohemian Highway

Sonoma's wild western side has been the place to let loose for over a century. Easy living along the Russian River was first fueled by hard cider, then bubbly wine. Heirloom apple orchards line rolling vineyards producing California's finest cult pinot noir. Come as you are and do your thing – paddle canoes, wander winding country lanes and dream days away in redwood forests.

1 Sebastopol

No amount of fermented grapes can explain free-spirited Sebastopol. In the 19th century, independent Pomo villagers and immigrant apple farmers formed a US township in the Pomo homeland of Bitakomtara. According to legend, an epic local bar brawl was jokingly compared to the famous Crimean War battlefront, and the nickname Sebastopol stuck.

While the rest of Wine Country started growing grapes, Sebastopol kept

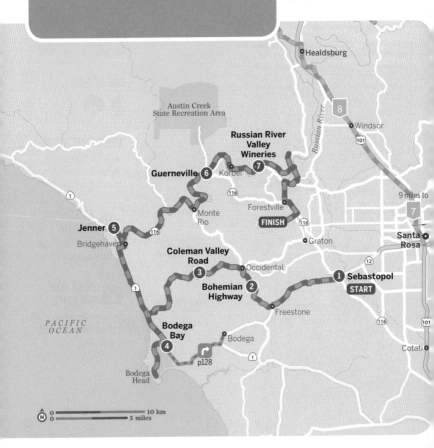

growing heirloom apples and wildflowers developed by local horticulture hero Luther Burbank at his **Gold Ridge Experiment Farm** (📞707-829-2361; www.wschs.org; 7777 Bodega Ave; ☻sunrise-sunset). Taste the difference heirloom Gravenstein apples make in the hard cider at **Horse & Plow** (📞707-827-3486; 1272 Gravenstein Hwy N; flights cider/wine/with cheese pairing $15/20/22; ☻11am-5pm; 🅿 ♿) and in the apple pie perfected by 'Mom' Betty Carr at Mom's Apple Pie (p129). When the apple-canning factory closed, the old sheds were creatively repurposed into **The Barlow** (📞707-824-5600; www.thebarlow.net; cnr Sebastopol Ave & Morris St; ☻hours vary; 🅿 ♿), an indie maker collective

LINK YOUR TRIP

8 **Healdsburg & Around**

East of Guerneville, follow River Rd (which becomes Eastside Rd) or scenic Westside Rd for 18 country miles to Healdsburg.

7 **Sonoma Valley**

From Sebastopol, head east on Hwy 12 for less than 20 miles, passing through Santa Rosa and into the Sonoma Valley for more wine tasting.

where creatives converge for local food and drink.

Back-to-the-land hippies brought fresh ideas to western Sonoma, including organic farming, home beekeeping and marijuana cultivation. You can visit many trailblazing local farms using the **Sonoma County Farm Trails Guide** (www.farmtrails.org), and admire the fruits of local labor at Sebastopol's organic **Farmers Market** (📞707-522-9305; www.sebastopolfarmmarket.org; 6932 Sebastopol Ave; ☻10am-1:30pm Sun; ♿), **BeeKind** (📞707-824-2905; www.beekind.com; 921 Gravenstein Hwy S; ☻10am-6pm Mon-Sat, to 4pm Sun) beekeping boutique, and **Solful** (📞707-596-9040; www.solful.com; 785 Gravenstein Ave; ☻10am-6pm) farm-to-spliff cannabis dispensary.

To meet more local characters, check out jam sessions at **People's Music** (📞707-823-7664; www.peoplesmusic.com; 122 N Main St; ☻noon-6pm; ♿), where you might meet Grateful Dead drummer Mickey Hart. Or take a walk down Florence Ave, lined with **recycled-art creatures** (📞707-824-9388; www.patrickamiot.com; 382 Florence Ave; 🅿 ♿ 🐕) Patrick Amiot made for his neighbors: a milk-jug cow rides a tractor, tin-can firefighters leap from a refrigerator-sized fire truck, and an auto-parts

dinosaur grabs a red convertible for lunch.

🍴 p129

The Drive » From the central intersection of Hwys 116 and 12, head west on Bodega Ave (signed Bodega Bay) for 6 miles, passing apple orchards en route to tiny Freestone.

-----

❷ Bohemian Highway

Follow your bliss north of Freestone along the aptly named Bohemian Hwy, passing shaggy barns in Occidental, winding through dense redwoods and emerging at the vintage Russian River resort of Monte Rio.

Pull over in **Freestone** for organic, nutty buns at Wild Flour Bread (p129), or for the full Freestone immersion experience, take a warm bath in soft, fermenting cedar chips at **Osmosis** (📞707-823-8231; www.osmosis.com; 209 Bohemian Hwy; individual bath $109, spa packages from $235; ☻by appointment 9am-8pm Thu-Mon, to 7pm Tue & Wed). Three miles north in **Occidental**, you can meet local artists at **Hinterland & Neon Raspberry** (📞707-599-0573; www.hinterlandempire.com; 3605 Main St; ☻10am-5pm Thu-Sun), and browse recycled, organic and women-made goods sporting Hinterland's motto: 'The future is feral.' On Fridays during summer and fall, everyone emerges from the woods for Occidental's **farmers market** (707-874-8478; www.occidental communityfarmersmarket. com; 3611 Bohemian Hwy; 4pm-dusk Fri mid-May–Oct; 👪), a free-form street party featuring local musicians, crafts and homemade food. Meanwhile in **Monte Rio**, everyone's at the **beach** (www.mrrpd.org/ monteriobeach.html; under Monte Rio Bridge; late May–late Sep; P 👪 🐾).

🍴 p129

The Drive ≫ In the center of Occidental, turn west onto well-signed Coleman Valley Rd.

---

❸ Coleman Valley Road

Sonoma County's most scenic drive isn't through the grapes, but along these 10 miles of winding byway from Occidental to the sea. It's best in the late morning, when the fog has lifted and the sun's filtering through the tree canopy.

Once you reach the ridgeline on Coleman Valley Rd, jog left onto Joy Rd and right onto Fitzpatrick Lane to find a hidden glory: the **Grove of the Old Trees** (707-544-7284; www.landpaths. org; 17599 Fitzpatrick Lane; dawn-dusk; 👪). This peaceful, 48-acre redwood forest was once owned by local lumberjacks, yet they couldn't bear to cut down these ancient giants. Environ-

mental activists rallied to save the trees, and conservation nonprofits purchased the entire grove. On the easy 1-mile loop trail, you'll spot faint blue marks on towering trees once destined for lumberyards. Today they're thriving in this designated 'Forever Wild' conservation site.

Back on Coleman Valley Rd, you'll dip into lush valleys where Douglas firs are cloaked in sphagnum moss – an eerie sight in the fog. Pass gnarled oaks and craggy rock formations as you ascend 1000ft, until finally you see the vast blue Pacific, unfurling at your feet.

The Drive ≫ The road ends at coastal Hwy 1 in the midst of Sonoma Coast State Park, which stretches 17 miles from Bodega Head to just north of Jenner. From Hwy 1, head 2.5 miles south, then west onto Eastshore Rd. Go right at the stop sign onto Bay Flat Rd and along the harbor until road's end.

TRIP HIGHLIGHT

❹ Bodega Bay

The town of Bodega Bay signals your approach to **Sonoma Coast State Park**, where rocky headlands lean into the horizon over hidden beach coves, and coastal hiking trails wind along wildflower-carpeted bluffs. Go all the way to the tip of the peninsula to reach **Bodega Head**, rising 265ft above sea level for sweeping ocean views,

GARY SAKE / SHUTTERSTOCK ©

exciting close-up whale-watching, kite-flying and hiking as seals bark approval from the rocks below.

🍴 p129

The Drive ≫ Return to Hwy 1 and trace the coastline 8 miles north toward Jenner, turning left onto Goat Rock Rd.

TRIP HIGHLIGHT

❺ Jenner

The charming fishing village of Jenner marks the spot where the Russian River flows into the ocean. At the end of Goat Rock Rd, bear left for **Blind Beach**, where

Johnson's Beach, Guerneville

the views are dominated by looming Goat Rock overhead and Arched Rock on the ocean's horizon. Double back and turn left (north) to **Goat Rock Beach**, where your arrival is greeted by the raucous barks of a harbor seal colony – pups are born here from March to August. Get to know your new marine mammal friends better by renting a kayak from **Water Treks EcoTours** (☎707-865-2249; www.watertreks.com; 2hr kayak rental from $50, 4hr guided tours from $120; ⊗hours vary), where you can get tips on river routes and navigating harbor seal habitats.

🛏 p129

The Drive ≫ After crossing the last bridge over the Russian River before it joins the sea, go east on Hwy 116/River Rd, a well-paved country road sandwiched between the river and hillsides that leads to Guerneville.

- - - - - - - - - - - - - - - - - -

TRIP HIGHLIGHT

⑥ Guerneville

The Russian River's biggest vacation destination almost doubles in size some hot summer weekends, when vacationers arrive to hike redwoods, canoe and hammer cocktails. This town is a good time had by all since the 1870s – it's been an LGBTQ resort destination for over a century, and a biker pit stop since the '50s. Downtown Guerneville is lined with cafes, indie maker boutiques, straight-friendly gay bars, down-home dining, and wine tasting for a cause at **Equality Vines** (☎877-379-4637; www.equalityvines.com; 6215 Main St; tastings $15; ⊗1-8pm Thu, noon-8pm Fri & Sat, to 6pm Sun, to 5pm Mon).

During summer and fall, the absolute best thing to do on the Russian River is to float down it, on an inner tube, raft or inflatable flamingo, with some friends

DETOUR: BLOODTHIRSTY BIRDS OF BODGE

Start: ④ Bodega Bay

As pretty much everyone in Bodega Bay will tell you, this was the setting for Alfred Hitchcock's classic thriller *The Birds* (1963). It's easy to see why, with all the boisterous gulls flapping around windswept coastal farmsteads. Venture 5 miles inland (south on Hwy 1) to the tiny town of **Bodega** and you'll find two icons from the film: the schoolhouse (now a private home) and St Teresa of Avila Church. Both look just as they did in the movie – and a crow overhead may make the hairs rise on your neck.

and a flask in hand. If you're feeling ambitious, rent kayaks and canoes on **Johnson's Beach** (☏707-869-2022; www. johnsonsbeach.com; 16215 & 16217 1st St; kayak & canoe rental per hour/day $15/40; ◷10am-6pm May to Oct; 🚶).

✕ 🛏 p129

The Drive » Follow Main St east of central Guerneville onto River Rd and drive almost 3 miles to Korbel on your left.

- - - - - - - - - - - - - - - - - -

⑦ Russian River Valley Wineries

There are 50 wineries within a 20-minute drive of Guerneville. The Russian River AVA (American Viticulture Area) produces California's cult-favorite pinot noir and chardonnay, thanks to nighttime coastal fog that swirls through the

redwoods, then burns off midday in dramatic silvery haloes of mist.

The highest concentration of wineries is along Westside Rd, between Guerneville and Healdsburg. Where Westside Rd turns northeast, 5 miles from Guerneville, you'll find low-key **Porter Creek** (☏707-433-6321; www. portercreekvineyards.com; 8735 Westside Rd; tastings $20; ◷10:30am-4:30pm; P), where pioneering biodynamic wines are served in a 1930s tool shed. From family vineyards Demeter-certified in 2003, Alex Davis crafts sensational, sustainable pinot noir, syrah, viognier and chardonnay – step up to the tasting bar to try his latest creations.

Backtrack south just over a mile on Westside Rd, then jog left onto

Wohler Rd and right back onto River Rd, then follow Mirabel Rd south toward the hamlet of Forestville. Turn right onto Hwy 116, and drive just over 4 miles west to the turnoff to Mays Canyon Rd to enter the hidden valley home of **Porter-Bass** (☏707-869-1475; www.porter-bass.com; 11750 Mays Canyon Rd; tastings $15; ◷10am-4pm). Mists swirl around redwoods above, with sunny vineyards below – and under a walnut tree, farmer Sue Bass pours wine that captures this splendid scenery in organic, biodynamic sauvignon blanc, chardonnay, pinot noir and zinfandel.

Head back onto Hwy 116 east, and after a mile, turn right onto sun-dappled, winding Green Valley Rd. Continue 8 miles to Thomas Rd, which bends three times before reaching the entry to **Iron Horse** (☏707-887-1507; www.ironhorsevineyards. com; 9786 Ross Station Rd; by appointment tastings $30, incl tour $50; ◷10am-4:30pm, last tastings 4pm; P) vineyards. Drive to the hilltop barn for drop-dead views over the county, and toast with bubbly pinot noir – including special cuvées celebrating LGBTQ Pride and climate resilience.

Eating & Sleeping

Sebastopol ❶

✖ Mom's Apple Pie
Desserts $

(☎707-823-8330; www.momsapplepieusa.com; 4550 Gravenstein Hwy N; pies $7-17; ⊙10am-6pm; 🖋🚼) 'Mom' Betty Carr began her search for the ultimate all-American pie in the 1960s, leading from her native Japan to Sonoma, where she fell in love with an apple farmer – and the rest is edible history. Enjoy her signature cinnamon-sprinkled Gravenstein pie or seasonal-favorite olallieberry still warm, piled with vanilla ice cream.

✖ Fern Bar
Californian $$

(☎707-861-9603; https://fernbar.square.site; 6780 Depot St No 120; shared plates $9-27; ⊙5-11pm Tue-Sun; 🅿❄🖋) Come for '70s fern-bar atmosphere, with stained glass and amber lighting – stay for the food. Choose your Sonoma-proud shared plates: seasonal standouts include local trout with green garlic and 'umami bomb' mushroom-cream broccolini on yeast-dusted sticky rice.

Bohemian Highway ❷

✖ Wild Flour Bread
Bakery $

(☎707-874-2938; www.wildflourbread.com; 140 Bohemian Hwy, Freestone; items from $3; ⊙8am-6pm Fri-Mon; 🚼) The West goes wild for organic artisan breads, mushroom fougasse glossy with olive oil, and sticky buns the size of throw pillows, all hot from the brick oven. Picnic table seating here is more sought after than royal thrones – regulars loll on grassy lawns or stroll through the gardens, which are the only possible post–Wild Flour activities anyway.

✖ Hazel
Californian $$

(☎707-874-6003; www.restauranthazel.com; 3782 Bohemian Hwy, Occidental; shared plates $18-36; ⊙5-9pm Wed-Sat, 10am-2pm & 5-9pm Sun; 🅿❄) Whenever you arrive, you're right on time for another fabulous dinner party at Jim and Michele Wimborough's cottage restaurant. Wine flows and oooOoooh! choruses erupt as dishes arrive bubbling from wood-fired ovens: caramelized Brussels sprouts, herb-roasted chicken, wild-mushroom pizzas and strawberry-

rhubarb crisp. Dishes are generous and your hosts unfailingly delightful – all you have to do is make happy noises.

Bodega Bay ❹

✖ Spud Point Crab Company
Seafood $

(☎707-875-9472; www.spudpointcrab.com; 1910 Westshore Rd; mains $8-13; ⊙9am-5pm) In the classic tradition of dockside crab shacks, Spud Point serves salty-sweet crab sandwiches and *real* clam chowder (that consistently wins local culinary prizes). You can also buy a crab to take home if you fancy. Eat at picnic tables overlooking the marina. Take Bay Flat Rd to get here.

Jenner ❺

⛺ River's End Inn
Cottage $$

(☎707-865-2484; www.ilovesunsets.com; 11048 Hwy 1; cottages $160-250; 🐾) These ocean-view cottages are wood-paneled and have no TVs, wi-fi or phones; however, many do come with fireplaces, breezy decks and breathtaking ocean views, complete with harbor seals. To preserve the romantic atmosphere, bringing children under 12 years old is not recommended.

Guerneville ❻

✖ Boon Eat + Drink
Californian $$

(☎707-869-0780; www.eatatboon.com; 16248 Main St; mains $12-28; ⊙11am-3pm & 5-9pm Sun-Tue & Thu, to 10pm Fri & Sat; 🖋) Good vibes are the not-so-secret ingredient in this tiny, always-packed bistro. Hyperlocal flavor bombs like mycopia-mushroom mac and cheese and preserved Meyer lemon chicken satisfy lumberjack appetites, while checking environmental scorecards. Chef/owner/dynamo Crista Luedtke uses homegrown ingredients from her **Boon Hotel + Spa** (☎707-869-2721; www.boonhotels.com; 14711 Armstrong Woods Rd; tents $175-230, d $195-400; 🅿🐾📶🏊🐕) and pours her own Big Bottom Market wines – her cooking has sustained Guerneville through firestorms and floods, not to mention first dates.

Mendocino & Anderson Valley

The uninitiated might roll their eyes at 'Mendocino Magic,' but spend a few days here cruising two-lane blacktop and you'll discover the enchantment of this place is undeniable.

10

TRIP HIGHLIGHTS

70 miles

Mendocino
A seaside gem of historic buildings and excellent B&Bs

6

105 miles

Orr Hot Springs
Soak among redwoods at this magical getaway

8
FINISH

Philo●

2

Hopland ●
START

Boonville
Learn to speak Boontling and sip excellent local brew

25 miles

3–4 DAYS
105 MILES / 170KM

GREAT FOR...

BEST TIME TO GO
In fall, when skies are clear and apples harvested.

ESSENTIAL PHOTO
Otters swimming alongside your canoe on the Big River.

BEST DAY
Hike through pygmy forests in Van Damme State Park and canoe up the Big River.

10

Mendocino & Anderson Valley

This trip is about family-operated vineyards, hushed stands of redwoods and a string of idiosyncratic villages perched in the border area between California's rolling coastal hills and the jagged cliffs of the Pacific. Just far enough out of the Bay Area orbit to move to its own relaxed rhythm, this makes an unforgettable trip filled with low-key pampering, specialty pinot noir, sun-drenched days and romantic, foggy nights.

1 Hopland

Tired of treading over the same ground in Napa and Sonoma? Make for adorable little Hopland, the wine hub of the Mendocino County. Just 100 miles north of San Francisco, this unsung winemaking region offers a lighter, more delicate style of pinot noir and chardonnay. You can taste the wines from many of the family farms you'll approach en route at the downtown

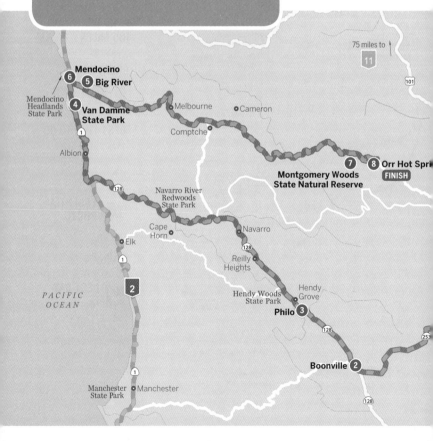

wine shop **Sip Mendocino** (📞707-744-8375; www.sipmendocino.com; 13420 S Hwy 101; tastings $5-10; 🕑11am-6pm). Its expert staff pour hand-picked flights that include rare vintages you might not even taste at the wineries themselves.

The Drive » Head north on Hwy 101 about 10 miles before exiting on Hwy 253, a beautiful serpentine route southwest through the hills. Hwy 253 ends at Hwy 128, just south of Boonville by the brewery.

TRIP HIGHLIGHT

② Boonville

Descending from the hills, visitors spill out into the sun-washed village of Boonville, a short main street with historical buildings, boutiques and artisanal ice cream. The town's most famous taste is just a mile down the road at the **Anderson Valley Brewing Company** (📞707-895-2337; www.avbc.com; 17700 Hwy 253; tastings from $10; 🕑11am-8pm Sat-Thu, to 9pm Fri, tours 1pm Sat). The Bavarian-style brewhouse sits on a big corner lot overlooking the valley, and the grounds are complete with a sparsely furnished tasting room, copper-clad brewing vats and beefy, grazing draft horses. The place also includes a disc-golf course, and players can buy beer inside the tasting room to drink as they play. The brewery's long-standing green credentials include a solar array that generates much of its power.

🍴 🛏 p137

The Drive » Drive just north out of town on Hwy 128, passing a number of family wineries and fruit stands. The best fruit is ahead, in Philo, only 6 miles north of Boonville.

③ Philo

The gorgeous **Philo Apple Farm** (📞707-895-2333; www.philoapplefarm.com; 18501 Greenwood Rd; 🕑10am-5pm) is a bit like something out of a storybook: a dreamy patch of green run by warm-hearted staff and scented with apple blossoms. It's worth skipping over the other farm stands on the way here for its organic preserves, chutneys and heirloom apples and pears. (If you get here after hours, you're likely to be able to leave a few dollars in a jar and take some goodies along for the ride.) Those who linger can take cooking classes with some of the Wine Country's best chefs. For a swim, the rocky shallow waters of

● Redwood Valley

● Calpella (20)

Lake Mendocino

101

h

101

START
① Hopland

LINK YOUR TRIP

2 Pacific Coast Highways

Can't get enough beachcombing and breathtaking cliffs? Join California's most epic drive along Hwy 1.

11 Lost Coast & Southern Redwoods

The northern edge of this trip nears California's wildest shores, perfect for travelers with sturdy hiking boots and a thirst for untouched wilds. Continue up Hwy 101 to connect with this trip.

133

the Navarro River are just a short stroll up the road.

📑 p137

The Drive » Take the twisting drive west along Hwy 128 through majestic fog-shrouded stands of redwood and you'll eventually emerge at Hwy 1. Go north on Hwy 1 through the seaside town of Albion and on toward Van Damme State Park.

④ Van Damme State Park

After emerging on one of California's most serene stretches of Hwy 1, a stroll by the waves seems mandatory. Three miles south of Mendocino, this sprawling 1831-acre **park** (📞707-937-4016; www.mendoparks.org/van-damme; 8125 N Hwy 1, Little River; per car $8; ⏰ hours vary; P) draws beachcombers, divers and kayakers to its easy-access beach, and hikers to its pygmy forest. The latter is a unique and precious place, where acidic soil and an impenetrable layer of hardpan have created a miniature forest of decades-old trees. You can reach the forest on the moderate 2.5-mile Fern Canyon Scenic Trail, which crosses back and forth over Little River and past the Cabbage Patch, a bog of skunk cabbage that's rich with wildlife. The **visitor center** (📞707-937-4016; www.mendoparks.org/van-damme; 8125 N Hwy 1; ⏰ hours vary) has nature exhibits and programs.

📑 p137

The Drive » A short 2-mile drive north along Hwy 1 brings you to the bridge over the Big River. Just before the bridge, take a right on Comptche Ukiah Rd.

⑤ Big River

A lazy paddle up the Big River is a chance to get an intimate look at the

TOP ANDERSON VALLEY WINERIES

The valley's cool nights yield high-acid, fruit-forward, food-friendly wines. Pinot noir, chardonnay and gewürztraminer grapes flourish. Most **Anderson Valley wineries** (www.avwines.com) sit outside Philo. Many are family-owned and offer tastings, and some give tours. The following are particularly noteworthy:

Toulouse Vineyards (📞707-895-2828; www.toulousevineyards.com; 8001 Hwy 128, Philo; tastings $10; ⏰11am-5pm Thu-Mon) Sample standout (and organic!) pinot gris, valdiguié and pinot noir from a stunning hilltop tasting room tucked into the forest.

Navarro Vineyards (📞707-895-3686; www.navarrowine.com; 5601 Hwy 128, Philo; ⏰9am-6pm Jun-Oct, to 5pm Nov-May) One of the most visitor-friendly options around, with award-winning pinot noir and dry gewürztraminer; has twice-daily free tours (10:30am and 2pm).

Pennyroyal Farm (📞707-895-2410; www.pennyroyalfarm.com; 14930 Hwy 128, Boonville; tastings $10; ⏰10am-5pm, cheese tastings until 4:30pm) You'll get the highlights reel of Anderson Valley at this sustainable farm, creamery and vineyard where you can pair small-batch cheeses with Alsatian-style wines.

WALTER BIBIKOW / GETTY IMAGES ©

NORTHERN CALIFORNIA **10** MENDOCINO & ANDERSON VALLEY

North Coast, Mendocino

border between land and sea – a place where otters, sea lions and majestic blue herons keep you company as you drift silently by. Although the area near the mouth of the river is an excellent place to watch the waves or catch the sunset, more adventurous travelers can check in at **Catch A Canoe & Bicycles, Too!** (707-937-0273; www. catchacanoe.com; 10051 S Big River Rd, The Stanford Inn & Resort; 3hr kayak, canoe or bicycle rental adult/child $35/15; 9am-5pm), a friendly riverside outfit that rents bikes, kayaks and canoes (including redwood outriggers) for trips up the 8-mile Big River tidal estuary, the longest undeveloped estuary in Northern California. Years of conservation efforts have protected this area from highways and buildings. Bring a picnic and a camera to enjoy the marshes, log-strewn beaches, abundant wildlife and ramshackle remnants of century-old train trestles.

The Drive >> The next stop, Mendocino, is just north of the bridge over the Big River.

TRIP HIGHLIGHT

6 Mendocino

Perched on a gorgeous headland, Mendocino is the North Coast's salt-washed gem, with B&Bs and rose gardens, white picket fences and New England–style redwood water towers. Bay Area weekenders walk along the headland among berry bramble and wildflowers, where cypress trees stand over dizzying cliffs. A stroll through this dreamy little village is a highlight of a trip through the region.

To get a sense for the village's thriving art scene, drop in at the **Mendocino Art Center** (☎707-937-5818; www.mendocinoartcenter.org; 45200 Little Lake St; ⊙11am-4pm), a hub for visual, musical and theatrical arts. The center is also home to the **Mendocino Theatre Company** (www.mendocinotheatre.org), which stages contemporary plays in the 81-seat Helen Schoeni Theatre.

The town itself is loaded with galleries, all of which host openings on the second Saturday evening of the month, when doors are thrown open to strolling connoisseurs of art and wine, and Mendocino buzzes with life. Of course, the natural setting here is a work of art itself. The spectacular **Mendocino Headlands State Park** (☎707-937-5804; www.parks.ca.gov) surrounds the village, with trails crisscrossing the bluffs and rocky coves. Ask at the **Ford House Museum & Visitor Center** (☎707-937-5397; www.mendoparks.org; 45035 Main St; ⊙11am-4pm) about guided weekend walks, including spring wildflower walks and whale-watching jaunts.

✕ 🛏 p137

The Drive 》 Just south of town, turn inland at Comptche Ukiah Rd. It will make a loop taking you back toward the trip's beginning. All the turns make the next 30 miles eastbound slow going, but the views are impressive.

---

❼ Montgomery Woods State Natural Reserve

Two miles west of Orr, this 2743-acre **park** (☎707-937-5804; www.parks.ca.gov; 15825 Orr Springs Rd) protects some of the best old-growth redwood groves within a day's drive from San Francisco. A 2-mile loop trail, starting near the picnic tables and toilets, crosses the creek, winding through the serene forest. It's out of the way, so visitors are likely to have it mostly to themselves. The trees here are impressive – some up to 367ft tall – but remember to admire them from the trail, both to protect the trees' root systems and to protect yourself from poison oak, which is all over the park.

The Drive 》 Continue 2 miles east on Comptche Ukiah Rd (which may be called Orr Springs Rd on some maps) to reach Orr Hot Springs.

TRIP HIGHLIGHT

❽ Orr Hot Springs

After all the hiking, canoeing and beachcombing, a soak in the thermal waters of this rustic **resort** (☎707-462-6277; www.orrhotsprings.org; 13201 Orr Springs Rd; day use adult/child $35/25; ⊙by appointment 10am-10pm) is heavenly, the ultimate zen-out to end the journey. While it's not for the bashful, this clothing-optional resort is beloved by locals, back-to-the-land hipsters, backpackers and liberal-minded tourists. Still, you don't have to let it all hang out to enjoy Orr Hot Springs. The place has private tubs, a sauna, a spring-fed rock-bottomed swimming pool, a steam room, massage and lovely, slightly shaggy gardens. Soaking in the rooftop stargazing tubs on a clear night is magical. Reservations are almost always necessary, even for day visits.

🛏 (p137)

Eating & Sleeping

Boonville ❷

✕ Paysanne — Ice Cream $

(📞707-895-2210; www.sweetpaysanne.com; 14111 Hwy 128; ice cream from $2.50; ⊙11am-6pm Fri-Mon Apr-Nov) Boonville's fantastic sweets shop serves the innovative flavors of Three Twins Ice Cream, with delightful choices including Lemon Cookie and Strawberry Je Ne Sais Quoi (which has a hint of balsamic vinegar); it's the best ice cream in the Anderson Valley.

🛏 Boonville Hotel — Boutique Hotel $$

(📞707-895-2210; www.boonvillehotel.com; 14050 Hwy 128; d $165-325; ⊙ ❄ 🛜) Decked out in contemporary American-country style with sea-grass flooring, pastel colors and fine linens, this historical hotel's rooms and suites are safe for urbanites who refuse to abandon style just because they've gone to the country. The hotel also has beautiful gardens and an inviting sitting room with board games and books. The **restaurant** (mains $20-30, dinner tasting menu $78; ⊙6-8pm Thu-Mon Apr-Nov, 6-8pm Fri & Sat, noon-2pm Sun Dec-Mar; 🛜) comes highly recommended.

Philo ❸

🛏 Philo Apple Farm Guest Cottages — Cottage $$$

(📞707-895-2333; www.philoapplefarm.com; 18501 Greenwood Rd,; d $300; ⊙) Set within the orchard, guests of bucolic Philo Apple Farm (p133) choose from four exquisite cottages, each built with rustic materials. With bright, airy spaces, polished plank floors, simple furnishings and views of the surrounding trees, each one is an absolute dream.

Van Damme State Park ❹

🛏 Van Damme State Park Campgrounds — Campground $

(📞800-444-7275; www.reservecalifornia. com; 8125 N Hwy 1, Little River; tent & RV sites from $40; 👪) Great for families, the main campground has lots of space and hot pay showers, but limited parking. Some sites are just off Hwy 1, while others are in a meadow.

Mendocino ❻

✕ Café Beaujolais — Californian $$$

(📞707-937-5614; www.cafebeaujolais.com; 961 Ukiah St; mains lunch $11-20, dinner $24-50; ⊙11:30am-3pm Wed-Sun, 5:30-9pm daily, closed Jan) Mendocino's iconic, beloved country-Cal–French restaurant occupies an 1893 farmhouse restyled into a monochromatic urban-chic dining room, perfect for holding hands by candlelight. The refined, inspired cooking draws diners from San Francisco, who make this the centerpiece of their trip.

🛏 Mendocino Grove — Campground $$

(www.mendocinogrove.com; 9601 Hwy 1; tent from $140; ⊙May-Oct; 🛜) Sleep amid the woods a quick stroll from town at this hipster-friendly glamping resort.

Orr Hot Springs ❽

🛏 Orr Hot Springs — Spa Hotel $$

(📞707-462-6277; www.orrhotsprings.org; 13201 Orr Springs Rd; tent sites per adult/child $75/35, r & yurt $230, cottages $300; 🛜) Elegantly rustic rooms are a good match for this earthy spa. Accommodations include use of the spa and communal kitchen, while some share bathrooms; cottages have their own kitchens. There are also six yurts tucked into the woods here, offering total privacy.

Lost Coast & Southern Redwoods

Get lost along the empty shores of this pristine coastal area, then cruise under the ancient trees of the Avenue of the Giants, putting the charms of NorCal center stage.

11

TRIP HIGHLIGHTS

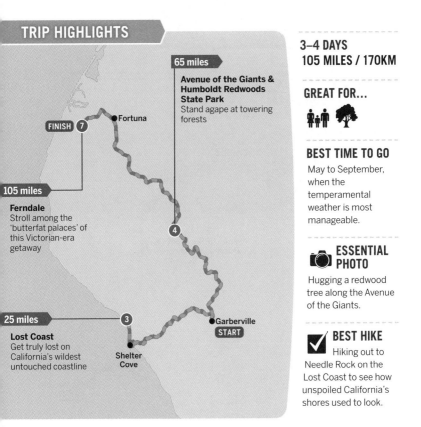

65 miles

Avenue of the Giants & Humboldt Redwoods State Park
Stand agape at towering forests

● Fortuna

FINISH **7**

105 miles

Ferndale
Stroll among the 'butterfat palaces' of this Victorian-era getaway

4

25 miles

Lost Coast
Get truly lost on California's wildest untouched coastline

3

● Shelter Cove

● Garberville
START

3–4 DAYS
105 MILES / 170KM

GREAT FOR...

BEST TIME TO GO
May to September, when the temperamental weather is most manageable.

ESSENTIAL PHOTO
Hugging a redwood tree along the Avenue of the Giants.

BEST HIKE
Hiking out to Needle Rock on the Lost Coast to see how unspoiled California's shores used to look.

11

Lost Coast & Southern Redwoods

With its secluded trails and pristine beaches, the gorgeous 'Lost Coast' is one of the state's most untouched coastal areas and most exciting hiking adventures. The region became 'lost' when the state highway system bypassed it in the 20th century and it has since developed an outsider culture of political radicals, marijuana farmers and nature lovers. Inland, take a magical drive through the big trees of California's largest redwood park.

① Garberville

The introductory stop on a Lost Coast romp is scrappy little Garberville, the first town beyond the so-called 'Redwood Curtain' of Humboldt County. It has an alluring laissez-faire attitude, but is not everyone's cup of tea. There's an uneasy relationship here between the old-guard loggers and the hippies, many of whom came in the 1970s to grow marijuana after the feds chased them out of Santa Cruz. The three-block downtown works

best as a pit stop to grab lunch and stock up on supplies before you zip over to the coast.

 p145

The Drive >> Take it easy and in a low gear on the steep, twisting drive down Briceland Rd (which becomes Shelter Cove Rd eventually) – managing the 21 miles from Redway to Shelter Cove can be a challenge. Best to heed the 'No Trespassing' signs on this part of the drive, as the local marijuana farmers don't take kindly to strangers.

---

② Shelter Cove

At the end of the road – and what seems like the end of the earth! – is the isolated community of Shelter Cove, gateway to the Lost Coast. The tiny encampment of restaurants and shops sometimes seems equally

LINK YOUR TRIP

12 Northern Redwood Coast

Link this trip with a jaunt to the forests of the Redwood National Park by continuing north past Ferndale on Hwy 101.

2 Pacific Coast Highways

Keep riding along the Pacific edge of California, either north toward Redwood National Park or south to San Diego.

---

populated by humans and Roosevelt elk. Although primarily used as a launching point for the nearby wilds, it makes a relaxing destination in its own right. From town, scan the water for migrating gray whales (look for mothers and their calves in early spring) and explore tide pools teeming with crabs, snails, sea stars and sponges; locals even spot an octopus on occasion.

 p145

The Drive >> There are trailheads for exploring the Lost Coast Trail both north and south of town. That's where the drive pauses; the trail has to be done on foot.

TRIP HIGHLIGHT

③ Lost Coast

The North Coast's superlative backpacking destination is a rugged, mystifying stretch of coast with trails crossing seafront peaks and volcanic black-sand beaches. The King Range boldly rises 4000ft within 3 miles of the coast, which became 'lost' when the state's highway system deemed the region impassable in the mid-20th century.

Made up of Sinkyone Wilderness State Park and the King Range National Conservation Area, the region is best explored on a multiday hike. Leaving from Shelter Cove, a three-day

trek north on the **Lost Coast Trail** ends at the mouth of the Mattole River. Equally challenging and rewarding, it passes the abandoned **Punta Gorda Lighthouse** near the end. You can arrange shuttle service back to your car through **Lost Coast Adventure Tours** (707-986-9895; www.lostcoastadventures.com; 210 Wave Dr; shuttle from $85; 10am-2pm Mon-Fri). From Shelter Cove, you can take a day hike to **Black Sand Beach**, or overnight at **Needle Rock Campground** (707-986-7711; www.parks.ca.gov; Bear Harbor Rd; tent sites $35), about 9 miles south of the Hidden Valley Trailhead. The **visitor center** (707-986-7711; www.parks.ca.gov; Bear Harbor Rd; per car $6; hours vary) there affords gorgeous coastal views.

The Drive >> Retrace the twisting drive back to Garberville, then continue north on Hwy 101. Exit Hwy 101 when you see the 'Avenue of the Giants' sign, 6 miles north of Garberville, near Phillipsville, and be sure to pick up one of the free driving guides at the roadside stand by the exit. This is the heart of the big-tree country.

TRIP HIGHLIGHT

④ Avenue of the Giants & Humboldt Redwoods State Park

The incredible, 32-mile, two-lane stretch of highway known as the **Avenue of the Giants** is

141

one of the most justifiably celebrated drives in California, and a place where travelers stand with jaws agape and necks craned upward at the canopy. The route connects a number of small towns with mid-20th-century motels, diners serving 'lumberjack' meals and pull-offs parked with Harleys. Visitors would be remiss to drive right past these majestic groves along the avenue without stopping at the **California Federation of Women's Clubs Grove**, home to an interesting four-sided hearth designed by renowned architect Julia Morgan, and the **Founders Grove**, where the 370ft **Dyerville Giant** was knocked down in 1991 by another falling tree.

Much of the Avenue of the Giants snakes in and out of **Humboldt Redwoods State Park** (☏707-946-2409; www.parks.ca.gov; Hwy 101). At 53,000 acres – 17,000 of which are old-growth – it boasts three-quarters of the world's tallest 100 trees. These groves rival (and

may surpass) those in Redwood National Park further north. The 100-plus miles of trails can be taken on foot, horse or bike and range in difficulty from the kid-friendly **Drury-Chaney Loop Trail** (with thimble berry picking in summer) to the rugged **Grasshopper Peak Trail**, which climbs to a fire lookout (3379ft). The primeval **Rockefeller Forest**, 4.5 miles west of the avenue via the incredibly picturesque Mattole Rd, appears as it did a century ago. It's the world's largest contiguous old-growth redwood forest, and contains about 20% of all such remaining trees.

🛏 p145

The Drive » From the Avenue of the Giants, follow signs to the groves in the park. You'll pass a number of small villages along the way that are ramshackle collections of mid-20th-century tourist traps, woodsy lodges and huge stands of trees. The Avenue of the Giants ends at Hwy 101 near Pepperwood, from where it's a 5-mile drive north to Scotia.

⑤ Scotia

For years, Scotia was California's last 'company town,' entirely owned and operated by the Pacific Lumber Company, which built cookie-cut houses and had an open contempt for long-haired outsiders who liked to get between their saws and the big trees. The company went belly-up in 2008, sold the mill to another redwood company and, though the town still has a creepy *Truman Show* vibe, you no longer have to operate by the company's posted 'Code of Conduct.'

TOP TIP: ACCESSING THE LOST COAST

Backpackers who wish to hike the entirety of the Lost Coast often go from north to south in order to avoid northerly winds. Many hikers start at the Mattole Campground, just south of Petrolia, which is on the northern border of the King Range.

Ferndale main street

There are dingy diners and a couple of bars in **Rio Dell**, across the river from Scotia. Back in the day, this is where the debauchery went down: because it wasn't a company town, Rio Dell had saloons and prostitutes. In 1969 the freeway bypassed the town and it withered.

The Drive » Follow Hwy 101 for almost 8 miles north to exit 687 for Kenmar Rd. At the south end of the town in Fortuna, turn right onto Alamar Way.

- - - - - - - - - - - - - - - - -

6 Fortuna

The penultimate stop is at **Eel River Brewing**
Company (☎702-725-2739; www.eelriverbrewing.com; 1777 Alamar Way; ⏰11am-11pm) in Fortuna for a cold, refreshing pint of beer. This place is completely in step with its amazing natural surrounds – it was the USA's first certified organic brewery and uses 100% renewable energy (there's a bit of irony in the fact that most of their beer is brewed in an old redwood mill that formerly belonged to the Pacific Lumber Company). The breezy beer garden and excellent burgers make it an ideal pit stop.

The Drive » Back on Hwy 101, go just over 2 miles north and take exit 691 for Fernbridge/Ferndale. Follow Hwy 211 for 5 miles southwest past rolling dairy farms to Ferndale.

- - - - - - - - - - - - - - - - -

TRIP HIGHLIGHT

7 Ferndale

The trip ends at one of the region's most charming towns, stuffed with impeccable Victorians – known locally as 'butterfat palaces' because of the dairy wealth that built them. The entire town is a State Historical Landmark with several nationally registered historic sites. A stroll down Main St offers a taste of super wholesome, small-town America, from galleries to old-world emporiums and soda fountains. Half a mile from downtown via Bluff St, enjoy short tramps through fields of wildflowers, beside ponds and past a mature Sitka spruce forest at 110-acre **Russ Park**. The **cemetery**, also on Bluff St, has graves dating to the 1800s and expansive views to the ocean.

To end the trip with whimsy, show up over Memorial Day weekend to see the fanciful, astounding, human-powered contraptions of the annual **Kinetic Grand Championship** (☏707-786-3443; www.kineticgrand-championship.com; ⏱ late May) race from Arcata to Ferndale. Shaped like giant fish and UFOs, these colorful piles of junk propel racers over roads, water and marsh in a three-day event.

✕ ⛏ p145

Eating & Sleeping

Garberville ❶

✕ Woodrose Café
American $

(☎707-923-3191; www.thewoodrosecafe.com; 911 Redwood Dr; mains $9-18; ☺8am-2pm; �) Garberville's beloved cafe serves organic omelets, veggie scrambles and buckwheat pancakes with *real* maple syrup in a cozy room. Lunch brings crunchy salads, sandwiches with all-natural meats and good burritos.

⛔ Benbow Historic Inn
Historic Hotel $$$

(☎707-923-2124; www.benbowinn.com; 445 Lake Benbow Dr, Benbow; d $175-475; ☺❄🖥♨🐾) This inn is a monument to 1920s rustic elegance; the area's first luxury resort is a National Historic Landmark. Hollywood's elite once frolicked in the Tudor-style resort's lobby, where you can now play chess by the crackling fire, and enjoy complimentary afternoon tea and scones. The window-lined **dining room** (breakfast and lunch $14 to $19, dinner mains $28 to $39) serves excellent meals; the steaks earn raves.

Shelter Cove ❷

✕ Gyppo Ale Mill
American $$

(☎707-986-7700; www.gyppo.com; 1661 Upper Pacific Dr; mains $10-20; ☺4-8pm Mon-Fri, noon-8pm Sat & Sun) Gyppo injects a jolt of youthful energy into this aging community, brewing a dozen of its own ales and showcasing them alongside local wines and ciders. There's all-you-can-eat popcorn, but the burgers, brats and salads are recommended. Ping-Pong, lawn games, fire pits and a serene ocean view complete the picture.

⛔ Tides Inn
Hotel $$

(☎707-986-7900; www.sheltercovetidesinn.com; 59 Surf Pt; r/ste from $170/220; ☺📶) Perched above tide pools teeming with starfish and sea urchins, the squeaky-clean rooms here offer excellent views (go for the minisuites on the 3rd floor with fireplaces).

Avenue of the Giants & Humboldt Redwoods State Park ❹

⛔ Humboldt Redwoods State Park Campgrounds
Campground $

(☎info 707-946-1811, reservations 800-444-7275; www.reservecalifornia.com; tent & RV sites $35, trail/environmental campsites $5/20; 🐾) The park runs three campgrounds, along with environmental camps, trail camps and a horse camp. Year-round Burlington Campground is beside the visitor center and near a number of trailheads; Hidden Springs Campground is 5 miles south along the Avenue of the Giants; and Albee Creek Campground is on Mattole Rd past Rockefeller Forest.

⛔ Miranda Gardens Resort
Resort $$

(☎707-943-3011; www.mirandagardens.com; 6766 Avenue of the Giants, Miranda; cottages $125-300; ☺♨🐾) The best indoor stay along the avenue. The cozy, dark, slightly rustic spotless cottages have redwood paneling; some have fireplaces and kitchens. The grounds – replete with outdoor Ping-Pong, a seasonal swimming pool and a play area for kids amid swaying redwoods – have wholesome appeal for families.

Ferndale ❼

✕ Tuyas
Mexican $

(☎707-786-5921; www.tuyasferndale.com; 553 Main St; mains $9-18; ☺11:30am-8pm Sun-Thu, to 9pm Fri & Sat; 📶) A classy Mexican spot with art-filled walls and sultry Latin music to set the mood. The elevated cuisine (think spicy-sweet mole and tangy shrimp ceviche) is a fine match for the superbly executed margaritas.

⛔ Victorian Inn
Historic Hotel $$

(☎707-786-4949; www.victorianvillageinn.com; 400 Ocean Ave; r $125-250; ☺📶) The bright, sunny rooms inside this venerable two-story former bank building (1890) are comfortably furnished with thick carpeting, period-style wallpaper, fantastic linens and funky antiques.

Northern Redwood Coast

Hug 800-year-old trees, stroll moody bluffs and visit roadside attractions of yesteryear on this trip through verdant redwood parks and personality-packed villages.

TRIP HIGHLIGHTS

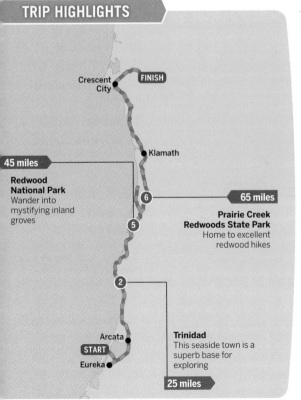

Crescent City **FINISH**

Klamath

45 miles

Redwood National Park
Wander into mystifying inland groves

6

65 miles

Prairie Creek Redwoods State Park
Home to excellent redwood hikes

5

2

Arcata

START

Eureka

Trinidad
This seaside town is a superb base for exploring

25 miles

3–4 DAYS
110 MILES / 175KM

GREAT FOR...

BEST TIME TO GO

April to October for usually clear skies and the region's warmest weather.

ESSENTIAL PHOTO

Misty redwoods clinging to rocky cliffs at Del Norte Coast Redwoods State Park.

BEST SCENIC DRIVE

Howland Hill Rd through dense old-growth redwood forests.

trick's Point State Park Agate Beach

Northern Redwood Coast

This trip may have been charted in the glory days of the mid-20th-century American road trip – roadside attractions include a giant Paul Bunyan statue, drive-through trees and greasy burger stands – but that might as well be yesterday in this land of towering, mystical, ancient redwood forests. Curving roads and misty trails bring visitors to lush, spectacular natural wonders that are unlike any other place on earth. Prepare to be impressed.

❶ Samoa Peninsula

Even though this trip is about misty primeval forest, the beginning is a study of opposites: the grassy dunes and windswept beaches of the 10-mile long Samoa Peninsula. At the peninsula's south end is **Samoa Dunes Recreation Area** (☑707-825-2300; www.blm. gov; 1400 Bay St; ☺sunrise-sunset), part of a 34-mile-long dune system. It's great for picnicking or fishing, and the wildlife viewing is excellent.

Or, leave the landlubbers behind and take a **Harbor Cruise** (Madaket Cruises; ☑707-445-1910; www.humboldtbaymaritime-museum.com; 1st St; narrated cruises adult/child $22/18; ☺1pm, 2:30pm & 4pm Wed-Sat, 1pm & 2:30pm Sun-Tue mid-May–mid-Oct) aboard the 1910 *Madaket,* America's oldest continuously operating passenger vessel. Leaving from the foot of C St in the nearby city of Eureka, it ferried mill workers before the Samoa Bridge was built in 1971. The $10 sunset cocktail cruise serves drinks from the smallest licensed bar in the state.

✗ p153

The Drive » Head north on Hwy 101 from Eureka (p153), passing myriad views of Humboldt Bay. Fifteen miles north of Arcata, take the first Trinidad exit. Note that the corridor between Eureka and Arcata is a closely watched safety corridor (aka speed trap).

- - - - - - - - - - - - - - - - - -

TRIP HIGHLIGHT

❷ Trinidad

Perched on an ocean bluff, cheery Trinidad somehow manages an off-the-beaten-path feel despite a constant flow of visitors. A free town map available at the tiny **Trinidad Museum** (☑707-677-3883; www.trinidadmuseum. org; 400 Janis Ct; ☺noon-4pm Thu-Sun) will help you navigate the town's cute little shops and several fantastic hiking trails, most notably the **Trinidad Head Trail** with superb coastal views and excellent whale-watching (December to April). If the weather is nice, stroll the exceptionally beautiful cove at **Trinidad State Beach**.

✗ ⊨ p153

The Drive » Head back north of town on Patrick's Point Dr to hug the shore for just over 5 miles.

- - - - - - - - - - - - - - - - - -

❸ Patrick's Point State Park

Coastal bluffs jut out to sea at 640-acre **Patrick's Point State Park** (☑707-677-3570; www.parks.ca.gov; 4150 Patrick's Point Dr; per car $8; ☺sunrise-sunset) where sandy beaches abut rocky headlands. Easy access to dramatic coastal bluffs makes this the best bet for families, but any age

will find a feast for the senses as they climb rock formations, search for breaching whales, carefully navigate tide pools and listen to barking sea lions and singing birds. The park also features **Sumêg**, an authentic reproduction of an indigenous Yurok village, with hand-hewn redwood buildings. The 2-mile **Rim Trail**, a former Yurok trail around the bluffs, circles the point with access to huge rocky outcrops. Don't miss **Wedding Rock**, one of the park's most romantic points, or **Agate Beach**, where lucky visitors spot bits of jade and sea-polished agate.

The Drive » Make your way back out to Hwy 101 through thick stands of redwoods. North

LINK YOUR TRIP

11 Lost Coast & Southern Redwoods

Head south on Hwy 101 from Eureka for more redwood wonders and the untouched Lost Coast for the North Coast's best hiking adventures.

13 Trinity Scenic Byway

Cut inland on Hwy 299 from Arcata and get lost in the wild country of California's northern mountains.

149

another 5 minutes will bring you to the sudden clearing of Big Lagoon, part of Humboldt Lagoons State Park. Continue 6 more miles north to the visitor center, which is closed, but has toilets and an information board.

④ Humboldt Lagoons State Park

Stretching out for miles along the coast, Humboldt Lagoons State Park has long, sandy beaches and a string of coastal lagoons. **Big Lagoon** and prettier **Stone Lagoon** are both excellent for kayaking and bird-watching. Sunsets are spectacular, with no structures in sight. At the Stone Lagoon Visitor Center, on Hwy 101, there are restrooms plus a bulletin board displaying information. Just south of Stone Lagoon, tiny **Dry Lagoon** (a freshwater marsh) has a fantastic day hike. Park at Dry Lagoon's picnic area and hike north on the unmarked trail to Stone Lagoon; the trail skirts the southwestern shore and ends up at the ocean, passing through woods and marshland rich with wildlife. Mostly flat, it's about 2.5 miles one way.

The Drive » Keep driving north on Hwy 101. Now, at last, you'll start to lose all perspective among the world's tallest trees. This is likely the most scenic part of the entire trip; you'll emerge from mist-shrouded shores dotted with rocky islets into curvy two-lane

roads through awing redwood groves.

TRIP HIGHLIGHT

⑤ Redwood National Park

Heading north, **Redwood National Park** (☎707-464-6101, 707-465-7335; www.nps.gov/redw; Hwy 101, Orick) is the first park in the patchwork of state and federally administered lands under the umbrella of Redwood National & State Parks. After picking up a map at the **Thomas H Kuchel Visitor Center** (☎707-465-7765; www.nps.gov/redw; Hwy 101, Orick; ⊙9am-5pm Apr-Oct, to 4pm Nov-Mar), you'll have a suite of choices for hiking. A few miles further north along Hwy 101, a trip inland on Bald Hills Rd will take you to **Lady Bird Johnson Grove**, with its 1.5-mile kid-friendly loop trail, or get you lost in the secluded serenity of **Tall Trees Grove**. To protect the latter grove, a limited number of cars per day are allowed access; get free permits at the visitor center. This can be a half-day trip itself, but you're well rewarded after the challenging approach (a 6-mile rumble on an old logging road behind a locked gate, then a moderately strenuous 4.5-mile round-trip hike).

The Drive » Back on Hwy 101, less than 2 miles north of Bald Hills Rd, turn left onto Davison

STEPHANIEFARRELL / SHUTTERSTOCK ©

Rd, which trundles for 7 miles (mostly unpaved) out to Gold Bluffs Beach.

TRIP HIGHLIGHT

⑥ Prairie Creek Redwoods State Park

The short stroll to **Gold Bluffs Beach** will lead you to the best spot for a picnic. Past the campground, you can take a longer hike beyond the end of the road into **Fern Canyon**; its 60ft-high fern-covered sheer rock walls appear in *The Lost World: Jurassic Park*. This is one of the most photographed spots on the North Coast – damp

Roosevelt Elk in Prairie Creek Redwoods State Park

and lush, all emerald green – and totally worth getting your toes wet to see.

Back on Hwy 101, head 2 miles further north and exit onto the 8-mile **Newton B Drury Scenic Parkway**, which runs parallel to the highway through magnificent untouched ancient redwood forests. Family-friendly nature trails branch off from roadside pullouts, including the wheelchair-accessible Big Tree Wayside, and also start outside the **Prairie Creek Redwoods State Park Visitor Center** (📞707-488-2039; www. parks.ca.gov; Prairie Creek Rd; ⏰9am-5pm Apr-Oct, to 4pm Nov-Mar), including the Revelation Trail for visually impaired visitors.

🛏 p153

The Drive » Follow the winding Newton B Drury Scenic Parkway through beautiful inland forests with views of the east and its layers of ridges and valleys. On returning to Hwy 101, head north to Klamath, with its bear bridge. Del Norte Coast Redwoods State Park is just a few minutes further north.

- - - - - - - - - - - - - - - - - - -

7 Del Norte Coast Redwoods State Park

Marked by steep canyons and dense woods, this park (📞707-464-6101; www. nps.gov/redw; Mill Creek Rd) contains 15 miles of hiking trails and several old logging roads that are a mountain biker's dream. Tall trees cling precipitously to canyon walls that drop to the rocky, timber-strewn coastline. It's almost impossible to get to the water, except via gorgeous but steep **Damnation Creek Trail** or **Footsteps Rock Trail**. The former may be only 4 miles round trip, but the 1100ft elevation change and cliffside redwoods make it the park's best hike. The unmarked trailhead is at a parking

DRIVE-THRU TREES & GONDOLA RIDES

With lots of kitschy mid-20th-century appeal, the following destinations are a throwback to those bygone days of the great American road trip.

Trees of Mystery (📞707-482-2251; www.treesofmystery. net; 15500 Hwy 101; museum free, gondola adult/child $18/9; ⏰9am-4:30pm; 🚻) In Klamath, it's hard to miss the giant statues of Paul Bunyan and Babe the Blue Ox towering over the parking lot at this shameless, if lovable, tourist trap. It has a gondola running through the redwood canopy.

Tour Thru Tree (430 Hwy 169; per car $5; ⏰hours vary; 🚻) In Klamath, squeeze through a tree and check out the emus.

Chandelier Drive-Thru Tree Park (📞707-925-6363; www.drivethrutree.com; 67402 Drive Thru Tree Rd; per car $10; ⏰8:30am-dark; 🚻) Fold in your mirrors and inch forward, then cool off in the uber-kitschy gift shop, in Leggett.

Shrine Drive Thru Tree (📞707-943-1975; 13078 Avenue of the Giants, Myers Flat; per car $6; ⏰sunrise-sunset Apr-Oct; 🚻) Look up to the sky as you roll through, on the Avenue of the Giants in Myers Flat. It's the oldest but least impressive of the three drive-thru trees.

pull-out along Hwy 101 near mile marker 16.

The Drive » Leaving Del Norte Coast Redwoods State Park and continuing on Hwy 101, you'll enter dreary little Crescent City, a fine enough place to gas up or grab a bite, but not worth stopping long. About 4 miles northeast of town, Hwy 199 splits off from Hwy 101; follow it east for 6 miles to Hiouchi.

- - - - - - - - - - - - - - - - - - -

8 Jedediah Smith Redwoods State Park

The final stop on the trip is loaded with worthy superlatives – the northernmost park has the densest population of redwoods and the largest natural undammed free-flowing river in California, the sparkling Smith. **Jedediah Smith Redwoods State Park** (📞707-464-6101; www.nps. gov/redw; Hwy 199, Hiouchi; ⏰sunrise-sunset) is a treat for the senses. The redwood stands here are so dense that few hiking trails penetrate the park, so drive the outstanding 10-mile **Howland Hill Rd**, which cuts through otherwise inaccessible areas, heading back toward Crescent City. It's a rough, unpaved road, and it can close if there are fallen trees or washouts, but you'll feel as if you're visiting from Lilliput as you cruise under the gargantuan trunks. To spend the night, reserve a site at the park's fabulous campground tucked along the banks of the Smith River.

Eating & Sleeping

Samoa Peninsula ❶

✕ Samoa Cookhouse — American $

(☎707-442-1659; www.samoacookhouse.
net; 908 Vance Ave; all-you-can-eat meals per
adult $14-18, child $7-8; ⏰7am-3pm & 5-8pm,
closed Mon & Tue Nov-Apr; 🚼) On the Samoa
Peninsula, the popular Samoa Cookhouse is
the dining hall of an 1893 lumber camp. Hikers,
hippies and lumberjacks get stuffed while
sharing long red-checked oilcloth-covered
tables.

Eureka

✕ Humboldt Bay Provisions — Seafood $$

(☎707-672-3850; www.humboldtbayprovisions.
com; 205 G St; half-dozen oysters $13; ⏰4-9pm
Mon-Fri, from 1pm Sat & Sun) Sit at the long
redwood bar at this rustic-chic establishment
and watch as experts shuck local oysters and
top them off with intriguing sauces such as
habanero and peach juice.

🛏 Carter House Inns — B&B $$$

(☎707-444-8062; www.carterhouse.com;
301 L St; r $184-395; 😀🛜🚼) Constructed in
period style, this aesthetically remodeled hotel
is a Victorian look-alike. Rooms have modern
amenities and top-quality linens; suites have
in-room Jacuzzis and marble fireplaces.

Trinidad ❷

✕ Larrupin Cafe — Californian $$$

(☎707-677-0230; www.thelarrupin.com; 1658
Patrick's Point Dr; mains $32-47; ⏰5-9pm)
Everybody loves Larrupin, where Moroccan
rugs, chocolate-brown walls, gravity-defying
floral arrangements and deep-burgundy
Oriental carpets create a moody atmosphere
perfect for a lovers' tryst. The smoked beef
brisket is truly amazing.

🛏 Trinidad Inn — Inn $

(☎707-677-3349; www.trinidadinn.com; 1170
Patrick's Point Dr; r $90-245; 😀🛜🚼) Sparkling

clean and attractively decorated rooms fill this
upmarket gray-shingled motel under tall trees.

Prairie Creek Redwoods State Park ❻

🛏 Elk Prairie Campground — Campground $

(☎reservations 800-444-7275; www.
reservecalifornia.com; Prairie Creek Rd; tent & RV
sites $35, hike-in sites $5 per person, cabins $80;
🐾) Elk roam this popular campground, where
you can sleep under redwoods or at the prairie's
edge. There are hike-in sites, four six-person
cabins and hot showers, plus a shallow creek to
splash in.

Klamath

🛏 Historic Requa Inn — Historic Hotel $$

(☎707-482-1425; www.requainn.com; 451 Requa
Rd; r $130-250; 😀🛜) A woodsy country lodge
on bluffs overlooking the mouth of the Klamath,
the creaky and bright 1914 Requa Inn is a North
Coast favorite. The dining room serves locally
sourced, organic New American cuisine.

Crescent City

✕ SeaQuake Brewing — American $

(☎707-465-4444; www.seaquakebrewing.com;
400 Front St; mains $10-17; ⏰11:30am-9pm
Tue-Thu, to 10pm Fri & Sat; 🛜) Easily the most
happening place in town thanks to its inventive
pizzas, creative salads and appealing barn-like
atmosphere. Oh, and did we mention the 12 taps
of home-brewed ales?

🛏 Curly Redwood Lodge — Motel $

(☎707-464-2137; www.curlyredwoodlodge.com;
701 Hwy 101 S; r $60-107; 😀🛜) This motel is
a gem of mid-20th-century kitsch. Its paneling
came from a single curly redwood tree that
measured more than 18ft thick in diameter.

Trinity Scenic Byway

13

Cruising this secluded corner of California you'll pass majestic peaks, tranquil lakes and historic mountain towns, experiencing both rugged nature and backcountry hospitality.

TRIP HIGHLIGHTS

0 miles

Mt Shasta
Explore Northern California's volcanic beauty

START
1

Arcata
FINISH

6

Shasta Lake

4

Redding

145 miles

Weaverville
Rugged little mountain town with a fascinating history

95 miles

Whiskeytown National Recreation Area
Camp on the shore of a scenic lake

3 DAYS
245 MILES / 395KM

GREAT FOR...

BEST TIME TO GO
June through October, when the lakes and rivers are full and the air is crisp and clean.

ESSENTIAL PHOTO
Santiago Calatrava's futuristic Sundial Bridge.

BEST FOR FAMILIES
Lake Shasta Caverns admission includes a boat ride, wildlife-watching and a cave tour.

13 Trinity Scenic Byway

The back-to-landers, outdoorsy types and new-age escapists in this remote corner of Northern California proudly count the number of stoplights and fast-food joints in their counties on one hand. An epic cruise along the Trinity Scenic Byway takes visitors from one of California's most distinctive mountains to the Pacific shore, passing ample natural wonders and sophisticated small towns along the way.

TRIP HIGHLIGHT

① Mt Shasta

'When I first caught sight of it I was 50 miles away and afoot, alone and weary. Yet all my blood turned to wine, and I have not been weary since,' wrote naturalist John Muir in 1874 of **Mt Shasta** (📞530-926-4511; www.fs.usda.gov/stnf; Everitt Memorial Hwy; 🅿 ♿). Though not California's highest (at 14,179ft it ranks fifth), the sight of this solitary peak is truly intoxicating. Start this

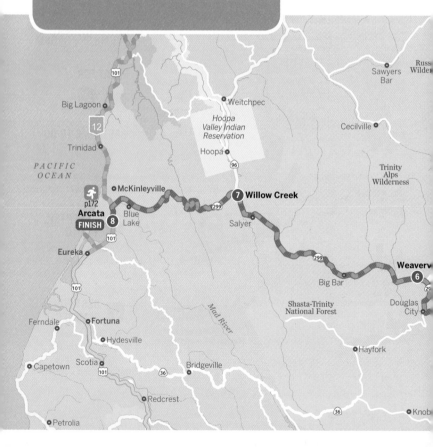

trip near the top: you can drive almost all the way up via the Everitt Memorial Hwy (Hwy A10) to enjoy exquisite views any time of year. By the time you reach **Bunny Flat** (6860ft) you'll be gasping at the sights (and the thin air), but if the road is clear of snow continue the ascent for more amazing views. You'll see Lassen Peak to the south. Look west for a bird's-eye preview of the rest of this trip, toward the Marble Mountains and the green hills along the Trinity Scenic Byway. For

information about hikes, contact the in-town **Mt Shasta Ranger Station** (✆530-926-4511; www. fs.usda.gov/stnf; 204 W Alma St; ☉8am-4:30pm Mon-Fri), which issues permits and good advice.

🛏 p161

The Drive » Follow Everitt Memorial Hwy back down the mountain. It'll take about 30 minutes to get down to Mt Shasta City, a new-agey town that's easy to love. Go south on I-5 for more than 40 miles to Shasta Lake.

❷ Shasta Lake

The largest reservoir in California, Shasta Lake has the state's biggest population of bald eagles, an endless network of hiking trails, and great fishing. On the north side, stop to tour the crystalline caves of the **Lake Shasta Caverns** (✆530-238-2341; www. lakeshastacaverns.com; 20359 Shasta Caverns Rd, Lakehead; 2hr tour adult/child 3-15yr $30/18; ☉tours every 30min 9am-4pm late May-early Sep, hourly 9am-3pm Apr-late May & early-late Sep, 10am, noon & 2pm Oct-Mar; P ♿). Tours include a boat ride that's great for families (bring a sweater – it's chilly!). The **Shasta Dam visitors center** (✆530-247-8555; www.usbr.gov/mp/ncao/

S LINK YOUR TRIP

12 **Northern Redwood Coast**

Head north on Hwy 101 from Arcata to link this epic mountain journey with a visit to the proud redwood stands of the far North Coast.

14 **Volcanic Legacy Byway**

Take a trip around California's untouched northern volcanic wilds by going east of Redding on Hwy 44.

157

shasta-dam.html; 16349 Shasta Dam Blvd; ⌚visitor center 8am-5pm; P 👪) to the south has maps of hiking trails and a view of **Shasta Dam**. The colossal, 15-million-ton dam is second only in size to Hoover Dam in Nevada; its 487ft spillway is nearly three times as high as Niagara Falls. At the visitor center, join a fascinating free guided tour of the structure's rumbling interior.

🛏 p161

The Drive » Retrace your path back to I-5 and head south about 9 miles to Redding.

3 Redding

Redding's sprawl – malls, big-box stores and large housing developments – might be discordant with the north's natural wonders, but it's the launching point for the Trinity Scenic Byway, which starts west of town. It's worth stopping for the **Turtle Bay Exploration Park** (☎530-243-8850; www.turtlebay.org; 844 Sundial Bridge Dr; adult/child $16/12, after 2:30pm $11/7; ⌚9am-5pm Mon-Sat, from 10am Sun late Mar-Oct, 9am-4:30pm Wed-Fri, from 10am Sat & Sun Nov–late Mar; 👪). Situated on 300 acres, the complex has an art and natural-science museum with interactive exhibits for kids, extensive gardens, a butterfly conservatory and a 22,000-gallon, walk-through river aquarium with regional aquatic life. The futuristic **Sundial Bridge** connects the park to the north bank of the Sacramento River and was designed by renowned Spanish architect Santiago Calatrava.

🍴 p161

The Drive » The banner stretch of the trip starts here: the Trinity Scenic Byway (Hwy 299) begins west of Redding and traces a winding path through the mountains to the Pacific Coast. Forests, mountain lakes, crumbling cabins and rushing rivers accompany the drive.

TRIP HIGHLIGHT

4 Whiskeytown National Recreation Area

An old mining town lent the rich name to **Whiskeytown Lake** (☎530-242-3400; www.nps.gov/whis; off Hwy 299, Whiskeytown; 7-day pass per car $10; P 👪), this lovely, multi-use reservoir. Much of the lake's serene 36 miles of forested shoreline was devastated in the 2018 Carr fire but it's slowly opening up as an excellent place to camp, swim, sail, mountain bike and pan for gold. The **visitor center** (☎530-246-1225; www.nps.gov/whis; 14412 Kennedy Memorial Dr, Whiskeytown; ⌚10am-4pm), on the northeast point, provides information and free maps. From here, the hike to roaring

MA'BADREE MASAE / SHUTTERSTOCK ©

Whiskeytown Falls (3.4 miles round trip) follows a former logging road. On the western side, the **Tower House Historic District** contains the El Dorado Mine ruins and the pioneer Camden House, open for summer tours. In winter, it's an atmospheric place to explore.

The Drive » Leaving Whiskeytown Lake, Hwy 299 enters more-remote country – cellphone service gets iffy. About 10 miles west of the lake the road becomes steep with white-knuckled turns and excellent lake vistas. Cut north on Trinity Dam Blvd for Lewiston.

Weaverville Joss House State Historic Park

⑤ Lewiston

Blink and you might miss Lewiston, a collection of buildings beside a rushing stretch of the Trinity River known for fishing. Stop at the **Country Peddler** (☎530-778-3325; 4 Deadwood Rd; ⏱May-Oct, hours vary; 🐾), a drafty old barn filled with antiques. The owners, avid outdoor enthusiasts, know the area like the backs of their hands. **Lewiston Lake** is about 1.5 miles north of town and is a serene alternative to the other area lakes. Early in the evening you may see ospreys and bald

eagles diving for fish. Still, the best natural sights are deeper afield – particularly the **Trinity Alps Wilderness**, west of Hwy 3. Look no further for rugged adventure: it hosts excellent hiking and backcountry camping, with over 600 miles of trails that cross granite peaks and skirt deep alpine lakes.

🛏 p161

The Drive 》 Take Lewiston Lake Rd back south to Hwy 299, then head west about 12 miles to Weaverville, the next village on this trip.

TRIP HIGHLIGHT

⑥ Weaverville

The walls of the **Weaverville Joss House State Historic Park** (☎530-623-5284; www.parks.ca.gov; 630 Main St; tours adult/child $4/2; ⏱tours hourly 10am-5pm Thu-Sun; 🅿) actually talk – they're papered inside with 150-year-old donation ledgers from the once thriving Chinese community, a testament to the rich culture of immigrants who built Northern California's infrastructure. The rich blue-and-gold Taoist shrine contains an

159

DETOUR: DUNSMUIR

Start: ❶ Mt Shasta

Built by Central Pacific Railroad, Dunsmuir (population 1570) was originally named Pusher, for the auxiliary 'pusher' engines that muscled the heavy steam engines up the steep mountain grade. The town's reputation is still inseparable from the trains, making the stop essential for rail buffs. You can also stop here to quench your thirst; it could easily be – as locals claim – 'the best water on earth.' Maybe that water is what makes the beer at **Dunsmuir Brewery Works** (📞530-235-1900; www.dunsmuirbreweryworks.com; 5701 Dunsmuir Ave; mains $13-15; ⏰11am-9pm Sun-Thu, to 10pm Fri & Sat, extended hours Apr-Sep; 📶) so damn good. The crisp ales and malty porter are perfectly balanced. Go south from Mt Shasta on I-5 for almost 8 miles and take exit 730 for central Dunsmuir.

---

ornate 3000-year-old altar, which was brought here from China. Sadly, state budget issues have made the future of this park uncertain, but it still makes a surprising gem within this far-flung mountain community.

🛏️ p161

The Drive » Gas up and get ready for awe-inspiring views of granite mountains, the nationally designated Wild and Scenic Trinity River and sun-dappled forest in every direction. There are no turnoffs; simply continue west on Hwy 299.

---

❼ Willow Creek

Stay sharp as you navigate the road to Willow Creek – this remote little community was the site of some of the most convincing homemade footage ever captured of a Sasquatch. This makes an obligatory stop of the **Willow Creek–China Flat Museum** (📞530-629-2653; www.bigfootcountry.net; 38949 Hwy 299; donation suggested; ⏰10am-4pm Wed-Sun May-Sep, from noon Fri-Sun Oct; 🅿️ 👶) for the fun Big Foot Exhibit that includes casts of very large footprints and some provocative (if blurry) photos. The 25ft-tall redwood sculpture of the hairy beast in the parking lot is hard to miss. Willow Creek is also the beginning of the Bigfoot

Scenic Byway (Hwy 96) – a route that winds north through breathtaking mountain and river country, with the most Bigfoot sightings in the country.

The Drive » About 10 miles west of Willow Creek, you'll pass the Berry Summit Vista Point (Mile 28.4) and then start to drop toward the Pacific. Continue just over 25 twisting miles on Hwy 299 to Hwy 101, turning south to Arcata.

---

❽ Arcata

Congratulations, you've finally arrived in Arcata, an idiosyncratic college town on the sparkling shores of the Pacific and in the middle of California's majestic redwood country. Park at **Arcata Plaza** (www.northcoastgrowersassociation.org; btwn 8th & 9th Sts; ⏰9am-2pm Sat Apr-Nov, from 10am Dec-Mar) and stroll around the historic downtown to find a bite to eat (the restaurants are top-notch) or explore the campus of **Humboldt State University** (HSU; 📞707-826-3551; https://ccat.humboldt.edu; 1 Harpst St), home to a world-class environmental sustainability program.

🍴 🛏️ p161

Eating & Sleeping

Mt Shasta ❶

🛏 Shasta MountInn   B&B $$

(📞530-261-1926; www.shastamountinn.com; 203 Birch St; d $150-175; P ⊖ 📶) Only antique on the outside, this bright Victorian 1904 farmhouse is all relaxed minimalism, bold colors and graceful decor on the inside. Each airy room has a great bed and exquisite views of the luminous mountain. Enjoy the expansive garden, the wraparound deck, the outdoor hot tub and sauna. Not relaxed enough yet? Chill on the perfectly placed porch swings.

Shasta Lake ❷

🛏 US Forest Service Campgrounds   Campground $

(📞info 530-275-1587, reservations 877-444-6777; www.recreation.gov; tent sites free-$46; P 📶) About half of the campgrounds around Shasta Lake are open year-round. The lake's many fingers have a huge range of camping, with lake and mountain views, and some of them are very remote. Free boat-in sites are first-come, first-served – sites without boat launches will be far less busy.

Redding ❸

🍴 Jack's Grill   Steak $$$

(📞530-241-9705; www.jacksgrillredding.com; 1743 California St; mains $21-46; ⊗4-10pm Mon-Sat) This funky little place doesn't look so inviting – the windows are blacked out and it's dark as a crypt inside – but its popularity with locals starts with its stubborn ain't-broke-don't-fix-it ethos and ends with its steak – a big, thick, charbroiled decadence.

Lewiston ❺

🛏 Lewiston Hotel   Historic Hotel $

(📞530-778-3823; www.lewistonhotelca.com; 125 Deadwood Rd; d without bath $85-95;

⊗restaurant 4-8pm Tue-Fri, from noon Sat, 11.30am-7:30pm Sun; P ⊖ 📶) This 1862 rambling, ramshackle hotel has small, rustic rooms with quilts, historica photos and river views – all have tons of character but none have attached bathrooms. Ask (or don't ask) for the room haunted by George. Explore the building to find giant stuffed moose heads, old girly calendars, rusty saws and so much more.

Weaverville ❻

🛏 Weaverville Hotel   Historic Hotel $$

(📞30-623-2222; www.weavervillehotel.com; 481 Main St; d $110-285; P ⊖ ❄ 📶) Play like you're in the Old West at this upscale hotel and historic landmark, refurbished in grand Victorian style. It's luxurious but not stuffy, and the very gracious owners take great care in looking after you. Guests may use the local gym, and a $10 credit at local restaurants is included in the rates. Kids under 12 years are not allowed.

Arcata ❽

🍴 Slice of Humboldt Pie   Californian $

(📞707-630-5100; 828 I St; pies $4.50-7.50; ⊗11am-6pm Tue-Thu, to 8pm Fri & Sat) Pies are the mainstays here, ranging from chicken pot pie to Mexican chocolate pecan pie. Savory empanadas also shine and include everything from vegan chipotle black bean to pulled pork with green chili. Ciders are the welcome accompaniment and cover mostly local varieties. The decor is pure industrial chic with exposed pipes and soft gray paintwork.

🛏 Hotel Arcata   Historic Hotel $

(📞707-826-0217; www.hotelarcata.com; 708 9th St; r $85-200; ⊖ 📶🛁) Anchoring the plaza, this renovated 1915 brick landmark has friendly staff, high ceilings and comfortable, old-world rooms of mixed quality. The rooms in front are an excellent perch for people-watching on the square, but the quietest face the back.

Volcanic Legacy Byway

Even in summer, the view-filled byways of Northern California's inland wilderness are largely empty. This loop skirts Mt Lassen, the southernmost active volcano in the Cascades.

TRIP HIGHLIGHTS

85 miles

Ahjumawi Lava Springs State Park
Paddle these rarely visited waters

Mt Shasta

FINISH 7

McCloud

2

225 miles

Castle Lake
After hiking, take a dip with mountain views

1 **START**

Lassen Volcanic National Park
Wander simmering landscapes of volcanic wonders

0 miles

3 DAYS
225 MILES / 360KM

GREAT FOR...

BEST TIME TO GO

July and August when the snow finally clears from the highest passes.

ESSENTIAL PHOTO

Snowcapped Mt Shasta at sunset.

BEST ADVENTURE

Renting a boat and making the trip to Ahjumawi Lava Springs State Park.

14 Volcanic Legacy Byway

Looping the big, green patches of the map is perfect for hiking, fishing, camping or getting lost. This is a place where few people venture, but those who do come back with stories. Settlements in this neck of the woods are mostly just places to gas up and buy some jerky, but adventurers are drawn here for just that reason. This is the deeply satisfying final frontier of California's wilderness.

TRIP HIGHLIGHT

1 Lassen Volcanic National Park

As you drive through the surrounding fields studded with volcanic boulders, **Lassen Volcanic National Park** (📞530-595-4480; www.nps.gov/lavo; 38050 Hwy 36 E, Mineral; 7-day entry per car mid-Apr–Nov $30, Dec–mid-Apr $10; **P**) glowers in the distance. Lassen Peak rises 2000 dramatic feet over the surrounding landscape to 10,457ft above sea level. Lassen's

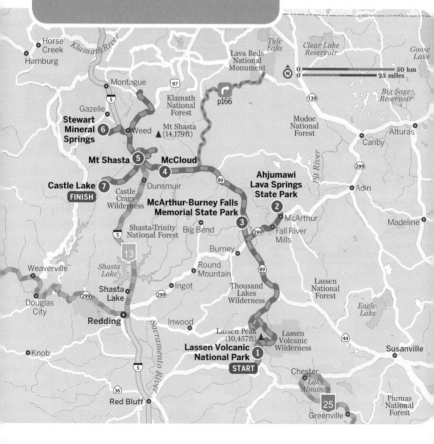

dome has a volume of half a cubic mile, making it one of the world's largest plug-dome volcanoes – its most recent eruption took place in 1915, when it blew a giant billow of smoke, steam and ash many miles high into the atmosphere.

Approaching the park, the road begins to climb, entering corridors of dense forest and emerging at the LEED platinum-certified **Kohm Yah-mah-nee Visitor Facility**. Stop in to pick up maps and the handy park newspaper, which outlines campsites and over 150 miles of hiking trails. Heading north, you can roam through the tawny stone slopes of burbling **Sulphur Works** – you'll know it by the ripe scent in the air and

the gaseous bursts hissing over the roadway. The moderate 1.5-mile hike to **Bumpass Hell** traverses an active geothermal area festooned with otherworldly colored pools and billowing clouds of steam.

🛏 p169

The Drive ⟫ Follow Hwy 89 for 29 miles through the park, looping east of Lassen Peak. Go right on Hwy 299 for Fall River Mills, where you may be able to rent a kayak or canoe. Entering McArthur, turn left onto Main St by the Inter-Mountain fairgrounds, cross a canal and continue on a dirt road to the Rat Farm boat launch.

TRIP HIGHLIGHT

❷ Ahjumawi Lava Springs State Park

Of all the stops along this trip, none is more remote and more rewarding than the **Ahjumawi Lava Springs State Park** (☎530-335-2777; www.parks.ca.gov; ☼sunrise-sunset). A visit here comes with serious bragging rights as the abundant springs, aquamarine bays and islets, and jagged flows of black basalt lava are truly off the beaten path, and can be reached only by boat. The best way to visit is to silently glide across these waters in a canoe or kayak. These can often be rented in nearby towns such as Fall River Mills. After you paddle out, the hikes are glorious: there are

basalt outcroppings, lava tubes, cold springs bubbling and all kinds of volcanic features. For more information about boat rentals and primitive camping, contact McArthur-Burney Falls Memorial State Park.

The Drive ⟫ Backtrack more than 20 miles west of McArthur on Hwy 299, then turn right on Hwy 89 and take it 6 miles north to McArthur-Burney Falls Memorial State Park.

---

❸ McArthur-Burney Falls Memorial State Park

After all the volcanic rock and sulfur fields, there's a soothing stop up the road in **McArthur-Burney Falls Memorial State Park** (☎530-335-2777; www.parks.ca.gov; Hwy 89, Burney; per car $10; 🅿 ♿). Fed by a spring, the splashing 129ft-tall waterfalls flow at the same temperature, 42°F (5.5°C), year-round. Rangers are quick to point out that it might not be California's highest waterfall, but it may be the most beautiful (Teddy Roosevelt called it the 'eighth wonder of the world.') Clear, lava-filtered water surges over the top and also from springs in the waterfall's face. Hiking trails include a portion of the Pacific Crest Trail, which continues north to Castle Crags State Park. The 1.3-mile **Burney**

LINK YOUR TRIP

25 Feather River Scenic Byway

Join this epic mountain journey 40 miles southeast of Lassen National Park in Chester for an inland trip along Hwy 70 and the river.

13 Trinity Scenic Byway

From Mt Shasta, go via the rugged Trinity Alps to the sparkling sea, following Hwy 299 past pristine wilderness.

Falls Trail is the one you shouldn't miss. Upgraded with guardrails, it's an easy loop for families and allows close-up views of water rushing right out of the rock.

🛏 p169

The Drive » Continue northwest on Hwy 89 for about 40 miles to McCloud.

---

④ McCloud

An old logging town, McCloud sits serenely on the southern slopes of Mt Shasta, with the peak looming in the distance. It is a mellow, comfortable place from which to explore the pristine wilderness that surrounds it. Bump along the tiny, partially paved **McCloud River Loop**, which begins off Hwy 89 about 11 miles east of McCloud, to find the lovely **McCloud River Trail**, which passes three waterfalls on the lower reaches of Mt Shasta. The easy 1.8-mile trail passes gorgeous, secluded falls, and you'll discover a lovely habitat for bird-watching in Bigelow Meadow. Other good hiking trails include the **Squaw Valley Creek Trail** (not to be confused with the ski area near Lake Tahoe), an easy 5-mile loop trail south of town, with options for swimming, fishing and picnicking.

🛏 p169

The Drive » Hwy 89 climbs steeply to reach the city of Mt Shasta. Along the way you'll pass Mt Shasta Ski Park, which has ski and snowboard trails that are converted into awesome mountain-biking runs in summer.

SARA HAHN / SHUTTERSTOCK ©

---

⑤ Mt Shasta

Still classified as an active volcano, **Mt Shasta** (📞530-926-4511; www.fs.usda.gov/stnf; Everitt Memorial Hwy; P 🚻) remains a mecca for mystics. Seekers are attracted to the 14,179ft peak's reported cosmic properties, but this reverence for the great mountain is nothing new: for centuries Native Americans have honored it as sacred, considering it to be no less than the Great Spirit's wigwam. Reach its highest drivable point by heading through Mt Shasta City to Everitt

---

DETOUR: LAVA BEDS NATIONAL MONUMENT

Start: ④ McCloud

Lava Beds National Monument (📞530-667-8113; www.nps.gov/labe; 1 Indian Well HQ, Tulelake; 7-day entry per car $25; P 🚻), perched on a shield volcano, is a truly remarkable 72-sq-mile landscape of geological features – lava flows, craters, cinder cones, spatter cones and amazing lava tubes. Nearly 750 caves have been found in the monument and they average a comfortable 55°F (13°C) no matter what the outside temperature. Spy Native American petroglyphs throughout the park too. From McCloud, go southeast several miles on Hwy 89, then take Harris Spring Rd northeast; the one-way drive takes about 2¼ hours.

Bumpass Hell in Lassen Volcanic National Park

Memorial Hwy, which leads to **Bunny Flat**, one of the lower access points on the mountain for excellent hikes. An amble around the town at the base of the mountain will provide you with an opportunity to duck into book shops and excellent eateries. Visitors can also fill their water bottles at the **Sacramento River Headwaters** off Mt Shasta Blvd, about a mile north of downtown. Pure water gurgles up from the ground in a large, cool spring amid a city park with walking trails, picnic spots and a children's playground.

✕ 🛏 p169

The Drive ›› From the north side of Mt Shasta City go 10 miles north on I-5, past Weed to the Edgewood exit, then turn left at Stewart Springs Rd and follow the signs.

- - - - - - - - - - - - - - - - -

❻ Stewart Mineral Springs

Make all the jokes you want about the name of the little town of Weed, but a visit to **Stewart Mineral Springs** (📞530-938-2222; www.stewart mineralsprings.com; 4617 Stewart Springs Rd; sauna/mineral baths $18/30; ⏱10am-6pm Thu-Sun, from noon Mon) will only inspire

a satisfied sigh. At this popular alternative (read clothing optional) hangout on the banks of a clear mountain stream guests soak in a private claw-foot tub or cook in the dry-wood sauna. There's also massage, body wraps, a Native American–style sweat lodge and a riverside sunbathing deck. You'll want to call ahead to be sure there is space in the steam and soaking rooms, especially on busy weekends.

While in the area, tickle your other senses at **Mt Shasta Lavender Farms** (📞530-926-2651;

www.mtshastalavenderfarms.
com; 9706 Harry Cash Rd,
Montague; ⊙9am-4pm mid-
Jun–early Aug; 🅿), about
19 miles northeast of
Weed off Hwy 97. You can
harvest your own sweet
French lavender during
the June and July bloom-
ing season.

✕ 🍽 p169

The Drive » Castle Lake can
be reached by driving south on

I-5 and taking exit 736. Go under
the highway and the service
road to the north on the west
side of the highway to connect
with Castle Lake Rd. The lake is
approximately 7 miles beyond
Lake Siskiyou. En route you'll
pass Ney Springs and the short
hike to Faery Falls.

`TRIP HIGHLIGHT`

❼ Castle Lake

Castle Lake is an easily
accessible yet pristine

mountain pool surround-
ed by granite formations
and pine forest. In the
distance you'll see two of
Northern California's
most recognizable
rocks: Castle Crags and
Mt Shasta. Swimming,
fishing, picnicking and
camping are popular in
summer.

Eating & Sleeping

Lassen Volcanic National Park ❶

🛏 Manzanita Lake Camping Cabins
Cabin $

(📞May-Oct 530-779-0307, Nov-Apr 877-622-0221; www.lassenlodging.com; Hwy 89, near Manzanita Lake; cabins $71-95; ⊙May-Oct; P ☺) These log cabins enjoy a lovely position on one of Lassen's lakes, and come in one- and two-bedroom options and slightly more basic eight-bunk configurations (a bargain for groups). They all have bear boxes, propane heaters and fire rings, but no bedding, electricity or running water. Shared bathrooms and coin-op hot showers are nearby.

McArthur-Burney Falls Memorial State Park ❸

🛏 McArthur-Burney Falls Memorial State Park Campground
Cabin, Campground $

(📞informati 530-335-2777, summer reservations 800-444-7275; www.reserveamerica.com; off Hwy 89, Burney; tent & RV sites $35, cabins $94-116; P 🐾) The park campground has hot showers, propane-heated bunk-bed cabins (bring your own sleeping bags) and campsites. It's open year-round, even when there's snow on the ground.

McCloud ❹

🛏 McCloud River Mercantile Hotel
Inn $$

(📞530-964-2330; www.mccloudmercantile.com; 241 Main St; d $139-275; P ☺ 🐾 🐾) Stroll into McCloud's 2nd-story Mercantile Hotel and try not to fall in love; it's all high ceilings and exposed brick done in modern preservationist class. All rooms have sublime antique furnishings and an open floor plan. Guests drift to sleep on feather beds after soaking in claw-foot tubs. A pet-friendly two-bedroom cabin is also available nearby.

Mt Shasta ❺

🍴 Berryvale Grocery
Market $

(📞530-926-1576; www.berryvale.com; 305 S Mt Shasta Blvd; cafe items from $3; ⊙ store 8am-8pm, cafe to 7pm; 🖉 🚻) This market sells groceries and organic produce to health-conscious eaters. The excellent cafe serves good coffee, fresh juices and an array of tasty – mostly veggie – salads, sandwiches and wraps.

🛏 LOGE Mt Shasta
Lodge $

(📞530-926-5596; www.logecamps.com/mtshasta; 1612 S Mt Shasta Blvd; campsites $35-40, dm/d/q $50/72/92; 🛜 🐾) An excellent choice geared toward active folks who want to mingle after exploring the mountain all day. Dorms are spacious with gear lockers, shared bathrooms and a kitchen, while there's space for après-hike yoga in the modern rooms and all have indoor hammocks. Covered camping sites have access to an outdoor kitchen and hotshower bathrooms.

Stewart Mineral Springs ❻

🍴 Mt Shasta Brewing Company Alehouse & Bistro
Pub Food $

(📞530-938-2394; www.weedales.com; 360 College Ave, Weed; mains $11-20; ⊙noon-9pm or 10pm) Try a tasty Shastafarian Porter or the rich, amber-colored Mountain High IPA. Brats, flatbread pizzas and grilled panini round out the brewpub menu; the kitchen closes an hour before the pub.

🛏 Stewart Mineral Springs
Cabin $

(📞530-938-2222; httpstewartmineralsprings.com; 4617 Stewart Springs Rd, Weed; tent & RV sites $40, tipis $50, d $95-200, cabins $120-140; P ☺) Basic accommodations available at the springs include a rough-cut lodge, rustic cabins and canvas tipis. Book ahead.

Start/Finish Chinatown Gate

Distance 3.3 miles

Duration 4–5 hours

Limber up and look sharp: on this walk, you'll pass hidden architectural gems, navigate the winding alleys of Chinatown and catch shimmering views of the bay. Along the way, enjoy controversial art, savory street snacks and a flock of parrots.

Take this walk on Trips

Chinatown Gate

The elaborate threshold of the **Dragon's Gate**, donated by Taiwan in 1970, graces the entrance to Chinatown. Beyond the gate was once a notorious red-light district – but forward-thinking businessmen reinvented the area in the 1920s, hiring architects to create a signature 'Chinatown Deco' look.

The Walk >> Huff it uphill from Chinatown Gate, past gilded dragon lamps on Grant Ave to Old St Mary's Square. Two blocks beyond earthquake-survivor Old St Mary's Church, take a left on Clay St.

Chinese Historical Society of America Museum

Picture what it was like to be Chinese during the gold rush, the Transcontinental Railroad construction and the Beat heyday. The intimate **Chinese Historical Society of America Museum** (CHSA; ☏415-391-1188; www.chsa.org; 965 Clay St; ☺11am-4pm Wed-Sun; ♿; ☐1, 8, 30, 45, ☐California, Powell-Mason, Powell-Hyde, MT) hosts rotating exhibits in a graceful building built in 1932 as Chinatown's YWCA by California's first licensed woman architect, Julia Morgan.

The Walk >> Backtrack past Stockton St and turn left down Spofford Alley, where you'll overhear epic mah-jongg games in the spot where Sun Yat-sen plotted the 1911 overthrow of China's last dynasty. At Washington St, take a right. Then go left on Ross Alley.

Golden Gate Fortune Cookie Factory

Murals on Ross Alley might look familiar to movie buffs; it's been the backdrop for flicks like *Karate Kid, Part II* and *Indiana Jones and the Temple of Doom*. Stop at No 56 to get your fortune while it's hot, folded into warm cookies at the **Golden Gate Fortune Cookie Factory** (☏415-781-3956; www.goldengatefortunecookies. com; 56 Ross Alley; ☺9am-6pm).

The Walk >> Go right on Jackson St and left on Grant Ave. You'll pass a number of Chinese bakeries with piping hot *char siu bao* (BBQ pork buns). Take a shortcut through Jack Kerouac Alley, where the *On the Road* author's words are embedded in the sidewalk.

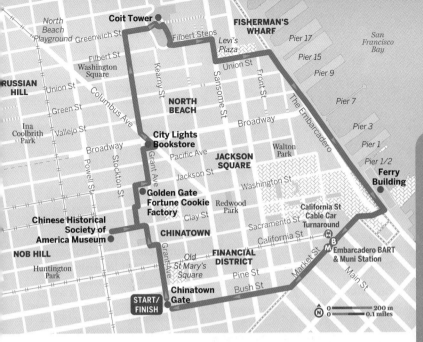

City Lights Bookstore

Ever since manager Shigeyoshi Murao and Beat poet Lawrence Ferlinghetti successfully defended their right to 'willfully and lewdly print' Allen Ginsberg's magnificent *Howl and Other Poems* in 1957, **City Lights Books** (☎415-362-8193; www.citylights.com; 261 Columbus Ave; ☺10am–midnight; ☂; ☐10, 12, 41) has been a free-speech landmark. Perch in the Poet's Chair upstairs overlooking Jack Kerouac Alley. When you get thirsty, join local authors for a pint at Vesuvio next door.

The Walk » Go left on Columbus Ave. Make a slight right on Grant Ave and walk for five blocks, then take a right and head up the Greenwich St steps.

Coit Tower

Adding an exclamation mark to SF's landscape, **Coit Tower** (☎415-249-0995; www.sfrecpark.org; Telegraph Hill Blvd; nonresident elevator fee adult/child $9/6, mural tour full/2nd fl only $8/5; ☺10am–6pm Apr–Oct, to 5pm Nov–Mar; ☐39) is a peculiar 210ft-projectile commissioned by millionaire fire survivor Lillie Coit as a monument to San Francisco firefight-

ers. When it was completed in 1934, the government-funded murals lining the lobby were denounced as communist, but now they're a national monument. To see murals inside Coit Tower's stairwell, take a free guided tour at 11am on Wednesday or Saturday.

The Walk » Take the Filbert Steps downhill past wild parrots and hidden cottages to Levi's Plaza. Head right on the Embarcadero to the Ferry Building.

Ferry Building

The historic **Ferry Building** (☎415-983-8000; www.ferrybuildingmarketplace.com; cnr Market St & the Embarcadero; ☺10am–7pm Mon–Fri, 8am–6pm Sat, 11am–5pm Sun; ☂; ☐2, 6, 9, 14, 21, 31, Ⓜ Embarcadero, Ⓑ Embarcadero) is a transit hub imaginatively transformed into a destination for local food. Bay Area artisan food producers, award-winning restaurants and a thrice-weekly **farmers market** (☎415-291-3276; www.cuesa.org; street food $3-12; ☺10am–2pm Tue & Thu, from 8am Sat; ☂☂) make this a memorable, mouthwatering stop.

The Walk » Walk down Market St. Turn right on Bush St back to Chinatown Gate.

STRETCH YOUR LEGS
ARCATA

Start/Finish Arcata Plaza

Distance 4 miles

Duration 4–6 hours

The North Coast's colorful college town offers a stroll on the most progressive edge of America, an artsy community – with visionary sustainability practices, excellent parks, amazing food and a wealth of historical buildings – that marches proudly to its own beat.

Take this walk on Trips

172

Arcata Plaza

The buzzing hub of Arcata is a place where young students toss Frisbees, farmers hawk crops and bearded professors saunter by dreadlocked vagabonds. Lined with boutiques and bars, the plaza bears witness to one festival after another. The 1915 **Hotel Arcata** (☎707-826-0217; www.hotelarcata.com; 708 9th St; r $85-200; ⊖🛜🐾), on the National Register of Historic Places, is on the northeast corner.

The Walk » Walk up G St past a number of excellent, cheap restaurants and take the pedestrian bridge over the highway at 17th St, which brings you to campus.

Humboldt State University

Humboldt State University (HSU; ☎707-826-3551; https://ccat.humboldt.edu; 1 Harpst St) is the North Coast's secluded intellectual center. Its **Campus Center for Appropriate Technology** (CCAT) is a world leader in developing sustainable technologies; on the first Friday of the month at noon and the third Friday of the month at 2pm, you can take a tour of CCAT's house, a converted residence that uses less than 5% of the energy consumed by the average American home.

The Walk » Walk south through campus to reach 14th St. Take a left to enter Redwood Park.

Arcata Community Forest

Few city parks hold a candle to **Redwood Park**, adjacent to 790 acres of community forest crossed by trails for biking, hiking and horseback riding. Without the big stands of trees common to the region, it doesn't have an untamed feel, but trail No 1 is a 0.6-mile loop that's an enjoyable hike for kids. Despite a few scruffy, semipermanent residents, whose tents flout the 'no camping' ordinance, the place feels magical, particularly during a performance on the park's stage.

The Walk » Retrace your path on 14th St and continue, crossing over the highway. When you reach G St, take a left. Eventually, this will

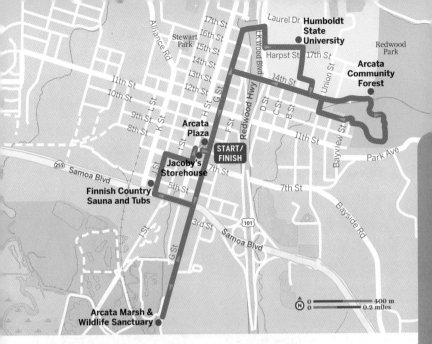

cross Samoa Blvd and take you onward to an interpretive center and trailhead for Arcata Marsh.

Arcata Marsh & Wildlife Sanctuary

On the shores of Humboldt Bay, the **Arcata Marsh & Wildlife Sanctuary** (www.cityofarcata.org; 569 South G St) has 5 miles of walking trails and outstanding bird-watching. During sunset it can be arrestingly beautiful – particularly when you consider that it was once the site of lumber mills, and that the water originates at Arcata's water treatment system. The Redwood Region Audubon Society and the Friends of Arcata Marsh (at the Arcata Marsh Interpretive Center) offer guided walks on Saturdays.

The Walk » Trails through the marshes will bring you near a colorful array of migratory and shore birds. Walk north from the marsh, take a left on Samoa Blvd and then a right on J St.

Finnish Country Sauna & Tubs

The private, open-air redwood tubs at the **Finnish Country Sauna and Tubs** (☏707-822-2228; www.cafemokkaarcata.com; 495 J St; per 30min adult/child $10.25/2; ⏰11am-11pm Sun-Thu, to midnight Fri & Sat) make an ideal place to rest your legs. The hot tubs and sauna are situated around a frog pond, and birds flutter in the redwood branches above. The attached coffeehouse has a mellow, old-world vibe.

The Walk » Continue north on J St and take a right at 7th St, then a left on H St.

Jacoby's Storehouse

The final stop returns to another corner of Arcata Plaza and another nationally registered historical place, **Jacoby's Storehouse** (☏707-826-2426; Arcata Plaza; ⏰hours vary). The creaking halls of this 1857 mercantile building lead to standout restaurants, some tasteful history displays and several closet-sized boutiques.

Central California Trips

The fairy-tale stretch of coast between San Francisco and LA is a road tripper's dream. Packed with beautiful beaches, historic lighthouses and tall redwood forests that hide magical waterfalls and hot springs, especially in bohemian Big Sur, it's a place for adventure as well as contemplation.

Explore central California's agricultural heartland while driving inland highways. At vineyards and farms you can taste the goodness of the land, from juicy strawberries to prickly artichokes to wine, including around Santa Barbara and Santa Cruz.

Further east rises the Sierra Nevada, uplifted along faultlines and weathered by glaciers, wind and rain. Soothe your soul with natural wonders, from Yosemite Valley to Lake Tahoe. Then drop into the foothills for gold-rush history and summertime swimming holes.

Alabama Hills with Sierra Nevada in the background
BON9 / SHUTTERSTOCK ©

Central California Trips

☑ DON'T MISS

Pfeiffer Beach

Catch sunset shining through a sea arch in the Pacific and dig into the purple-tinged sand. **15**

Vikingsholm Castle

Tour this Scandinavian-style mansion at Emerald Bay, Lake Tahoe's most captivating shoreline, which you can also hike along. **20**

Kings Canyon Scenic Byway

Wind down into one of the USA's deepest canyons, carved by glaciers and the mighty Kings River. **21**

Alabama Hills

Explore the terrain where Hollywood Western movies and TV shows have been filmed outside Lone Pine, just below Mt Whitney. **22**

South Yuba River State Park

Swim, hike and photograph the USA's longest covered wooden bridge, near the 19th-century mining town of Nevada City. **23**

Big Sur

Nestled up against mossy redwood forests, the rocky Big Sur coast is a secretive place. Get to know it like locals do, visiting wild beaches, waterfalls and hot springs.

15

TRIP HIGHLIGHTS

10 miles

Andrew Molera State Park
Condors glide above ocean beaches

START
Bixby Bridge

3 4
5
7

14 miles

Pfeiffer Big Sur State Park
Trails to tall redwood trees

18 miles

Pfeiffer Beach
Purplish sand in a photographer's dream seascape

• Lucia

• Gorda

FINISH

Julia Pfeiffer Burns State Park
Peer at McWay Falls

30 miles

2–3 DAYS
60 MILES / 95KM

GREAT FOR...

BEST TIME TO GO

April to May for waterfalls and wildflowers; September to October for sunny, cloudless days.

 ESSENTIAL PHOTO

McWay Falls dropping into the Pacific.

✓ **BEST FOR FAMILIES**

Pfeiffer Big Sur State Park for camping, cabins and easy hikes.

15 | Big Sur

Much ink has been spilled extolling the raw beauty of this craggy land shoehorned between the Santa Lucia Mountains and the Pacific. Yet nothing quite prepares you for that first glimpse through the windshield of Big Sur's wild, unspoiled coastline. There are no traffic lights, banks or strip malls, and when the sun goes down, the moon and the stars are the only streetlights – if coastal fog hasn't extinguished them.

❶ Bixby Bridge

Big Sur is more a state of mind than a place you can pinpoint on a map, but the photogenic Bixby Bridge lets you know you've finally arrived. Arching above Rainbow Canyon, this landmark is one of the world's highest single-span bridges, completed in 1932 by prisoners eager to lop time off their sentences. Off-road parking is limited and can create a traffic hazard, so consider stopping at other safer pull-offs taking in equally stellar

coastal scenery further south.

The Drive › From Bixby Bridge, it's about 6 miles south along Hwy 1, rolling beside pastureland, to Point Sur State Historic Park. Watch out for cyclists and use signposted roadside pull-offs to let fast-moving traffic pass by.

----

② Point Sur State Historic Park

Rising out of the sea, **Point Sur State Historic Park** (☑831-625-4419; www.pointsur.org; off Hwy 1; adult/child 6-17yr from $15/5; ☺tours 10am & 2pm Wed & Sat, 10am Sun Apr-Sep, 1pm Wed, 10am Sat & Sun Oct-Mar) looks like an island, but it's connected to the mainland by a sandbar. On the volcanic rock sits California's only

LINK YOUR TRIP

2 Pacific Coast Highways

Big Sur is just one famous stretch of Hwy 1 along the California coast, which you can drive along from Mexico to Oregon.

17 Around Monterey & Carmel

From Bixby Bridge, drive almost 20 miles north on Hwy 1 to Monterey for maritime-history lessons and one of the world's best aquariums.

turn-of-the-20th-century light station that's still open to the public. Ocean views combine with engrossing tales of the facility's importance in tracking Soviet submarines during the Cold War. Call ahead to confirm schedules; arrive early, because space is limited (no reservations).

The Drive › Lighthouse tours meet at the locked farm gate a quarter-mile north of Point Sur Naval Facility. Afterwards, drive south on Hwy 1 another 2 miles along the coast to Andrew Molera State Park.

TRIP HIGHLIGHT

③ Andrew Molera State Park

Named after the farmer who first planted artichokes in California, **Andrew Molera State Park** (☑831-667-2315; www.parks.ca.gov; Hwy 1; day use per car $10, cash only; ☺30min before sunrise-30min after sunset; ℗ 🚻) is a trail-laced collage of grassy meadows, ocean bluffs and sandy beaches, all offering excellent wildlife-watching. Hike for about a mile to where the Big Sur River meets the driftwood-strewn beach, whipped by surf and strong winds. At the parking lot, walk south to the **Big Sur Discovery Center** (☑831-620-0702; www.ventanaws.org/discovery_center; Andrew Molera State Park; ☺10am-4pm Sat & Sun late May-early Sep; ℗ 🚻) to learn all about

endangered California condors.

The Drive › Speeds rarely top 35mph along Hwy 1, which narrows and becomes curvier further south. A few miles beyond the state park, watch for pedestrians in 'the village,' Big Sur's hub for shops, services, motels and cafes. About 5 miles south of Andrew Molera State Park, the entrance to Pfeiffer Big Sur State Park is on the inland side of the highway.

TRIP HIGHLIGHT

④ Pfeiffer Big Sur State Park

Big Sur's biggest draw is **Pfeiffer Big Sur State Park** (☑831-667-2315; www.parks.ca.gov; Hwy 1; per car $10; ☺30min before sunrise-30min after sunset; ℗ 🚻). Named after Big Sur's first European settlers, who arrived in 1869, it's the largest state park along this coast. Hiking trails loop through redwood groves and run uphill to 60ft-high **Pfeiffer Falls**, a delicate forested cascade that usually flows between December and May. Near the park entrance, inside a rustic lodge built in the 1930s by the Civilian Conservation Corps (CCC), is a general store selling drinks, snacks, camping supplies and road-trip souvenirs.

📖 p185

The Drive › Just 2 miles south of Pfeiffer Big Sur State Park, about half a mile past ranger-staffed Big Sur Station, make a sharp right turn off Hwy 1 onto Sycamore Canyon Rd, marked

only by a small yellow sign saying 'Narrow Road.' Partly unpaved, this road (RVs and trailers prohibited) corkscrews down for over 2 miles to Pfeiffer Beach.

TRIP HIGHLIGHT

⑤ Pfeiffer Beach

Pfeiffer Beach (☏805-434-1996; www.campone.com; Sycamore Canyon Rd; day use per car $12, cash and credit cards; ☻9am-8pm; [P][♿][🐾]) is definitely worth the trouble it takes to reach it. This crescent-shaped strand is known for its huge double rock formation, through which waves crash powerfully. It's often windy, and the surf is too dangerous for swimming. Dig into the wet sand to find sand that's purple because manganese garnet washes down from hillsides above.

The Drive » Backtrack up Sycamore Canyon Rd for more than 2 miles, then turn right

onto Hwy 1 southbound. After two more twisting, slow-moving miles, look for Nepenthe restaurant on your right. The Henry Miller Memorial Library is another 0.4 miles south, at a hairpin turn on your left.

⑥ Henry Miller Memorial Library

'It was here at Big Sur that I first learned to say Amen!' wrote Henry Miller in *Big Sur and the Oranges of Hieronymus Bosch*. A surrealist novelist, Miller was a local from 1944 to 1962. A beatnik memorial, alt-cultural venue and bookshop, the **Henry Miller Memorial Library** (☏831-667-2574; www.henrymiller.org; 48603 Hwy 1; donations accepted; ☻11am-5pm Wed-Sun) was never actually the writer's home. The house belonged to a friend of his, painter Emil White. Inside are copies of all of Miller's published books, many of his paintings and a collection of Big Sur and Beat Generation material. Stop by to browse and hang out on the front deck with coffee, or join the bohemian carnival of live music, open-mic nights and independent-film screenings.

✕ ⌖ p185

The Drive » You'll leave most of the traffic behind as Hwy 1 continues southbound, curving slowly along the vertiginous cliffs, occasionally opening up for ocean panoramas. It's fewer than 8 miles to Julia Pfeiffer Burns State Park; the entrance is on the inland side of Hwy 1.

DETOUR: ESALEN HOT SPRINGS

Start: ⑦ Julia Pfeiffer Burns State Park

Ocean beaches and waterfalls aren't the only places to get wet in Big Sur. At the private Esalen Institute, clothing-optional **baths** (☏831-667-3047; www.esalen.org; 55000 Hwy 1; per person $30; ☻by reservation only) fed by a natural hot spring sit on a ledge high above the ocean. Dollars to donuts you'll never take another dip that compares scenery-wise, especially on stormy winter nights. Only two small outdoor pools perch directly over the waves, so once you've stripped and taken a quick shower, head outside immediately. Advance reservations are required. The signposted entrance is on Hwy 1, about 3 miles south of Julia Pfeiffer Burns State Park.

Point Sur light station in Point Sur State Historic Park

7 Julia Pfeiffer Burns State Park

If you've got an appetite for chasing waterfalls, swing into **Julia Pfeiffer Burns State Park** (☎831-667-2315; www.parks.ca.gov; Hwy 1; day use per car $10, cash only; ☉30min before sunrise-30min after sunset; P 🚻). From the parking lot, the short Overlook Trail rushes downhill towards the sea, passing through a tunnel underneath Hwy 1. Everyone is in a hurry to see **McWay Falls**, which tumbles year-round over granite cliffs and free falls into the ocean or onto the beach, depending on the tide. This is the classic Big Sur postcard shot, with tree-topped rocks jutting above a golden beach next to swirling blue pools and crashing white surf. During winter, watch for migrating whales offshore.

The Drive » The tortuously winding stretch of Hwy 1 southbound is sparsely populated, rugged and remote, running through national forest. Make sure you've got enough fuel in the tank to at least reach the expensive gas station at Gorda, over 20 miles south of Julia Pfeiffer Burns State Park.

8 Los Padres National Forest

If you have any slivers of sunlight left, keep trucking down Hwy 1 approximately 8 miles past Gorda to **Salmon Creek Falls** (https://visitsansimeonca.com/what-to-do/salmon-creek-falls; Hwy 1; P 🚻 🐾), which usually runs from December through May. Take a short hike to splash around in the pools at the base of this double-drop waterfall, tucked uphill in a forested canyon. In a hairpin turn of Hwy 1, the roadside turnoff is marked only by a small brown trailhead sign.

🛏 p185

Eating & Sleeping

Big Sur Village

✗ Big Sur Deli & General Store
Sandwiches $

(☎831-667-2225; www.bigsurdeli.com; 47520 Hwy 1, Big Sur Village; sandwiches $5-11; ⊙7am-8pm; P 🛜 🖟) Put together a picnic of freshly made sandwiches from this family-owned deli and pair them with drinks and chips from the attached store, which also carries other essentials from beer to batteries. Easily the best-value food along this part of Hwy 1.

✗ Big Sur Roadhouse
Californian $

(☎831-667-2370; www.glenoaksbigsur.com/big-sur-roadhouse; 47080 Hwy 1; snacks & mains $8-16; ⊙8am-2:30pm; 🛜 🖟) This modern roadhouse glows with color-splashed artwork and an outdoor fire pit. At riverside tables, tuck into upscale California-inspired bar food such as spicy wings, pork sliders and gourmet burgers, with craft beer on tap. It's also a top spot for coffee and cake.

✗ Fernwood Tavern
Pub Food $$

(☎831-667-2422; www.fernwoodbigsur.com; 47200 Hwy 1; mains $12-20; ⊙11am-11pm Sun-Thu, to 1am Fri & Sat; P 🛜 🖟 🍽) Hearty burgers, burritos and build-your-own pizzas combine with regular weekend live music at this laid-back and welcoming tavern. Adjourn to the rear deck to cozy up to the fire pits or take on your traveling companions at the table-tennis table. Check the website to see what's scheduled – usually on Friday and Saturday nights.

✗ Big Sur River Inn
American $$$

(☎831-667-2700; www.bigsurriverinn.com; 46840 Hwy 1; mains breakfast & lunch $12-28, dinner $21-32; ⊙8am-9pm; P 🛜 🖟) Woodsy restaurant with a deck, overlooking a creek teeming with throaty frogs. The food is standard American – burgers, steak, sandwiches, roast chicken and salads – and there are a few vegetarian dishes. Breakfast features breakout options such as the utterly irresistible carrot-cake French toast with maple-caramel sauce. Great apple pie, too. Rooms (starting at $150), a general store and gas station are also available.

✗ Big Sur Bakery & Restaurant
Californian $$$

(☎831-667-0520; www.bigsurbakery.com; 47540 Hwy 1; bakery items $5-12, mains $22-38; ⊙bakery from 8am daily, restaurant 9:30am-2pm Mon-Fri, 10am-2:30pm Sat & Sun, 5:30pm-late Wed-Sat) Behind the Shell station, this warmly lit, funky house has seasonally changing menus, on which wood-fired pizzas share space with rustic dishes like grilled swordfish or wood-roasted chicken. Fronted by a pretty patio, the bakery makes addictive cinnamon buns and stuffed sandwiches. Expect occasional longish waits. Dinner reservations are essential.

🏕 Big Sur Campground & Cabins
Cabin, Campground $$

(☎831-667-2322; www.bigsurcamp.com; 47000 Hwy 1; tent/RV sites from $70/80, cabins $185-440; P ♿) Situated on the Big Sur River and shaded by redwoods, cozy cabins sport full kitchens and fireplaces, while canvas-sided tent cabins share bathroom facilities. The riverside campground, where neighboring sites have little privacy, is popular with RVers. There are hot showers and a coin-operated laundry, a playground and a general store.

🏕 Glen Oaks Big Sur
Boutique Hotel $$$

(☎831-667-2105; www.glenoaksbigsur.com; 47080 Hwy 1; d $310-660; P ♿ 🛜) At this 1950s redwood-and-adobe motor lodge, rooms and cabins are rustic yet exude effortless chic. Dramatically transformed by eco-conscious design, each of these romantic hideaways has a gas fireplace and unique design features. For more space, book into the woodsy cottages in a redwood grove that come with kitchenettes and shared fire pits.

Pfeiffer Big Sur State Park ④

🏕 Pfeiffer Big Sur State Park Campground
Campground $

(☎reservations 800-444-7275; www.reservecalifornia.com; 47225 Hwy 1; tent & RV sites $35-50; P 🍽) These 169 campsites (without hookups) nestle in a redwood-shaded valley and are good for novice campers and families with young kids. Facilities include toilets, drinking water, fire pits and coin-operated hot showers.

🛏 Big Sur Lodge   Lodge $$$

(☎831-667-3100; www.bigsurlodge.com; 47225 Hwy 1; d $299-383; 🅿 ❤ 🛜 🏊) What you're paying for here is the peaceful location inside Pfeiffer Big Sur State Park (p181). Duplexes each have a deck or balcony looking out into the redwood forest, while family-size rooms may have a kitchenette or wood-burning fireplace. Note that the outdoor swimming pool is closed in winter. There are excellent walking trails close by and an on-site restaurant (mains $16 to $32).

Henry Miller Memorial Library ⑥

✕ Nepenthe   Californian $$$

(☎831-667-2345; www.nepenthebigsur.com; 48510 Hwy 1; mains lunch $18-25, dinner $18-53; ⊙11:30am-10pm; 🛜 ♿ 👶) Nepenthe comes from a Greek word meaning 'isle of no sorrow,' and indeed it's hard to feel blue while sitting by the fire pit on this aerial terrace. Just-OK California cuisine (try the renowned Ambrosia burger) takes a back seat to the views and Nepenthe's history – Orson Welles and Rita Hayworth briefly owned a cabin here in the 1940s. Kids menu available. Downstairs, casual Café Kevah serves coffee, baked goods, light brunches and the same head-spinning ocean views on its deck (closed during winter and bad weather).

✕ Sur House   Californian $$$

(☎831-667-4242; www.ventanabigsur.com/dining/the-sur-house; 48123 Hwy 1; mains $19-40, 4-course dinner menu $95; ⊙7:30-10:30am, 11:30am-4:30pm & 6-9pm; 🅿 🛜) Ventana's clifftop terrace restaurant is Big Sur's gathering spot for foodies. Feast on steamed

mussels with harissa or halibut with Sicilian pistachios, or enjoy the four-course tasting menu. Lunch options include falafel wraps and a great cheeseburger. Herbs and vegetables often come from the on-site organic garden, and the chefs work closely with local farming and fishing communities. Reservations essential.

🛏 Post Ranch Inn   Luxury Hotel $$$

(☎831-667-2200; www.postranchinn.com; 47900 Hwy 1; d from $1095; 🅿 ❤ ❄ @ 🛜 🏊) The last word in luxurious coastal getaways, this adult-only ranch retreat pampers guests with private hot tubs, wood-burning fireplaces, decks and a free minibar. Enjoy dreamy sunset views from the ocean-facing units or fall asleep 9ft off the forest floor in a tree house. The clifftop infinity pool invites chilling, perhaps after a shamanic-healing session or yoga class. Breakfast included. Lunch and dinner reservations are essential for the panoramic sea-view Sierra Mar restaurant; the gourmet breakfast buffet is available to guests only.

Los Padres National Forest ⑧

🛏 Treebones Resort   Cabin $$$

(☎805-927-2390; www.treebonesresort.com; 71895 Hwy 1; tent sites $95, yurts with shared bath from $320; 🅿 ❤ 🛜 🏊) Don't let the word 'resort' mislead you. Yes, it has an ocean-view hot tub, a heated pool and massage treatments. But a unique woven 'human nest' and canvas-sided yurts with polished pine floors, quilt-covered beds, sink vanities and redwood decks offer an experience more akin to glamping, with little privacy. Communal bathrooms and showers are a short stroll away. Basic walk-in campsites (no vehicle access) are also available. Children must be at least six years old. The on-site restaurant, serving salads and burgers, offers panoramic views and is a handy lunchtime pit stop. After the signposted turnoff a mile north of Gorda, the resort is a steep quarter mile uphill.

Along Highway 1 to Santa Cruz

16

South of San Francisco to Santa Cruz, you'll travel one of the most jaw-dropping stretches of scenic highway on California's coast, passing farmstands, lighthouses and beaches.

TRIP HIGHLIGHTS

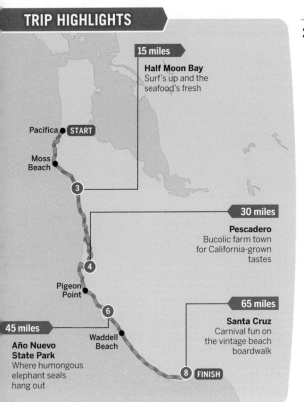

15 miles

Half Moon Bay
Surf's up and the seafood's fresh

Pacifica • **START**

Moss Beach •

3

30 miles

Pescadero
Bucolic farm town for California-grown tastes

4

Pigeon Point •

6

65 miles

Santa Cruz
Carnival fun on the vintage beach boardwalk

45 miles

Waddell Beach •

Año Nuevo State Park
Where humongous elephant seals hang out

8 **FINISH**

**2–3 DAYS
75 MILES / 120KM**

GREAT FOR...

BEST TIME TO GO
July to October gives you the best chance of sunshine.

 ESSENTIAL PHOTO

Elephant seal antics at Año Nuevo's beaches.

 BEST FOR FOODIES

Pescadero's bakery, goat dairy and roadside farms.

16 Along Highway 1 to Santa Cruz

A lazily flowing river of tourism, serpentine Hwy 1 is most celebrated for its scenic charms along the Big Sur coast. But some locals say that the most enchanting stretch of this iconic road starts just south of San Francisco, winding its way slowly down to Santa Cruz. Most beaches are buffeted by wild and unpredictable surf, making them better for tidepooling than swimming or sunbathing. But, oh, the views!

1 Pacifica

In often fog-bound Pacifica, the divided four-lane highway from San Francisco peters out at an intersection overlooking pounding waves, a portent of things to come. Narrowing to two lanes, Hwy 1 jogs inland through thick eucalyptus groves before turning back to the coast. Downhill at **Pacifica State Beach**, stretch your legs or surf, and breath the sea-salted air. Then swerve up through the new tunnels to **Devil's Slide**, where a stretch of the old highway has been converted into a popular hiking and cycling path.

The Drive » As Hwy 1 keeps heading south, you'll be enjoying the sea views. In the next 6 miles, you'll pass Gray Whale Cove and Montara State Beaches. In Moss Beach, turn right onto Vermont Ave, then follow Lake St to its end.

2 Moss Beach

South of Point Montara Lighthouse, **Fitzgerald Marine Reserve** (☎650-728-3584; www.fitzgerald reserve.org; 200 Nevada Ave, Moss Beach; ⊙8am-8pm Apr-Aug, closes earlier Sep-Mar; P 🚻) is a thriving habitat for harbor seals and natural tidepools. Walk out among the pools at low tide to observe (but never pick up) myriad crabs, sea stars, mollusks and rainbow-colored sea

anemones. It's illegal to remove creatures, shells or even rocks. Back on Hwy 1 southbound, take the next right onto Cypress Ave, turning left onto Beach Way to find **Moss Beach Distillery** (650-728-5595; www.mossbeachdistillery.com; 140 Beach Way, Moss Beach; from noon Mon-Sat, from 11am Sun, closing time varies; 👪). Overlooking the cove where bootleggers used to unload Prohibition-era liquor, the heated ocean-view deck is perfectly positioned for sunset cocktails.

The Drive » Continue south on Hwy 1 past the airport. Pillar Point Harbor is on the right after 2 miles. For downtown Half Moon Bay, go four more miles south on Hwy 1, turn left onto Hwy 92, then right onto Main St.

LINK YOUR TRIP

4 Marin County

Starting in San Francisco, follow Hwy 1 in the other direction by crossing north over the Golden Gate Bridge to find redwood groves, beaches and lighthouses.

17 Around Monterey & Carmel

From Santa Cruz, Hwy 1 winds 40 miles south to Monterey, passing more beaches, fishing ports and farms.

TRIP HIGHLIGHT

③ Half Moon Bay

Offshore from the western end of Pillar Point Harbor lies **Mavericks**, a serious surf break that attracts big-wave riders to battle steep wintertime swells more than 50ft high. Not feeling brave? Paddle in calmer waters with **Half Moon Bay Kayak** (☏650-773-6101; www.hmbkayak.com; 2 Johnson Pier; kayak or SUP set rental per day $25/75, bicycle rental $20/50; ☺9am-5pm Jun-Sep, rest of the year Wed-Mon, winter hours 10am-4pm), which rents kayaks and guides tours. Further south down Hwy 1, detour inland to amble down this Victorian-era seaside resort's quaint Main St, its tree-lined blocks overstuffed with bookstores, antiques shops and cafes.

✖ ⌫ p193

The Drive » For the next 11 miles heading south, Hwy 1 gently follows the contours of the coast. Vistas of pounding surf, unspoiled shores and dramatic rock outcrops seem boundless. Turn inland onto Hwy 84 at San Gregorio, then right after less than a mile onto Stage Rd, which narrowly winds through the hills for 7 miles south to Pescadero.

TRIP HIGHLIGHT

④ Pescadero

With its long coastline and mild weather, Pescadero has always been prime real estate. Spanish for 'fishmonger,' Pescadero was formally established in 1856, when it was mostly a farming and dairy settlement with a key location along the stagecoach route. Munch on a fresh-baked, pull-apart loaf of Italian garlic-and-herb bread stuffed with juicy artichokes from **Arcangeli Grocery Co** (Norm's Market; ☏650-879-0147; www.norms-market.com; 287 Stage Rd; sandwiches $8-10; ☺10am-6pm; ⓟ) before traipsing around downtown's art galleries and antiques shops. At the north end of the main drag, turn right onto North St and drive a mile to steal-your-heart **Harley Farms Goat Dairy** (☏650-879-0480; www.harleyfarms.com; 250 North St; ☺11am-4pm Fri-Sun; ⓟ). The farm shop sells artisanal goat cheeses festooned with fruit, nuts and edible flowers. Call ahead for a weekend farm tour or show up anytime to chill with goats.

✖ ⌫ p193

The Drive » Continue driving past the goat farm on North St to Pescadero Rd. Turn right and head west 2 miles to Pescadero State Beach, passing marshlands where bird-watchers spot waterfowl. Turn left back onto Hwy 1, driving south beside pocket beaches and coves for almost 6 miles to the Pigeon Point turnoff.

⑤ Pigeon Point

One of West Coast's tallest lighthouses stands in **Pigeon Point Light Station State Historic Park** (☏650-879-2120; www.parks.ca.gov; 210 Pigeon Point Rd; ☺8am-sunset, visitor center 10am-4pm Thu-Mon; ⓟ). The 1872 landmark had to close access to its Fresnel lens when chunks of its cornice began to rain from the sky, but the beam still flashes brightly and the bluff is a prime though blustery spot to scan for breaching gray whales.

⌫ p193

Seals in Año Nuevo State Park

The Drive >> Back at Hwy 1, turn right and cruise south along the coast, curving inland as the wind howls all around you, for about 5 miles to Año Nuevo State Park's main entrance.

TRIP HIGHLIGHT

6 Año Nuevo State Park

During winter and early spring, thousands of enormous northern elephant seals noisily mate, give birth, learn to swim, battle for dominance or just laze around on the sands at **Año Nuevo State Park** (☏ park office 650-879-2025, recorded info 650-879-0227, tour reservations 800-444-4445; www.parks.ca.gov/anonuevo; 1 New Years Creek Rd; per car $10, 2½hr tour per person incl reservation fee $11; ⊙8:30am-sunset Apr-Nov, 8:30am-3:30pm Dec 15–Mar 31 (guided tours only); **P**). Join park rangers for a guided hike (reservations required) through the sand dunes for up-close views of the huge pinnipeds – a mature male weighs twice as much as your car!

The Drive >> Over the next 6 miles, Hwy 1 southbound traces the coast. As you descend a long hill bordered by a sheer cliff face that recalls Devil's Slide, look for Waddell Beach on your right.

7 Waddell Beach

These thrilling breaks are usually alive with windsurfers, kitesurfers and other daredevils. Wander the chilly sands and get blasted by the winds and you'll quickly understand that without a wet suit, you won't be hankering to swim here. Across Hwy 1 is the end of the popular Skyline-to-the-Sea Trail that descends from Big Basin State Park's redwoods. Just inland, **Rancho del Oso Nature and History Center** (☏831-427-2288; http://ranchodeloso.org; 3600 Hwy 1, Davenport; ⊙ noon-4pm

Sat & Sun; [P] [⚲]) has two kid-friendly nature trails through the marshlands behind the beach.

The Drive >> Hwy 1 begins slowly moving away from the rocky shoreline as the coast's limestone and sandstone cliffs regularly shed chunks into the white-capped waters below. Motor past roadside farmstands and barns and more pocket beaches before rolling into Santa Cruz after 15 miles.

- - - - - - - - - - - - - - - - - - -

TRIP HIGHLIGHT

8 Santa Cruz

SoCal beach culture meets NorCal counter-culture in Santa Cruz. Witness the old-school radical and freak-show weirdness along **Pacific Ave**, downtown's main drag. Tumble downhill to the West Coast's oldest oceanfront amusement park, **Santa Cruz Beach Boardwalk** ([☎]831-423-5590; www.beachboardwalk.com; 400 Beach St; boardwalk free, per ride $4-7, all-day pass $40-50; [☺]daily late May-Aug, most weekends Sep-Apr, weather permitting; [P] [⚲]), where the smell of cotton candy mixes with the salt air. Continue up W Cliff Dr, which winds for a mile to Lighthouse Point. Join the gawkers on the cliffs peering down at the floating kelp

beds, hulking sea lions, playful sea otters and black wet-suit-clad surfers riding **Steamer Lane** surf break. Inside the 1960s-era lighthouse is the memorabilia-packed **Santa Cruz Surfing Museum** ([☎]831-420-6289; 701 W Cliff Dr; entry by donation; [☺]10am-5pm Thu-Tue Jul 4-early Sep, noon-4pm Thu-Mon early Sep-Jul 3; [P] [⚲]). Almost 2 miles further west, W Cliff Dr dead-ends at **Natural Bridges State Beach** ([☎]831-423-4609; www.parks.ca.gov; 2531 W Cliff Dr; day use per car $10; [☺] beach 8am-sunset, visitor center 10am-4pm; [P] [⚲]), named for its sea arches. Starfish, anemones, crabs and more inhabit myriad tidepools carved into the limestone rocks. Find out about sea creatures both great (look at that blue-whale skeleton!) and small at the nearby **Seymour Marine Discovery Center** ([☎]831-459-3800; http://seymourcenter.ucsc.edu; 100 McAllister Way; adult/child 3-16yr $9/7; [☺]10am-5pm Tue-Sun Sep-Jun, daily Jul & Aug; [P] [⚲]).

[✕] [🛏] p193

DETOUR: SANTA CRUZ MOUNTAINS

Start: 8 **Santa Cruz**

Hwy 9 is a sun-dappled backwoods byway into the Santa Cruz Mountains, passing towering redwood forests and a few fog-blessed vineyards (estate-bottled pinot noir is a specialty). Seven miles north of Santa Cruz, **Henry Cowell Redwoods State Park** ([☎]info 831-335-4598, reservations 800-444-7275; www.parks.ca.gov; 101 N Big Trees Park Rd, Felton; entry per car $10, tent & RV sites $35; [☺]sunrise-sunset; [P][⚲]) has hiking trails through old-growth redwood trees. Nearby in Felton, **Roaring Camp Railroads** ([☎]831-335-4484; www.roaringcamp.com; 5401 Graham Hill Rd, Felton; adult/child 2-12yr from $33/24, parking $10; [⚲]) operates narrow-gauge steam trains up into the redwoods. It's another 7 miles up to Boulder Creek, a tiny mountain town with simple cafes and a grocery store for picnic supplies. Take Hwy 236 northwest for 10 more twisty miles to **Big Basin Redwoods State Park** ([☎]831-338-8860; www.parks.ca.gov; 21600 Big Basin Way, Boulder Creek; entry per car $10, tent & RV sites $35; [☺]sunrise-sunset; [P][⚲]), where misty nature trails loop past skyscraping redwoods.

Eating & Sleeping

Half Moon Bay ❸

✗ Half Moon Bay Brewing Company   Pub Food $$

(☏650-728-2739; www.hmbbrewingco.com; 390 Capistrano Rd; mains $15-27; ⊙11am-9pm Mon-Fri, 10am-10pm Sat, 10am-8pm Sun; 🛜👶) Chomp on seafood and burgers while you swill pints from a respectable menu of local brews and gaze out at the bay from a sheltered, heated outdoor patio. Live music every weekend.

🛏 Beach House at Half Moon Bay   Hotel $$$

(☏650-712-0220, 800-315-9366; www.beach-house.com/half-moon-bay; 4100 Cabrillo Hwy; r from $235; P👶🛜🏊) Overlooking the bay from the bluffs near Pillar Point Harbor, all these loft-style suites have down comforters and wood-burning fireplaces to keep you toasty in the fog, but not all have ocean views. The outdoor heated pool and hot tub will soothe your aching muscles after a day of paddling, surfing or hiking.

Pescadero ❹

✗ Duarte's Tavern   American $$

(☏650-879-0464; www.duartestavern.com; 202 Stage Rd; mains $9-42; ⊙7am-8pm Wed-Mon) You'll rub shoulders with fancy-pants foodies, spandex-swathed cyclists and dusty cowboys at this casual, surprisingly unpretentious fourth-generation family restaurant. Duarte's is this town's culinary magnet, though some critics say it's resting on its laurels. Feast on crab cioppino and a half-and-half split of cream of artichoke and green-chili soups, then bring it home with a wedge of olallieberry pie.

🛏 Costanoa   Lodge $$

(☏650-879-1100; www.costanoa.com; 2001 Rossi Rd; tent bungalows/cabin from $145/175, lodge r from $175; P👶🛜) Although this coastal resort, about 10 miles south of Pescadero, includes a **campground** (☏650-879-7302; http://koa.com/campgrounds/santa-cruz-north; 2001 Rossi Rd; tent/RV sites with hookups from $42/82; P🛜👶), nobody can pull a straight face and declare they're actually roughing it here. Down bedding swaddles guests in canvas-sided tent bungalows with shared bathrooms, and in hard-sided Douglas-fir cabins with private ones.

Pigeon Point ❺

🛏 HI Pigeon Point Lighthouse   Hostel $

(☏650-879-0633; www.norcalhostels.org/pigeon; 210 Pigeon Point Rd; dm $38, r with shared bath $96-134, r with private bath $228; ⊙reception 7:30am-10:30pm; P👶@🛜) Not your workaday hostel, this highly coveted coastside lodging is all about its absolutely stunning location. Book ahead and check in early to snag a spot in the outdoor hot tub ($8 per person per 30 minutes) and contemplate roaring waves as the lighthouse beacon races through a starburst sky.

Santa Cruz ❽

✗ Bad Animal   Bistro $$

(☏831-900-5031; www.badanimalbooks.com; 101 Cedar St; shared plates & mains $12-23; ⊙5-10pm Wed-Sat, 11am-2pm & 5-9pm Sun; 🍴) A thoroughly modern menu – including contemporary interpretations of French flavors and natural and organic wines – complements this brilliant bookshop showcasing Santa Cruz' bohemian and counter-culture roots. Try the mussel cassoulet or yuzu-tinged steak tartare for dinner, or enjoy a leisurely Sunday brunch with the duck hash.

🛏 Pacific Blue Inn   B&B $$$

(☏831-600-8880; www.pacificblueinn.com; 636 Pacific Ave; r $229-285; P👶🛜👶) This downtown courtyard B&B is an eco-conscious gem, with water-saving fixtures and renewable and recycled building materials. Refreshingly elemental rooms have pillowtop beds, electric fireplaces and flat-screen TVs with DVD players.

Around Monterey & Carmel

Briny sea air and drifting fog define Monterey, a fishing village holding relics of California's Spanish and Mexican past. As you explore, witness the scenery lauded by artists and writers.

17

TRIP HIGHLIGHTS

9 miles

17-Mile Drive
Ocean-view toll road to ritzy Pebble Beach

FINISH ● Moss Landing

Pacific Grove · Cannery Row

1
START

3

4

5

0 miles

Monterey
Maritime city evokes Spanish and Mexican colonial history

Carmel Valley

Point Lobos State Natural Reserve
Oceanfront trails for wildlife watchers

25 miles

Carmel-by-the-Sea
Erstwhile bohemian artists' village with a gorgeous mission

17 miles

2–3 DAYS
70 MILES / 115KM

GREAT FOR...

BEST TIME TO GO

August to October for sunniest skies; December to April for whale-watching.

ESSENTIAL PHOTO

Pebble Beach's trademarked lone cypress tree.

BEST FOR FAMILIES

Spend the day at the Monterey Bay Aquarium.

17

Around Monterey & Carmel

Tourist-choked Cannery Row isn't actually the star attraction on the Monterey Peninsula. Much more memorable are ocean panoramas caught from roadside pull-offs on the edge of the bay, from the hiking trails of Point Lobos or from the open-air decks of a winter whale-watching boat. Historical roots show all along this drive, from well-preserved Spanish Colonial adobe buildings in downtown Monterey to Carmel's jewel-box Catholic mission.

PACIFIC OCEAN

Paci
Grov
2

Cannery Row

Monterey

17-Mile Drive **3**
Pebble Beach

S

Carmel-by-the-Sea
4

1

5
Point Lobos State Natural Reserve

9 miles to

15

TRIP HIGHLIGHT

① Monterey

Working-class Monterey is all about the sea. Start exploring by walking around **Old Monterey**, downtown's historic quarter (p284), which preserves California's Mexican and Spanish colonial roots. It's just inland from the salt-sprayed **Municipal Wharf II**, overlooking Monterey Bay National Marine Sanctuary, which protects kelp forests, seals, sea lions, dolphins and whales.

Less than 2 miles northwest of downtown via Lighthouse Ave,

Cannery Row was the hectic, smelly epicenter of the sardine-canning industry, Monterey's lifeblood till the 1950s, as immortalized by novelist John Steinbeck. Today the eco-conscious **Monterey Bay Aquarium** (🛈info 831-648-4800, tickets 866-963-9645; www.monterey-bayaquarium.org; 886 Cannery Row; adult/child 3-12yr/13-17yr $50/30/40, tours $15; ⏰9:30am-6pm May-Aug, 10am-5pm Sep-Apr; 👶) puts aquatic creatures on educational display

Walking south along Cannery Row, peek into the one-room shacks of former cannery workers. Further south along Cannery Row, stop at

Steinbeck Plaza (Cannery Row) to soak up bay views.

🍴 🛏 p201

The Drive » From Cannery Row, Ocean View Blvd slowly traces the bayfront coastline for 2.5 miles west to Point Pinos, curving left onto Sunset Dr. Watch out for cyclists along this route.

196

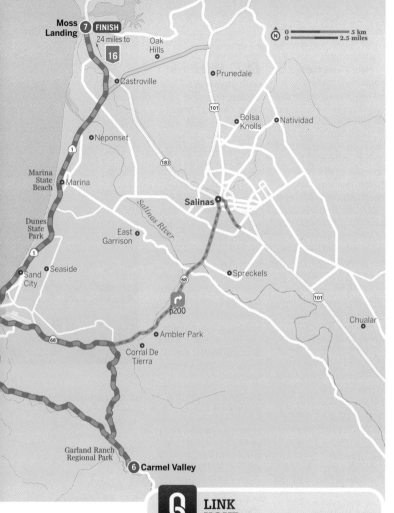

2 Pacific Grove

Pacific Grove was where John Steinbeck's family once had a summer cottage. Ocean View Blvd runs from Lovers Point west to Point Pinos, where it becomes Sunset Dr heading south to Asilomar State Beach. Tempting turnoffs

LINK YOUR TRIP

 Big Sur
Big Sur's vertiginous coastal cliffs, hippie-beatnik retreats and redwood forests alongside Hwy 1 start 15 miles south of Carmel-by-the-Sea.

 Along Highway 1 to Santa Cruz
Santa Cruz's 'Surf City' beaches are about 25 miles north of Moss Landing via Hwy 1, which curves around Monterey Bay.

197

showcase pounding surf, rocky outcrops and teeming tide pools.

Point Pinos Lighthouse (☎831-648-3176; www.pointpinoslighthouse.org; 80 Asilomar Ave; suggested donation adult/child 7-17yr $5/2; ⏰1-4pm Thu-Mon; P) has been warning ships of this peninsula's hazards since 1855. Nearby, golfers crowd the windy **Pacific Grove Golf Links** (☎831-648-5775; www.playpacificgrove.com; 77 Asilomar Blvd; green fees $49-69), a penny-pincher's version of Pebble Beach.

Follow Lighthouse Ave east, turning right onto Ridge Rd after half a mile. Park to stroll around the **Monarch Grove Sanctuary** (www.cityofpacificgrove.org/visiting; 250 Ridge Rd; ⏰dawn-dusk; 👪) between October and March, when thousands of migratory monarch butterflies cluster in tall eucalyptus trees.

🍴 p201

The Drive » Drive back north on Ridge Rd to Lighthouse Ave, which heads east toward leafy downtown Pacific Grove, with its shops, cafes and a natural-history museum for kids. To bypass downtown PG, take the next right after Ridge Rd onto 17-Mile Dr. Drive another mile southwest, crossing Sunset Dr/Hwy 68, to the Pacific Grove toll gate.

TRIP HIGHLIGHT

❸ 17-Mile Drive

Once promoted as 'Mother Nature's Drive-Thru,' **17-Mile Drive** (www.pebblebeach.com; per car/bicycle $10.50/free) is a spectacularly scenic private toll road (motorcyclists prohibited) that loops around the Monterey Peninsula, connecting Pacific Grove with Pebble Beach and Carmel-by-the-Sea. Using the self-guided tour map handed out at the toll gates, motor past postcard vistas of the ocean and Monterey cypress trees, world-famous golf courses, a luxury lodge and the bay where Spanish explorer Gaspar de Portolá dropped anchor in 1769.

The Drive » 17-Mile Dr is actually only 9 miles long between the Pacific Grove and Carmel toll gates. After exiting the toll road, continue south to Ocean Ave, then turn left for downtown Carmel-by-the-Sea.

TRIP HIGHLIGHT

❹ Carmel-by-the-Sea

Once an artists' colony, this quaint village now has the manicured feel of a country club.

On the west side of town, **Carmel Beach City Park** (off Scenic Rd; 👪 🐾) is a gorgeous white-sand strand where pampered pups run off-leash. Just

LUCKY PHOTOGRAPHER / SHUTTERSTOCK ©

inland, 20th-century poet Robinson Jeffers' **Tor House** (☎844-285-0244; www.torhouse.org; 26304 Ocean View Ave; adult/child 12-17yr $12/7; ⏰tours hourly 10am-3pm Fri & Sat) offers insights into bohemian Old Carmel.

Further east, off Rio Rd, the arched basilica and flowering garden courtyard of **Mission San Carlos Borroméo de Carmelo** (☎831-624-1271; www.carmelmission.org; 3080 Rio Rd; adult/child 7-17yr $10/7; ⏰9:30am-5pm; P) will make you feel as if you've landed in old Spain. Established in 1772, this is the second-

Point Pinos Lighthouse in Pacific Grove

oldest California mission. Padre Junípero Serra is buried here.

🍴 🛏 p201

The Drive » From the mission, continue southeast down Rio Rd to the intersection with Hwy 1. Turn right and drive about 2 miles south to the turnoff for Point Lobos State Natural Reserve on your right.

TRIP HIGHLIGHT

⑤ Point Lobos State Natural Reserve

Sea lions are the stars here at Punta de los Lobos Marinos (Point of the Sea Wolves), where a rocky coastline offers excellent tide-pooling. Short walks around **Point Lobos State Natural Reserve** (☎831-624-4909; www.pointlobos.org; Hwy 1; per car $10; ◷8am-5pm, last entry 4:30pm; 🅿 🚻) take in wild scenery and wildlife-watching, including Bird Island, shady cypress groves, the historic Whaler's Cabin and the Devil's Cauldron, a whirlpool that gets splashy at high tide.

The Drive » Back at the park entrance, turn left onto Hwy 1 northbound. Wind 2.5 miles uphill away from the coast to the stoplight intersection with Carmel Valley Rd. Turn right and drive east through farmlands and vineyards toward Carmel Valley village, about 11.5 miles away.

⑥ Carmel Valley

Carmel Valley is a peaceful and bucolic side trip. At organic **Earthbound Farm** (☎805-625-6219; www.ebfarm.com; 7250 Carmel Valley Rd; ◷8am-6pm Mon-Sat, 9am-6pm Sun; 🚻), sample fresh-fruit smoothies and homemade soups. Wineries further east offer tastings. The pinot noir bottled by **Boeke-noogen** (☎831-659-4215; www.boekenoogenwines.com; 24 W Carmel Valley Rd; tasting flights $15-20; ◷11am-5pm;

DETOUR: SALINAS

Start: ⑥ Carmel Valley

From Salinas farmhands to Monterey cannery workers, the sun-baked Central Valley hills to the fishing coastline, Nobel Prize–winning author John Steinbeck drew a perfect picture of the landscapes and communities he knew. His hometown, Salinas, is a 25-minute drive east of Monterey via Hwy 68.

Downtown, the **National Steinbeck Center** (☎831-775-4721; www.steinbeck.org; 1 Main St; adult/child 6-17yr $13/7; ☺10am-5pm, to 9pm first Friday of each month; ♿) brings the novels to life with interactive exhibits and short movie clips. Look for Rocinante, the camper Steinbeck drove across America while writing *Travels with Charley*. Take a moment and listen to Steinbeck's Nobel acceptance speech – it's grace and power combined.

A few blocks west, **Steinbeck House** (☎831-424-2735; www.steinbeckhouse.com/about-us; 132 Central Ave; ☺restaurant 11:30am-2pm Tue-Sat, gift shop to 3pm) is the author's childhood home. A classic Queen Anne Victorian with dainty bird-patterned lace curtains, it's both a mini museum and a high-tea restaurant.

Two miles southeast of downtown, Steinbeck pilgrims can pay their respects at **Garden of Memories Memorial Park** (Memory Dr). An iron sign points the way to the Hamilton family plot, where a simple grave marker identifies where some of Steinbeck's ashes were buried.

Around 20 miles southeast of Salinas is the **River Road Wine Trail** (www.riverroadwinetrail.com).

♿) is excellent, and both **I Brand & Family** (☎831-298-7227; www.ibrandwinery.com; 19 E Carmel Valley Rd; tastings $20; ☺noon-6pm Wed-Sun) and **Joyce Wine Company** (☎831-659-2885; www.joycewineco.com; 1 E Carmel Valley Rd; tastings $15-20; ☺noon-5:30pm; ♿) feature stylish tasting rooms. Carmel Valley village is also chock-a-block with excellent cafes. Try **Corkscrew Cafe** (☎831-659-8888; www.corkscrewcafe.com; 55 W Carmel Valley Rd; mains $18-30; ☺11:30am-9pm Thu-Mon; ♿) for Mediterranean flavors and wood-fired pizza.

The Drive » Backtrack 2 miles west of the village along Carmel Valley Rd, then turn right onto Laureles Grade. After 6 miles, turn left on Hwy 68, driving west to join Hwy 1 northbound. After passing sand dunes, suburbs and strawberry fields, Hwy 1 swings back towards the coast. Turn left onto Moss Landing Rd.

---

❼ Moss Landing

Time to meet the local wildlife. Rent a kayak from outfitters on Hwy 1 and paddle past harbor seals into **Elkhorn Slough National Estuarine Research Reserve** (☎831-728-2822; www.elkhornslough.org; 1700 Elkhorn Rd,

Watsonville; adult/child under 16yr $4/free; ☺9am-5pm Wed-Sun; ♿), or take a guided weekend hike and go bird-watching. From the fishing harbor on Moss Landing Rd, **Sanctuary Cruises** (☎info 831-917-1042, tickets 831-350-4090; www.sanctuarycruises.com; 7881 Sandholdt Rd; tours $40-55; ♿) operates year-round whale-watching and dolphin-spotting cruises aboard biodiesel-fueled boats (make advance reservations).

 p201

Eating & Sleeping

Monterey ❶

✗ Alta Bakery & Cafe
Cafe $

(☎831-920-1018; www.altamonterey.com; 502 Munras Ave; snacks & mains $8-12; ⏰7am-4pm; 🅿🚻) In the restored **Cooper-Molera Adobe** (☎831-223-0172; www.coopermolera. org; 525 Polk St; ⏰11am-4pm Tue-Sat, to 2:30pm Sun), Alta Bakery & Cafe's excellent baking is showcased with brunch options including orange marmalade and ricotta on sourdough, while daily donut, strudel and muffin specials are always worth trying. The kombucha on tap and organic and fair-trade coffee, and interesting historic photos in the main dining area. In warmer weather, adjourn to the lovely gardens.

✗ Montrio Bistro
Californian $$$

(☎831-648-8880; www.montrio.com; 414 Calle Principal; shared plates $6.50-20, mains $20-46; ⏰4:30-10pm Sun-Thu, to 11pm Fri & Sat; 🛜) With 'clouds' hanging from the ceiling and tube sculptures wriggling towards them, it's apparent that much thought has gone into the design of this dining-scene stalwart set inside a 1910 firehouse. Fortunately, the New American fare, prepared with ingredients hunted and gathered locally, measures up nicely. Drink and snack prices during happy hour (daily until 6:30pm) are practically a steal.

🛏 Jabberwock
B&B $$$

(☎831-372-4777; www.jabberwockinn.com; 598 Laine St; r $239-379; @🛜) Barely visible behind a shroud of foliage, this 1911 khaki-shingled arts-and-crafts-style house hums a playful *Alice in Wonderland* tune through seven immaculate rooms, a few with fireplaces and Jacuzzis for two. Over afternoon wine and hors d'oeuvres, ask the genial hosts about the house's many salvaged architectural elements. Weekends have a two-night minimum. Breakfast included.Also available is Tumtum Tree, a stand-alone cottage cradled by Monterey Cypress trees, accommodating up to four guests.

Pacific Grove ❷

✗ Crema
Cafe $$

(☎831-324-0347; www.cremapg.com; 481 Lighthouse Ave; mains $11-18; ⏰7am-4pm; 🅿🚻) Our pick for Pacific Grove's best coffee, with expertly prepared lattes and macchiatos complemented by delicious brunch plates guaranteed to set you up for the day. If you're planning on cycling 17-Mile Drive (p198), you could do worse than Crema's crab cakes and eggs or the waffles with spiced apple and toasted pecans. Cocktails and craft beer are particularly popular on weekends.

Carmel-by-the-Sea ❹

✗ La Bicyclette
French $$$

(☎831-622-9899; www.labicycletterestaurant. com; cnr Dolores St & 7th Ave; mains lunch $21-31, dinner $21-48; ⏰8am-10pm) Rustic French comfort food using seasonal local ingredients and an open kitchen baking wood-fired-oven pizzas packs couples into this bistro. Excellent local wines by the glass. It's also a top spot for a leisurely lunch.

🛏 Cypress Inn
Boutique Hotel $$$

(☎831-624-3871; www.cypress-inn.com; cnr Lincoln St & 7th Ave; r/ste from $299/499; 🅿🐕🛜🍽) Done up in Spanish Colonial style, this 1929 inn was co-owned by movie star Doris Day for 20 years. Airy terracotta hallways with colorful tiles give it a Mediterranean feel, while sunny rooms face the courtyard. Pet fee $30.

Moss Landing ❼

✗ Phil's Fish Market
Seafood $$

(☎831-633-2152; www.philsfishmarket.com; 7600 Sandholdt Rd; mains $12-28; ⏰10am-9pm; 🚻) Devour buckets of crab, mussels, squid, scallops and prawns covered in San Francisco–style cioppino sauce at this warehouse-size eatery right by the harbor. Meals are absolutely huge, so you may want to combine lunch and dinner.

Around San Luis Obispo

18

It's nothing but all-natural fun in SLO County, with sunny beaches and rolling vineyard roads. Slow down – this idyllic coast deserves to be savored, not gulped.

TRIP HIGHLIGHTS

95 miles

Paso Robles Wine Country
Rural vineyards off Hwy 46

Paso Robles

FINISH

7

33 miles

Avila Beach
Sunny shores by an old fishing port

Cayucos

Morro Bay

San Luis Obispo

START

55 miles

Montaña de Oro State Park
Peak hikes and tide-pooling coves

5

4

3

Pismo Beach
Rockin' retro California beach town

Arroyo Grande

25 miles

2–3 DAYS
115 MILES / 185KM

GREAT FOR...

BEST TIME TO GO
July through October brings sunniest skies.

ESSENTIAL PHOTO
Morro Rock silhouetted at sunset.

BEST FOR WINERIES
Hwy 46 east and west of Paso Robles.

Surfers at Pismo Beach

203

Around San Luis Obispo

Halfway between San Francisco and LA, the laid-back college town of San Luis Obispo (aka 'SLO') is a gateway to coastal adventures. Beach towns and fishing villages offer a bucketful of outdoor pursuits, both on land and at sea — and wherever there's natural beauty, it's never too far from Hwy 1. Farm-to-table locavorian restaurants and vineyards abound, especially in Paso Robles' wine country, ideal for lazy weekend or weekday drives.

❶ San Luis Obispo

Oprah called it 'the happiest city in America,' and once you spend a few hours downtown, you might agree. CalPoly university students inject a healthy dose of hubbub into the streets, shops, pubs and cafes, especially during the weekly **farmers market** (www. downtownslo.com; Higuera St btwn Nipomo & Osos Sts; snacks from $5; ⏰6-9pm Thu; 🖉 🚻), which turns downtown's Higuera St into a street festival with live music and sidewalk

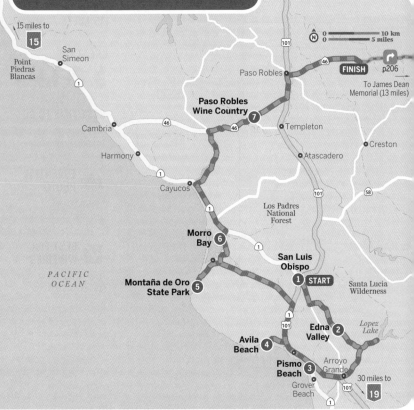

food stalls. Like many other California towns, SLO grew up around a Spanish Catholic mission, **Mission San Luis Obispo de Tolosa** (☎805-543-6850; www.missionsanluisobispo.org; 751 Palm St; suggested donation $5; ⊙9am-5pm late Mar-Oct, to 4pm Nov–mid-Mar; ⬛), founded in 1772 by missionary Junípero Serra. The creek that once used to irrigate mission orchards still flows through downtown, beside tranquil, shaded walking paths.

✕ ⤙ p209

The Drive ≫ From downtown SLO, follow Broad St/Hwy 227 for 2.5 stop-and-go miles southeast, turning left before the airport onto Tank Farm Rd. After a mile, curve right and continue onto Orcutt Rd, which

LINK YOUR TRIP

19 **Santa Barbara Wine Country**

Want more good grapes? Follow Hwy 101 south of Pismo Beach for 45 miles to the Santa Ynez Valley.

15 **Big Sur**

From Cayucos, cruise Hwy 1 north for 45 miles to the southern Big Sur coast, passing Hearst Castle halfway along.

rolls up and down past vineyards into Edna Valley.

- - - - - - - - - - - - - - - - - -

2 **Edna Valley**

Cradled by the rich volcanic soil of the Santa Lucia foothills, thriving **Edna Valley wineries** (www.slocoastwine.com) are known for their crisp, often unoaked chardonnay and subtle syrah and pinot noir. Pick up a free map from any tasting room. All are signposted along Orcutt Rd and Edna Rd/Hwy 227. These roads run parallel through the peaceful valley, which is cooled by drifting coastal fog in the morning before being brightened by afternoon sunshine. **Niven Family Wine Estates** (☎805-269-8200; www.nivenfamilywines.com; 5828 Orcutt Rd; tastings $15-30; ⊙10am-5pm; ⬛) pours inside a 20th-century wooden schoolhouse, while **Edna Valley Vineyard** (☎805-544-5855; www.ednavalleyvineyard.com; 2585 Biddle Ranch Rd; tastings from $25; ⊙10am-5pm) has panoramic windows that overlook vineyards. Further southeast, **Talley Vineyards** (☎805-489-0446; www.talleyvineyards.com; 3031 Lopez Dr, Arroyo Grande; tasting fee $12-18; ⊙10:30am-4:30pm) offers winery tours by appointment.

The Drive ≫ From Talley Vineyards, Lopez Rd winds west toward Arroyo Grande, just over 6 miles away. Turn left onto Branch St, then merge onto

Hwy 101 north to Pismo Beach. Exit at Price St, which enters downtown Pismo Beach. Turn left onto Pomeroy Ave and roll downhill to the ocean.

- - - - - - - - - - - - - - - - - -

TRIP HIGHLIGHT

3 **Pismo Beach**

By a wooden pier that stretches towards the setting sun, James Dean once trysted with Pier Angeli. Today this classic California beach town feels like somewhere straight out of a 1950s hot-rod dream. Pismo likes to call itself the 'Clam Capital of the World.' Across recent years, clams have been rare on the wide, sandy beach, but the tasty mollusc is now making a slow comeback. To ride the waves, rent a wet suit and board from any surf shop, or negotiate the hilltop walking trails of the **Pismo Preserve** (www.lcslo.org; Mattie Rd; ⊙6am-9:30pm Mar-Oct, to 7pm Nov-Apr; ⬛⬛⬛) for excellent coastal views. After dark, go bar hopping or knock down pins at the retro bowling alley. The next day, drive a mile south of downtown to the **Monarch Butterfly Grove** (☎805-773-5301; www.monarchbutterfly.org; Hwy 1; ⊙10am-4pm late Oct-Feb; ⬛⬛), where migratory monarchs roost in eucalyptus trees, usually from November through February. Join a free docent tour at 11am and 2pm.

p209

The Drive » Follow Hwy 1 north through downtown Pismo Beach, then follow the signs to rejoin Hwy 101 northbound for almost 4 miles to exit 195 for Avila Beach Dr. Keep left at the fork, then wind slowly west downhill to Avila Beach, about 3 miles away.

- - - - - - - - - - - - - - - - - -

TRIP HIGHLIGHT

❹ Avila Beach

For a perfectly lazy summer day at the beach, rent beach chairs and umbrellas underneath Avila Pier, off downtown's sparkling new waterfront promenade. Two miles further west, the coastal road dead-ends at Port San Luis. The barking of sea lions echoes as you stroll past seafood shacks and restaurants to the end of creaky, weather-worn **Harford Pier**, where you can while away time gazing out over the choppy

waters. If you'd like to visit 1890 **Point San Luis Lighthouse** (🔌 guided hike reservations 805-528-8758, trolley tour reservations 805-540-5771; www.pointsanluislighthouse.org; Wild Cherry Canyon parking area, Avila Beach Dr; lighthouse $5, trolley tours incl lighthouse adult/child 3-12yr $25/20; ⊘ guided hikes 8:45am-1pm Wed & Sat, trolley tours noon, 1pm & 2pm Wed & Sat; 🚍), guided-tour reservations are required.

Back uphill near Hwy 101, you can pick your own fruit and feed the goats at **Avila Valley Barn** (🔌805-595-2816; www.avilavalleybarn.com; 560 Avila Beach Dr; ⊘9am-6pm May-Sep, to 5pm Apr, Oct & Nov, to 5pm Thu-Mon Dec-Mar; 🅿 🚍) farm stand, or do some stargazing from a private redwood hot tub at **Sycamore Mineral Springs** (🔌805-595-7302; www.sycamoresprings.com; 1215 Avila Beach Dr; 1hr per person $17.50-22.50; ⊘8am-

MATTHEW BAUGH PHOTOGRAPHY / SHUTTERSTOCK ©

midnight, last reservation 10:30pm).

The Drive » Take Hwy 101 back northbound toward San Luis Obispo. Exit after 4.5 miles at Los Osos Valley Rd, which leaves behind stop-and-go strip-mall traffic to slowly roll past farmland for about 11 miles. After passing through downtown Los Osos, curve left onto Pecho Valley Rd, which enters Montaña de Oro State Park a few miles later.

- - - - - - - - - - - - - - - - - -

TRIP HIGHLIGHT

❺ Montaña de Oro State Park

In spring, the hillsides of **Montaña de Oro State Park** (🔌805-772-6101; www. parks.ca.gov; 3550 Pecho Val-

DETOUR: JAMES DEAN MEMORIAL

Start: ❼ Paso Robles Wine Country

On Hwy 46 about 25 miles east of Paso Robles, there's a monument near the spot where *Rebel Without a Cause* star James Dean fatally crashed his Porsche on September 30, 1955, at the age of 24. Ironically, the actor had recently filmed a public-safety-campaign TV spot against drag racing and speeding on US highways. Look for the shiny brushed-steel memorial wrapped around an oak tree outside the Jack Ranch Cafe truck stop, which has a few old photographs and some dusty movie-star memorabilia inside.

Sunrise at Morro Baye

ley Rd, Los Osos; ⏱6am-10pm; P ♿) are blanketed by bright California native poppies, wild mustard and other wildflowers, giving this park its Spanish name, which means 'mountain of gold.' Along the winding access road, sand dunes and the wind-tossed bluffs of the Pacific appear. Pull over at Spooner's Cove, a postcard-perfect sandy beach once used by smugglers. Here the grinding of the Pacific and North American plates has uplifted and tilted sedimentary layers of submarine rock, visible from shore. Hike along the beach and

the park's grassy ocean bluffs, or drive uphill past the visitor center to tackle the 4-mile round-trip trail up rocky Valencia Peak – the summit views are exhilarating.

The Drive » Backtrack on Pecho Rd out of the park, curving right onto Los Osos Valley Rd. East of Los Osos, turn left onto Bay Blvd, winding north alongside Morro Bay's estuary. Before reaching Hwy 101, turn left onto Morro Bay State Park Rd, continuing on Main St into downtown Morro Bay. Turn left on Marina St and drive downhill to the Embarcadero.

---

6 Morro Bay

This fishing village is home to **Morro Rock**, a volcanic peak jutting up from the ocean floor. (Too bad about those power-plant smokestacks obscuring the views, though.) You're likely to spot harbor seals and sea otters as you paddle around the bay in a kayak rented from the waterfront Embarcadero, crowded with seafood shacks. Or drive a mile north of the marina to walk partway around the base of the landmark rock. West of downtown in **Morro Bay State Park**

CRAFT BEER & DISTILLING

Craft beer and distilleries are both very popular around Paso Robles. Around 7 miles south of downtown, the interesting Tin City Neighbourhood includes **BarrelHouse Brewing Co** (☑805-296-1128; www.barrelhousebrewing.com; 3055 Limestone Way, Tin City; ⊗11am-9pm; 🚻🐾), **Tin City Cider Co** (☑805-293-6349; www.tincitycider.com; 3005a Limestone Way, Tin City; ⊗11am-8pm Sun-Wed, to 9pm Thu-Sat) and the **Wine Shine** (☑805-286-4453; www.wineshine.com; 3064 Limestone Way, Tin City; ⊗1-5pm Fri-Sun) distillery. Nearby, **Kilokilo Brewing** (☑805-296-3670; www.kilokilobrewing.com; 3340 Ramada Dr; ⊗3-8pm Wed & Thu, 2-9pm Fri, 11am-9pm Sat, to 7pm Sun) is a smaller craft brewery, making delicious IPAs with citrusy New Zealand hops, while closer to downtown Paso, the focus at **Silva Brewing** (☑805-369-2337; www.silvabrewing.com; 525 Pine St; ⊗2-7pm Wed-Fri, noon-7pm Sat, to 5pm Sun) is bold, hop-forward styles and Belgian-influenced beers.

See www.brewpaso.com for information on the brewing, distilling and coffee-roasting scenes in and around the city. For more on the growing Paso Robles distillery scene, see www.pasorublesdistillerytrail.com, and download a touring map listing 10 distilleries.

(☑museum 805-772-2694, park 805-772-6101; www.parks.ca.gov; 60 State Park Rd; park entry free, museum adult/child under 17yr $3/free; ⊗park 6am-10pm, museum 10am-5pm; 🅿🚻) is the **Museum of Natural History**, where kids can touch interactive models of the bay's ecosystem and stuffed wildlife mounts.

✖ p209

The Drive » Follow Main St north to Hwy 1. For 4 miles, Hwy 1 northbound rides above ocean beaches. In Cayucos, turn right onto Old Creek Rd, a winding, narrow back road, passing citrus farms and cattle ranches. Turn right after 9 miles onto Hwy 46, which heads east through wine country for 11 miles to meet Hwy 101 in Paso Robles.

TRIP HIGHLIGHT

❼ Paso Robles Wine Country

Franciscan missionaries brought the first grapes to this region in the late 18th century, but it wasn't until the 1920s that the now-famous zinfandel vines took root in Paso Robles. Coasting through golden-brown hills and grassy pasture lands, Hwy 46 passes family-owned vineyards, olive orchards and rustic farm stands. Pick up a free **winery tour map** (www.pasowine.com) from any tasting room and sniff out boutique winemakers such as **Chronic Cellars** (☑805-237-7848; www.chroniccellars.com; 2020 Nacimiento Lake Dr; tasting fee $10; ⊗11am-5pm) as well as big-name producers like **Eberle Winery** (☑805-238-9607; www.eberlewinery.com; 3810 E Hwy 46; tastings free-$25; ⊗10am-6pm Apr-Oct, to 5pm Nov-Mar; 🅿). For many more wine-tasting rooms and bars, restaurants and urbane boutiques, explore around downtown Paso's leafy central park square.

 p209

Eating & Sleeping

San Luis Obispo ❶

✕ Mint + Craft — Cafe $

(☏805-632-9191; www.mintandcraft.com; 848 Monterey St; mains $11-16; ⊙8am-8pm; 🖨) Often bathed in morning sunshine, this versatile all-day eatery kicks off with eggy breakfasts before segueing to salads, wellness bowls and interesting flatbreads and sandwiches later in the day. Beer and wine are both served, making it a good option for a well-priced dinner in the early evening.

✕ Mestiza — Mexican $$

(☏805-592-3201; www.mestizaslo.com; 858 Monterey St; lunch mains $10-16, dinner mains $22-29; ⊙11:30am-9pm Tue-Thu & Sun, to 10pm Fri & Sat) Modern Mexican flavors shine at Mestiza. Secure a booth or sit at the bar and enjoy the *molcajete*, a complex dish named after a traditional Mexican mortar and pestle and crammed with steak, chorizo, rice and shrimp. It's definitely a dish for sharing; for a lighter end-of-day snack pair shrimp *taquitos* with a smokey mezcal cocktail.

🛏 Hotel Cerro — Boutique Hotel $$$

(☏805-548-1000; www.hotelcerro.com; 1125 Garden St; r $228-399, ste $380-630; ⊙restaurant 7:30am-9:30pm Mon-Sat, to 3pm Sun; P 🛜 ♨) Hotel Cerro combines luxury boutique style with a significant commitment to sustainable design. The hotel has been constructed around a restored heritage brick facade, and suites look over an inner garden enlivened with fresh herbs used by the on-site Brasserie SLO. There's a spa and wellness center, and the hotel's own compact distillery crafts artisan spirits for its cocktail bar.

Pismo Beach ❸

✕ Cracked Crab — Seafood $$

(☏805-773-2722; www.crackedcrab.com; 751 Price St; mains $16-61; ⊙11am-9pm Sun-Thu, 11am-10pm Fri & Sat; 🖨) Fresh seafood and regional wines are staples at this super-casual family-owned grill. When the famous Big Bucket – a messy bonanza of crab, clams, shrimp and mussels accompanied by Cajun sausage, red potatoes and cob corn – gets dumped on your butcher-paper-covered table, make sure you're wearing one of those silly-looking plastic bibs. No reservations, but the wait is worth it.

✕ Oyster Loft — Californian, Seafood $$$

(☏805-295-5104; www.oysterloft.com; 101 Pomeroy Ave; mains $20-45; ⊙5-9pm Sun-Thu, to 10pm Fri & Sat) Delve into the appetizers menu – including crab cakes and orange-glazed octopus – or kick off with tuna tataki or fresh oysters from the crudo raw bar. Mains including pan-fried halibut are still seafood heavy, but they do venture successfully into steak and chicken. Look forward to excellent views of the surf and the Pismo Beach pier from the restaurant's elevated position.

Morro Bay ❻

✕ House of JuJu — Californian $$

(☏805-225-1828; www.houseofjuju.com; 945 Embarcadero; mains $12-18; ⊙11am-9:30pm Sun-Thu, to 10:30pm Fri & Sat) Friendly service lifts this waterfront spot above other nearby bars and eateries. House of JuJu's signature gourmet burgers are deservedly world-famous-in-Morro Bay. Our favourite is the JuJu Bleu with caramelized onions, bacon and blue cheese. Salads and wraps are good options for smaller appetites. Ask for a table with views of Morro Rock.

Paso Robles Wine Country ❼

✕ Hatch Rotisserie & Bar — American $$

(☏805-221-5727; www.hatchpasorobles.com; 835 13th St; mains $17-30; ⊙4:30-9pm Mon-Wed, to 10pm Thu, to 11pm Fri & Sat) Wood-fired treats in this heritage location, which combines shimmering chandeliers and rustic bricks, include grilled octopus, rotisserie chicken and creamy bone marrow. It adds a sly sophistication to American comfort food including shrimp and grits and buttermilk fried chicken. Craft beer, cocktails and local wines are all tasty diversions. Check the website for nightly dinner specials.

Santa Barbara Wine Country

Oak-dotted hillsides, winding country roads, rows of sweetly heavy grapevines stretching into the distance – let yourself veer sideways into the Santa Maria and Santa Ynez Valleys.

19

TRIP HIGHLIGHTS

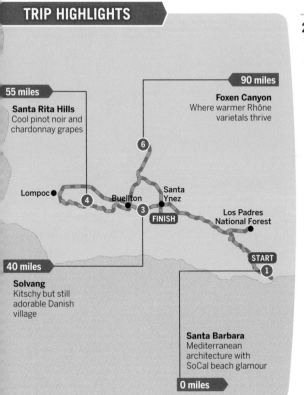

55 miles

Santa Rita Hills
Cool pinot noir and chardonnay grapes

90 miles

Foxen Canyon
Where warmer Rhône varietals thrive

6

Lompoc

4 Buellton

Santa Ynez

3

FINISH

Los Padres National Forest

START
1

40 miles

Solvang
Kitschy but still adorable Danish village

Santa Barbara
Mediterranean architecture with SoCal beach glamour

0 miles

2–3 DAYS
145 MILES / 235KM

GREAT FOR...

BEST TIME TO GO
April to October for optimal sunshine.

ESSENTIAL PHOTO

Danish windmills in Solvang.

BEST FOR WALKING

Los Olivos' wine-tasting rooms and boutique shops.

19 Santa Barbara Wine Country

The 2004 Oscar-winning film *Sideways*, an ode to wine-country living as seen through the misadventures of middle-aged buddies Miles and Jack, may have brought the spotlight to Santa Barbara's wine country. But passionate winegrowers and vintners direct the ongoing viticultural play in this gorgeous, climactically blessed setting. More than 100 wineries spread across the landscape, with five small towns all clustered within a 10-mile drive of one another.

TRIP HIGHLIGHT

❶ Santa Barbara

Start pretending to live the luxe life in Santa Barbara, a coastal Shangri-la where the air is redolent with citrus, and flowery bougainvillea drapes whitewashed buildings with Spanish Colonial-style red-tiled roofs, all fringed with beaches and oceanside bluffs. Before heading out of town into the wine country for the day or weekend, make time to visit landmark **Mission Santa Barbara**

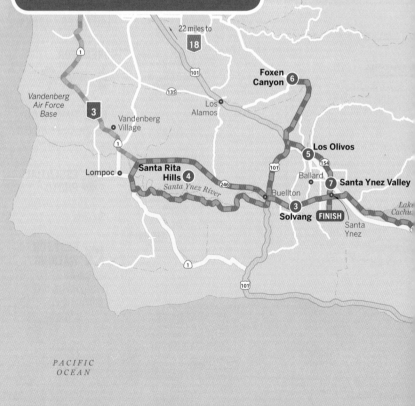

(☎805-682-4713; www.santabarbaramission.org; 2201 Laguna St; adult/child 5-17yr $12/7; ☻9am-4:15pm Sep-Jun, to 5:15pm Jul & Aug; ℗), California's 'Queen of the Missions.' Then walk around downtown's courthouse, historical buildings and museums (p286), all on or just off **State St**, which leads downhill to the ocean and splintered wooden **Stearns Wharf** (www.stearnswharf.org; ☻8am-10pm; ℗ 👶), the West Coast's oldest continuously operating pier. A few blocks inland from

the beach, follow Santa Barbara's **Urban Wine Trail** (www.urbanwinetrailsb.com), where boutique wine-tasting rooms are typically open from noon to 6pm daily (tasting fees $10 to $20).

✗ 🛏 p217

The Drive » In the morning, take a short drive north on Hwy 101, then follow winding, narrow Hwy 154 up into the Santa Ynez Mountains and over San Marcos Pass. About 9 miles from Hwy 101, turn left onto Stagecoach Rd, passing the 1860s Cold Springs Tavern. After 2 miles, turn right onto Paradise Rd.

----

❷ Los Padres National Forest

Off Paradise Rd, the oak-covered hills of **Los Padres National Forest** (☎805-967-3481; www.fs.usda.gov/lpnf; 3505 Paradise Rd; daily pass per car $5; ☻8am-4:30pm Mon-Fri, plus Sat late May-early Sep; 👶) contain several good hiking trails for all ages, all easily accessed off Hwy 154. Starting beyond the family campgrounds and

river crossing on Paradise Rd, the creekside Red Rock Trail leads for a mile to rocky pools and waterfalls where you can sunbathe or swim.

The Drive » Backtrack along Paradise Rd, then turn right and follow Hwy 154 northbound past Lake Cachuma and the rolling hillsides for over 13 miles. Turn left onto Hwy 246 and keep motoring five more flat miles through the Santa Ynez Valley west to Solvang.

TRIP HIGHLIGHT

❸ Solvang

Loosely translated as 'sunny fields,' this touristy Danish village was founded in 1911 on what was once a Mexican *rancho* (land grant). Filled with knickknack stores and storybook motels, the town is almost as sticky-sweet as the Scandinavian pastries gobbled by day-trippers. Wine-tasting rooms and windmills decorate the village's pedestrian-friendly streets. For a break from the grapes, seek out tiny speakeasy

🔗 LINK YOUR TRIP

18 Around San Luis Obispo

Want more wine, but beaches too? Drive Hwy 101 north of the Santa Ynez Valley for 45 miles to Pismo Beach.

3 Mission Trail
Trace the path of Spanish-colonial history at La Purísima Mission, 18 miles northwest of Solvang via Hwy 246.

the **Backroom** (Valley Brewers; 805-691-9160; www.valleybrewers.com/the-backroom; 515 Fourth Pl; 1-6pm Sun & Mon, to 8pm Wed-Sat), where locals cozy up with pints from a rotating selection of intriguing local and international beers. Of cultural interest is the petite **Wildling Museum** (805-688-1082; www.wildlingmuseum.org; 1511-B Mission Dr; adult/child under 17yr $5/free; 11am-5pm Mon & Wed-Fri, from 10am Sat & Sun; P), exhibiting nature-themed California and American Western art. On a residential side street, the tiny **Elverhøj Museum of History & Art** (805-686-1211; www.elverhoj.org; 1624 Elverhoy Way; suggested donation adult/child under 13yr $5/free; 11am-4pm Wed-Sun;) uncovers the real roots of Danish life in Solvang. Tranquil today, **Old Mission Santa Ínes** (805-688-4815; www.missionsantaines.org; 1760 Mission Dr; adult/child under 12yr $6/free; 9am-5pm, closed for services; P) witnessed an 1824 Chumash revolt against Spanish colonial cruelty.

✗ ⌂ p217

The Drive » Continue west on Hwy 246 past equestrian ranches and the famous ostrich farm (as seen during Jack's predawn run in *Sideways*) for just a few miles to Buellton. Continue across Hwy 101 and drive west toward Lompoc.

TRIP HIGHLIGHT

④ Santa Rita Hills

When it comes to rolling scenery, eco-conscious farming practices and top-notch pinot noir and chardonnay grapes kissed by coastal fog, the **Santa Rita Hills** (www.staritahills.com) undoubtedly hold their own. Almost a dozen tasting rooms open their doors daily along this 36-mile scenic loop west of Hwy 101. Be prepared to share these slow-moving roads with sweaty cyclists, Harley Davidson bikers and an occasional John Deere tractor. Head west of Buellton on Hwy 246 into the countryside to small-lot estate winery **Melville** (805-735-7030; www.melvillewinery.com; 5185 E Hwy 246, Lompoc; tastings $15-20; 11am-4pm Sun-Thu, to 5pm Fri & Sat; P), which talks about pounds per plant, not tons per acre. Turn left onto Hwy 1 south, then left again on Santa Rosa Rd, where **Sanford Winery** (800-426-9463; www.sanfordwinery.com; 5010 Santa Rosa Rd, Lompoc; tastings $20-30; 10am-4pm Wed-Sun, by appointment Mon & Tue) was the first to plant pinot noir in the Santa Rita Hills; stop to taste the wine and the vineyard scenery. Just west of Hwy 101 by a hillside olive orchard, **Mosby Winery** (805-688-2415; www.mosbywines.com; 9496 Santa Rosa Rd;

tasting fee $15; 10am-4pm Mon-Thu, to 4:30pm Fri-Sun; P) pours unusual Cal-Italian varietals inside a red carriage house.

The Drive » At the eastern end of Santa Rosa Rd, merge onto Hwy 101 northbound. After 6 miles, take the Hwy 154 exit for Los Olivos, driving 3 miles further east past more rolling vineyards.

⑤ Los Olivos

The local saddlery occupies the same block as one of the best restaurants in the ranching town of Los Olivos. Its four-block-long downtown is bursting with

Solvang in Santa Ynez Valley

wine-tasting rooms, little eateries, art galleries and fashionable shops seemingly airlifted straight out of Napa Valley. You can easily walk between downtown's inviting tasting rooms and brewery on a long, lazy afternoon. Taste estate small-lot artistry at **Blair Fox** (☏805-691-1678; www.blairfoxcellars.com; 2477 Alamo Pintado Ave; ⏱noon-5pm Thu-Mon) and compare nuances of terroir at **Liquid Farm** (☏805-697-7859; www.liquidfarm.com; 2445 Alamo Pintado Ave, Suite 101; tasting $20; ⏱11am-5pm Mon-Thu, to 7pm Fri-Sun), among the numerous diverse tasting rooms in town.

✗ p217

The Drive >> From Los Olivos, drive west on Hwy 154 for 3 miles. Before reaching Hwy 101, turn right onto Zaca Station Rd, then follow it for three winding miles northwest onto Foxen Canyon Rd.

TRIP HIGHLIGHT

❻ Foxen Canyon

On the celebrated wine trail through **Foxen Canyon** (www.foxencanyonwinetrail.com), tidy rows of grapevines border some of Santa Barbara County's prettiest wineries. This country lane meanders north all the way to the Santa Maria Valley before finally reaching the 1875 **San Ramon Chapel** (☏805-937-1334; Foxen Canyon Rd; ⏱grounds 6:30am-6:30pm; P), a good turnaround point after about 15 miles.

Furthest south, tour buses crowd **Firestone Vineyards** (☏805-688-3940; www.firestonewine.com; 5017 Zaca Station Rd; tastings $10-15, incl tour $20; ⏱11am-5pm; P), Santa Barbara's oldest estate winery (it's where Miles, Jack and their dates sneak into the barrel room in *Sideways*). You'll have to

215

LOCAL KNOWLEDGE: WINE-TASTING TIPS

To make the most of your wine tour, travel the wine country in small groups and with an itinerary focused on just a handful of wineries. Keep an open mind: don't tell the staff you never drink chardonnay or merlot – who knows, the wine you try that day may change your mind. Picnicking is usually cool, if you complement your lunch with a bottle of wine purchased on the premises. Not so cool? Heavy perfume and smoking. Otherwise, enjoy yourself and don't be afraid to ask questions – most tasting rooms welcome novices. And be sure to tip your knowledgeable server.

make an appointment to visit the hidden beauty of **Demetria Estate** (☑805-686-2345; www.demetria estate.com; 6701 Foxen Canyon Rd, Los Olivos; tastings $25; ☺by appointment; P), where Rhône varietals and pinot grapes are farmed biodynamically. On a former cattle ranch, sustainable **Foxen** (☑805-937-4251; www.foxenvineyard. com; 7200 & 7600 Foxen Canyon Rd, Santa Maria; tastings $15-20; ☺11am-4pm; P) pours chardonnay and full-fruited pinot noir in a solar-powered tasting room; up the road, Foxen's old 'shack' – with a corrugated-metal roof and funky decor – pours award-winning Bor-

deaux-style and Italian varietals.

The Drive ≫ Backtrack just over 17 miles along Foxen Canyon Rd, keeping left at the intersection with Zaca Station Rd to return to Los Olivos. Turn left onto Hwy 154 southbound for 2 miles, then turn right onto Roblar Ave for Ontiveros Rd.

🄻 Santa Ynez Valley

Further inland in the warm Santa Ynez Valley, Rhône-style grapes do best, including syrah and viognier. Some of the most popular tasting rooms cluster between Los Olivos, Solvang and Santa Ynez, but noisy tour groups, harried staff and stingy pours too often disappoint.

Thankfully, that's not the case at **Beckmen Vineyards** (☑805-688-8664; www.beckmenvineyards. com; 2670 Ontiveros Rd; tastings $20; ☺11am-5pm; P 🖐 🖼), where biodynamically farmed, estate-grown varietals flourish on the unique terroir of Purisima Mountain. For more natural beauty, backtrack east on Roblar Ave to family-owned **Clairmont Farms** (☑805-688-7505; www. clairmontfarms.com; 2480 Roblar Ave; ☺11am-5pm Wed-Mon; P 🖐), where purple lavender fields bloom like a Monet masterpiece in early summer.

Turn right onto Refugio Rd, which flows south past more vineyards, fruit orchards and farms and straight across Hwy 154 to **Kalyra Winery** (☑805-693-8864; www.kalyra winery.com; 343 N Refugio Rd, Santa Ynez; tastings $20; ☺noon-5pm Tue-Fri, from 10am Sat & Sun; P), where an Australian traveled halfway around the world to combine two loves: surfing and winemaking. Try his shiraz made with imported Australian grapes or locally grown varietals, all in bottles with Aboriginal art–inspired labels.

Eating & Sleeping

Santa Barbara ❶

✗ Corazon Cocina   Mexican $

(📞805-845-0282; https://corazoncocinasb.
com; 38 W Victoria St; mains $5.50-16.50;
🕐11am-9pm Mon-Fri, 10am-9pm Sat & Sun)
Mexican regional favorites, elevated: al pastor
tacos with pineapple and habanero salsa,
delicate wild-shrimp ceviche laden with chili-
spiked mango and cucumber, grilled Oaxacan
quesadillas featuring local veggies...*sí, por
favor*. Head into the Santa Barbara Public
Market and prepare to get food drunk (and to
wait a while – it's popular for very good reason).

✗ Santa Barbara
Shellfish Company   Seafood $$

(📞805-966-6676; http://shellfishco.com; 230
Stearns Wharf; dishes $4-24; 🕐11am-9pm;
👶🐕) 'From sea to skillet to plate' sums up
this end-of-the-wharf seafood shack that's
more of a buzzing counter joint than a sit-down
restaurant. Chase away the seagulls as you
chow down on garlic-baked clams, crab cakes
and coconut-fried shrimp at wooden picnic
tables outside. Awesome lobster bisque, ocean
views and the same location for almost 40
years.

🛏 Harbor House Inn   Inn $$

(📞805-962-9745; www.harborhouseinn.
com; 104 Bath St; r from $224; P👶❄🛜)
Two blocks from the beach, this meticulously
run inn offers bright, individually decorated
sandy-hued studios with hardwood floors, small
kitchens, and amenities such as SmartTVs
with free Netflix and Hulu. If you're staying two
nights or more, rates include a welcome basket
of breakfast goodies. Make use of free loaner
beach towels, chairs, umbrellas and three-
speed bicycles.

Solvang ❸

✗ El Rancho
Marketplace   Supermarket $

(📞805-688-4300; http://elranchomarket.com;
2886 Mission Dr; 🕐6am-11pm) On the eastern

outskirts of Solvang, this upscale supermarket
– with a full deli, smokin' barbecued meats, a
wine shop and an espresso bar – is the best
place to fill your picnic basket before heading
out to the wineries.

🛏 Hadsten House   Boutique Hotel $$

(📞805-688-3210; www.hadstenhouse.com;
1450 Mission Dr; r $197-297; P👶❄🛜🐕)
This revamped motel has luxuriously updated
just about everything, except for its routine
exterior. Inside, rooms are surprisingly plush,
with flat-screen TVs, comfy duvets and high-end
bath products. Spa suites come with jet tubs.
There's a good in-house restaurant (Tuesday to
Saturday). Pet fee $50.

🛏 Hamlet Inn   Motel $$

(📞805-688-4413; www.thehamletinn.com;
1532 Mission Dr; r $99-229; P👶❄🛜) This
remodeled motel is to wine-country lodging
what IKEA is to interior design: a budget-
friendly, trendy alternative. Crisp, modern
rooms have bright Danish-flag bedspreads and
iPod docking stations. Free loaner bicycles
and a super-central location add to the appeal.
Rates include coffee and a pastry from Olsen's
Bakery across the street.

Los Olivos ❺

✗ Los Olivos Wine
Merchant & Café   Californian $$

(📞805-688-7265; www.winemerchantcafe.
com; 2879 Grand Ave; mains $15-28; 🕐11:30am-
8pm Mon-Thu, to 8:30pm Fri, 11am-8:30pm Sat,
11am-8pm Sun) This wine-country landmark
(seen in the film *Sideways*) swirls up a casual-
chic SoCal ambience with its wisteria-covered
trellis entrance. The food is bold, complex and
addictive, prepared with organic ingredients
from Los Olivos' own farm and harmoniously
paired with its exceptional wine selection. Sit
inside in the elegant dining room or outside on
the covered patio.

Lake Tahoe Loop

Shimmering in bright blues and greens, and astounding in its clarity, Lake Tahoe is the USA's second-deepest lake. Adventure beckons from trailheads, parks and beaches along its 72-mile shoreline.

20

TRIP HIGHLIGHTS

55 miles

Truckee
Near Donner Lake, relive Old West history

70 miles

Kings Beach & Tahoe Vista
Paddle off sandy beaches

Incline Village

Squaw Valley

Crystal Bay

Tahoe City

Lake Tahoe Nevada State Park

FINISH

20 miles

Emerald Bay & DL Bliss State Parks
Hike the shoreline Rubicon Trail

START

South Lake Tahoe
Take a cruise, swim or ski

0 miles

2–3 DAYS
105 MILES / 170KM

GREAT FOR...

BEST TIME TO GO

May to September for sunshine; January to March for snow.

ESSENTIAL PHOTO

Inspiration Point above Emerald Bay.

✓ BEST ROADSIDE VIEWS

South Lake Tahoe to Tahoe City.

ndola ride over Lake Tahoe

20 Lake Tahoe Loop

Encircled by mountains, Lake Tahoe is open for adventure year-round. During summer hit the cool sapphire waters fringed by sandy beaches or trek and mountain-bike forest trails. In winter, powder-hungry skiers and boarders bombard scores of slopes. Year-round, the north shore is quiet and upscale; the west shore, rugged and old-timey; the east shore, blissfully undeveloped; and the south shore, always busy. The lake straddles the California–Nevada state line.

TRIP HIGHLIGHT

❶ South Lake Tahoe

South Lake Tahoe is a chockablock commercial strip bordering the lake, which is framed by post-card-pretty mountains. In winter, go swooshing down the double-black diamond runs and monster vertical drops of **Heavenly** (☏775-586-7000; www.skiheavenly. com; 3860 Saddle Rd; adult/child 5-12yr/youth 13-18yr $154/85/126; ⏰9am-4pm Mon-Fri, 8:30am-4pm Sat, Sun & holidays; 👪), a behemoth

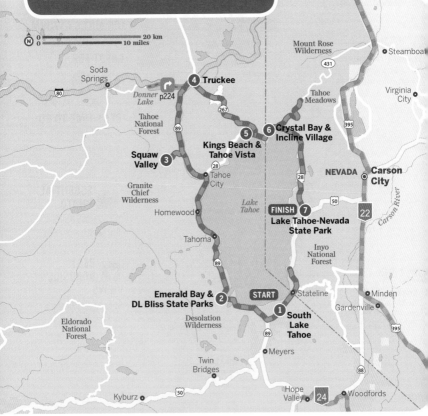

ski resort. From the top, you're on the spine of the Sierra Nevada between mountains and desert flatlands. For killer lake views in summer, ascend the **gondola** (www.ski heavenly.com; adult/child 5-12yr/youth 13-18yr from $64/39/50; ⏱10am-5pm Jun-Aug, reduced off-season hours;) from Heavenly Village, or board the paddle wheelers of **Lake Tahoe Cruises** (🕿775-586-4906; www.zephyrcove.com; 760 Hwy 50; adult/child from $68/38) that ply the 'Big Blue.' Survey the azure expanse of the lake at eye level from in-town beaches or aboard a kayak launched from **Zephyr Cove** (🕿775-589-4901; www.zephyrcove.com; 760 Hwy 50; per car May-Sep $10; ⏱sunrise-sunset), which also has sandy swimming beaches. It's about 3 miles north of

LINK YOUR TRIP

22 Eastern Sierra Scenic Byway

Downtown Reno's casinos are just over 30 miles northeast of Truckee via I-80.

24 Ebbetts Pass Scenic Byway

From South Lake Tahoe, it's 20 miles south along Hwy 89 to Hope Valley, although Ebbetts Pass is closed during winter and spring.

Stateline, NV, where you can bet a stack of chips at the hulking casinos, all buzzing with bars, nightclubs and 24-hour restaurants.

✕ 🛏 p225

The Drive » Unless the road has been closed by heavy snowfall, set a course heading northwest from South Lake Tahoe's 'The Y' intersection onto scenic lakeside Hwy 89. You'll pass USFS Tallac Historic Site and Taylor Creek Visitor Center, both of which have nature trails and educational exhibits, before reaching Inspiration Point and, further along, the parking lot of Vikingsholm Castle ($10 per vehicle).

- - - - - - - - - - - - - - - - -

TRIP HIGHLIGHT

② Emerald Bay & DL Bliss State Parks

Sheer granite cliffs and a jagged shoreline mark glacier-carved **Emerald Bay** (🕿530-541-6498; www.parks.ca.gov; parking $10; ⏱sunrise-sunset), a teardrop cove that will get you digging for your camera. Panoramic pullouts all along Hwy 89 peer over the uninhabited granite speck of **Fannette Island**, which harbors the vandalized remains of a 1920s teahouse once belonging to heir Lora Knight. She also built **Vikingsholm Castle** (🕿530-525-7232; www.vikingsholm.com; tours adult/child 7-17yr $15/12; ⏱10:30am-4pm late May-Sep; P), a Scandinavian-style mansion on the bay that's reached via a steep

2-mile round-trip hiking trail. Heading north, the 4.5-mile **Rubicon Trail** ribbons along the lakeshore past hidden coves to **DL Bliss State Park** (🕿530-525-7277; www.parks.ca.gov; Hwy 89; per car $10; ⏱late May–mid-Oct; P), with its old lighthouse and sandy beaches.

The Drive » Head north on Hwy 89 past the sandy beach at Meeks Bay, forested Ed Z'berg Sugar Pine Point State Park and the lakeshore hamlets of Tahoma and Homewood. At the intersection with N Lake Blvd/Hwy 28, Tahoe City's commercial strip, turn left to stay on Hwy 89 for another 5 miles northwest to Squaw Valley Rd.

- - - - - - - - - - - - - - - - -

③ Squaw Valley

After stopping in Tahoe City for supplies and to refuel your stomach and the car, it's a short drive up to **Squaw Valley Alpine Meadows** (🕿800-403-0206; www.squawalpine.com; 1960 Squaw Valley Rd, off Hwy 89, Olympic Valley; adult/child 5-12yr/youth 13-22yr $169/110/144; ⏱9am-4pm;), a mega-size ski resort that hosted the 1960 Winter Olympics. You could spend a whole winter weekend here and not ski the same run twice. Hold on tight as the aerial tram rises over the granite ledges of the Tram Face to High Camp at a lofty 8200ft, where you can sip a cocktail while being mesmerized by vistas of the lake so very far below. In summer, families crowd the outdoor swimming pool, disc-golf course, ziplines and the hiking and mountain-biking trails radiating from High Camp. The thrilling **Tahoe Via Ferrata** (877-873-5376; www.tahoevia.com; 1985 Squaw Valley Rd; half-day/full day $99/149) takes climbers, who are clipped to cables, along a network of steel anchors ascending the afore-mentioned Tram Face, which looms over the ski village. Hold on tight – there's more than 1000ft of elevation gain!

The Drive » Backtrack out of Squaw Valley, turning left onto Hwy 89 and driving north for about 8 miles. Before reaching I-80, turn right onto W River St for another mile to downtown Truckee.

- - - - - - - - - - - - - - - - - -

TRIP HIGHLIGHT

❹ Truckee

Cradled by mountains and forests, this speck of a town is steeped in Old West history. Truckee was put on the map by the railroad, grew rich on logging and ice harvesting, and found Hollywood fame with the 1924 filming of Charlie Chaplin's *The Gold Rush*.

The aura of the Old West still lingers over Truckee's teensy one-horse downtown, where railroad workers and lumberjacks once milled about in raucous saloons, bawdy brothels and

shady gambling halls. But an influx of entre-preneurs and youthful newcomers from the San Francisco Bay Area and beyond has infused the town with a fun-loving energy. Most of the late 19th-century buildings now contain festive restaurants and bars, and upscale boutiques.

Truckee is close to a dozen downhill and cross-country ski resorts, most famously **Northstar California** (530-562-1010; www.northstarcalifornia.com; 5001 Northstar Dr, off Hwy 267; adult/child 5-12yr/youth 13-18yr $169/100/139; 8am-5pm), where ski lifts also transport summer hikers and mountain bikers into the highlands.

p225

The Drive » In downtown Truckee, cross over the railroad tracks and the river, following Brockway Rd southeast for 1.5 miles. Turn right onto Hwy 267 back toward Lake Tahoe, passing Northstar ski resort before cruising downhill to the lakeshore town of Kings Beach, 10 miles away.

- - - - - - - - - - - - - - - - - -

TRIP HIGHLIGHT

❺ Kings Beach & Tahoe Vista

On summer weekends, sun-seekers converge on picturesque **Kings Beach State Recreation Area** (530-523-3203; www.parks.ca.gov; off Hwy 28; per car May-Sep $10, Oct-Apr $5; 6am-10pm; P 🚻 🐶), especially the picnic

tables, barbecue grills and boat rentals. **Adrift Tahoe** (530-546-4112; www.standuppaddletahoe.com; 8338 N Lake Blvd; rentals per hour $25-50, per day from $80; 8am-6pm Jun-Aug, 10am-6pm Sep-May; 🚻) handles kayak, outrigger canoe and stand-up paddle-boarding (SUP) rentals, paddling lessons and tours. Just inland, the 1920s **Old Brockway Golf Course** (530-546-9909; www.oldbrockwaygolf.com; 400 Brassie Ave, cnr Hwys 267 & 28; green fees $40-70, club/cart rental from $25/20) runs along pine-bordered fair-ways where Hollywood celebs once hobnobbed.

Lake Tahoe

Spread southeast along Hwy 28, **Tahoe Vista** has more public beaches than any other lakeshore town. Lose the crowds on the hiking and mountain-biking trails or disc-golf course at **North Tahoe Regional Park** (📞530-546-4212; www.northtahoeparks.com; 6600 Donner Rd, off National Ave; per car $5; ⏰7am-9pm Jun-Aug, 7am-7pm Sep & Oct, 7am-5pm Nov-May; P 🚻 👪), which also has a snow-sledding hill and cross-country ski and snowshoe trails in winter. In summer, local hikers, picnickers and disc-golf fans keep the park just as busy.

🍴 🛏 p225

The Drive » East of Kings Beach, Hwy 28 barrels uphill across the California–Nevada border past the small-potatoes casinos of Crystal Bay before reaching Incline Village just a few miles later.

6 Crystal Bay & Incline Village

Crossing into Nevada, the neon starts to flash and old-school gambling palaces appear. Try your luck at the gambling tables or catch a live-music show at the **Crystal Bay Casino** (📞775-833-6333; www.crystalbaycasino.com; 14 Hwy 28; P). Straddling the state border, the currently closed **Cal-Neva Resort & Casino** evokes a colorful history of ghosts, mobsters and ex-owner Frank Sinatra. Oracle cofounder and billionaire Larry Ellison purchased the property in 2018, and slow-moving plans are afoot to develop a new resort here. Ask about the secret tunnels if it ever reopens.

One of Lake Tahoe's ritziest communities, **Incline Village** is a gateway to winter ski resorts. During summer, you can tour the eccentric **Thunderbird Lodge** (📞800-468-2463; www.thunderbirdtahoe.org;

DETOUR: DONNER LAKE

Start: **4** Truckee

Donner Summit is where the infamous Donner Party became trapped during the fierce winter of 1846–47. Their grisly tale of survival – and cannibalism – is chronicled inside the visitor center at **Donner Memorial State Park** (☏530-582-7892; www.parks.ca.gov; Donner Pass Rd; per car May-Sep $10, Oct-Apr $5; ☉visitor center 10am-5pm; P🚻), where tree-lined **Donner Lake** (www.donnerlakemarina.com; P🚻) offers sandy beaches. Further west, popular municipal **West End Beach** (☏530-582-7777; www.tdrpd.com; 15888 S Shore Dr, off Donner Pass Rd; adult/child 2-17yr $6/5; ☉sunrise-sunset; 🚻) has a roped-off swimming area for kids, and kayak, paddleboat and stand-up paddleboarding (SUP) rentals. Pull over for delicious homemade ice cream at **Little Truckee Ice Creamery** (☏530-587-2884; www.truckeeicecream.com; 15628 Donner Pass Rd; one scoop $5; ☉12:30-8pm Fri-Mon), a nice pit stop on the way back to Truckee from West End Beach. The state park and lakeshore are just a few miles east of Truckee via Donner Pass Rd.

The Drive » Beyond the stop-and-go traffic of Incline Village, Hwy 28 winds south, staying high above Lake Tahoe's east shore, offering peekaboo lake views and roadside pull-offs, from where locals scramble down the cliffs to hidden beaches. It's a slow-moving 13 miles south to Spooner Lake.

----

7 Lake Tahoe-Nevada State Park

With pristine beaches and miles of wilderness trails for hikers, mountain bikers, skiers and snowshoers, **Lake Tahoe-Nevada State Park** (☏775-831-0494; www.parks.nv.gov; per car/bicycle $10/2; ☉8am-1hr after sunset; P) is the east shore's big draw. Summer crowds splash in the warm, turquoise waters and sun themselves on the white, boulder-strewn beaches of **Sand Harbor**, a few miles south of Incline Village. The 15-mile **Flume Trail**, a mountain biker's holy grail, starts further south at **Spooner Lake**, where anglers fish along the shore (no swimming – too many leeches!). It's just north of the Hwy 50 junction.

adult/child 6-12yr from $45/19; ☉tours 10am-2pm Tue-Sat late Jun-late Sep, Tue, Fri & Sat mid-May–mid-Jun & late Sep–mid-Oct; 🚻), a historical mansion only accessible by bus, boat or kayak. Or drive northeast up Hwy 431 into the Mt Rose Wilderness, a gateway to miles of unspoiled terrain, including easy wildflower walks at **Tahoe Meadows**. The new **East Shore Trail** (www.tahoefund.org; Hwy 28) is a paved 3-mile path linking Incline Village with Sand Harbor State Park. Open to walkers and cyclists, the trail overlooks the lake and is lined with viewpoints and interpretive markers.

Eating & Sleeping

South Lake Tahoe ❶

✗ Sprouts Vegetarian $

(✎530-541-6969; www.sproutscafetahoe.com; 3123 Harrison Ave; mains $8-12; ⊘8am-8pm; 🅟 ♿) Cheerful chatter greets you at this energetic, mostly organic cafe that gets extra kudos for its juices and smoothies. A healthy menu will have you noshing happily on satisfying soups, rice bowls, sandwiches, burrito wraps, tempeh burgers and fresh salads.

✗ Naked Fish Sushi $$

(✎530-541-3474; www.thenakedfish.com; 3940 Lake Tahoe Blvd; sushi $6-12, mains $16-23; ⊘5-10pm Mon-Thu, 5-10:30pm Fri & Sat) With sushi chefs in ski caps, 'Rock the Casbah' rolling from the speakers and eclectic art adorning the walls, it's easy to feel not quite cool enough as you enter this oft-recommended raw fish joint. But then you taste the Hidden Dragon roll and you know you're right where you should be.

▭ Coachman Hotel Boutique Hotel $$

(✎530-545-6460; www.coachmantahoe.com; 4100 Pine Blvd; r $224-278, ste $314; 🅟 🛜 ♨ ♿) This modernly reimagined motel sports a hunting-lodge chic. Wooden pegs for your clothes and rubber mats for your boots give rooms a functional feel, but thoughtful amenities such as free nightly s'mores by the fire pit, a breakfast room and a welcoming bar for coffee and alcohol encourage conversation and community.

▭ Alder Inn Motel $$

(✎530-544-4485; www.alderinn.com; 1072 Ski Run Blvd; r $190-225; 🅟 🛜 ♨ ♿) This hospitable inn on the Heavenly ski-shuttle route charms with color schemes that pop, pillow-top mattresses, organic bath goodies, mini-refrigerators, microwaves and flat-screen TVs. Dip your toes in the pool in summer.

Truckee ❹

✗ Moody's Bistro & Lounge Californian $$

(✎530-587-8688; www.moodysbistro.com; 10007 Bridge St; mains lunch $15-19, dinner

$17-49; ⊘11:30am-10pm) With its sophisticated supper-club looks and live jazz (Thursday through Saturday evenings), this gourmet restaurant in the **Truckee Hotel** (www.truckeehotel. com; r $149-229; 🛜) oozes urban flair. Convivial weekend crowds bring the fun. Only fresh, organic and locally grown ingredients appear in the chef's concoctions, such as pork loin with sweet potato puree, Neapolitan pizza with wild mushrooms and baby kale, and a Gruyère cheeseburger.

▭ Cedar House Sport Hotel Boutique Hotel $$

(✎530-582-5655; www.cedarhousesporthotel. com; 10918 Brockway Rd; r/ste from $195/315; 🅟 @ 🛜 ♨) This chic, environmentally conscious contemporary lodge aims at getting folks out into nature. It boasts countertops made from recycled paper, 'rain chains' that redistribute water from the green roof garden, low-flow plumbing and in-room recycling. However, it doesn't skimp on plush robes, sexy platform beds with pillow-top mattresses, flat-screen TVs or the outdoor hot tub. It also houses **Stella** (mains $12-28; ⊘5-9pm Wed-Sun) dining room.

Kings Beach & Tahoe Vista ❺

✗ Old Post Office Cafe American $

(✎530-546-3205; 5245 N Lake Blvd; mains $10-16; ⊘6:30am-2pm; ♿) Head west of town toward Carnelian Bay, where this always-packed wooden shack serves scrumptious breakfasts: buttery potatoes, eggs Benedict, biscuits with gravy, fluffy omelets with lotsa fillings and fresh-fruit smoothies. Waits for a table get long on summer and winter weekends, so roll up early.

▭ Franciscan Lakeside Lodge Cabin $$

(✎530-546-6300; www.franciscanlodge.com; 6944 N Lake Blvd; cabins $186-493; 🅟 🛜 ♨) Spend the day on a private sandy beach or in the outdoor pool, then light the barbecue grill after sunset – now that's relaxation. All of the simple cabins, cottages and suites have kitchenettes. Lakeside lodgings have better beach access and views, but roomier cabins near the back of the complex tend to be quieter.

Classic Trip

Yosemite, Sequoia & Kings Canyon National Parks

21

Drive up into the lofty Sierra Nevada, where glacial valleys and ancient forests overfill the windshield scenery. Go climb a rock, pitch a tent or photograph wildflowers and wildlife.

TRIP HIGHLIGHTS

50 miles

Tunnel View
Iconic view of the valley from this spectacular perch

START
Tuolumne Meadows

55 miles

Yosemite Valley
Where waterfalls tumble over giant granite cliffs

2 **3**
Wawona Glacier Point

320 miles

Cedar Grove
Drop into one of the USA's deepest canyons

Grant Grove **8**

Fresno

9

FINISH
Mineral King Valley

Giant Forest
Circumambulate the world's biggest trees

390 miles

**5–7 DAYS
450 MILES / 725KM**

GREAT FOR...

BEST TIME TO GO

April and May for waterfalls; June to September for full access.

ESSENTIAL PHOTO

Yosemite Valley from panoramic Tunnel View.

BEST SCENIC DRIVE

Kings Canyon Scenic Byway to Cedar Grove.

Yosemite, Sequoia & Kings Canyon National Parks

21

Glacier-carved valleys resting below dramatic peaks make Yosemite an all-ages playground. Here you can witness earth-shaking waterfalls, clamber up granite domes and camp out by high-country meadows where wildflowers bloom in summer. Home to the USA's deepest canyon and the biggest tree on the planet, Sequoia and Kings Canyon National Parks justify detouring further south into the Sierra Nevada, which conservationist John Muir called 'The Range of Light.'

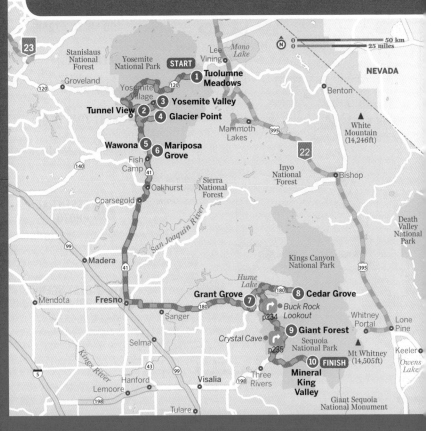

① Tuolumne Meadows

Tuolumne Meadows makes for an impressive introduction to the Yosemite area. These are the Sierra Nevada's largest subalpine meadows, with fields of wildflowers, bubbling streams, ragged granite peaks and cooler temperatures at an elevation of 8600ft. Hikers can find a paradise of trails to tackle, or unpack a picnic basket by the stream-fed meadows.

Note that the route crossing the Sierra and passing by the meadows, **Tioga Rd** (a 19th-century wagon road and Native American trading route),

LINK YOUR TRIP

22 Eastern Sierra Scenic Byway

From Yosemite's Tuolumne Meadows, roll over high-elevation Tioga Pass and downhill toward Mono Lake, a 20-mile trip.

23 Highway 49 Through Gold Country

En route between Yosemite Valley and Tuolumne Meadows, turn west onto Hwy 120, then follow Hwy 49 north to Sonora, a 70-mile drive away.

is completely closed by snow in winter. It usually reopens in May or June and remains passable until October or November.

Nine miles west of the meadows, a sandy half-moon beach wraps around **Tenaya Lake**, tempting you to brave some of the park's coldest swimming. Sunbathers lie upon rocks that rim the lake's northern shore. A few minutes further west, stop at **Olmsted Point**. Overlooking a lunar-type landscape of glaciated granite, you can gaze deeply down Tenaya Canyon to Half Dome's backside.

🛏 p236

The Drive » From Tuolumne Meadows it's 50 miles to Yosemite Valley, following Tioga Rd (Hwy 120), turning south onto Big Oak Flat Rd, then east onto El Portal Rd. There's one must-do stop before entering the valley proper, Tunnel View, so follow Wawona Rd west for a few miles where it forks with Southside Dr. You'll know you've arrived when you see all the other parked cars.

TRIP HIGHLIGHT

② Tunnel View

For your first, spectacular look into Yosemite Valley, pull over at Tunnel View, a vista that has inspired painters, poets, naturalists and adventurers for centuries. On the right, Bridalveil Fall swells with snowmelt in late spring, but by late summer it's a mere

whisper, often lifted and blown aloft by the wind. Spread below you are the pine forests and meadows of the valley floor, with the sheer face of El Capitan rising on the left and, in the distance straight ahead, iconic granite Half Dome.

The Drive » Merge carefully back onto eastbound Wawona Rd, which continues downhill into Yosemite Valley, full of confusingly intersecting one-way roads. Drive east along the Merced River on Southside Dr past the Bridalveil Fall turnoff. Almost 6 miles from Tunnel View, turn left and drive across Sentinel Bridge to Yosemite Village's day-use parking lots. Ride free shuttle buses that circle the valley.

TRIP HIGHLIGHT

③ Yosemite Valley

From the bottom looking up, this dramatic valley cut by the meandering Merced River is song-inspiring, and not just for birds: rippling meadow grasses; tall pines; cool, impassive pools reflecting granite monoliths; and cascading, glacier-cold white-water ribbons.

At busy Yosemite Village, start inside the **Yosemite Valley Visitor Center** (☏209-372-0200; www.nps.gov/yose; 9035 Village Dr; ☺9am-5pm), with its thought-provoking history and nature displays and free *Spirit of Yosemite* film screenings. At the nearby **Yosemite Museum** (www.nps.gov/yose; 9037 Village Dr; ☺9am-5pm

summer, 10am-4pm rest of year, often closed noon-1pm), Western landscape paintings are hung beside Native American baskets and beaded clothing.

The valley's famous waterfalls are thunderous cataracts in May but mere trickles by late July. Triple-tiered **Yosemite Falls** is North America's tallest, while **Bridalveil Fall** is hardly less impressive. A strenuous, often slippery staircase beside Vernal Fall leads you,

gasping, right to the top edge of the waterfall, where rainbows pop in clouds of mist. Keep hiking up the same Mist Trail to the top of **Nevada Fall** for a heady 5.5-mile round-trip trek.

In midsummer you can rent a raft at Curry Village and float down the Merced River. The serene stretch between Stoneman Bridge and Sentinel Beach is gentle enough for kids. Or take the whole family to see the stuffed wildlife mounts at the hands-on **Nature Center at Happy Isles** (☎209-372-4207; artcenter@ yosemiteconservancy.org; Happy Isle Loop Rd; classes

$10-20), east of Curry Village.

✕ 🛏 p236

The Drive ⟫ Use Northside Dr to loop round and join Wawona Rd again. Follow Wawona Rd/ Hwy 41 up out of the valley. After 9 miles, turn left onto Glacier Point Rd at the Chinquapin intersection, driving 15 more miles to Glacier Point.

❹ Glacier Point

In just over an hour you can zip from Yosemite Valley up to head-spinning Glacier Point. Note that the final 10 miles of Glacier Point Rd is closed by snow in winter, usually from November through April or May.

HIKING HALF DOME & AROUND YOSEMITE VALLEY

Over 800 miles of hiking trails in Yosemite National Park fit hikers of all abilities. Take an easy half-mile stroll on the valley floor or underneath giant sequoia trees, or venture out all day on a quest for viewpoints, waterfalls and lakes in the mountainous high country.

Some of the park's most popular hikes start right in Yosemite Valley, including to the top of **Half Dome** (16-mile round trip), the most famous of all. It follows a section of the John Muir Trail and is strenuous, difficult and best tackled in two days with an overnight in Little Yosemite Valley. Reaching the top can only be done in summer after park rangers have installed fixed cables; depending on snow conditions, this may occur as early as late May and the cables usually come down in mid-October. To limit the cables' notorious human logjams, the park now requires permits for day hikers, but the route is still nerve-racking because hikers must share the cables. Advance permits go on sale by preseason lottery in early spring, with a limited number available via another daily lottery two days in advance during the hiking season. Permit regulations and prices keep changing; check the park website (www.nps.gov/yose) for current details.

The less ambitious or physically fit will still have a ball following the **Mist Trail** as far as Vernal Fall (2.5-mile round trip), the top of Nevada Fall (5.5-mile round trip) or idyllic Little Yosemite Valley (8-mile round trip). The **Four Mile Trail** (9-mile round trip) up to Glacier Point is a strenuous but satisfying climb to a glorious viewpoint. If you've got the kids in tow, nice and easy valley walks include to **Mirror Lake** (2-mile round trip) and viewpoints at the base of thundering **Yosemite Falls** (1-mile round trip) and lacy **Bridalveil Fall** (0.5-mile round trip).

During winter the road remains open as far as the Badger Pass Ski Area, but snow tires and tire chains are required.

Rising over 3000ft above the valley floor, dramatic **Glacier Point** (7214ft) practically puts you at eye level with Half Dome. Glimpse what John Muir and US president Teddy Roosevelt saw when they camped here in 1903: the waterfall-strewn Yosemite Valley below and the distant peaks ringing Tuolumne Meadows. To get away from the crowds, hike a little way down the Panorama Trail, just south of the crowded main viewpoint.

On your way back from Glacier Point, take time out for a 2-mile hike up **Sentinel Dome** or out to **Taft Point** for incredible 360-degree valley views.

The Drive » Drive back downhill past Badger Pass Ski Area, turning left at the Chinquapin intersection and winding south through thick forest on Wawona Rd/Hwy 41. After almost 13 curvy miles you'll reach Wawona, with its lodge, visitor center, general store and gas station, all on your left.

---

5 Wawona

At Wawona, a 45-minute drive south of the valley, drop by the **Pioneer Yosemite History Center** (www.nps.gov/yose/plan yourvisit/upload/pyhc.pdf; rides adult/child $5/4; ⏱24hr,

rides 10am-2pm Wed-Sun May-Sep; P ♿), with its covered bridge, pioneer-era buildings and historic Wells Fargo office. In summer you can take a short, bumpy stagecoach ride and really feel like you're living in the past. Peek inside the **Wawona Visitor Center** (☎209-375-9531; ⏱8:30am-5pm May-Oct) at the recreated studio of 19th-century artist Thomas Hill, hung with romantic Sierra Nevada landscape paintings. On summer evenings, imbibe a civilized cocktail in the lobby lounge of the Wawona Hotel (p237), where pianist Tom Bopp often plays tunes from Yosemite's bygone days.

🛏 p237

The Drive » By car, follow Wawona Rd/Hwy 41 south for 4.5 miles to the park's south entrance, where you must leave your car at the new parking lot. A free shuttle will take you to Mariposa Grove.

6 Mariposa Grove

Wander giddily around the **Mariposa Grove** (⏱8am-8pm summer, hours vary rest of year), home of the 1800-year-old Grizzly Giant and 500 other monumental sequoias that tower above your head. Nature trails wind through this popular grove, but you can only hear yourself think above the noise of vacationing crowds during the early morning or evening. Notwithstanding a cruel hack job back in 1895, the walk-through California Tunnel Tree continues to survive, so pose your family in front and snap away. If you've got the energy, make a round-trip pilgrimage on foot to the fallen Wawona Tunnel Tree in the upper grove.

The Drive » From Yosemite's south entrance station, it's a 115-mile, three-hour trip to Kings Canyon National Park.

WINTER WONDERLANDS

When the temperature drops and the white stuff falls, there are still tons of fun outdoor activities around the Sierra Nevada's national parks. In Yosemite, strap on some skis or a snowboard and go tubing downhill off Glacier Point Rd; plod around Yosemite Valley on a ranger-led snowshoe tour; or just try to stay upright on ice skates at Curry Village. Further south in Sequoia and Kings Canyon National Parks (p233), the whole family can go snowshoeing or cross-country skiing among groves of giant sequoias. Before embarking on a winter trip to the parks, check road conditions on the official park websites or by calling ahead. Don't forget to put snow tires on your car, and always carry tire chains too.

Classic Trip

WHY THIS IS A CLASSIC TRIP
BY MICHAEL GROSBERG, WRITER

When city life gets claustrophobic, the Sierra Nevada region beckons me. This drive takes you through scenery out of an Albert Bierstadt painting or a CGI version of the American West. Out of the car and into the wilderness, your thoughts become meditative as the rhythm of your walking pace and the challenge of the terrain are the only concerns.

Above: Pioneer Yosemite History Center, Wawona
Left: Tioga Pass, Yosemite National Park
Right: Giant sequoia in Sequoia National Park

DAVIDHOFFMANN PHOTOGRAPHY / SHUTTERSTOCK ©

Follow Hwy 41 south 60 miles to Fresno, then slingshot east on Hwy 180 for another 50 miles, climbing out of the Central Valley back into the mountains. Keep left at the Hwy 198 intersection, staying on Hwy 180 toward Grant Grove.

----

❼ Grant Grove

Through **Sequoia and Kings Canyon National Parks** (📞559-565-3341; www.nps.gov/seki; 7-day entry per car $35; P 🚹), roads seem barely to scratch the surface of the twin parks' beauty. To see real treasures, you'll need to get out and stretch your legs. North of Big Stump entrance station in Grant Grove Village, turn left and wind downhill to **General Grant Grove** (N Grove Trail; P 🚹), where you'll see some of the park's landmark giant sequoia trees along a paved path. You can walk right through the Fallen Monarch, a massive, fire-hollowed trunk that's done duty as cabin, hotel, saloon and horse stable. For views of Kings Canyon and the peaks of the Great Western Divide, follow a narrow, winding side road (closed in winter; no RVs or trailers) starting behind the John Muir Lodge for over 2 miles up to **Panoramic Point** (🕒summer only).

The Drive >> Kings Canyon National Park's main visitor areas, Grant Grove and Cedar Grove, are linked by the narrow, twisting Kings Canyon

Classic Trip

Scenic Byway (Hwy 180), which dramatically descends into the canyon. Expect spectacular views all along this outstandingly scenic 30-mile drive. Note: Hwy 180 from the Hume Lake turnoff to Cedar Grove is closed during winter (usually mid-November through mid-April).

TRIP HIGHLIGHT

8 Cedar Grove

Serpenting past chiseled rock walls laced with waterfalls, Hwy 180 plunges down to the Kings River, where roaring white water ricochets off the granite cliffs of North America's deepest canyon, technically speaking. Pull over partway down at **Junc-**

tion View overlook for an eyeful, then keep rolling down along the river to **Cedar Grove Village**. East of the village, **Zumwalt Meadow** is the place for spotting birds, mule deer and black bears. If the day is hot and your swimming gear is handy, stroll from Road's End to **Muir Rock**, a large flat-top river boulder where John Muir once gave outdoor talks that's now a popular summer swimming hole. Starting from **Road's End**, a very popular day hike climbs 4 miles each way to **Mist Falls**, which thunders in late spring.

The Drive >> Backtrack from Road's End nearly 30 miles up Hwy 180. Turn left onto Hume Lake Rd. Curve around the lake past swimming beaches and campgrounds, turning right onto 10 Mile Rd. At Hwy 198, turn left and follow the Generals Hwy

(often closed from January to March) south for about 23 miles to the Wolverton Rd turnoff on your left.

TRIP HIGHLIGHT

9 Giant Forest

We dare you to try hugging the trees in Giant Forest, a 3-sq-mile grove protecting the park's most gargantuan specimens. Park off Wolverton Rd and walk downhill to reach the world's biggest living tree, the **General Sherman Tree**, which towers 275ft into the sky. With sore arms and sticky sap fingers, you can lose the crowds on any of many forested trails nearby. The trail network stretches all the way south to Crescent Meadow, a 5-mile one-way ramble.

By car, drive 2.5 miles south along the Generals Hwy to get schooled on sequoia ecology and fire cycles at the **Giant Forest Museum** (☎559-565-3341; www.nps.gov/seki; 47050 Generals Hwy; ⊙9am-4:30pm winter, to 6pm summer; P). Starting outside the museum, Crescent Meadow Rd makes a 6-mile loop into the Giant Forest, passing right through **Tunnel Log**. For 360-degree views of the Great Western Divide, climb the steep quarter-mile staircase up **Moro Rock**. Note: Crescent Meadow Rd is closed to traffic by winter snow; during summer, ride the free

---

DETOUR: BUCK ROCK LOOKOUT

Start: 8 Cedar Grove

To climb one of California's most evocative fire lookouts, drive east of the Generals Hwy on Big Meadows Rd into the Sequoia National Forest between Grant Grove and the Giant Forest. Follow the signs to staffed **Buck Rock Fire Lookout** (☎559-901-8151; www.buckrock.org; FR-13S04; ⊙10am-4pm mid–May-Oct). Constructed in 1923, this active fire lookout allows panoramic views from a dollhouse-sized cab lording it over the horizon from 8500ft atop a granite rise, reached by 172 spindly stairs. It's not for anyone with vertigo. Opening hours may vary seasonally, and the lookout closes during lightning storms and fire emergencies.

shuttle buses around the loop road.

The Drive » Narrowing, the Generals Hwy drops for more than 15 miles into the Sierra Nevada foothills, passing Amphitheater Point and exiting the park beyond Foothills Visitor Center. Before reaching the town of Three Rivers, turn left on Mineral King Rd, a dizzyingly scenic 25-mile road (partly unpaved, no trailers or RVs allowed and closed in winter) that switchbacks up to Mineral King Valley.

🔟 Mineral King Valley

Navigating over 700 hairpin turns, it's a winding 1½-hour drive up to the glacially sculpted Mineral King Valley (7500ft), a 19th-century silvermining camp and lumber settlement, and later a mountain retreat. Trails into the high country begin at the end of Mineral King Rd, where historic private cabins dot the valley floor, flanked by massive mountains.

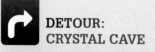

DETOUR: CRYSTAL CAVE

Start: 9 Giant Forest

Off the Generals Hwy, about 2 miles south of the Giant Forest Museum, turn right (west) onto twisting 6.5-mile-long Crystal Cave Rd for a fantastical walk inside 10,000-year-old **Crystal Cave** (www.recreation. gov; tours adult/child/youth from $16/5/8; ⊙late May-late Sep; P), carved by an underground river. Stalactites hang like daggers from the ceiling, and milky-white marble formations take the shape of ethereal curtains, domes, columns and shields. Bring a light jacket – it's 50°F (10°C) inside the cave. Buy tour tickets a month or more in advance online at www. recreation.gov; during October and November, tickets are only sold in person at the Giant Forest Museum and Foothills Visitor Center. Tour tickets are *not* available at the cave itself.

Your final destination is just over a mile past the ranger station, where the valley unfolds all of its hidden beauty, and hikes to granite peaks and alpine lakes beckon.

Note that Mineral King Rd is typically open only from late May through late October. In summer, Mineral King's marmots like to chew on parked cars, so wrap the undercarriage of your vehicle with a tarp and rope (which can be bought, though not cheaply, at the hardware store in Three Rivers).

Eating & Sleeping

Tuolumne Meadows ❶

🛏 Tioga Pass Resort   Cabin $$

(www.tiogapassresort.com; Hwy 120; d $145, cabins $180-280; ☺Jun-Sep) Situated at a whopping 9550ft and only 2 miles east of Tioga Pass, this is as close to a Yosemite experience as you can get without staying in the park. Founded in 1914, this high-country resort attracts a fiercely loyal clientele to its quiet, comfortable, woodsy cabins (most with full kitchen) beside Lee Vining Creek. Walk-ins can sometimes snag a cancellation.

🛏 Tuolumne Meadows Lodge   Cabin $$

(☎reservations 888-413-8869; www. travelyosemite.com; tent cabins $160; ☺mid-Jun–mid-Sep) Set amid the magnificent high country, about 60 miles from Yosemite Valley off Tioga Rd, this option attracts hikers to its 69 canvas tent cabins with two or four beds each, a wood-burning stove and candles (no electricity); showers available. Breakfast and dinner are offered (surcharge applies; dinner reservations required). A fork of the Tuolumne River runs through the property.

Yosemite Valley ❸

✗ Mountain Room Restaurant   American $$$

(☎209-372-1281; www.travelyosemite.com; Yosemite Valley Lodge, 9006 Yosemite Lodge Dr; mains $22-50; ☺5-9pm; 🖉 🐾) With a killer view of Yosemite Falls, the window tables at this casual yet elegant contemporary restaurant are a hot commodity. Plates of NY strip steak, roasted acorn squash and locally caught mountain trout woo diners, who are seated beside gallery-quality nature photographs. Reservations accepted only for groups larger than eight.

🛏 Curry Village   Cabin $$

(☎front desk 209-372-8333, reservations 888-413-8869; www.travelyosemite.com; tent cabins from $135, r from $260, cabins with bath from $209; ☺daily mid-Mar–late Nov, Sat & Sun early Jan–mid-Mar; 🅿 😅 🛜 🐾) Founded in 1899 as summertime Camp Curry, this 'village' has hundreds of units squished together beneath towering evergreens. The canvas cabins (heated or unheated) – basically glorified tents – are an atmospheric compromise for those who crave a few creature comforts (bed, sheets, shelving units and safe). There are 18 motel-style rooms in Stoneman House, including a loft suite that sleeps six. For more comfort, quiet and privacy, get one of the cozy wood cabins, which have vintage posters. Cabin 819, with its fireplace, sofa bed and king-size bed, is probably the most luxurious of the bunch. The village, which has an amphitheater for naturalist talks, several eating options, a small grocery, and bike and raft rental kiosks, is off Southside Dr.

🛏 Ahwahnee   Historic Hotel $$$

(☎reservations 888-413-8869; www. travelyosemite.com; r/ste from $580/1400; 🅿 😅 @ 🛜 🐾) The crème de la crème of Yosemite's lodging, this sumptuous historic property (briefly renamed the Majestic Hotel) dazzles with soaring ceilings and atmospheric lounges featuring mammoth stone fireplaces. Classic rooms have inspiring views of Glacier Point, Half Dome and Yosemite Falls. Cottages are scattered on the immaculate lawn next to the hotel. For high season and holidays, book a year ahead.

🛏 Yosemite Valley Lodge   Motel $$$

(☎209-372-1001, reservations 888-413-8869; www.travelyosemite.com; 9006 Yosemite Lodge Dr; r from $260; 🅿 😅 @ 🛜 🐾) A short walk from Yosemite Falls, this low-slung complex contains a wide range of eateries, a lively bar, a big pool and other amenities. The rooms, spread out over 15 buildings, feel like they're a cross between a motel and a lodge, with rustic wooden furniture and nature photography. Rooms have cable TV, fridge and coffeemaker, and small patios or balcony panoramas. Check-in can take a long time, and wi-fi is available but spotty and slow. Parking is free but fills up quickly for the day. Around 8pm it becomes easy to find a spot.

Wawona ⑤

⭐ Wawona Hotel   Historic Hotel $$
(⌨ reservations 888-413-8869; www.travelyosemite.com; 8308 Wawona Rd; r with/without bath from $220/150; ⌚ mid-Mar–late Nov & mid-Dec–early Jan; 🅿 ⊖ 🐾 📷) This National Historic Landmark, dating from 1879, is a collection of six graceful, whitewashed New England–style buildings flanked by wide porches. The 104 rooms – with no phone or TV – have Victorian-style furniture and other period items, and about half the rooms share bathrooms, with nice robes provided for the walk there. Wi-fi is available in the annex building only.
The grounds are lovely and fairly idyllic on sunny spring days, with a spacious lawn dotted with Adirondack chairs.

Kings Canyon National Park

⭐ John Muir Lodge   Lodge $$$
(⌨ 877-436-9617; www.visitsequoiakingscanyon.com; 86728 Hwy 180, Grant Grove Village; r $250-280; 🅿 ⊖ 🐾) An atmospheric building hung with historical black-and-white photographs, this is a place to lay your head and still feel like you're in the forest. Wide porches have rocking chairs, and homespun rooms contain rough-hewn wooden furniture and patchwork bedspreads. On chilly nights, cozy up to the big stone fireplace with a board game.

⭐ Hume Lake Campground   Campground $
(www.fs.usda.gov; Hume Lake Rd; tent & RV sites $27; ⌚ mid-May–mid-Sep; 🐾) Almost always full, yet still managing a laid-back atmosphere, this campground operated by California Land Management offers 65 relatively uncrowded, shady campsites at 5250ft. A handful come with views of the lake, which is good for swimming. It's on the northern shore and has picnic tables,

campfire rings, flush toilets and drinking water. Reservations highly recommended. Bookable online at www.recreation.gov.

Sequoia National Park

⭐ Lodgepole Campground   Campground $
(www.nps.gov/seki; Lodgepole Rd; tent & RV sites $22; ⌚ mid-Apr–late Nov; 🐾) Closest to the Giant Forest area, with more than 200 closely packed sites, this place fills quickly because of its proximity to Kaweah River swimming holes and Lodgepole Village amenities. The 16 walk-in sites are more private. Flush toilets, picnic tables, fire rings, drinking water and bear lockers are available. Reservations are possible (and strongly recommended) from late May through late September.

⭐ Wuksachi Lodge   Lodge $$
(⌨ info 866-807-3598, reservations 888-252-5757; www.visitsequoia.com; 64740 Wuksachi Way; r $123-340; ⌚ restaurant 7-10am, noon-2pm & 5:30-8pm; 🅿 ⊖ 🐾 🐕) Built in 1999, Wuksachi Lodge is the park's most upscale option. But don't get too excited: the wood-paneled atrium lobby has an inviting stone fireplace and forest views, but the motel-style rooms are fairly generic, with coffeemakers, mini-fridges, oak furniture and thin walls. The location near Lodgepole Village, however, is lovely, and staff members are friendly and accommodating.

⭐ Silver City Mountain Resort   Cabin $$
(⌨ 559-561-3223; www.silvercityresort.com; Mineral King Rd; cabins with/without bath from $205/165, largest cabin from $495; ⌚ late May–late Oct; 🐾) The only food-and-lodging option anywhere near these parts, this rustic, old-fashioned place rents everything from cute and cozy 1950s-era cabins to modern chalets sleeping up to eight. Bring your own sheets and towels for some of the cabins (or rent linens for $45 per cabin). It's 3.5 miles west of the ranger station. Minimum two-night booking may be required. There's a Ping-Pong table, a playground and a small pond. Some cabins don't have electricity and the property's generator usually shuts off in the evenings.

Eastern Sierra Scenic Byway

22

A straight shot north along California's arched geological backbone, Hwy 395 dazzles with high-altitude vistas, crumbling Old West ghost towns and limitless recreational distractions.

TRIP HIGHLIGHTS

FINISH ● Reno

● Carson City

220 miles

Bodie State Historic Park
A haunting and solitary Wild West ghost town

Bridgeport ● ⑩

⑨

190 miles

Mono Lake
An eerie blue desert basin sprouting towers of tufa

⑦ ⑥

130 miles

Bishop ●

Mammoth Lakes
A snow-sports resort with summertime mountain biking

140 miles

Reds Meadow
Shuttle to an ancient volcanic formation and a splendid waterfall

● Lone Pine
START

3–5 DAYS
360 MILES / 580KM

GREAT FOR...

BEST TIME TO GO
June to September for warm days and (mostly) snow-free mountain ramblings.

 ESSENTIAL PHOTO
Sunrise or sunset in the Alabama Hills, framed by the snowy Sierra Nevada.

☑ **BEST FOR OUTDOORS**
Hike tranquil mountain trails and camp in Mammoth Lakes.

22 Eastern Sierra Scenic Byway

The gateway to California's largest expanse of wilderness, Hwy 395 – also called the Eastern Sierra Scenic Byway – borders towering mountain vistas, glistening blue lakes and the seemingly endless forests of the eastern Sierra Nevada mountains. A lifetime of outdoor activities beckons beyond the asphalt (parts of which get traffic clogged in summer), and desolate Old West ghost towns, unique geological formations and burbling natural hot springs await exploration.

① Lone Pine

The diminutive town of Lone Pine stands as the southern gateway to the craggy jewels of the Eastern Sierra. At the southern end of town, drop by the **Museum of Western Film History** (☎760-876-9909; www.museumof westernfilmhistory.org; 701 S Main St; adult/under 12yr $5/ free; ◷10am-5pm Mon-Sat, to 4pm Sun; 🅿 ♿ 🐾), which contains exhibits of paraphernalia from the over 450 movies shot in the area. Don't miss the occasional screenings in its theater or the tricked-out Cadillac convertible in its foyer.

Just outside the center of town on Whitney Portal Rd, an otherworldly orange alpenglow makes the **Alabama Hills** a must for watching a slow-motion sunset. A frequent backdrop for movie Westerns and the *Lone Ranger* TV series, the rounded earthen-colored mounds stand out against the steely gray foothills and jagged pinnacles of the Sierra range, and a number of graceful rock arches are within easy hiking distance of the roads.

🍴 p247

The Drive ❯❯ From Lone Pine, the jagged incisors of the Sierra surge skyward in all their raw and fierce glory. Continue west past the Alabama Hills and then brace yourself for the dizzying ascent to road's end – a total

of 13 miles from Hwy 395. The White Mountains soar to the east, and the dramatic Owens Valley spreads below.

----

❷ Whitney Portal

At 14,505ft, the celestial granite giant of **Mt Whitney** (www.fs.usda.gov/inyo; Whitney Portal Rd) stands as the loftiest peak in the lower 48 and the obsession of thousands of high-country hikers every summer. Desperately coveted permits (assigned by advance lottery) are your only passport to the summit, though drop-in day trippers can swan up the mountain as far as Lone Pine Lake – about 6 miles round trip – to kick up some dust on the iconic Whitney Trail. Ravenous hikers can stop by the **Whitney Portal Store** (☏760-876-0030; www.facebook.com/WhitneyPortalStore;

CENTRAL CALIFORNIA **22** EASTERN SIERRA SCENIC BYWAY

LINK YOUR TRIP

21 Yosemite, Sequoia & Kings Canyon National Parks

In Lee Vining, go west on Hwy 120 to enter Yosemite National Park via the 9945ft Tioga Pass.

31 Life in Death Valley

From Lone Pine, head southeast on Hwys 136 and 190 to reach Panamint Springs, a western access point for Death Valley.

241

⊙ hours vary May-Nov) for enormous burgers and plate-size pancakes.

As you get a fix on this majestic megalith cradled by scores of smaller pinnacles, remember that the country's lowest point is only 80 miles (as the crow flies) east of here: Badwater in Death Valley.

The Drive ≫ Double back to Lone Pine and drive 9 miles north on divided Hwy 395. Scrub brush and tumbleweed desert occupy the valley between the copper-colored foothills of the Sierra Nevada and the White Mountain range. Well-signed Manzanar sits along the west side of the highway.

- - - - - - - - - - - - - - - - -

❸ Manzanar National Historic Site

A monument to one of the darkest chapters in US history, Manzanar unfolds across a barren and windy sweep of land cradled by snow-dipped peaks. During the height of WWII, the federal government interned more than 10,000 people of Japanese ancestry here following the attack on Pearl Harbor. Though little remains of the infamous war concentration camp, the camp's former high-school auditorium houses a superb **interpretive center** (📋760-878-2194; www.nps.gov/manz; 5001 Hwy 395; ⊙9am-4:30pm; P). Watch the 22-minute documentary film, then explore the thought-provoking

exhibits chronicling the stories of the families that languished here yet built a vibrant community. Afterwards, take a self-guided 3.2-mile driving tour around the grounds, which include a recreated mess hall and barracks, vestiges of buildings and gardens, as well as the haunting camp cemetery.

Often mistaken for Mt Whitney, 14,375ft Mt Williamson looms above this flat, dusty plain, a lonely expanse that bursts with yellow wildflowers in spring.

The Drive ≫ Continue north 6 miles on Hwy 395 to the small town of Independence. In the center of town, look for the columned Inyo County Courthouse and turn left onto W Center St. Drive six blocks through a residential area to the end of the road.

- - - - - - - - - - - - - - - - -

❹ Independence

This sleepy highway town has been a county seat since 1866 and is home to the **Eastern California Museum** (📋760-878-0258; www.inyocounty.us/ecmsite; 155 N Grant St; donation requested; ⊙10am-5pm; P 🚻). An excellent archive of Eastern Sierra history and culture, it contains one of the most complete collections of Paiute and Shoshone baskets in the country, as well as historic photographs of local rock climbers scaling Sierra peaks – including

Mt Whitney – with huge packs and no harnesses. Other highlights include artifacts from Manzanar and an exhibit about the fight to keep the region's water supply from being diverted to Los Angeles.

Fans of Mary Austin (1868–1934), renowned author of *The Land of Little Rain* and vocal foe of the desertification of the Owens Valley, can follow signs leading to her former house at **253 Market St**.

The Drive ≫ Depart north along Hwy 395 as civilization again recedes amid a buffer of dreamy granite mountains, midsize foothills and (for most

Mountain-biking around the Mammoth Lakes

of the year) an expanse of bright blue sky. Tuffs of blackened volcanic rock occasionally appear roadside. Pass through the blink-and-you'll-miss-it town of Big Pine, and enter Bishop.

5 Bishop

The second-largest town in the Eastern Sierra and about a third of the way north from Lone Pine to Reno, Bishop is a major hub for hikers, cyclists, anglers and climbers. To get a taste of what draws them here, head to the Happy and Sad Boulders areas in the strikingly unique rocky **Volcanic Tablelands** not far north of town.

Where Hwy 395 swings west, continue northeast for 4.5 miles on Hwy 6 to reach the **Laws Railroad Museum & Historic Site** (☎760-873-5950; www.lawsmuseum.org; Silver Canyon Rd; suggested donation $10; ☺10am-4pm Sep-May; ♿), a remnant of the narrow-gauge Carson and Colorado rail line that closed in 1960. Train buffs will hyperventilate over the collection of antique railcars, and kids love exploring the 1883 depot and clanging the brass bell. Dozens of historic buildings from the region have been reassembled with period artifacts to create a time-capsule village.

✕ ⊨ p247

The Drive » Back on Hwy 395, continue over 40 miles north to Hwy 203, passing Lake Crowley and the southern reaches of the Long Valley Caldera seismic hot spot. On Hwy 203 before the center of town, stop in at the Mammoth Lakes Welcome Center for excellent local and regional information.

TRIP HIGHLIGHT

6 Mammoth Lakes

Splendidly situated at 8000ft, Mammoth Lakes is an active year-round outdoor-recreation town

DETOUR: ANCIENT BRISTLECONE PINE FOREST

Start: ➍ **Independence**

For encounters with some of the earth's oldest living things, plan at least a half-day trip to the **Ancient Bristlecone Pine Forest** (☎760-873-2500; www. fs.usda.gov/inyo; White Mountain Rd; ⏲trails year-round, visitor center Fri-Mon mid-May–early Nov; P♿). These gnarled, otherworldly-looking trees thrive above 10,000ft on the slopes of the seemingly inhospitable White Mountains, a parched and stark range that once stood even higher than the Sierra. One of the oldest trees – called Methuselah – is estimated to be over 4700 years old, beating even the Great Sphinx of Giza by about two centuries.

To reach the groves, take Hwy 168 east 12 miles from Big Pine to White Mountain Rd, then turn left (north) and climb the curvy road 10 miles to **Schulman Grove**, named for the scientist who first discovered the trees' biblical age in the 1950s. The entire trip takes about one hour one way from Independence. There's access to self-guided trails near the solar-powered **Schulman Grove Visitor Center** (☎760-873-2500; www.fs.usda.gov/inyo; White Mountain Rd; per person/car $3/6; ⏲10am-5pm Jun-Aug, to 4pm Fri-Sun May-Jun). White Mountain Rd is usually closed from November to April.

buffered by alpine wilderness and punctuated by its signature 11,053ft peak, Mammoth Mountain. This ever-growing **resort complex** (☎760-934-2571, 760-934-2571, 24hr snow report 888-766-9778; www.mammothmountain.com; adult/13-17yr/5-12yr/under 5yr from $79/65/32/free) has 3100 vertical feet – enough to whet any snow-sports appetite – and an enviably long season that may last from November to June.

When the snow finally melts, the ski and snowboard resort does a quick costume change and becomes the massive **Mammoth Mountain Bike Park** (☎800-626-6684; www.mammothmountain.com; day pass adult/7-12yr $45/24; ⏲9am-6pm Jun-Sep), and with a slew of mountain-bikers decked out in body armor, it could be mistaken for the set of an apocalyptic *Mad Max* sequel. With more than 80 miles of well-tended single-track trails and a crazy terrain park, it draws those who know their knobby tires.

Year-round, a vertiginous **gondola** (☎800-626-6684; www.mammothmountain.com; Minaret Rd; adult/13-18yr/5-12yr $34/29/12; ⏲hours vary; P♿) whisks sightseers to the apex for breathless views of snow-speckled mountaintops.

✗ ⬛ p247

The Drive » Keep the car parked at Mammoth Mountain and catch the mandatory Reds Meadow shuttle bus from the Gondola Building. However, you may want to drive up 1.5 miles west and back on Hwy 203 as far as Minaret Vista to contemplate eye-popping views of the Ritter Range, the serrated Minarets and the remote reaches of Yosemite National Park.

- - - - - - - - - - - - - - - - - - -

TRIP HIGHLIGHT

➐ Reds Meadow

One of the most beautiful and varied landscapes near Mammoth is the Reds Meadow Valley, west of Mammoth Mountain. The most fascinating attraction in Reds Meadow is the surreal 10,000-year-old volcanic formation of **Devils Postpile National Monument** (☎760-934-2289; www.nps.gov/depo; shuttle day pass adult/child $8/4; ⏲Jun-Oct, weather depending). The 60ft curtains of near-vertical, six-sided basalt columns formed when rivers of molten lava slowed, cooled and cracked with perplexing symmetry. This honeycomb design is best appreciated from atop the columns, reached by a short trail. The columns are an easy half-mile hike from the **Devils Postpile Ranger Station** (📞760-934-2289; www.nps.gov/depo; Postpile Ranger Station Rd; 🕙9am-5pm mid-Jun–Sep).

From the monument, a 2.5-mile hike passing through fire-scarred forest leads to the spectacular **Rainbow Falls**, where the San Joaquin River gushes over a 101ft basalt cliff. Chances of actually seeing a rainbow forming in the billowing mist are greatest at noon. The falls can also be reached via an easy 1.5-mile walk from the Reds Meadow shuttle stop.

The Drive >> Back on Hwy 395, continue north to Hwy 158 and pull out the camera for the alpine lake and peak vistas of the June Lake Loop.

---

⑧ June Lake Loop

Under the shadow of massive Carson Peak (10,909ft), the stunning 16-mile **June Lake Loop** (Hwy 158) meanders through a picture-perfect horseshoe canyon, past the relaxed resort town of June Lake and four sparkling, fish-rich lakes: Grant, Silver, Gull and June. It's especially scenic in fall when the basin is ablaze with golden aspens. Hardy ice climbers scale its frozen waterfalls in winter.

June Lake is backed by the Ansel Adams Wilderness, which runs into Yosemite National Park. From Silver Lake, Gem and Agnew Lakes make spectacular day hikes, and boat rentals and horseback rides are available.

The Drive >> Rejoin Hwy 395 heading north, where the rounded Mono Craters dot the dry and scrubby eastern landscape and the Mono Lake Basin unfolds into view.

TRIP HIGHLIGHT

⑨ Mono Lake

North America's second-oldest lake is a quiet and mysterious expanse of deep blue water, whose glassy surface reflects jagged Sierra peaks, young volcanic cones and the unearthly tufa (*too*-fah) towers that make the lake so distinctive. Protruding from the water like drip sand castles, tufas form when calcium bubbles up from subterranean springs and combines with carbonate in the alkaline lake waters.

The salinity and alkaline levels are unfortunately too high for a pleasant swim. Instead, paddle a kayak or canoe around the weathered towers of tufa, drink in wide-open views of the Mono Craters volcanic field, and discreetly spy on the water birds that live in this unique habitat.

EASTERN SIERRA HOT SPRINGS

Nestled between the White Mountains and the Sierra Nevada near Mammoth is a tantalizing slew of natural pools with snowcapped panoramic views. When the high-altitude summer nights turn chilly and the coyotes cry, you'll never want to towel off. About 9 miles southeast of Mammoth Lakes, Benton Crossing Rd juts east off Hwy 395, accessing a delicious bounty of hot springs.

To overnight with your very own private hot-springs tub, head to the **Inn at Benton Hot Springs** (📞760-933-2287; www.bentonhotsprings.org; Hwy 120, Benton; tent & RV sites per 2 people $60-70, B&B r $92-225; 🅿❄🛜🐾), a small, historic resort in a 150-year-old former silver-mining town nestled in the White Mountains.

For detailed directions and maps, pick up Matt Bischoff's excellent *Touring Hot Springs California and Nevada: A Guide to the Best Hot Springs in the Far West* or see www.mammothweb.com/recreation/hottubbing.cfm for directions to a few.

245

The **Mono Basin Scenic Area Visitor Center** (☎760-647-3044; www.fs.usda.gov/inyo; 1 Visitor Center Dr; ⏰8am-5pm May-Sep, hours vary Oct-Dec, closed Jan-Apr; 🚹), half a mile north of Lee Vining, has interpretive displays, a bookstore and a 20-minute movie about Mono Lake.

✖ p247

The Drive » About 10 miles north of Lee Vining, Hwy 395 arrives at its highest point, Conway Summit (8148ft). Pull off at the vista point for awe-inspiring panoramas of Mono Lake, backed by the Mono Craters and June and Mammoth Mountains. Continue approximately 8 miles north, and go 13 miles east on Hwy 270 (closed in winter); the last 3 miles are unpaved.

TRIP HIGHLIGHT

⑩ Bodie State Historic Park

For a time warp back to the gold-rush era, swing by **Bodie** (☎760-616-5040; www.parks.ca.gov/bodie; Hwy 270; adult/child $8/5; ⏰9am-6pm Apr-Oct, to 4pm Nov-Mar, road often closed winter; 🅿 🐾), one of the West's most authentic and best-preserved ghost towns. Gold was discovered here in 1859, and the place grew from a bare-bones mining camp to a lawless boomtown of 10,000. Fights and murders occurred almost daily, fueled by liquor from 65 saloons, some of which doubled as brothels, gambling halls or opium dens.

The hills disgorged some $35 million worth of gold and silver in the 1870s and '80s, but when production plummeted, Bodie was abandoned, and about 200 weather-beaten buildings now sit frozen in time in this cold, barren and windswept valley. Peering through dusty windows you'll see stocked stores, furnished homes, a schoolhouse with desks and books, the jail and many other buildings. The former Miners' Union Hall now houses a **museum** and **visitor center**, and rangers conduct free tours in summer.

The Drive » Retrace your way back to Hwy 395, where you'll soon come to the big-sky settlement of Bridgeport. From here, it's approximately two hours to Reno along a lovely two-lane section of the highway that traces the bank of the snaking Walker River.

----

⑪ Reno

Nevada's second-largest city has steadily carved a non-casino niche as an all-season outdoor-recreation spot. The Truckee River bisects the heart of the mountain-ringed city, and in the heat of summer the **Truckee River Whitewater Park** (☎775-334-2270; www.reno.gov; Wingfield Park) teems with urban kayakers and swimmers bobbing along on inner tubes. Two kayak courses wrap around Wingfield Park, a small river island that hosts free concerts in summertime. **Sierra Adventures** (☎775-323-8928; www.wildsierra.com; 11 N Sierra St; kayak/inner tube per day from $39/19) offers kayak rentals, tours and lessons.

🛏 p247

Eating & Sleeping

Lone Pine ❶

✗ Alabama Hills Cafe   Diner $
(☎760-876-4675; www.alabamahillscafe.com; 111
W Post St; breakfast items $9.50-14; ⊙6am-3pm
Fri-Sun, to 2pm Mon-Thu; 🛜🚲) Just off the main
streets, the portions are big, the bread is freshly
baked and the soups are hearty. Sandwiches and
fruit pies make lunch an attractive option too. You
can also plan your drive through the **Alabama
Hills** (Movie Flat Rd/Whitney Portal Rd; 🅿)
with the help of the map on the menu and rock
formations painted on the walls.

Bishop ❺

✗ Erick Schat's Bakery   Bakery $
(☎760-873-7156; www.schatsbakery.com; 763
N Main St; sandwiches $6-10; ⊙8:30am-3:30pm
Mon-Thu, to 4pm Fri, 6am-5pm Sat & Sun; 🖪)
A deservedly hyped tourist mecca filled to the
rafters with racks of fresh bread, dipping oil, jams
and other goodies, Schat's has been making
baked goods since 1938. Some of the desserts,
including the crispy cookies and bear claws, are
addictive, and call for repeated trips. Also has a
popular sandwich bar and outdoor tables.

🛏 Eastside
Guesthouse & Bivy   Guesthouse $
(☎760-784-7077; www.eastsideguesthouse.com;
777 N Main St; dm $25-35, r $120-480; ❄🛜)
With an airy blonde-wood common area for
pre- and post-hike confabs, this new guesthouse
is easily Bishop's best for laid-back travelers
who also want some creature comforts. The
young owners have designed the property with
features such as the idyllic backyard deck,
barbecue spot and pond, inspired by their own
world travels. Room furnishings are Ikea-like,
with more upscale bathroom fixtures.

Mammoth Lakes ❻

✗ Dos Alas CubaRican Cafe   Cuban $$
(☎760-965-0345; Sherwin Creek Rd; sandwiches
$12, mains $17; ⊙11:30am-2pm & 4:30-9pm
Wed, Thu & Sun, to 10pm Fri & Sat; 🛜) While its

setting, in a frontier-style timber building with
stunning mountain views, doesn't evoke the
Caribbean, this restaurant brings Cuba's flavors
alive in dishes such as *escabeches* (pickled-base
marinade with chicken, shrimp or vegetables) and
a tasty *picadillo con arroz* (ground-beef stew).
Live music from 6:30pm Wednesday.

🛏 Tamarack Lodge   Lodge, Cabin $$
(☎760-934-2442; www.tamaracklodge.com; 163
Twin Lakes Rd; r from $140, without bathroom
from $110, cabins $255-425; 🅿🐾@🛜🖪) In
business since 1924, this charming year-round
resort on Lower Twin Lake has a cozy fireplace
lodge, a bar and an excellent restaurant, and 11
rustic-style rooms and 35 cabins. The cabins
range from very simple to simply deluxe, and
have full kitchen, private bathroom, porch and
wood-burning stove. Some can sleep up to 10.
Daily resort fee around $20.

Mono Lake ❾

✗ Whoa Nellie Deli   American $$
(☎760-647-1088; www.whoanelliedeli.com;
Tioga Gas Mart, 22 Vista Point Rd; mains $7.50-
19; ⊙6:30am-9pm late Apr-Oct; 🖪) Years
after its famed chef moved on to **Toomey's**
at Mammoth Lakes, this Mobil-gas-station
restaurant off Hwy 120 is still, surprisingly, a darn
good place to eat. Stop in for delicious burgers,
fish tacos, wild-buffalo meatloaf and other tasty
morsels, and Mono Lake views from outdoor
picnic tables. There are live bands some nights.

Reno ⓫

🛏 Whitney Peak   Design Hotel $$
(☎775-398-5400; www.whitneypeakhotel.
com; 255 N Virginia St; r $237-280, ste $323;
🅿❄🛜🖪) What's not to love about this
independent, inventive, funky, friendly,
nonsmoking, non-gambling downtown hotel?
Spacious guest rooms have a youthful, fun vibe
celebrating the great outdoors and don't skimp
on designer creature comforts. With an external
climbing wall, a decent on-site restaurant and
friendly, professional staff, Whitney Peak is
unbeatable in Reno.

Classic Trip

Highway 49 Through Gold Country

A trip through Gold Country on winding Hwy 49 shows off California's early days, when hell-raising prospectors rushed helter-skelter into the West. Burgeoning wine regions bring modern pizzazz.

23

TRIP HIGHLIGHTS

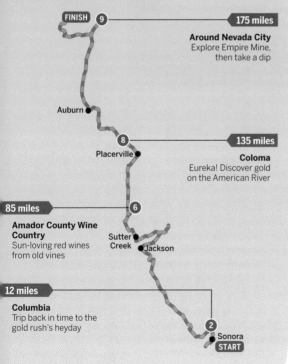

FINISH **9** ——————— **175 miles**

Around Nevada City
Explore Empire Mine, then take a dip

Auburn

8 ——————— **135 miles**

Placerville

Coloma
Eureka! Discover gold on the American River

85 miles **6**

Amador County Wine Country
Sun-loving red wines from old vines

Sutter Creek ● Jackson

12 miles

Columbia
Trip back in time to the gold rush's heyday

2 Sonora
START

3–4 DAYS
200 MILES / 322KM

GREAT FOR...

BEST TIME TO GO

May to October for sunny skies

ESSENTIAL PHOTO

Sutter's Mill, California's original gold discovery site

✓ BEST FOR SWIMMING

South Yuba River State Park

Classic Trip

23 Highway 49 Through Gold Country

When you roll into Gold Country on a sunny afternoon, the adventures along Hwy 49 recall the days when newspaper headlines screamed about gold discoveries and the Golden State was born. Today this rural region offers different riches: exploring crumbling false-front saloons, rusting mining parks, wineries in the Sierra Nevada foothills and a parade of patinaed bronze historical markers along Hwy 49, one of California's most enchantingly scenic byways.

❶ Sonora

Settled in 1848 by Mexican miners, Sonora soon became a cosmopolitan center with ornate saloons patronized by gamblers, drunkards and gold diggers. Its downtown district is so well preserved that it's frequently a location for Hollywood films, such as Clint Eastwood's *Unforgiven*. Likewise, **Railtown 1897 State Historic Park** (☏20 9-984-3953; www.parks.ca.gov; 10501 Reservoir Rd, Jamestown; adult/child $5/3, incl train ride $15/10; ⏰9:30am-4:30pm

Apr-Oct, 10am-3pm Nov-Mar, train rides 10:30am-3pm Sat & Sun Apr-Oct; P ♿) and the surrounding hills of **Jamestown**, about 4 miles southwest of Sonora along Hwy 49, have been a backdrop for more than 200 Western movies and TV shows, including *High Noon*. There's a lyrical romance to the historical railway yard, where orange poppies bloom among the rusting shells of steel goliaths. On some weekends and holidays, you can board the narrow-gauge railroad that once transported ore, lumber and miners. Making a 45-minute, 6-mile circuit, it's the best train ride in Gold Country. The park is five blocks east of Jamestown's pint-size Main St.

✕ ⊨ p258

The Drive » Follow Hwy 49 just over 2 miles north of Sonora, then turn right onto Parrots Ferry Rd at the sign for Columbia. The state historic park is 2 miles further along this two-lane country road.

TRIP HIGHLIGHT

2 Columbia

Grab suspenders and a floppy hat for **Columbia State Historic Park** (☏209-588-9128; www.parks.ca.gov; 11255 Jackson St; ⊘most businesses 10am-5pm; P ♿), near the so-called 'Gem of the Southern Mines.' It's like a miniature

🔗 LINK YOUR TRIP

24 Ebbetts Pass Scenic Byway

From Columbia, wind 13 miles northwest on Parrots Ferry Rd and Hwy 4 to Murphys, in Calaveras County wine country.

26 Sacramento Delta & Lodi

Sacramento is an hour's drive or less from such Gold Country towns as Placerville via Hwy 50 or Auburn via I-80.

251

Classic Trip

gold-rush Disneyland, but with more authenticity and heart. Four blocks of town have been preserved, around which volunteers perambulate in 19th-century dress and demonstrate gold panning. The blacksmith's shop, theater, hotels and saloon are all carefully framed windows into California's past. The yesteryear illusion of Main St is shaken only a bit by fudge shops and the occasional banjo picker or play-acting 49er whose cell phone rings. Stop by the **Columbia Museum** (209-532-3184; www.parks.ca.gov; cnr Main & State Sts; 10am-5pm Apr-Sep, to 4pm Oct-Mar) inside Knapp's Store to learn more about historical mining techniques and let your kids dress up in Old West attire. According to the hotel manager and past guests, there are two ghosts in the atmospheric Fallon Hotel. You'll have to spend the night to see if the rumors are true.

p258

The Drive » Backtrack south on Parrots Ferry Rd, veering right and then turning right to stay on Springfield Rd for just over a mile. Rejoin Hwy 49 northbound, which crosses a long bridge over an artificial reservoir. After a dozen miles or so, Hwy 49 becomes Main

St through the small town of Angels Camp.

---

❸ Angels Camp

On the southern stretch of Hwy 49, one literary giant looms over all other Western tall-tale tellers: Samuel Clemens, aka Mark Twain, who got his first big break with the short story *The Celebrated Jumping Frog of Calaveras County,* written in 1865 and set in Angels Camp. With a mix of Victorian and art-deco buildings that shelter antiques shops and cafes, this 19th-century mining town makes the most of its Twain connection. Visit the engaging **Angels Camp Museum** (209-736-2963; http://angelscamp.gov/museum; 753 S Main St; adult/child 5-11yr $7/3; 10am-4pm Thu-Mon;) for a good overview of Twain and local mining-era history. The annual **Calaveras County Fair & Jumping Frog Jubilee** (www.frogtown.org; 2465 Gun Club Rd; from $10; May;) is held at the fairgrounds just south of town on the third weekend in May. You could win $5000 if your frog beats the world-record jump (over 21ft) set by 'Rosie the Ribeter' back in 1986.

The Drive » Hwy 49 heads north of Angels Camp through rolling hillside farms and ranches. Past San Andreas, make a short detour through Mokelumne ('Moke') Hill, another historic mining town.

In Jackson, turn right onto Hwy 88 east. After 9 miles, turn left on Pine Grove-Volcano Rd for 3 miles to reach Volcano, passing Indian Grinding Rock State Historic Park en route.

---

❹ Volcano

Although the village of Volcano once yielded tons of gold and saw Civil War intrigue, today it slumbers in solitude. Huge sandstone rocks lining Sutter Creek were blasted from the surrounding hills using a hydraulic process before being scraped clean of gold-bearing dirt. Hydraulic mining had dire environmental consequences, but at its peak, miners raked in nearly $100 a day. Less than a mile southeast of town, **Black Chasm Cavern** (888-488-1960; www.caverntouring.com; 15701 Pioneer Volcano Rd, Pine Grove; adult/child $6-12yr $18.50/10; 9am-5pm Jun–mid-Sep, 10am-4pm mid-Sep–May;) has the whiff of a tourist trap, but one look at the helictite crystals – sparkling white formations in rare horizontal clusters – makes the crowds bearable. For eye-catching rock formations just outside the cavern, head to the on-site Zen Garden, where a short trail twists through a cluster of Tolkien-esque marble slabs.

Two miles southwest of town at **Indian Grinding Rock State Historic Park** (Chaw'se; 209-296-7488;

www.parks.ca.gov; 14881 Pine Grove-Volcano Rd; per car $8; ⏱ park sunrise to sunset; museum 10am-4pm; P), a limestone outcrop is covered with petroglyphs and more than 1000 *chaw'se* (mortar holes) used for grinding acorns into meal. Learn more about the Sierra Nevada's indigenous tribes inside the park's museum, shaped like a Native American *hun'ge* (roundhouse).

🛏 p258

The Drive » Backtrack along Pine Grove-Volcano Rd, turning right onto Hwy 88 for about half a mile, then turn right onto Ridge Rd, which winds for around 8 miles back to Hwy 49. Turn right and head north about a mile to Sutter Creek.

- - - - - - - - - - - - - - - - - -

⑤ Sutter Creek

Perch on the balcony of one of Main St's gracefully restored buildings and view this gem of a Gold Country town, boasting raised, arcaded sidewalks and high-balconied, false-fronted buildings that exemplify California's 19th-century frontier architecture. Pick up self-guided walking and driving tour maps at the **visitor center** (📞209-267-1344; www.suttercreek.org; 71a Main St; ⏱10am-6pm). The nearby **Sutter Creek Theatre** (📞916-425-0077; www.suttercreektheater.com; 44 Main St; tickets from $22), an 1860s saloon and billiards hall, now hosts live-music

concerts and occasionally plays, films and cultural events. The rest of the town's four-block-long Main St is crowded with antiques shops, county boutiques, cafes and tasting bars pouring regional wines and craft spirits. Welcoming **Yorba Wines** (📞209-267-8190; www.yorbawines.com; 51 Hanford St; ⏱11am-5pm) is a good place to start your tasting. You can learn more about the town's mining past at the new **Miners Bend Park** (www.suttercreekfoundation.org; Old Hwy 49; P) at the southern end of downtown. It's loaded with old mining equipment and informative signage.

The Drive » Follow Main St north of Sutter Creek for 3 miles through quaint Amador City. Back at Hwy 49, turn right and continue north toward Plymouth and Shenandoah Valley Rd.

- - - - - - - - - - - - - - - - - -

TRIP HIGHLIGHT

⑥ Amador County Wine Country

Amador County is an underdog among California's winemaking regions, but a circuit of welcoming wineries and local characters make for great sipping without any pretension. Planted with California's oldest surviving zinfandel vines, the countryside has a lot in common with its most celebrated grape varietal – bold, richly colored and earthy. Many

➡ **DETOUR: CALIFORNIA CAVERN**

Start: ③ Angels Camp

A 20-minute drive east of San Andreas via Mountain Ranch Rd, off Hwy 49 about 12 miles north of Angels Camp, **California Cavern State Historic Landmark** (📞209-736-2708; www.cavetouring.com; 9565 Cave City Rd, Mountain Ranch; adult/child from $16/8.50; ⏱10am-5pm Jun-Sep, to 4pm early Sep–mid-May; P♿) has the mother lode's most extensive system of natural underground caverns. John Muir described them as 'graceful flowing folds deeply plicated like stiff silken drapery.' Regular tours take 60 to 80 minutes, or get a group together and reserve ahead for a three- to five-hour 'Middle Earth Expedition' ($130), which includes some serious spelunking (no children under age 16 allowed). There's also a three-hour Mammoth Expedition ($89). The Trail of Lakes walking tour, available only during the wet season in winter and spring, is magical.

Classic Trip

WINE TASTING

OPEN

WHY THIS IS A CLASSIC TRIP
AMY C BALFOUR,
WRITER

Highway 49 rolls through Old West towns and crusty mining sites – all looking much like they did during their gold-rush heyday and offering a fascinating window on the past. The vineyards and wineries scattered near Plymouth, Sutter Creek and Placerville are gorgeous places to savor the history, the old vine grapes and the sweeping views of the Sierra Nevada mountains.

Above: The preserved town of Columbia
Left: Wine-tasting in Amador County
Right: Restored Shell station in the South Yuba River State Park

ALESSANDRAC / SHUTTERSTOCK ©

wineries are found along Shenandoah Valley Rd and its offshoots. For a true family affair going back 150 years stop by **Deaver Vineyards** (☏20 9-245-4099; www.deavervine-yards.com; 12455 Steiner Rd, Plymouth; tasting fee $5; ⊙10:30am-5pm; P), where nearly everyone pouring has their last name on the bottles. Down the road is chic **Iron Hub Winery** (www.ironhubwines. com; 12500 Steiner Rd; tastings $10-15; ⊙11am-5pm Fri-Mon; P🐾). With its hilltop perch and sweeping views of the Sierra Nevada foothills, this is a pretty place to sample wines and social-ize. Continue east on Shenandoah Rd to **Sobon Estate** (☏209-245-6554; www.sobonwine.com; 14430 Shenandoah Rd, Plymouth; ⊙10am-5pm Apr-Oct, to 4:30pm Nov-Mar), an envi-ronmentally conscious family-run estate with a wine-making history dat-ing to the 1850s. There's a small local history museum on-site. Back-track to **Jeff Runquist Wines** (☏209-245-6282; www.jeffruhnquistwines.com; 10776 Shenandoah Rd, Plym-outh; ⊙11am-5pm), which dominates the double-gold winners list at the San Francisco Chronicle Wine Competition every year. Locally sourced favorites here include the zinfandel and barbera.

✕ 🛏 p258

CENTRAL CALIFORNIA **23** HIGHWAY 49 THROUGH GOLD COUNTRY

255

Classic Trip

The Drive >> Turn left back onto Shenandoah Rd for 3 miles, then turn right onto Hwy 49 northbound. Less then 20 miles later, after up-and-down roller-coaster stretches, you'll arrive in downtown Placerville, south of Hwy 50.

- - - - - - - - - - - - - - - - - -

➐ Placerville

Things get livelier in 'Old Hangtown,' a nickname Placerville earned for the vigilante-justice hangings that happened here in 1849. Most buildings along Placerville's Main St date from the 1850s. Poke around antiques shops or ho-hum **Placerville Hardware** (✆530-622-1151; 441 Main St; ⊗8am-6pm Mon-Sat, 9am-5pm Sun), the oldest continuously operating hardware store west of the Mississippi River. Downtown dive bars get an annual cleaning at Christmas and are great for knocking elbows with odd birds.

For family-friendly shenanigans, head 1 mile north of town via Bedford Ave to **Hangtown's Gold Bug Park & Mine** (✆530-642-5207; www.goldbugpark.org; 2635 Gold Bug Lane; tour adult/child $9/5; ⊗10am-4pm Apr-Oct, noon-4pm Sat & Sun Nov-Mar; P 🚻), where hard-hatted visitors can descend into a 19th-century mine shaft, or try gem panning (per hour $2).

Around Placerville, El Dorado County's mountainous terrain and volcanic soil combine with intense summertime heat and cooling night breezes off the Sierra Nevada to produce some noteworthy wines. Welcoming wineries on Apple Hill north of Hwy 50 include **Lava Cap Winery** (✆530-621-0175; www.lavacap.com; 2221 Fruit Ridge Rd; tasting fee $5; ⊗10am-5pm; P), which sells well-stocked picnic baskets, and **Boeger Winery** (✆530-622-8094; www.boegerwinery.com; 1709 Carson Rd; tasting $5-15; ⊗10am-5pm; P), whose vineyards were first planted during the gold rush.

✖ p259

The Drive >> Back on Hwy 49 northbound, you'll ride along one of the most scenic stretches of the Gold Country's historic route. Patched with shade from oak and pine trees, Hwy 49 drifts beside Sierra Nevada foothills for the next 9 miles to Coloma.

- - - - - - - - - - - - - - - - - -

TRIP HIGHLIGHT

➑ Coloma

At pastoral, low-key **Marshall Gold Discovery State Historic Park** (✆530-622-3470; www.parks.ca.gov; Hwy 49, Coloma; per car $8; ⊗8am-8pm late May-early Sep, to 6pm early Sep-Oct, Mar-late May, to 5pm Nov-Feb; P 🚻 🐾), a simple dirt path leads to the place along the banks of the American River where James Marshall made his famous discovery of gold flecks below Sutter's Mill on January 24, 1848. Today, several reconstructed and restored historical buildings are all within a short stroll along grassy trails that pass mining artifacts, a blacksmith's shop, pioneer houses and the **Gold Discovery Museum & Visitor Center** (✆530-622-6198; http://marshallgold.com; 310 Back St, Coloma; free with park entry, guided tour adult/child $3/2; ⊗10am-5pm Mar-Oct, 9am-4pm Nov-Feb, guided tours 11am & 1pm year-round; P 🚻). Panning for gold is always popular at **Bekeart's Gun Shop** (329

CHASING THE ELEPHANT

Every gold prospector in the Sierra Nevada foothills came to 'see the elephant,' a colloquialism of the '49ers that captured the adventurous rush for gold. Those on the overland California Trail were 'following the elephant's tracks,' and when they hit it rich, they'd seen the beast from 'trunk to tail.' Like hunting a rare wild animal, rushing Gold Country's hills was a once-in-a-lifetime risk, with potential for a jumbo reward.

Hwy 49, Coloma; per person $7; ⏱10am-3pm Sat & Sun; ♿). Opposite the pioneer cemetery, you can walk or drive up Hwy 153 – the sign says it's California's shortest state highway (but it's not really) – to where the **James Marshall Monument** marks Marshall's final resting place. Ironically, he died bankrupt, penniless and a ward of the state.

 p259

The Drive » Rolling northbound, Hwy 49 unfolds more of the region's historical beauty over the next 18 miles. In Auburn, drive across I-80 and stay on Hwy 49 north for another 22 miles, gaining elevation while heading toward Grass Valley. Exit onto Empire St, turning right to follow the signs for Empire Mine State Historic Park's visitor center.

TRIP HIGHLIGHT

9 Around Nevada City

The biggest bonanza of the mother lode is **Em-pire Mine State Historic Park** (☎530-273-8522; www.parks.ca.gov; 10791 Empire St; adult/youth 6-16yr $7/3; ⏱10am-5pm Mar-Oct, to 4pm Nov-Feb; P ♿), where California's richest hard-rock mine produced 5.8 million ounces of gold between 1850 and 1956. The mine yard is littered with massive mining equipment and buildings constructed from waste rock.

Backtrack west, then follow the Golden Chain Hwy (Hwy 49) about 5 miles further north to Nevada City. On the town's quaint main drag, hilly Broad St, the **National Exchange Hotel** (211 Broad St; www.thenationalexchangehotel.com) was built in 1856. It was scheduled to re-open in 2021, after a renovation. Walk to historic **Firehouse No 1 Museum** (☎530-265-3937; www.nevadacountyhistory.org; 214 Main St; by donation; ⏱1-4pm Wed-Sun May-Oct, by appt

Nov-Apr), where Native American artifacts join displays about Chinese laborers and creepy Donner Party relics.

Last, cool off with a refreshing dip at **South Yuba River State Park** (☎530-432-2546; www.parks.ca.gov; 17660 Pleasant Valley Rd, Penn Valley; parking $10 Jun-Aug, $5 Sep-May; ⏱park sunrise-sunset, visitor center 11am-4pm May-Sep, to 3pm Thu-Sun Oct-Apr; P ♿ 🎫), which has popular swimming holes and forest hiking trails near Bridgeport, the USA's longest covered wooden bridge (temporarily closed for restoration at the time of research). It's a 30-minute drive northwest of Nevada City or Grass Valley.

🍴 🛏 p259

Eating & Sleeping

Sonora ❶

✖ Diamondback Grill ⠀⠀⠀⠀⠀⠀American $

(☏209-532-6661; www.thediamondbackgrill.com; 93 S Washington St, Sonora; mains $13-17; ⏱11am-9pm Mon-Thu, to 9:30pm Fri & Sat, to 8pm Sun; 🖐) With exposed brick, modern fixtures, fresh menu and contemporary details, this cafe and wine bar is a reprieve from occasionally overbearing Victorian frill along Hwy 49. Sandwiches and burgers dominate the menu (the salmon and eggplant-mozzarella are both great) and everything is homemade.

🛏 Bradford Place Inn ⠀⠀⠀⠀⠀B&B $$

(☏209-536-6075; www.bradfordplaceinn.com; 56 W Bradford St, Sonora; r $145-265; ✳@🛜) Gorgeous gardens and inviting porch seats surround this four-room B&B, which is under new and on-the-ball ownership. With a two-person claw-foot tub, the Bradford Suite is the definitive, romantic B&B experience. Gourmet breakfasts can be served on the verandah: try the crème brûlée French toast or the filling Mother Lode Skillet.

Columbia ❷

🛏 Fallon Hotel ⠀⠀⠀⠀⠀⠀Historic Hotel $

(☏information 209-532-1470, reservations 800-444-7275; www.reserveamerica.com; 11175 Washington St; r $66-127; ✳🛜) The historic Fallon Hotel hosts the most professional theater troupe in the region, the **Sierra Repertory Theatre** (☏209-532-3120; www.sierrarep.org; 11175 Washington St). The building is done out in period style, with floral wallpaper, glass lanterns and gleaming wooden furnishings. Rooms have a toilet and sink, but showers are down the hall. Ask about the ghosts if you're so inclined.

Volcano ❹

🛏 Volcano Union Inn ⠀⠀⠀⠀Historic Hotel $$

(☏209-296-7711; www.volcanounion.com; 21375 Consolation St; r $139-165; P✳🛜) The more comfortable of the two historic hotels in Volcano: there are four lovingly updated rooms with crooked floors and private bathrooms and a large, shared balcony facing the street. Flat-screen TVs and modern touches are a bit incongruous in the old building, but it's a cozy place to stay. The on-site **Volcano Union Pub** (☏209-296-7711; www.volcanounion.com; 21375 Consolation St; mains $10-28; ⏱5-8pm Mon, Wed & Thu, 5-9pm Fri, noon-9pm Sat, to 8pm Sun; 🍽) has the best food in town and a lovely patio garden. The lamb burger earns raves.

Amador County Wine Country ❻

✖ Taste ⠀⠀⠀⠀⠀⠀Californian $$$

(☏209-245-3463; www.restauranttaste.com; 9402 Main St, Plymouth; small plates $9-15, dinner mains $30-53; ⏱11:30am-2pm Fri-Sun, 5-9pm Mon, Tue, Thu & Fri, 4:30-9pm Sat & Sun) Book a table at Taste, where excellent Amador County wines are paired with a fine menu of California-style cooking (big on meat and game). There's open seating in the wine bar, where gregarious locals will gladly fill you in on local haunts – and maybe buy you a glass of wine. Don't miss the mushroom cigars.

🛏 Rest ⠀⠀⠀⠀⠀⠀Boutique Hotel $$

(☏209-245-6315; www.hotelnest.net; 9372 Main St; r $197-279. ste $329; P✳🛜🍽) Guests sip local wines and nibble gourmet snacks from sister-property Taste during the afternoon wine hour at this new boutique property in downtown Plymouth. Staff are helpful, and the 19 rooms blend comfort and modern style. We especially like the complimentary in-room snacks. A satisfying continental breakfast is also served.

Placerville ⑦

✕ Farm Table Restaurant
Mediterranean $$

(📞530-295-8140; https://ourfarmtable.com; 311 Main St; mains lunch $10-14, dinner $22-36; 🕐11am-3pm Mon, to 8pm Wed & Sun, to 9pm Thu-Sat; 🖋) A lovely deli-style place dishing up well-cooked farm-fresh food with a Mediterranean feel, alongside homespun fare such as duck confit raviolo. It specializes in charcuterie and preserving, and has plenty of gluten-free and veggie options on the menu too.

Coloma ⑧

✕ Argonaut Farm to Fork Cafe
American $

(📞530-626-7345; www.argonautcafe.com; 331 Hwy 49, Coloma; items $9-14; 🕐8am-4pm; 🛜🖋👶) Delicious soups, sandwiches, baked goods and coffee from well-known Sacramento and local purveyors find their way to this little wooden house in Marshall Gold Discovery State Historic Park (p256). Crowds of schoolkids waiting for gelato can slow things down.

Around Nevada City ⑨

✕ South Pine Cafe
Breakfast $

(📞520-265-0260; www.southpinecafe.com; 110 S Pine St; mains $9-18; 🕐8am-3pm) It may not be Instagram-pretty, but the lobster scramble here was the best thing we ate for breakfast across the Gold Country: chunks of lobster, jack cheese, mushrooms, scrambled eggs and hollandaise sauce. All breakfast options are equally decadent. The habanero sauce and ketchup are housemade. Enjoy a Bloody Mary or beer with your meal.

🛏 Outside Inn
Inn, Cottage $$

(📞530-265-2233; http://outsideinn.com; 575 E Broad St; r $99-175, cabin $180, cottage $230; 🅿❄🛜♨👶) The best option for active explorers, this is an unusually friendly and fun inn, with 13 rooms, one cabin and one cottage maintained by staff who love the outdoors. Some rooms have a patio overlooking a small creek; all have nice quilts and access to BBQ grills. It's a 10-minute walk from downtown and there's a small unheated outdoor pool.

Ebbetts Pass Scenic Byway

24

Follow this winding road over the rooftop of the Sierra Nevada, crossing from Gold Country to Lake Tahoe, passing lakes, giant sequoia groves, hot springs and all-seasons resorts.

TRIP HIGHLIGHTS

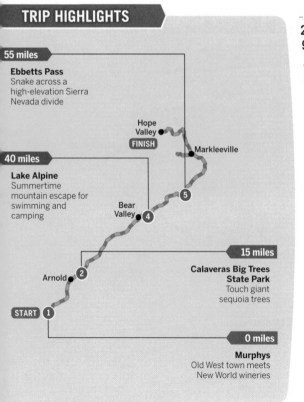

55 miles

Ebbetts Pass
Snake across a high-elevation Sierra Nevada divide

40 miles

Lake Alpine
Summertime mountain escape for swimming and camping

Hope Valley
FINISH

Markleeville

5

Bear Valley **4**

Arnold **2**

START **1**

15 miles

Calaveras Big Trees State Park
Touch giant sequoia trees

0 miles

Murphys
Old West town meets New World wineries

2 DAYS
95 MILES / 155KM

GREAT FOR...

BEST TIME TO GO
June to October, when the pass is open.

 ESSENTIAL PHOTO

Sierra Nevada peaks from Ebbetts Pass.

 BEST FOR FAMILIES

Bear Valley's ski resort and summertime trails and lakes.

lley views at a car camping site along Ebbets Pass

261

24 Ebbetts Pass Scenic Byway

Stretched along a gold-rush-era mining route, Hwy 4 jogs through a handful of mountain hamlets and forests before crossing Ebbetts Pass, which is only open in summer and fall. For outdoor fanatics, it's practically a road trip through paradise. Go hiking among giant sequoias and on the Sierra Crest, paddle tranquil lakes, climb granite boulders, splash in summer swimming holes, or strap on skis or snowshoes in winter.

TRIP HIGHLIGHT

❶ Murphys

With its white-picket fences, the 19th-century 'Queen of the Sierra' is one of the most picturesque towns along the southern stretch of California's Gold Country. Amble along Main St, which shows off plenty of historical charm alongside its wine-tasting rooms, art galleries, boutiques and cafes. These rocky, volcanic Sierra Nevada foothills are known for making brambly

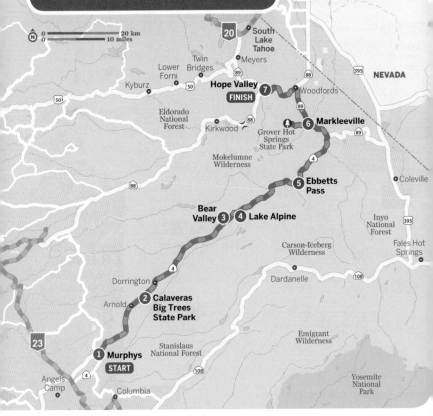

zinfandel and spicy syrah, which you can sample at a dozen wineries, most crowded together on a four-block stretch downtown. It's best to arrive early if you're visiting on the weekend. Don't miss the 'Drama Queen' chenin blanc at **Newsome-Harlowe** (209-728-9817; www.nhvino.com; 403 Main St; tasting $10; noon-5pm Mon-Thu, 11am-5:30pm Fri-Sun;). If you can, responsibly, hop in the car for the quick drive to **Ironstone Vineyards** (209-728-1251; www.ironstonevineyards.com; 1894 Six Mile Rd; tasting fee $5; 11am-5pm; P), with its enormous tasting room, natural-spring waterfall, and landmark amphitheater, which hosts outdoor concerts.

 p267

LINK YOUR TRIP

20 **Lake Tahoe Loop**
From Hope Valley, it's a 20-mile drive northwest on Hwy 89 past stream-fed meadows to South Lake Tahoe's beaches and ski resorts.

23 **Highway 49 Through Gold Country**
From Murphys, mosey 13 miles along Hwy 4 and Parrots Ferry Rd to old-time Columbia State Historic Park.

The Drive » Hwy 4 ascends through the workaday small town of Arnold, which has a few cafes and motels strung along the roadside 12 miles east of Murphys. After motoring another 3 miles uphill, turn right into Calaveras Big Trees State Park.

TRIP HIGHLIGHT

❷ Calaveras Big Trees State Park

An on-the-nose name if there ever was one, **Calaveras Big Trees State Park** (209-795-2334; www.parks.ca.gov; 1170 Hwy 4, Arnold; per car $10; sunrise-sunset, visitor center 10am-4pm; P) is home to giant sequoias. The most massive trees on earth, they grow only in the western Sierra Nevada range. Reaching up to 275ft tall here and with trunk diameters over 35ft, these leftovers from the Mesozoic era are thought to weigh upwards of 2000 tons, or more than 10 blue whales. Close to the park entrance, the **North Grove Big Trees Trail** is a 1.5-mile self-guided loop, where the air is scented with fresh pine, fir and incense cedar. To escape some of the crowds, drive 8.5 miles along the curving park road to the start of the **South Grove Trail**. This 3.5-mile loop ascends to a peaceful grove that protects 10 times as many giant sequoias; a 1.5-mile round-trip spur trail leads to the Agassiz

Tree, the big daddy of them all. Afterward, cool off with a summertime dip in Beaver Creek below the trail's footbridge or in the Stanislaus River along the main park road.

p267

The Drive » Back at Hwy 4, turn right and drive uphill past Dorrington, a 19th-century stagecoach stop and toll-road station, stopping at Hell's Kitchen Vista Point for panoramas of the glaciated volcanic landscape. About 22 miles northeast of the state park lies Bear Valley.

----

❸ Bear Valley

It's all about outdoor family fun here. Sniff out anything from rock climbing to mountain biking and hiking, all within a short distance of Bear Valley Village, which has a gas station, shops and casual restaurants. In winter, **Bear Valley Mountain** (209-753-2301; www.bearvalley.com; 2280 Hwy 207, Bear Valley; daily ski-lift ticket adult/6-12yr/13-19yr $105/42/85; lift 9am-3:30pm, resort end Nov-May;) ski area will get your brain buzzing with 2000ft of vertical rise and 12 lifts. The resort's somewhat off-the-beaten-track location gives it a beginner-friendly, locals-only feel. On your left as you pull into Bear Valley Village, **Bear Valley Adventure Company** (20 9-753-2834; www.bvadventures.com; 1 Bear Valley Rd,

Bear Valley; snowshoes/sleds/ mountain bikes/kayaks from $25/15/30/35; 🕑9am-5pm; 👤) is a one-stop shop for outdoor gear and supplies – kayak, stand-up paddle boarding (SUP), mountain-bike and cross-country-ski rentals – plus insider information on just about everything there is to do in the area. Staff also arrange mountain-bike shuttles and sell helpful maps.

The Drive » From the Bear Valley Village turnoff, it's less than 4 miles up Hwy 4 to Lake Alpine's beaches, campgrounds and day-use parking lots.

- - - - - - - - - - - - - - - - - -

TRIP HIGHLIGHT

4 Lake Alpine

Suddenly Hwy 4 reaches the shores of gaspworthy **Lake Alpine**, a reservoir skirted by slabs of granite and offering several sandy beaches and a handful of rustic US Forest Service (USFS) campgrounds. Paddling, swimming and fishing opportunities abound, which means that it's always jammed with people on summer weekends. No matter how many folks descend upon the lake (and there are far fewer midweek), it's still hard to beat the gorgeous Sierra Nevada setting, 7350ft above sea level. Of several nearby hiking trailheads, the scramble to Inspiration Point gets you spectacular views of lakes and the Dardanelles; this 3-mile round-trip hike starts from the lakeshore trail near Pine Marten Campground. Next to the boat ramp on the lake's northern shore, Lake Alpine Resort's summertime kiosk rents rowboats, paddleboats, kayaks and canoes.

🛏 p267

The Drive » Make sure you've got plenty of gas in the tank before embarking on the 33-mile drive over Ebbetts Pass downhill to Markleeville. There are campgrounds, but no services, gas stations, motels or places to eat along this high-elevation, twisting mountain road, which is only open seasonally during summer and fall.

TOP TIP: CROSSING EBBETTS PASS

Hwy 4 is usually plowed from the west as far as Lake Alpine year-round, but Ebbetts Pass closes completely after the first major snowfall in November, December or January. The pass typically doesn't open again until April, May or June. Check current road conditions with the **California Department of Transportation** (CalTrans; 📞800-427-7623; www.dot.ca.gov).

- - - - - - - - - - - - - - - - - -

TRIP HIGHLIGHT

5 Ebbetts Pass

Ebbetts Pass National Scenic Byway officially runs from Arnold to Markleeville, yet it's the dramatic stretch east of Lake Alpine that really gets drivers' hearts pumping. Narrowing, the highway continues 4 miles past **Cape Horn Vista** to **Mosquito Lakes** and over Pacific Grade Summit before slaloming through historic **Hermit Valley**, where the Mokelumne River meadow blooms with summer wildflowers. Finally, Hwy 4 winds

Mosquito Lakes National Forest

up and over the actual summit of **Ebbetts Pass** (elevation 8736ft), where the top-of-the-world scenery encompasses snaggletoothed granite peaks rising above the tree line. About 0.4 miles east of the signposted pass, the highway crosses the **Pacific Crest Trail** (PCT), which zigzags from Mexico to Canada. For wildflowers, volcanic cliffs and granite canyon views, take an 8-mile round-trip hike to Nobel Lake. Or park the car and have a picnic beside **Kinney Reservoir**, just over another mile east.

The Drive » With a maximum 24% grade (no vehicles with trailers or over 25ft long), Hwy 4 loses elevation via dozens of steep hairpin turns, crossing multiple creek and river bridges as forested valley views open up below bald granite peaks. After 13 miles, turn left onto Hwy 89 and drive almost 5 miles northwest to Markleeville.

- - - - - - - - - - - - - - - - -

⑥ Markleeville

Breathlessly coming down from Ebbetts Pass, Hwy 4 winds past remnants of old mining communities long gone bust, including a pioneer cemetery, ghost towns and cattle ranches. From the junction below Moni-

tor Pass, Hwy 89 runs gently north alongside the Carson River, where anglers fish for trout from pebble-washed beaches that kids love. Crossing Hangman's Bridge, Hwy 89 threads through **Markleeville**, a historic toll-road outpost that boomed with silver mining in the 1860s. Today it's a quiet spot to refuel and relax. Downtown, turn left onto Hot Springs Rd, then head up School St to **Alpine County Museum** (☏530-694-2317; www.alpinecounty museum.org; 1 School St, Markleeville; suggested donation $2; ☻10am-4pm Thu-Sun late May-Oct; **P**), with its one-room 1882 school-house, log-cabin jail and tiny museum displaying Native American baskets and pioneer-era artifacts. Back on Hot Springs Rd, drive 4 miles west through pine forests to **Grover Hot Springs State Park** (☏530-694-2248, 530-694-2249; www.parks. ca.gov; 3415 Hot Springs Rd, Markleeville; pool adult/child $10/5; ◷10am-7pm; ♿), which has a shady picnic area, a campground and a natural-spring-fed swimming pool. Carry tire chains in winter.

✕ p267

The Drive ❯❯ Drive north out of Markleeville for 6 miles to the unremarkable junction of Hwys 88 and 89 at Woodfords. Turn left and continue lazily west another 6 miles, crossing the bridge over the Carson River to Hope Valley, where Hwys 88 and 89 split at Picketts Junction.

- - - - - - - - - - - - - - - - - -

❼ Hope Valley

After all the fantastical scenery leading up to and over Ebbetts Pass, what's left? **Hope Valley**, where wildflowers, grassy meadows and burbling streams are bordered by evergreen pines and aspen trees that turn brilliant yellow in fall. This panoramic valley is ringed by Sierra Nevada peaks, which remain dusted with snow even in early summer. Incidentally, the historic Pony Express route once ran through this way. Today, whether you want to dangle a fishing pole or splash around in the chilly mountain waters, or just take a bird-watching stroll or snowshoe trek in winter around the meadows, Hope Valley can feel like the most magical place in Alpine County. Start exploring on the nature trails of **Hope Valley Wildlife Area** (☏916-358-2900; www.wildlife.ca.gov; **P**).

🛏 p267

Eating & Sleeping

Murphys ❶

✕ Alchemy Market & Cafe
Californian $$

(☏209-728-0700; www.alchemymurphys.com; 191 Main St; most mains $16-32; ◷11am-3pm Fri-Sun, 4-8pm Sun-Thu, 4-9pm Fri & Sat, bar 9pm-midnight Fri & Sat) The stellar cafe menu has a long wine list and many dishes, from calamari frites to green curry mussels, all great for sharing on the patio, plus gourmet comfort dishes. Live music every Friday night from 6pm to 8:30pm.

🛏 Victoria Inn
B&B $$

(☏209-728-8933; www.victoriainn-murphys. com; 402 Main St; r $143-197, ste $237-327, cottages from $302; P📶) This downtown B&B has glamorous rooms with claw-foot slipper tubs, sleigh beds and balconies. Some rooms have wood-burning stoves and balconies overlooking the courtyard fountain. The common spaces have chic, modern country appeal. The complimentary chocolate-chip cookies are delicious.

Calaveras Big Trees State Park ❷

🛏 Calaveras Big Trees State Park Campgrounds & Cabins
Campground, Cabin $

(☏reservations 800-444-7275; www. reserveamerica.com; off Hwy 4; tent & RV sites $25-35, cabins $185-205; ◷generally Mar-Nov; P) At the park (p263) entrance is busy North Grove Campground. Less crowded, hillside Oak Hollow Campground is about 4 miles further along the park's main road. Rustic two-bedroom cabins with kitchens are also rented. Walk-in primitive 'environmental' sites also available.

Lake Alpine ❹

🛏 Lake Alpine Resort
Cabin $$

(☏209-753-6350; www.lakealpineresort.com; 4000 Hwy 4, Bear Valley; tent cabins $89-99,

cabins with kitchenette or kitchen $189-339; ◷May-Oct; P🐕📶) If you're not ready to rough it at rustic lakeshore campgrounds, this lodge with general store, lake-view restaurant and bar has a handful of cozy wooden and canvas-tent cabins that suit families. Cabins vary in size, sleeping between one and 10 people. The place is closed during winter, when the area turns into a snow park and snowmobile route. The lodge also operates as the concessionaire for mostly first-come, first-served tent sites ($26) along the lakeshore. Some are available for reservation at www. recreation.gov.

Markleeville ❻

✕ Stone Fly
Californian $$

(☏530-694-9999; www.stoneflyrestaurant. com; 14821 Hwy 89, Markleeville; mains $15-36; ◷5-9pm Fri-Sun) Meaty mains like 16oz rib eyes, wood-fired chicken and spice-rubbed pork tenderloin join wood-fired pizzas and homemade desserts on this mouthwatering menu. Dishes are delivered to an open-air patio in summer. Reservations recommended.

Hope Valley ❼

🛏 Wylder Hotel Hope Valley
Chalet $$$

(☏530-694-2203; https://wylderhotels. com/hope-valley; 14255 Hwy 88; cabins & cottages/yurts from $275/350, campsites/ RV sites $105/130; P) Now under new ownership, the former Sorensen's Resort is a truly delightful option in the Hope Valley, with snug pine cottages and cabins decked out with fairy lights and hammocks. Plus yurts, an Airstream and camping. There's a wealth of activities, including hiking, mountain biking and snowshoeing. Magical in the snow, but just as lovely in summer. The on-site cafe serves three home-cooked meals daily (7:30am to 9pm).

Feather River Scenic Byway

25

Get ready for a winding journey into sheer-walled canyons, remote forests and scenic lakes. The northern Sierras are rich with wildlife and hiking opportunities abound.

TRIP HIGHLIGHTS

100 miles

Lake Almanor
Remote forest camping and excellent hiking

190 miles

Lakes Basin
A network of lakes makes a naturalist's playland

Quincy

START
Oroville

FINISH 7

Sierra City

225 miles

Downieville
Bomb down single-track mountain-bike trails

3–4 DAYS
215 MILES /
346 KM

GREAT FOR...

BEST TIME TO GO

April to June when hills are green, and September to October when oak leaves turn.

ESSENTIAL PHOTO

The crags of the Sierra Buttes.

BEST SWIMMING HOLE

At the riverside Feather River Hot Springs, fifteen miles east of Belden.

---

25 Feather River Scenic Byway

As you cruise the remote two-lane blacktop of the Feather River Scenic Byway you're surrounded by California's northern natural wonders – rushing streams, daunting mountains and forest lakes. Eventually, the route leads to characterful towns, where hikers and mountain bikers shovel down hearty fare and stock up on supplies. The best way to soak up the sights is by camping; a number of cheap (or free) federal campgrounds line the route.

① Oroville

This journey begins in Oroville, a little town that shares a name with the nearby lake that's filled by the Feather River. There's not much to see in Oroville, save the stunning **Chinese Temple & Museum Complex** (☎530-538-2496; 1500 Broderick St; adult/child $3/free; ⊗noon-4pm Tue, Wed Sat & Sun, Mar-Nov; ℗), a quiet monument to the 10,000 Chinese people who once lived here. During the 19th century, theater troupes from

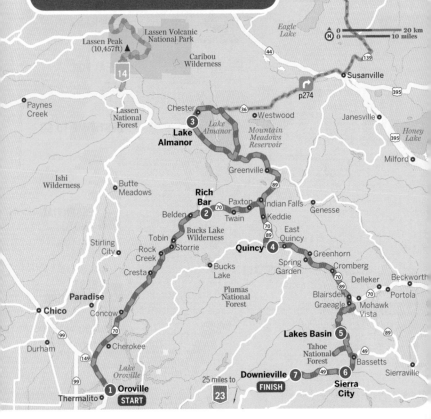

China toured a circuit of Chinatowns in California, and Oroville was the end of the line, which explains the unrivaled collection of 19th-century Chinese stage finery. The **Feather River Ranger District** (Plumas National Forest; 📞530-534-6500; www.fs.usda.gov; 875 Mitchell Ave; ⏰8am-4:30pm Mon-Fri) office is also in town; it issues permits and has a handout detailing historic stops along the byway. The nearby **Lake Oroville State Recreation Area** (📞530-538-2219; www.parks.ca.gov; 917 Kelly Ridge Rd; ⏰park 8am-8pm, visitor center 9am-5pm; 🅿 🚻) is an excellent place to hike, camp and hook bass; head north instead of east and you'll find the **North Table Mountain Ecological Reserves**,

LINK YOUR TRIP

23 **Highway 49 Through Gold Country**

More swimming holes, wild history lessons and winding byways await on the 'Golden Chain.' Link to Hwy 49 in Downieville.

14 **Volcanic Legacy Byway**

Skirt the volcanic domes of Mt Shasta and Mt Lassen, starting 30 miles northwest of Chester via Hwys 36 and 89.

which offers an off-the-beaten-track hiking experience through volcanic basalt rock formations and wildflower meadows.

🛏 p275

The Drive » Take Hwy 70 into the granite gorge, passing hydroelectric plants, mountain tunnels and historic bridges, including the Pulga Bridge. Four miles past the red bridge to Belden turn off Hwy 70 onto Rich Bar Rd, on your right.

---

❷ Rich Bar

Although the so-called Golden Chain, Hwy 49, is still further up the road, the Feather River area was dotted with its own rough-and-ready encampments of fortune hunters. One of the most successful of these was the aptly named **Rich Bar**, where little remains today except a crumbling graveyard and a historic marker. This quiet place wasn't so tame in the 1850s, when a resident named Dame Shirley chronicled life at Rich Bar as a part of her fascinating diary of life in California gold towns. Published as *The Shirley Letters,* her letters paint Rich Bar as a chaotic place of bloody accidents, a couple of murders, mob rule enforced by horse-whipping and hanging, an attempted suicide and a fatal duel. And she was only here a single month!

The Drive » Continue the lovely, sinuous drive on Hwy 70, catching quick views of Lassen and Shasta peaks in the rearview mirror. Go north on Hwy 89 to reach the south shore of Lake Almanor. Follow the shore around the lake clockwise.

TRIP HIGHLIGHT

❸ Lake Almanor

This artificial lake is a crystalline example of California's beautiful, if sometimes awkward, conservation and land-management policy: the lake was created by the now-defunct Great Western Power Company and is now ostensibly owned by the Pacific Gas & Electric (PG&E) Company. Lassen Peak's stark silhouette overlooks the lake, which is surrounded by lush meadows and stately pines, mostly in the **Lassen National Forest** and **Caribou Wilderness**. Both offer quiet camping with a permit from the **Almanor Ranger District** (Lassen National Forest; 📞530-258-2141; www.fs.usda.gov; 900 CA 36, Chester; ⏰8am-4:30pm Mon-Fri) office. The main town near the lake is **Chester**, and though you could whiz right by and dismiss it as a few blocks of nondescript roadside storefronts, don't – it's not. This robust little community has a fledgling art scene, decent restaurants and some comfy places to stay. You can rent bicycles for a cruise along the lakeshore at **Bodfish Bicycles & Quiet Mountain Sports** (☎530-258-2338; www.bodfishbicycles.com; 149 Main St, Chester; bicycle rental per hour/day $12/35; ⊘10am-5pm Tue-Sat, noon-4pm Sun, shorter off-season hours).

✕ ⊨ p275

The Drive » Continue around the lake and retrace the route south on Hwy 89, which will bring you back to the Feather River Scenic Byway. You'll hit Quincy after hanging left at the T-junction.

- - - - - - - - - - - - - - - -

④ Quincy

Idyllic Quincy (population 1858) is a mountain community that teeters on the edge of becoming an incorporated town. It's no metropolis, but after the route along the Feather River it may feel like one. Three streets make up Quincy's low-key commercial district, dotted with homey restaurants, bars and bakeries. One of the nicest community museums in the state is also located here, amid flowering gardens. Visit the **Plumas County Museum** (☎530-283-6320; www.plumasmuseum.org; 500 Jackson St, at Coburn St; adult/child $5/free; ⊘10am-4pm Tue-Sat & sometimes Sun; ℙ ♿) and you'll find that the building houses hundreds of historical photos and relics from the county's pioneer and

Maidu days, early mining and timber industries, and construction of the Western Pacific Railroad. The hills surrounding the town also harbor some lovely hiking trails.

✕ ⊨ p275

The Drive » Continue down Hwy 70/89 passing horse pastures and distant mountain views. At Graeagle take the fork in the road to the right to follow Hwy 89 south, then after less than 3 miles take a right on Gold Lake Hwy and start climbing. If traveling in shoulder season, check road conditions before you make the turnoff; an alternate route follows Hwy 89 until it hits Hwy 49 just north of Sattley.

- - - - - - - - - - - - - - - -

TRIP HIGHLIGHT

⑤ Lakes Basin

Haven Lake, Gold Lake, Rock Lake, Deer Lake: dotted with crystalline alpine waters, this area is a secluded corner of paradise. Over a dozen of these gems can be reached only on foot, and great trails are virtually endless – you can even connect to the Pacific Crest Trail. The most scenic hike in the area is the **Haskell Peak Trail**, which affords views of both Lassen and Shasta and, on a clear day, Mt Rose in Nevada. To reach the trailhead, turn right from Gold Lake Hwy at Haskell Peak Rd (Forest Rd 9) and follow it for 8.5 miles. The hike is only 4.5 miles round-trip, but

it's not for the faint of heart – you'll climb more than 1000ft through dense forest before it opens on an expansive view. From there you can see the rugged Sierra Buttes, distinguished from their surrounding mountains by jagged peaks, which look like a miniature version of the Alps.

⊨ p275

The Drive » Gold Lake Hwy will now descend and connect to Hwy 49 in Bassetts (a town that consists of little more than a gas station). Go right on Hwy 49 for 5 miles to reach Sierra City.

North Table, Oroville

❻ Sierra City

Sierra City is the primary supply station for people headed to the **Sierra Buttes** and offers more chances at amazing short hikes to summits with panoramic views. From the **Sierra Country Store** (📞530-862-1560; www.sierracountrystore.com; 213 Main St; 🕓8am-7pm May-Sep, 10am-6pm Oct-Apr; 🛜), there's a vast network of trails that is ideal for backpacking and casual hikes. They are listed in the *Lakes Basin, Downieville–Sierra City* map ($2), which is on sale at the store. Sierra City's local museum, the **Kentucky Mine** (📞530-862-1310; www.sierracountyhistory.org; 100 Kentucky Mine Rd; museum adult/child $2/50¢, tour adult/child 7-17yr $7/3.50; 🕓10am-4pm late May-early Sep; 🅿 ♿), is a worthy stop that introduces the famed 'Golden Chain Highway.' Its gold mine and stamp mill are just northeast of town.

🛏 p275

The Drive » Head west on Hwy 49 along the North Yuba River for a dozen miles to Downieville.

TRIP HIGHLIGHT

❼ Downieville

Even with a population smaller than 300, Downieville is the biggest town in the remote Sierra County, located at the junction of the North Yuba and Downie Rivers. With a reputation that quietly rivals Moab, Utah (before it got big), the town is the premiere place for trail riding in the state, and a staging area for true wilderness adventures. Brave souls bomb down the **Downieville Downhill**, a molar-rattling 4000ft

DETOUR:
EAGLE LAKE

Start: ❸ Lake Almanor

Those who have the time to get all the way out to Eagle Lake, California's second-largest natural lake, are rewarded with one of the most striking sights in the region: a stunningly blue jewel on the high plateau. From late spring until early fall, this lovely lake, over 15 miles northwest of Susanville, attracts a smattering of visitors who come to cool off, swim, fish, boat and camp. On the south shore, you'll find a pristine 5-mile paved recreational trail for cycling and hiking and several busy federal **campgrounds** (🖉information 530-257-4188, reservations 877-444-6777; www.recreation.gov; tent/RV sites from $20/30) managed by **Eagle Lake Marina** (🖉530-825-3454; www.eaglelakerecreationarea.com), which offers hot showers, laundry and boat rentals. It also can help you get out onto the lake with a fishing license. To get to Eagle Lake, take Hwy 36 northeast of Lake Almanor toward Susanville, then continue north on Eagle Lake Rd to the south shore.

vertical descent, which is rated among the best mountain-bike routes in the USA. **Downieville Outfitters** (🖉530-289-0155; www.downievilleout fitters.com; 312 Main St; bike rental per day $100-120, shuttle per person $30-40; ☺8am-5pm, shuttles Jun-Oct) is a good place to rent a bike and arrange a shuttle to make the one-way trip,

and the nonprofit **Yuba Expeditions** (🖉530-289-3010; www.yubaexpeditions. com; 208 Main St; bike/e-bike rentals $150/200 per day, shuttle per person $25; ☺8:30am-5:30pm Mon-Fri, 8am-6pm Sat & Sun May–mid-Nov) is a great resource for information on hiking and biking trails.

🛏 p275

Eating & Sleeping

Oroville ❶

🏕 Lake Oroville State Recreation
Area Campgrounds
Campground $

(📞information 530-538-2219, reservations 800-444-7275; www.reservecalifornia.com; tent & RV sites $20-45; P) Drive-in campgrounds aren't the most rustic choice, but there are good primitive campsites if you're willing to hike or boat. There are six campgrounds to choose from and a cove of floating platform sites (per night $175).

Lake Almanor ❸

✗ Red Onion Grill Modern American $$$
(📞530-258-1800; www.redoniongrill.com; 303 Peninsula Dr, Westwood; mains $16-39; ⏱11am-9pm, Wed-Sun, shorter hours Oct-Apr) The finest dining on the lake with upscale New American, Italian-influenced cuisine (like simply prepared shrimp scampi), and bar food that's executed with panache. The setting is casual and made all the more warm by the wine list.

🏕 PG&E Recreational
Area Campgrounds
Campground $

(📞916-386-5164; http://recreation.pge.com; tent & RV sites from $23; ⏱May-Sep; P 🐾) A favorite for tents and RVs, Rocky Point Campground is right on the lake. For something more remote, try Cool Springs Campground or Ponderosa Flat Campground, both at Butt Reservoir near the lake's south shore, at the end of Prattville Butt Reservoir Rd.

Quincy ❹

✗ Pangaea Cafe & Pub
Cafe $

(📞530-283-0426; www.pangaeapub.com; 461 W Main St; mains $11-14; ⏱11am-9pm Mon-Fri; 🛜🖉🐾) This earthy spot is committed to serving local produce. Choose from regional beef burgers, salmon sushi, a slew of sandwiches (many veggie), quesadillas and rice bowls. It's hopping with locals drinking craft brews, kids running around and lots of hugging.

🏨 Quincy
Courtyard Suites
Apartment $$

(📞530-283-1401; www.quincycourtyardsuites.com; 436 Main St; apt $149-189; P 🐾🛜) Staying in this beautifully renovated 1908 Clinch building feels just right, like renting the village's cutest apartment. The warmly decorated rooms are modern and apartments have spacious kitchens, claw-foot tubs and gas fireplaces.

Lakes Basin ❺

🏕 Salmon Creek
Campground
Campground $

(📞information 530-288-3231, reservations 877-444-6777; www.recreation.gov; Gold Lake Hwy, Calpine; tent & RV sites $24; ⏱mid-May–late Sep; P 🐾) With dramatic views of the Sierra Buttes, this USFS campground in the Tahoe National Forest is 2 miles north of Bassetts on Gold Lake Hwy, off Hwy 49. It has vault toilets, running water and sites for tents and RVs, but no hookups.

Sierra City ❻

🏨 Buttes Resort
Cabin, Lodge $$

(📞530-862-1170; www.buttesresort.com; 230 Main St; d $95-160; P 🐾) Buttes Resort occupies a lovely spot overlooking the river and is a favorite with hikers looking to recharge. Most cabins have a private deck and barbecue, and some have full kitchens. There's a communal area with a pool table.

Downieville ❼

🏨 Riverside Inn
Hotel $$

(📞530-289-1000; www.downieville.us; 206 Commercial St; r $105-135, ste $200, cottage $275; P 🛜🐾) There is a secluded, rustic charm to these 11 stove-warmed rooms and a suite. About half have kitchens and all have balconies. The innkeepers share information about local hiking and biking, and lend snowshoes. A nearby cottage sleeps eight.

Sacramento Delta & Lodi

Shady levy roads on the river delta bring you to an eccentric string of towns, with surprises around every bend. Then meander east into Lodi's family-owned vineyards.

26

TRIP HIGHLIGHTS

35 miles

Locke
Walk a hidden, historic town with Chinese roots

START
1

Sacramento
Stroll California's capital city down by the riverside

0 miles

Clarksburg

3

Isleton

6 FINISH

Lodi
Sip bold Zinfandel from some of California's oldest vines

90 miles

**2 DAYS
100 MILES / 160KM**

GREAT FOR...

BEST TIME TO GO

May to October when the 'Delta Breeze' keeps the sweltering heat at bay.

ESSENTIAL PHOTO

One of the many colored metal bridges along S River Rd.

BEST FOR CULTURE

The tiny town of Locke, California's last remaining rural Chinese American community.

cramento California State Capitol Building

26 Sacramento Delta & Lodi

When exploring the network of channels in the 750,000-acre Sacramento–San Joaquin River Delta, you'll take gently sweeping levy roads into a maze of orchards, vineyards and waterways. Although this region of California is squeezed between the crowded urban spaces of the Bay Area and Sacramento, it feels like it's a million miles away. So do the rural wineries of nearby Lodi, one of California's oldest grape-growing regions.

TRIP HIGHLIGHT

❶ Sacramento

At the confluence of two of California's most powerful waterways – the American and Sacramento Rivers – lies the tidy grid of streets that make up the state capital. The impressive **California State Capitol** (☎916-324-0333; http://capitol museum.ca.gov; 1315 10th St; ☻7:30am-6pm Mon-Fri, 9am-5pm Sat & Sun; ♿) is a mandatory stop, as is **Capitol Park**, the 40-acre

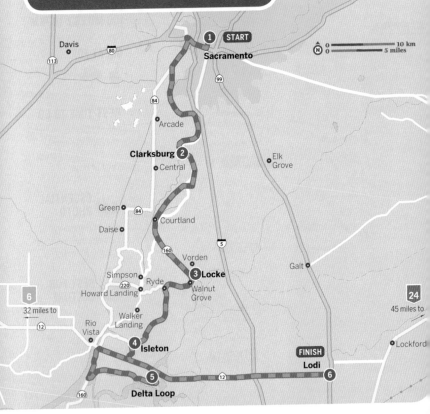

garden surrounding the dome.

At the river port neighboring downtown, **Old Sacramento State Historic Park** (☏916-442-8575; http://oldsacramento.com; 1124 2nd St; P ♿) remains the city's stalwart tourist draw. The old-fashioned gold-rush atmosphere makes it good for a stroll, especially on summer evenings. California's largest concentration of buildings on the National Register of Historic Places is found here. At the north end, the **California State Railroad Museum** (☏916-323-9280; www.csrmf.org; 125 I St; adult/child $12/6; ⊙10am-5pm; P ♿) displays a sizable collection of railcars and locomotives, including a

LINK YOUR TRIP

24 Ebbetts Pass Scenic Byway

Ready for another off-the-beaten-path excursion? Head east from Lodi via Hwys 12, 49 and 4 for 55 miles to Murphys in Gold Country.

6 Napa Valley

Contrasting with Lodi's humble charms, Northern California's most celebrated wine circuit is off Hwy 12, which runs west from Rio Vista.

fully outfitted Pullman sleeper and vintage dining cars. Foodies and beerheads will be content with a visit to Sac's buzzing Midtown, where they will find a large number of breweries and local restaurants sourcing fresh ingredients straight from the Central Valley.

✕ 🛏 p283

The Drive » Point the car west from over the golden Tower Bridge, a landmark on the Sacramento River that opened in 1935. Across the bridge, turn left by Raley Field onto 5th St, following it south until it connects with S River Rd. It's less than 20 miles to Clarksburg.

---

2 Clarksburg

The fields and arid heat surrounding West Sacramento offer little clue that the 'Thousand Miles of Waterways' is near. But as you follow River Rd into Clarksburg, the breeze begins to blow. Travelers can't miss the **Old Sugar Mill** (☏916-744-1615; www.oldsugarmill.com; 35265 Willow Ave, Clarksburg; ⊙11am-5pm; P), the hub of a thriving community of local winemakers. The wines made in the Clarksburg region of the Sacramento Valley have developed a lot over the last decades, benefiting from the blazing sun and cool breezes. A few miles southwest of town via County Rds 141 and 144, the region's best-known winery, **Bogle** (☏916-

744-1092; www.boglewinery. com; 37783 Country Rd 144, Clarksburg; ⊙10am-5pm Mon-Fri, from 11am Sat & Sun; P), is prettily set among the vineyards of a sixth-generation family farm.

The Drive » Just over a mile south of Bogle, turn east on County Rd 142 to return to S River Rd, which winds beside a wide stretch of the Sacramento River. At the next bridge you come to, cross over to the river's eastern side and continue south another 6 miles. Turn left onto Locke Rd to enter Locke's historic district.

TRIP HIGHLIGHT

3 Locke

Locke was founded by Chinese laborers who built the levies that line nearly every inch of this Delta drive. In its heyday, Locke had a fairly wild reputation; during Prohibition (1920–33) the town's lack of a police force and quiet nearby waterways made it a hotbed of boozing and gambling. As you drop off the main road that parallels the river down into the old town, the view is unlike anywhere else in the country: tightly packed rows of wooden structures with creaking balconies and architecture that blends Western and Chinese details. Locke's wild days are in evidence at the **Dai Loy Museum** (☏916-776-1661; www.locke-foundation.org; 13951 Main St, Locke; donations appreciated;

noon-4pm Fri-Sun;), a former gambling house with exhibits on regional history. Its humble displays are worth a peek, but the best part is the atmospheric building itself. Nearby, the Chinese cultural shop sells souvenirs, crafts, games, imported teas and books including *Bitter Melon: Inside America's Last Rural Chinese Town*, which contains luminous photographs and oral histories.

✕ p283

The Drive » Immediately south of Locke in Walnut Grove, cross west over the bridge, then keep motoring south on gently curving Hwy 160, running alongside the Sacramento River. As you approach Isleton, look for the yellow swing bridge, which turns on a pivot so that large ships can pass. Drive east over the bridge, then continue south on Hwy 160 into town.

❹ Isleton

Like Locke and Walnut Grove, Isleton also boasted a thriving Chinese community, which is evident in the historic storefronts that line its main drag. The town is a regular stop for weekend Harley cruisers and Delta boaters, who lend the streets an amiably scruffy atmosphere and ensure the bars are always busy. Isleton also holds the title of 'Crawdad Town USA' and hosts a festival to honor the crustacean every year. Fishers should drop in to **Bob's Bait Shop** (916-777-6666; http://the-masterbaiter.tripod.com; 302 2nd St, Isleton; 6am-4pm Thu & Fri, to 5pm Sat, to 3pm Sun) for advice from the self-described, ahem, 'Master Baiter.' As well as dispensing expert information on fishing in the

area, he sells live crayfish that you can cook up yourself for a riverside picnic.

✕ p283

The Drive » Take Jackson Slough Rd south out of town and go left on Hwy 12. Just before the next bridge, go right on Brannan Island Rd and follow it along the Delta Loop for views of bird-filled skies and marshy lowlands. With the air-conditioning off, the rush of heat through the open window smells of tilled earth and river water.

---

❺ Delta Loop

The drive along the Delta Loop is best taken at an unhurried pace – proof

---

LOCAL KNOWLEDGE: CALIFORNIA STATE FAIR

For two weeks every July, the **California State Fair** (916-263-3247; www.castatefair.org; 1600 Exposition Blvd; adult/child $14/10; Jul;) fills the Cal-Expo fairgrounds, east of I-80 on the north side of the American River, with a small city of cows and carnival rides. It's likely the only place on earth where you can plant a redwood tree, watch a pig give birth, ride a roller coaster, catch some barrel racing and taste exquisite Napa vintages and California craft beers all in one (exhausting) afternoon. Make time to see some of the auctions ($500 for a dozen eggs!) and the interactive agricultural exhibits run by the University of California, Davis.

Downtown Lodi

that sometimes the journey itself is as important as the destination. This is the heart of the Delta: marinas line the southern stretch where you can charter anything that floats, migratory birds fill the skies and cruisers meander the uncrowded roads. The loop ends at **Brannan Island State Recreation Area** (☎916-777-6671; www.parks.ca.gov; 17645 Hwy 160, Rio Vista; per car $10; ☉sunrise-sunset; P 👪), where sandy picnic areas and grassy barbecue spots draw hard-partying campers. By day, it's a great place for families:

it has lots of space in which to run around and a beach where little ones can wade into the reeds. The park offers excellent bird-watching at **Little Franks Tract**, a protected wetland marsh and riparian habitat, where keen-eyed visitors might also spot mink, beavers or river otters.

🛏 p283

The Drive » Take Hwy 160 north to connect with Hwy 12, just across the bridge from Rio Vista, a place to stop and grab a bite. Otherwise, turn right and head east on Hwy 12 for 17 miles toward Lodi, usually a 30-minute drive away. Less than 2 miles

east of I-5, look for Michael David winery on your right.

TRIP HIGHLIGHT

❻ Lodi

Lodi used to be the 'Watermelon Capital of the World,' but today wine grapes rule this patch of the valley. Breezes from the delta soothe the area's intensely hot vineyards, where more Zinfandel grapes are grown than anywhere else in the world. Some particularly old vines have been tended by the same families for more than a century.

The popular **Michael David** (☎209-368-7384; www.michaeldavidwinery.com; 4580 W Hwy 12; tasting $10; ⏰10am-5pm; 🅿) winery sits right off the highway on the way into town. Drive a few miles north-east to the **Lodi Wine & Visitor Center** (☎209-367-4727; www.lodiwine.com; 2545 W Turner Rd; ⏰10am-5pm) to snag a free map of Lodi's rural wineries or sample (responsibly) local vintages at the tasting bar. If you have time to spare, head out on the country lanes to atmospheric wineries like **Jessie's Grove** (☎209-368-0880; www.jessiesgrovewinery.com; 1973 W Turner Rd; ⏰noon-5pm) or **Bokisch Vineyards** (☎209-642-8880; www.bokischvineyards.com; 18921 Atkins Rd; tasting $10; ⏰11am-5pm Thu-Mon; 🚹🐾); if your schedule is tight, go straight downtown to sip some of the region's boutique wines and more famous labels at several tasting rooms within a few blocks of one another.

✕ 🛏 p283

Eating & Sleeping

Sacramento ❶

✕ Empress Tavern   New American $$$

(☎916-662-7694; www.empresstavern.com;
1013 K St; mains $24-41; ⊕11:30am-9pm Mon-
Thu, to 10pm Fri, 5-10pm Sat) In the catacombs
under the historic Crest Theater, this gorgeous
restaurant hosts a menu of creative, meat-
focused dishes (including beef-cheek stroganoff
and grilled pork chop). The space itself is just as
impressive as the food: the arched brick ceilings
and glittering bar feel like a speakeasy supper
club from a bygone era.

🛏 Citizen Hotel   Boutique Hotel $$

(☎916-442-2700; www.thecitizenhotel.com; 926
J St; d from $180; P 🐕 ❄ @ 🛜 🐾) After an
elegant upgrade, this long-vacant 1924 beaux
arts tower became downtown's coolest place to
stay. The details are spot-on: luxe linens, wide-
striped wallpaper and an atmospheric reception
area evoking the building's past. There's an
upscale farm-to-fork restaurant (☎916-492-
4450; www.grangerestaurantandbar.com; 926
J St; mains $27-56; ⊕6:30am-10pm Mon-Thu,
8am-11pm Sat, to 9pm Sun; 🛜) on the ground
floor. Wi-fi costs an additional $9.95 per day.

🛏 Delta King   B&B $$

(☎916-444-5464, 800-825-5464; www.
deltaking.com; 1000 Front St; d from $145;
P 🐕 ❄ 🛜) It's a kitschy treat to sleep aboard
the Delta King, a 1927 paddle wheeler docked
on the river in Old Sacramento. It lights up like a
Christmas tree at night.

Locke ❸

✕ Al's Place   American $

(☎916-776-1800; 13943 Main St, Walnut Grove;
mains $7-21; ⊕11am-9pm) This landmark Locke
bar is a magnet for amiable Harley crews. The
draw isn't the food so much as the ambience.
Above the creaking floorboards, the ceiling's
covered in wrinkled dollar bills, and stuffed
animal heads sport many a forgotten brassiere.

Isleton ❹

✕ Rogelio's   Fusion $

(☎916-777-5878; www.rogelios.net; 34 Main St,
Isleton; mains $8-17; ⊕4-8pm Tue & Wed, 11am-
8pm Thu & Sun, to 9pm Fri & Sat) Making the
most of the delta's multiethnic history, Rogelio's
hotel and casino restaurant serves a Mexican
and Chinese mash-up, with a few Italian and
American standards mixed in. Nothing beats
the carnitas.

Delta Loop ❺

🛏 Brannan Island State Park Recreation Area Campgrounds   Campground $

(☎800-444-7275; www.reservecalifornia.com;
17645 Hwy 160, Rio Vista; tent & RV sites $36-49,
cabin $56; P 🐾) A tidy facility in a protected
wetland marsh provides drive-in and walk-in
campsites. There's a hike-in log cabin with
electricity that sleeps four; bring sleeping bags.

Lodi ❻

✕ Dancing Fox Winery & Bakery   American $

(☎209-366-2634; www.dancingfoxwinery.com;
203 S School St; mains $11-14; ⊕11am-9pm Tue-
Thu, to 10pm Fri & Sat, 9am-3pm Sun) Everything
here celebrates grapes – from the Lewis Family
Estate's own wines to the bread cultures
created from the vineyard's petite sirah grapes.
Menu highlights include the grilled sandwiches
stuffed to max capacity (the tri tip green chili
melt is choice) and a tasty cabernet franc.

🛏 Poppy Sister Inn   B&B $$

(☎209-401-2502; www.poppysisterinn.com;
533 W Oak St; r $150) This buttercream-yellow
Victorian house is a welcoming, atmospheric
base for vineyard exploring. The home has four
cozy rooms (each with a private bathroom), and
your stay includes breakfast and wine social
hours in the afternoon. The wraparound porch
makes an ideal spot for relaxing after a long day.

STRETCH YOUR LEGS
MONTEREY

Start/Finish Municipal Wharf II

Distance 2 miles

Duration 3–4 hours

Old Monterey holds California's most extraordinary collection of 19th-century brick and adobe buildings, all located along the self-guided Path of History. Museums and hidden gardens are also within a fishing line's cast of Monterey Bay.

Take this walk on Trips

2 17

Municipal Wharf II

For an authentic look at Monterey, explore Municipal Wharf II. Fishing boats bob and sway, painters work on their canvases and seafood purveyors hawk fresh catches.

The Walk ≫ From the foot of the wharf, walk south and join the paved recreational trail heading west. Before reaching Fisherman's Wharf, turn south toward Custom House Plaza.

Pacific House

An 1847 adobe, **Pacific House** (☏831-649-7118; www.parks.ca.gov; 20 Custom House Plaza; walking tour adult/child $10/free; ☺10am-4pm Tue-Sun; 🚻) has museum exhibits on California's multicultural history. Grab a Path of History map, ask staff about other nearby historical houses, and buy guided-tour tickets.

The Walk ≫ Stroll north across the plaza to the Custom House.

Custom House

In 1846 when the US flag was raised over the **Custom House** (☏831-649-7111; www.parks.ca.gov; Custom House Plaza; ☺10am-4pm; 🚻), California was formally annexed from Mexico. This restored adobe building displays goods that traders brought to exchange for local cowhides, and there's a browse-worthy gift shop.

The Walk ≫ Head south through Portola Plaza onto Alvarado St. Turn right onto Jefferson St, then left onto Pacific St. Ahead on your right is Colton Hall.

Colton Hall & Old Monterey Jail

Colton Hall (☏831-646-5640; www.monterey.org/museums; 570 Pacific St; ☺10am-4pm) is where California's first constitutional convention took place, in 1849. Once the capitol of Alta (Upper) California, this building now houses a small historical museum. Just south is the **Old Monterey Jail** (☏831-646-5640; www.monterey.org; Dutra St; ☺10am-4pm), featured in John Steinbeck's novel *Tortilla Flat*.

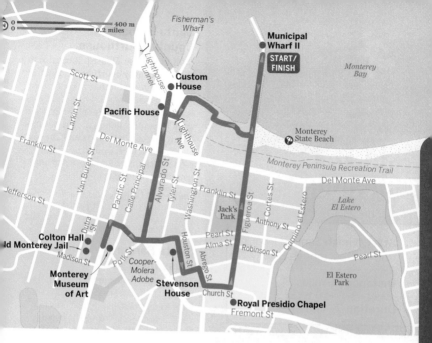

The Walk » On the opposite side of Pacific St is the art museum.

Monterey Museum of Art

Downtown's **Monterey Museum of Art** (☎831-372-5477; www.montereyart.org; 559 Pacific St; adult/child $10/free; ☺11am-5pm Thu-Tue; Ⓟ♿) showcases California contemporary art and the work of modern landscape painters and photographers, including Ansel Adams and Edward Weston.

The Walk » Retrace your steps up Pacific St, turning right onto Jefferson St back to Munras Ave, passing the Cooper-Molera Adobe on your right. Follow Pearl St two blocks east, then turn right onto Houston St.

Stevenson House

Writer Robert Louis Stevenson came to Monterey in 1879 to court his wife-to-be, Fanny Osbourne. **Stevenson House** (☎831-649-7118; www.parks.ca.gov; 530 Houston St; ☺1-4pm Sat Apr-Oct), then called the French Hotel, was where he stayed while reputedly devising *Treasure Island*. The restored interior is filled with memorabilia, including from the writer's later years in Polynesia. The gardens are also worth a look.

The Walk » Continue down Houston St, then turn left on Webster St, right on Abrego St, and left on Church St.

Royal Presidio Chapel

Today known as San Carlos Cathedral, **Royal Presidio Chapel** (☎831-373-2628; www.sancarloscathedral.org; 500 Church St; donations accepted; ☺10am-2pm Fri-Sun, to noon Wed, 1:15-3:15pm 2nd & 4th Mon of month; Ⓟ♿) is California's oldest continuously functioning church. As Monterey expanded under Mexican rule in the 1820s, older buildings were destroyed, leaving behind this National Historic Landmark as the strongest reminder of the defeated Spanish-colonial presence. Free guided tours leave from the adjacent Heritage Center Museum.

The Walk » Head north up Figueroa St for eight blocks back to the foot of Municipal Wharf II.

STRETCH YOUR LEGS
SANTA BARBARA

Start/Finish Santa Barbara County Courthouse

Distance 1.6 miles

Duration 3–4 hours

Frankly put, this chic SoCal city is damn pleasant to putter around. Low-slung between lofty mountains and the sparkling Pacific, downtown's red-tiled roofs, white stucco buildings and Mediterranean vibe make this an irresistible ramble on any sunny afternoon.

Take this walk on Trips

Santa Barbara County Courthouse

Built in Spanish-Moorish Revival style, the 1929 **county courthouse** (☏805-962-6464; http://sbcourthouse.org; 1100 Anacapa St; ◷8am-5pm Mon-Fri, 10am-5pm Sat & Sun) is an absurdly beautiful place to stand trial. It features hand-painted ceilings, wrought-iron chandeliers and Tunisian and Spanish tiles. Climb the *Vertigo*-esque clock tower for city, ocean and mountain panoramas.

The Walk » Exit the courthouse and head southwest along Anapamu St, passing the striking Italianate 1924 Santa Barbara Public Library. Turn left onto State St, downtown's main drag.

Santa Barbara Museum of Art

This compact **museum** (☏805-963-4364; www.sbma.net; 1130 State St; adult $10, child 6-17yr $6, 5-8pm Thu free; ◷11am-5pm Tue, Wed & Fri-Sun, to 8pm Thu; ♿) holds an impressive collection of the work of contemporary California artists, and modern European and American masters such as Matisse and O'Keeffe, as well as 20th-century photography and classical antiquities.

The Walk » Walk three blocks southeast on State St, jam-packed with cafes, restaurants and boutiques. Turn left onto Cañon Perdido St, passing the 1873 Lobero Theatre, then cross Anacapa St.

El Presidio de Santa Barbara State Historic Park

This 18th-century **fort** (☏805-965-0093; www.sbthp.org/presidio; 123 E Canon Perdido St; adult $5, child under 17yr free; ◷10:30am-4:30pm) was colonial Spain's last military stronghold in Alta California. Today this small park encloses several reconstructed adobe buildings. Peek inside the chapel, its interior radiant with gold and scarlet.

The Walk » On the opposite side of Cañon Perdido St, Handlebar Coffee Roasters is a refueling stop. Otherwise, walk one block southeast along Santa Barbara St, turning right onto De La Guerra St.

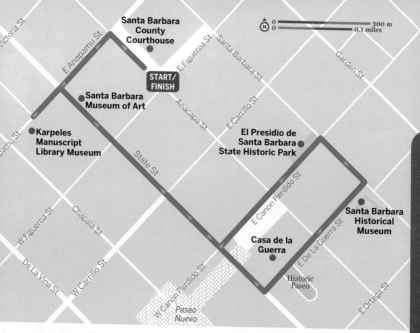

Santa Barbara Historical Museum

Embracing a romantic courtyard, this peaceful little **museum** (☏805-966-1601; www.sbhistorical.org; 136 E De La Guerra St; ⏱10am-5pm Tue-Sat, from noon Sun) has a collection of local memorabilia ranging from the simply beautiful, such as Chumash woven baskets and Spanish colonial-era textiles, to the simply odd, like an intricately carved coffer that belonged to missionary Junípero Serra. Learn about the city's involvement in toppling the last Chinese monarchy, among other footnotes in local history.

The Walk » Keep walking southwest on De La Guerra St, crossing Anacapa St. Casa de la Guerra stands on the north side of the street.

Casa de la Guerra

Your ticket to El Presidio includes entry to **Casa de la Guerra** (☏805-965-0093; www.sbthp.org/casa-de-la-guerra; 15 E De La Guerra St; adult $5, child under 17yr free; ⏱noon-4pm Tue-Sun), a grand 19th-century colonial home with Spanish, Mexican and American heritage exhibits. Authentically restored, this whitewashed adobe with red-tiled roofs was an architectural model for rebuilding all of downtown Santa Barbara after the 1925 earthquake.

The Walk » Continue walking southwest, crossing State St over to the Paseo Nuevo shopping mall. Head northwest four blocks along State St to Anapamu St and turn left.

Karpeles Manuscript Library Museum

This **museum** (☏805-962-5322; https://karpeles.com/museums/sb.php; 21 W Anapamu St; ⏱noon-4pm Wed-Sun) – one of a dozen Karpeles manuscript collections nationwide – is an embarrassment of riches for history nerds, science geeks, and literature- and music-lovers. Rotating exhibits often spotlight literary masterworks.

The Walk » Head northeast on Anapamu St. Turn right onto Anacapa St to return to the county courthouse.

Southern California Trips

Surf, sand and sex will always sell SoCal, especially in Hollywood's star-studded dreamscapes. The reality won't disappoint either: the swimsuits are smaller, the water warmer and summers less foggy here than in NorCal. Los Angeles is the place for celebrity spotting. Surf culture rules San Diego and Orange County, where Disneyland proves an irresistible attraction for kids.

You'll find even more road-tripping adventures inland. Turn up the heat in SoCal's deserts, at the chic resorts of Palm Springs. Then dig deep into the backcountry beauty of Death Valley and Joshua Tree, where dusty 4WD roads lead to remote ghost towns and hidden springs. Finally, leave the crowds behind on SoCal's most iconic road trip: Route 66.

Ventura
/ SHUTTERSTOCK ©

Southern California Trips

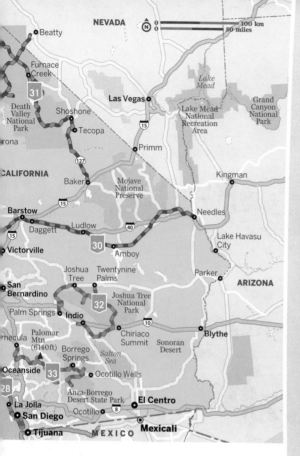

33 Temecula, Julian & Anza-Borrego
3 Days
Vineyards and apple farms, plus off-roading in California's biggest state park. (p349)

☑ **DON'T MISS**

Seal Beach

Slow way down for this old-fashioned beach town, just south of LA, where you can learn to surf by a weather-beaten pier on Trip 27

Sunny Jim Cave

In coastal La Jolla, walk down spooky steps through a tunnel into California's only sea cave accessible to landlubbers on Trip 28

Burbank

Take a behind-the-scenes movie studio tour, attend a live TV show taping or buy fashions worn by real-life stars on Trip 29

Amboy

Watch desert tumbleweeds blow by on Route 66 outside landmark Roy's Motel & Cafe, with its giant-sized neon sign, on Trip 30

Tecopa

Soak in hot-springs pools, then grab a craft beer in town or a snack at China Ranch Date Farm on Trip 31

Disneyland & Orange County Beaches

27

On this fun coastal getaway, let the kids loose at the 'Happiest Place on Earth,' then strike out for surf and sand on sunny SoCal beaches.

TRIP HIGHLIGHTS

0 miles

Disneyland
Party with Mickey Mouse and the Pixar gang

START 1

Seal Beach

Sunset Beach

30 miles

Huntington Beach
Laze on the golden sands of Surf City USA

3

40 miles

4

Newport Beach
Show off your bikini on Balboa Peninsula

Crystal Cove State Park

7

Laguna Beach
An artist's dreamy seascape

55 miles

FINISH
Dana Point

2–4 DAYS
65 MILES / 105KM

GREAT FOR...

BEST TIME TO GO
June to September for summer beach season.

ESSENTIAL PHOTO
Surfers at Huntington Beach Pier.

BEST FOR VIEWS
Corona del Mar's Lookout Point.

Huntington Beach

Classic Trip

Disneyland & Orange County Beaches

27

You'll find gorgeous sunsets, prime surf breaks and just-off-the-boat seafood when road-tripping down the OC's sun-kissed coastal Hwy 1. Yet it's the unexpected, serendipitous discoveries you'll remember long after you've left these blissful 42 miles of surf and sand behind. Start with a couple days at Disneyland's theme parks, and call it a wrap for the perfect SoCal family vacation.

TRIP HIGHLIGHT

❶ Disneyland Resort

The west coast's most popular attraction, **Disneyland** (☏714-781-4636; www.disneyland.com; 1313 Harbor Blvd; 1-day pass adult $104-149, child 3-9yr $96-141, 2-day pass adult/child 3-9yr $225/210; ⊙open daily, seasonal hours vary) has welcomed untold millions since opening in 1955. From the ghostly skeletons of Pirates of the Caribbean to the screeching monkeys of the Indiana Jones Adventure, the pure adrenaline of Space Mountain to the newest 'land,' Star Wars: Galaxy's Edge, there's magical detail everywhere. After dark,

LINK YOUR TRIP

2 Pacific Coast Highways

Orange County is California's official section of the Pacific Coast Hwy (PCH), running along Hwy 1 between Seal Beach and Dana Point.

28 Fun on the San Diego Coast

It's just a 30-mile drive from Dana Point along I-5 south to Carlsbad in San Diego's family-friendly North County.

watch fireworks explode over Sleeping Beauty's Castle.

Across the plaza, Disneyland's younger neighbor, **Disney California Adventure** (DCA; ☏714-781-4565; https://disneyland.disney.go.com; 1313 Harbor Blvd, Anaheim; 1-day pass adult $104-149, child 3-9yr $96-141, 2-day pass adult/child 3-9yr $225/210; 🅿🚻), highlights the best of the Golden State and moviedom in sections like Cars Land, Hollywoodland and Pixar Pier. Catch the *World of Color* special-effects show at night.

The adjacent, pedestrian **Downtown Disney District** is packed with souvenir shops, family restaurants, after-dark bars and entertainment venues.

🛏 p300

The Drive » Follow I-5 south, then take Hwy 22 west through inland Orange County, merging onto I-405 north. After another mile or so, exit onto Seal Beach Blvd, which crawls 3 miles toward the coast. Turn right onto Hwy 1, also known as the Pacific Coast Hwy (PCH) throughout Orange County, then take a left onto Main St in Seal Beach.

❷ Seal Beach

In the SoCal beauty pageant for pint-sized beach towns, Seal Beach takes the crown, a refreshingly unhurried alternative to the more crowded Orange County coast further south. Its

stoplight-free, three-block **Main St** bustles with mom-and-pop restaurants and indie shops that are low on 'tude and high on nostalgia. Follow barefoot surfers trotting toward the ocean where Main St ends, then walk out onto **Seal Beach Pier**. Down on the **beach**, you'll find families spread out on blankets, building sandcastles and playing in the water – all of them ignoring that hideous oil derrick offshore. The gentle waves make Seal Beach a great place to learn to surf. **M&M Surfing School** (☏714-846-7873; www.surfingschool.com; 802 Ocean Ave; 1hr/3hr group lesson $80/90; ⊙lessons 8am-noon early Sep–mid-Jun and Sat & Sun all year, to 2pm Mon-Fri mid-Jun–early Sep; 🚻) parks its van in the lot just north of the pier, off Ocean Ave at 8th St.

The Drive » Past a short bridge south along Hwy 1, drivers drop onto a mile-long spit of land known as Sunset Beach, with its biker bars and harborside kayak and stand-up paddleboarding (SUP) rental shops. Keep cruising Hwy 1 south another 6 miles past Bolsa Chica State Beach and Ecological Reserve to Huntington Beach Pier.

TRIP HIGHLIGHT

❸ Huntington Beach

In 'Surf City USA,' SoCal's obsession with wave riding hits its frenzied peak. There's

Classic Trip

a statue of Hawaiian surfer Duke Kahan-amoku at the intersection of Main St and PCH, and if you look down, you'll see names of legendary surfers in the sidewalk **Surfers' Hall of Fame** (www.hsssurf.com/shof; 300 Pacific Coast Hwy); find out more about them a few blocks east at the **International Surfing Museum** (📞714-960-3483; www.huntingtonbeachsurfing museum.org; 411 Olive Ave; $3; 🕐noon-5pm Tue-Sun). On **Huntington Beach Pier**, you can catch up-close views of daredevils barreling through tubes, though newbie surfers should try elsewhere – locals can be territorial. In summer, the US Open of Surfing draws more than 600 world-class surfers and 500,000 spectators with a minivillage of concerts and more. Otherwise, wide, flat **Huntington City Beach** is a perfect place to snooze on the sand on a giant beach towel. Snag a fire pit just south of the pier to build an evening bonfire with friends.

🍴 🛏 p300

The Drive ≫ From the Huntington Beach Pier at the intersection of Main St, drive south on Hwy 1 alongside the ocean for another 4 miles to Newport Beach. Turn right onto W Balboa Blvd, leading onto the Balboa Peninsula, squeezed between the ocean and Balboa Island, off Newport Harbor.

TRIP HIGHLIGHT

❹ Newport Beach

As seen on Bravo's *Real Housewives of Orange County* and Fox' *The OC* and *Arrested Development,* in glitzy Newport Beach wealthy social-ites, glamorous teens and gorgeous beaches all share the spotlight. Bikini vixens strut down the sandy beach stretching between the peninsula's twin piers, while boogie boarders brave human-eating waves at the **Wedge** and the ballet of yachts in the harbor makes you dream of being rich and famous. From the harbor, hop aboard a ferry over to old-fashioned **Balboa Island** (www.explorebalboa island.com; 🅿) or climb aboard the Ferris wheel at the pint-sized **Balboa Fun Zone** (www.thebalboa funzone.com; 600 E Bay Ave; Ferris wheel $4; 🕐Ferris wheel 11am-6pm Sun-Thu, to 9pm Fri, to 10pm Sat; 👪), near the landmark 1906 **Balboa Pavilion** (www.balboa pavilion.com; 400 Main St).

🍴 🛏 p300, p319

The Drive ≫ South of Newport Beach, prime-time ocean views are just a short detour off Hwy 1. First drive south across the bridge over Newport Channel, then after 3 miles turn right onto Marguerite Ave in Corona del Mar. Once you reach the coast, take another right onto Ocean Blvd.

----

❺ Corona del Mar

Savor some of SoCal's most celebrated ocean views from the bluffs of Corona del Mar, a chichi bedroom community south of Newport Channel. Several postcard beaches, rocky coves and child-friendly tide pools beckon along this idyllic stretch of coast. One of the best viewpoints is at breezy **Lookout Point** on Ocean Blvd near Heliotrope Ave. Below the rocky cliffs to the east is half-mile-long **Main Beach** (Big Corona Beach; 📞949-644-3151; www.newportbeachca.gov; off E Shore Ave; 🕐6am-10pm; 🅿 👪), with fire rings and volleyball courts (arrive early on week-ends to get a parking spot). Stairs lead down to **Pirates Cove**, a great, waveless pocket beach for families – scenes from the classic TV show *Gilligan's Island* were shot here. Head east on Ocean Blvd to **Inspira-tion Point**, near the corner of Orchid Ave, for more vistas of surf, sand and sea.

The Drive ≫ Follow Orchid Ave back north to Hwy 1, then turn right and drive southbound. Traffic thins out as ocean views become more wild and uncluttered by housing developments that head up into the hills on your left. It's just a couple of miles to the entrance of Crystal Cove State Park.

⑥ Crystal Cove State Park

With more than 3 miles of open beach and 2400 acres of undeveloped woodland, **Crystal Cove State Park** (☎949-494-3539; www.parks.ca.gov; 8471 N Coast Hwy; per car $15; ⏰6am-sunset; P ⛹) lets you almost forget that you're in a crowded metro area. It's also an underwater park where scuba enthusiasts can check out the wreck of a Navy Corsair fighter plane that went down in 1949. Or just go tide pooling, fishing, kayaking and surfing along Crystal Cove's exhilaratingly wild, windy shoreline. On the inland side of Hwy 1, miles of hiking and mountain-biking trails wait for landlubbers.

✗ 🛏 p301

The Drive ≫ Drive south on Hwy 1 for another 4 miles or so. As shops, restaurants, art galleries, motels and hotels start to crowd the highway once again, you've arrived in Laguna Beach. Downtown is a maze of one-way streets just east of the Laguna Canyon Rd (Hwy 133) intersection.

TRIP HIGHLIGHT

⑦ Laguna Beach

This early 20th-century artist colony's secluded coves, romantic-looking cliffs and arts-and-crafts bungalows come as a relief after miles of suburban beige-box architecture. Laguna celebrates its bohemian roots with summer arts festivals, dozens of galleries and the acclaimed **Laguna Art Museum** (☎949-494-8971; www.lagunaartmuseum.org; 307 Cliff Dr; adult/student & senior/child under 13yr $7/5/free, 5-9pm 1st Thu of month free; ⏰11am-5pm Fri-Tue, to 9pm Thu). In downtown's village, while away an afternoon browsing the chic boutiques. Along the shore, **Main Beach** is crowded with volleyball players and sunbathers. Just north atop the bluffs, **Heisler Park** winds past public art, palm trees, picnic tables and grand views of rocky shores and tide pools. Drop down to **Divers Cove**, a deep, protected inlet. Heading south, dozens of public beaches sprawl along just a few miles of coastline. Keep a sharp eye out for 'beach access' signs off Hwy 1, or pull into locals' favorite **Aliso Beach County Park** (☎949-923-2280; www.ocparks.com; 31131 S Pacific Coast Hwy; parking per hour $1; ⏰6am-10pm; P ⛹).

✗ 🛏 p301

The Drive ≫ Keep driving south of downtown Laguna Beach on Hwy 1 (PCH) for about 3 miles to Aliso Beach County Park, then another 4 miles into the town of Dana Point. Turn right onto Green Lantern St, then left onto Cove Rd, which winds past the state beach and Ocean Institute onto Dana Point Harbor Dr.

▶ DETOUR: PACIFIC MARINE MAMMAL CENTER

Start: ⑦ Laguna Beach

About 3 miles inland from Laguna Beach is the heart-warming **Pacific Marine Mammal Center** (☎949-494-3050; www.pacificmmc.org; 20612 Laguna Canyon Rd; donations welcome; ⏰10am-4pm; P ⛹), dedicated to rescuing and rehabilitating injured or ill marine mammals. This nonprofit center has a small staff and many volunteers who help nurse rescued pinnipeds (mostly sea lions and seals) back to health before releasing them into the wild. Stop by and take a self-guided facility tour to learn more about these marine mammals and to visit the 'patients' out back.

Classic Trip

ALAN BUDMAN / SHUTTERSTOCK ©

KGRIF / GETTY IMAGES ©

WHY THIS IS A CLASSIC TRIP
ANDREW BENDER, WRITER

The OC coast is a microcosm of the best of SoCal: 42 miles of gorgeous sunsets, prime surfing, just-off-the-boat seafood, secluded coves and sparkling white sands. Each town offers its own experience – surf lessons in Seal Beach, beach volleyball at Huntington Beach, boating around Newport Harbor, eclectic art in Laguna Beach, whale-spotting off Dana Point – but sometimes the best plan is no plan at all.

Above: Crystal Cove at Newport Beach
Left: Laguna Beach
Right: Newport Beach

DEBBIE ECKERT / SHUTTERSTOCK ©

8 Dana Point

Dana Point is all about family fun with whalewatching and sportfishing boats departing from its **harbor**. Designed for kids, the **Ocean Institute** (☏949-496-2274; www.ocean-institute.org; 24200 Dana Pt Harbor Dr; adult/child 2-12yr $10/7.50; ⊙10am-4pm Mon-Fri, to 3pm Sat & Sun, last entry 2:15pm; P ⚄) has replicas of historic tall ships, maritime-related exhibits and a floating research lab. East of the harbor, **Doheny State Beach** (☏949-496-6171; www.dohenystatebeach.org; 25300 Dana Point Harbor Dr; per car $15; ⊙park 6am-10pm, visitor center 10am-4pm Wed-Sun; P ⚄) offers picnic tables, volleyball courts, an oceanfront bike path and a sandy beach for swimming, surfing and tide pooling.

Eating & Sleeping

Disneyland ❶

🛏 Alpine Inn   Motel $

(☎714-535-2186; www.alpineinnanaheim.com;
715 W Katella Ave; r $99-399; P❄@🛜🏊)
Connoisseurs of kitsch will hug their Hummels
over this 42-room, snow-covered chalet facade
on an A-frame exterior and icicle-covered roofs
– framed by palm trees, of course. Bordering
Disney California Adventure, the inn also has
Ferris-wheel views. It's c 1958, and air-con
rooms are well kept and have fridges and
microwaves. Grab 'n' go breakfast is served in
the lobby.

🛏 Disney's Grand Californian
Hotel & Spa   Resort $$$

(☎info 714-635-2300, reservations 714-956-
6425; https://disneyland.disney.go.com/grand-
californian-hotel; 1600 S Disneyland Dr; r from
$586; P❄@🛜🏊) Soaring timber beams
rise above the cathedral-like lobby of the six-
story Grand Californian, Disney's homage to the
arts-and-crafts architectural movement. Cushy
rooms have triple-sheeted beds, down pillows,
bathrobes and all-custom furnishings. Outside
there's a faux-redwood waterslide into the pool.
At night, kids wind down with bedtime stories by
the lobby's giant stone hearth.

Huntington Beach ❸

🍴 Sugar Shack   Cafe $

(☎714-536-0355; www.hbsugarshack.com;
213½ Main St; mains $4-14; ⏰6am-2pm Mon,
Tue, Thu & Fri, to 8pm Wed, to 3pm Sat & Sun)
Expect a wait at this HB institution, or get here
early to see surfer dudes don their wetsuits.
Breakfast is served all day on the bustling Main
St patio and inside, where you can grab a spot at
the counter or a two-top. Photos of surf legends
plastering the walls raise this place almost to
shrine status.

🛏 Shorebreak
Hotel   Boutique Hotel $$$

(☎714-861-4470; www.shorebreakhotel.
com; 500 Pacific Coast Hwy; r from $269;
P☕❄@🛜🏊) Stow your surfboard
(lockers provided) as you head inside HB's
hippest hotel, a stone's throw from the pier.
The Shorebreak has 'surf ambassadors,' a
wetsuit mural in the lobby, a pseudo-steampunk
fitness center with climbing wall, and surfboard
headboards in geometric-patterned rooms.
Minibars stock temporary tattoos and
surfboard wax, in case you forgot yours.

Newport Beach ❹

🍴 Bear Flag Fish Company   Seafood $

(☎949-673-3474; www.bearflagfishco.com;
3421 Via Lido; mains $11-17; ⏰11am-9pm Tue-
Sat, to 8pm Sun & Mon; 🚲) This is *the* place for
generously sized, grilled and *panko*-breaded
fish tacos, ahi burritos, spankin' fresh ceviche
and oysters. Pick out what you want from the
ice-cold display cases, then grab a picnic-table
seat. About the only way this seafood could be
any fresher is if you caught and hauled it off the
boat yourself!

🛏 Bay Shores
Peninsula Hotel   Hotel $$$

(☎949-675-3463; www.thebestinn.com; 1800
W Balboa Blvd; r $175-300; P❄@🛜) With
a 50-plus-year history, this family-run, three-
story hotel flexes some surf-themed muscle.
From complimentary fresh-baked cookies
and free rental movies, it's beachy, casual and
customer-focused with surf-themed murals in
each room. Complimentary parking, beach gear
and continental breakfast buffet, best enjoyed
on the 360-degree-view sun deck. Coin-op
laundry available.

Crystal Cove State Park ⑥

✖ Crystal Cove

Shake Shack American $

(☎949-464-0100; 7703 E Coast Hwy; mains $5-9; ☺7am-8pm; 🚼) At this 1946-vintage wooden snack stand, the shakes – and the ocean views – are as good as ever. Don't fear the date shake; it's delish. They also serve snacks and simple meals (sandwiches, burgers, fries, chili etc) and a kids menu. Expect lunchtime waits during summer and on weekends.

🛏 Crystal Cove

Beach Cottages Cabin $$

(☎reservations 800-444-7275; www.crystalcovealliance.org; 35 Crystal Cove, Crystal Cove State Park Historic District; dm with shared bath from $38, cottages from $269; ☺check-in 4-9pm; 🅿) Right on the beach, these two dozen preserved cottages (c 1930s to '50s) now host guests for a one-of-a-kind stay. Each cottage is different, sleeping between two and nine people in a variety of private or dorm-style accommodations. To snag one, book six months before your intended stay – or pray for cancellations.

Laguna Beach ⑦

✖ Orange Inn Diner $

(☎949-494-6085; www.orangeinncafe.com; 703 S Coast Hwy; mains $7-13; ☺5:30am-5:30pm) Birthplace of the smoothie (it's in the *Guinness World Records*), this little 1931 shop continues to pack in surfers fueling up before hitting the waves. It also serves date shakes, big omelets and breakfast burritos, homemade muffins and deli sandwiches on whole-wheat or sourdough bread.

🛏 Laguna Beach House Hotel $$$

(☎949-497-6645; www.thelagunabeachhouse.com; 475 N Coast Hwy; r $205-419; 🅿 😋 ❄ 🛜 🐾 🐱) Be it good feng shui, friendly staff or proximity to the beach, this 36-room courtyard inn feels right. From the surfboards in the lobby to colorful throw pillows and clean white walls and linens, the decor is contemporary, comfy and clean. Enjoy the heated pool and fire pit.

Fun on the San Diego Coast

28

With 70 miles of coastline and a near-perfect climate, it's tough to know where to start. So just do as the locals do: grab a fish taco and a surfboard and head for the beaches.

TRIP HIGHLIGHTS

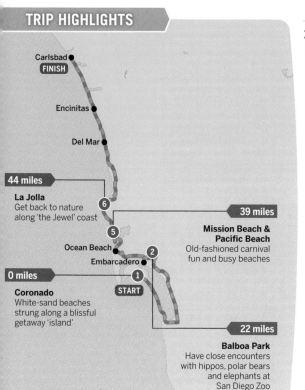

Carlsbad FINISH

Encinitas

Del Mar

44 miles

La Jolla
Get back to nature along 'the Jewel' coast

6

39 miles

Mission Beach & Pacific Beach
Old-fashioned carnival fun and busy beaches

5

Ocean Beach

Embarcadero

2

0 miles

Coronado
White-sand beaches strung along a blissful getaway 'island'

1

START

22 miles

Balboa Park
Have close encounters with hippos, polar bears and elephants at San Diego Zoo

2–4 DAYS
80 MILES / 130KM

GREAT FOR...

BEST TIME TO GO

June to September for prime-time beach weather.

 ESSENTIAL PHOTO

The red-turreted Hotel del Coronado.

 BEST FOR OUTDOORS

La Jolla's coves, beaches and nature preserves.

alboa Park Palm Canyon

Fun on the San Diego Coast

25 miles to
27

78

Carlsbad 9 *San Eli Lagoo*
FINISH

Leucadia

Encinitas

Cardiff-by-the-Se

Most Americans work all year for a two-week vacation. San Diegans work all week for a two-day vacation at the beach. Family-fun attractions found just off the county's gorgeous coastal highways include the USS Midway Museum, Balboa Park's zoo and the Legoland theme park, along with dozens of beaches from ritzy to raucous. With SoCal's most idyllic weather, it's time to roll down the windows and chill, dudes.

TRIP HIGHLIGHT

1 Coronado

With the landmark 1888 **Hotel del Coronado** (619-435-6611, tours 619-522-8100; www. hoteldel.com; 1500 Orange Ave; tours $40; tours 10am daily plus 2pm Sat & Sun; P) and one of the USA's top-rated beaches, the city of Coronado sits across San Diego Bay from Downtown. It's miles from the concrete jungle of the city and the chaos of more crowded beaches further north. After crossing the bay via the curved Coronado Bay Bridge, follow the tree-lined, manicured median strip of Orange Ave a mile toward Ocean Blvd, then park your car and walk around. Sprawling in front of the 'Hotel Del' is postcard-perfect **Coronado Municipal Beach** (P). Around 5 miles further south, **Silver Strand State Beach** (619-435-5184; www.parks. ca.gov; 5000 Hwy 75; parking per car Mon-Fri $10, Sat & Sun $12; 7am-sunset; P) offers calm waters for family-friendly swimming. The strand's long, narrow sand spit connects to the mainland, though people still call this 'Coronado Island.'

p312

The Drive » Follow Hwy 75 south of Silver Strand past San Diego Bay National Wildlife Refuge, curving inland by

PACIFIC OCEAN

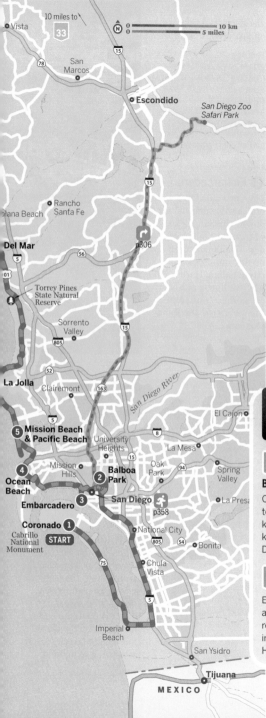

Imperial Beach. Merge onto I-5 northbound, then exit onto Hwy 163 northbound toward Balboa Park. Take exit 1C and follow the signs for the park and zoo.

TRIP HIGHLIGHT

② Balboa Park

Spanish Revival–style pavilions from the 1915–16 Panama-California Exposition add a dash of the exotic to a day spent in Balboa Park. This 1200-acre urban retreat is home to gardens, theaters, more than 16 museums and one giant outdoor organ pavilion, all of which you can see on foot (p358). Without a doubt, the highlight is the **San Diego Zoo** (☎619-231-1515; www.zoo. sandiegozoo.org; 2920 Zoo Dr; adult/child 3-11yr day pass from $58/48; 2-visit pass zoo

LINK YOUR TRIP

27 Disneyland & Orange County Beaches

Cruise 30 miles north on I-5 to Dana Point for another kid-friendly trip, combining knockout beaches with Disneyland's magic.

33 Temecula, Julian & Anza-Borrego

Escape to wine country, apple farms and desert resorts, starting 35 miles inland from Carlsbad via Hwy 76 east to I-15 north.

&/or safari park $92.80/82.80; ⊙9am-9pm mid-Jun–early Sep, to 5pm or 6pm rest of year; P ♿). If it slithers, crawls, stomps, swims, leaps or flies, chances are you'll find it living inside this world-famous zoo. Conservation-minded signs guide visitors through multilevel walkways, where face-to-snout encounters aren't uncommon. Arrive early, when the animal denizens are most active – though many perk up again in the afternoon. Nearby at the **Spanish Village Art Center** (📞619-233-9050; http://spanish villageart.com; 1770 Village Pl; ⊙11am-4pm), an enclave of small tiled cottages are rented out as artists' studios, you can watch potters, jewelry makers, glassblowers, sculptors and painters at work.

The Drive ›› Exit Balboa Park to the east via Zoo Pl, turning right onto Florida Dr and right again onto Pershing Dr. Merge onto I-5 north for over a mile, then take exit 17A. Drive almost another mile west on Hawthorn St toward the waterfront, then turn left onto Harbor Dr.

---

❸ Embarcadero

The Coronado ferry and cruise ships moor along downtown San Diego's waterfront Embarcadero. Well-manicured oceanfront promenades stretch along Harbor Dr, where a lineup of historical sailing ships points the way to the **Maritime Museum** (📞619-234-9153; www.sdmaritime.org; 1492 N Harbor Dr; adult/

MANUELA DURSON / SHUTTERSTOCK ©

child 3-12yr/child under 3yr $20/10/free; ⊙9am-9pm late May-early Sep, 9am-8pm rest of year; ♿). Climb aboard the 1863 *Star of India* and don't miss seeing the B-39 Soviet attack submarine. The even larger **USS Midway Museum** (📞619-544-9600; www.midway.org; 910 N Harbor Dr; adult/child 6-12yr/child under 6yr $26/12/free; ⊙10am-5pm, last admission 4pm; P ♿) is housed on the Navy's longest-serving aircraft carrier (1945–92); it saw action in WWII, Vietnam and the Gulf War. *Top Gun's* Goose and Maverick may spring to mind at

DETOUR: SAN DIEGO ZOO SAFARI PARK

Start: ❷ Balboa Park

Take a walk on the 'wild' side at **San Diego Zoo Safari Park** (📞760-747-8702, 619-231-1515; www.sdzsafaripark.org; 15500 San Pasqual Valley Rd, Escondido; adult/child 3-11yr day pass from $58/48, 2-visit pass safari park &/or zoo $92.80/82.80; ⊙9am-5pm; P ♿), where giraffes graze, lions lounge and rhinos romp across 1800 acres of open range. For that instant safari feel, board the Africa Tram, which tours some of the field exhibits in just 25 minutes. Elsewhere, animals are in giant outdoor enclosures so naturalistic it's as if the humans are guests. There's a petting kraal, zookeeper talks and animal encounters too. The park is in Escondido, 30 miles northeast of Balboa Park via Hwy 163 and I-15 northbound; alternatively, it's 25 miles east of coastal Carlsbad via Hwy 78. Parking costs $15.

La Jolla

the sight of this floating city. A self-guided tour is the best way to experience history: crawl into berthing spaces, the galley and sickbay and, of course, peer over the flight deck with its restored aircraft, including an F-14 Tomcat.

The Drive » Follow Harbor Dr northwest for 3 miles as it curves along the waterfront past the airport. Turn right onto Nimitz Blvd for another mile, then left onto Chatsworth Blvd and right on Narragansett Ave. After a mile, you'll intersect with Sunset Cliffs Blvd in Ocean Beach.

④ Ocean Beach

San Diego's most bohemian seaside community, OB is a place of seriously scruffy haircuts and tattooed and pierced skin. **Newport Ave**, the main drag, runs perpendicular to the beach through a downtown district of bars, street-food eateries, surf and music shops, and vintage-clothing and antique boutiques. Half-mile-long **Ocean Beach Pier** has all the architectural allure of a freeway ramp, but at its end you'll get a great perspective on the coast. A bait-and-tackle shop

rents fishing poles if you want to try your luck. Further north on **Dog Beach**, pups chase birds around the marshy area where the river meets the sea, or walk a few blocks south of the pier to **Sunset Cliffs Park** for surfing and, yes, brilliant sunsets.

✗ p312

The Drive » Follow stop-and-go Sunset Cliffs Blvd north. Merge onto W Mission Bay Dr, which crosses the water twice and curves past SeaWorld. Less than 4 miles from Ocean Beach, you'll intersect with Mission Blvd; turn left to reach the main beach and Belmont Park.

TRIP HIGHLIGHT

❺ Mission Beach & Pacific Beach

This is the SoCal of the movies: buffed surfers and bronzed sun worshippers pack the 3-mile-long stretch of beach from South Mission Jetty north to Pacific Beach Point. San Diego's best people-watching is along **Ocean Front Walk**, the boardwalk that connects the two beaches. For old-fashioned carnival fun in Mission Beach,

Belmont Park (☎858-488-1549; www.belmontpark.com; 3146 Mission Blvd; per ride or attraction $4-15, all-day ride pass incl attractions under/over 48in $56/46; ☺11am-6pm Mon-Thu,11am to 10pm Fri & Sat, 11am-9pm Sun, shorter hours during winter; P 🚼) has been giving kids a thrill with its Giant Dipper wooden roller coaster since 1925. There are bumper cars, a tilt-a-whirl, a carousel, other classic rides and an escape room. At the ocean end of Garnet Ave in Pacific Beach, **Crystal**

Pier is a mellow place to gaze out to sea or fish. Just inland at **Mission Bay** (www.sandiego.gov/park-and-recreation; P 🚼), you can play beach volleyball and zip around **Fiesta Island** on water skis or fly a kite at **Mission Bay Park**. Sailing, windsurfing and kayaking dominate northwest Mission Bay, and there's delightful cycling and inline skating on miles of paved recreational paths.

✖ 🛏 p312

TIJUANA, MEXICO

Just beyond the busiest land border in the western hemisphere is Tijuana, Mexico (population around 2 million). It was for decades a cheap, convivial escape for hard-partying San Diegans, Angelenos, sailors and college kids. Around two decades ago, a double-whammy of drug-related violence and global recession turned once bustling tourist areas into ghost towns. While there are pockets of hope around the city, there is also a very worrying local methamphetamine market. At the time of research, Tijuana had the highest murder rate in the world. The difference from squeaky-clean San Diego is palpable from the moment you cross the border. However, while travelers should maintain a decent level of caution, many visits are trouble-free and there are numer reasons to visit.

The main tourist drag is **Avenida Revolución** ('La Revo'), though its charm is marred by cheap clothing and souvenir stores, strip joints, pharmacies selling bargain-priced medications to Americans, and touts best rebuffed with a firm 'no.' It's a lot more appealing just beyond La Revo, toward and around **Avenida Constitución**, where sightseeing highlights include **Catedral de Nuestra Señora de Guadalupe**, the city's oldest church; **Mercado El Popo**, an atmospheric market hall selling everything from tamarind pods to religious iconography; and **Pasaje Rodríguez**, an arcade filled with youthful art galleries, bars and trendsetters. A short taxi ride away, **Museo de las Californias**, inside the architecturally daring **Centro Cultural Tijuana** (aka El Cubo, the Cube), offers an excellent history of the border region from prehistory to the present; there's signage in English.

A passport is required for the **border crossing** (☎619-690-8900; www.cbp.gov/contact/ports/san-ysidro-class; 720 E San Ysidro Blvd; ☺24hr). Driving into Mexico is not recommended. By public transportation, the San Diego Trolley Blue Line runs from downtown San Diego to **San Ysidro**, at the border. Cross the border on foot, and walk approximately 20 minutes to La Revo; follow signs reading 'Centro Downtown.' If traveling by taxi on the Mexican side, be sure to take a taxi with a meter.

The Drive >> Heading north of Pacific Beach on Mission Blvd, turn left onto Loring St, which curves right onto La Jolla Blvd. Winding through several traffic circles (roundabouts), the boulevard streams along the coast for 3 miles to downtown La Jolla, stretched along Pearl St east of the beach.

- - - - - - - - - - - - - - -

TRIP HIGHLIGHT

⑥ La Jolla

Sitting pretty and privileged on one of SoCal's loveliest sweeps of coast, La Jolla (say la-*hoy*-ah, if you please, similar to *joya*, the Spanish word for 'jewel') is a ritzy town of shimmering beaches, downtown fashionista boutiques and clifftop mansions. Take advantage of the sunshine by kayaking and snorkeling at **La Jolla Cove**, or go scuba diving and snorkeling in **San Diego-La Jolla Underwater Park**, a protected ecological zone harboring a variety of marine life, kelp forests, reefs and canyons. Waves have carved a series of caves into the sandstone cliffs east of La Jolla Cove. From land, you can walk down 145 spooky steps to the **Sunny Jim Cave**, accessed via the **Cave Store** (☎858-459-0746; www.cavestore.com; 1325 Coast Blvd; adult/child $5/3; ⊗10am-5:30pm, cave entry 5pm; 🚻).

Heading north along La Jolla Shores Dr, the oceanfront **Birch Aquari-**

LOCAL KNOWLEDGE: CHILDREN'S POOL

Along the coast in La Jolla, take your kids to the **Children's Pool** (850 Coast Blvd; ⊗24hr; 🚻). But not for swimming! For decades, seals and sea lions have been lolling on the protected beach, and children now come to watch the pinnipeds and their pups. Animal rights groups have duked it out in court to protect the cove as a rookery, while some local swimmers and divers want the seals removed. For now the seals remain, surrounded by a simple rope barrier during pupping season to keep humans at bay – you can also view them from the coast wall. The beach and cove are off Coast Blvd.

um at Scripps (☎858-534-3474; www.aquarium.ucsd.edu; 2300 Expedition Way; adult/child 3-17/child under 2yr $19.50/15/free; ⊗9am-5pm; 🅿🚻) has kid-friendly tidepool displays. Another 5 miles further north, **Torrey Pines State Natural Reserve** (☎858-755-2063; www.torreypine.org; 12600 N Torrey Pines Rd; ⊗7:15am-sunset, visitor center 9am-4pm Oct-Apr, to 6pm May-Sep; 🅿🚻) protects the endangered Torrey pine tree and offers nature walks above a state beach, where hang gliders dramatically soar in for a landing.

✕ p312

The Drive >> Driving below the natural preserve next to Torrey Pines State Beach, panoramic ocean views open up as the coastal highway narrows and crosses over a lagoon, then climbs the sandstone cliffs toward Del Mar, just over 10 miles away.

⑦ Del Mar

The ritziest of North County's seaside suburbs is home to the pink, Mediterranean-style **Del Mar Racetrack & Fairgrounds** (☎858-792-4242; www.dmtc.com; 2260 Jimmy Durante Blvd; from $6; ⊗race season mid-Jul–early Sep), cofounded in 1937 by celebrities including Bing Crosby and Oliver Hardy. It's worth braving the crowds on opening day, if nothing else to see the amazing spectacle of over-the-top hats. Brightly colored hot-air balloons are another trademark sight in Del Mar – book ahead for a sunset flight with **California Dreamin'** (☎951-699-0601; www.californiadreamin.com; per person from $148; ⊗from 5:45am). Downtown Del Mar (sometimes called 'the village') extends for about a mile along Camino del Mar. At its hub, **Del Mar Plaza** (📞858-847-2284; www.delmarplaza.com; 1555 Camino Del Mar) shopping center has restaurants, boutiques and upper-level terraces that look out to sea. At the west end of 15th St, beachfront **Seagrove Park** has grassy lawns, perfect for picnicking.

The Drive » Continue up the coast on Camino del Mar, leading onto S Coast Hwy 101 into Solana Beach, where the arts, fashion and antiques shops of Cedros Ave Design District are just one block inland. Continue north on S Coast Hwy 101 into Encinitas, about 6 miles north of Del Mar.

---

❽ Encinitas

Technically part of Encinitas, the southern satellite of **Cardiff-by-the-Sea** has groovy restaurants, surf shops and new-agey businesses lined up along the coast. Known for its surfing breaks and laid-back crowds, Cardiff sits by the coastal **San Elijo Lagoon** (📞760-623-3026; www.sanelijo.org; 2710 Manchester Ave; ⊙ nature center 9am-5pm; P ♿), a 979-acre ecological preserve that is popular with bird watchers and hikers. Stop by the nature center for kid-friendly educational exhibits and wide-angle views from the 2nd-floor observation deck.

Since Paramahansa Yogananda built his **Self-**

Realization Fellowship Retreat (📞760-436-7220; www.encinitastemple.org; 215 K St; ⊙ meditation garden 9am-5pm Tue-Sat, from 11am Sun) by the sea here in 1937, Encinitas has been a magnet for healers and spiritual seekers. The fellowship's compact but lovely meditation garden has wonderful ocean vistas, a stream and koi pond. The gold lotus domes of the hermitage mark the turn-out for **Swami's**, a powerful reef break surfed by territorial locals. Apart from outdoor cafes, bars, restaurants and surf shops, downtown's main attraction is the 1928 **La Paloma Theatre** (📞760-436-7469; www.lapalomatheatre.com; 471 S Coast Hwy 101; tickets $10), an arthouse cinema screening indie, international and cult films nightly.

✗ p312

The Drive » About 4 miles north of Encinitas, S Coast Hwy 101 becomes Carlsbad Blvd, slowly rolling north along the ocean cliffs for more than 5 miles into Carlsbad Village. If you go too far, you'll hit Oceanside, largely a commuter town for Marine Corps Base Camp Pendleton.

---

❾ Carlsbad

One of California's last remaining tidal wetlands, **Batiquitos Lagoon** (📞760-931-0800; www.batiquitosfoundation.org; Gabbiano Lane; ⊙ nature center 9am-12:30pm

Mon-Fri, 9am-3pm Sat & Sun subject to volunteer availability; P ♿) separates Carlsbad from Encinitas. Go hiking here to see prickly pear cactus, coastal sage scrub and eucalyptus trees, as well as great heron and snowy egrets. Then detour inland past the springtime blooms of **Carlsbad Ranch Flower Fields** (📞760-431-0352; www.theflowerfields.com; 5704 Paseo del Norte; adult/child 3-10yr $18/9; ⊙ usually 9am-6pm Mar–mid-May; P ♿) to **Legoland California Resort** (📞760-203-3604; www.legoland.com/california; 1 Legoland Dr; adult/child 3-12yr from $101/95, parking $25; ⊙10am-5pm; P ♿), a fun fantasy park of rides, shows and attractions for the elementary-school set. Tots can dig for dinosaur bones, pilot helicopters and earn their driver's license, while mom and dad will probably get a kick out of Miniland USA, recreating such national landmarks as the White House, the Golden Gate Bridge and Las Vegas, all made entirely of Lego blocks. Back at the coast, you can go beachcombing for seashells on the long, sandy beaches, off Carlsbad Blvd. The beaches run south of Carlsbad Village Dr, where a beach boardwalk beckons for sunset strolls.

🛏 p312

Eating & Sleeping

Coronado ❶

🛏 **Hotel del Coronado** Luxury Hotel **$$$**
(☑619-435-6611; www.hoteldel.com; 1500
Orange Ave; r from $382; 🅿 ⊖ ✳ @ 🤶 🐾 🥋)
Now managed by Hilton, San Diego's iconic hotel
provides the essential Coronado experience:
more than a century of history (p304), a pool, a
spa, a well-equipped gym, shops, restaurants,
manicured grounds and a white-sand beach. Book
a room in the main Victorian-era hotel, not in the
adjacent seven-story 1970s tower.

Ocean Beach ❹

✕ **Hodad's**   Burgers **$**
(☑619-224-4623; www.hodadies.com; 5010
Newport Ave; burgers $5-15; ⊖11am-9pm
Sun-Thu, 11am-9:30pm Fri & Sat) Since the flower-
power days of 1969, OB's legendary burger joint
has served great shakes, massive baskets of
onion rings and succulent hamburgers wrapped
in paper. The walls are covered in license plates;
grunge/surf-rock plays (loud!); and your bearded,
tattooed server might sidle into your booth to
take your order.

Mission Beach & Pacific Beach ❺

✕ **Kono's Surf Club**   Cafe **$**
(☑858-483-1669; www.konoscafe.com; 704
Garnet Ave, Pacific Beach; mains $5.50-12; ⊖7am-
3pm Mon-Fri, 7am-4pm Sat & Sun; 🖶) This place
makes five kinds of breakfast burritos that you
eat out of a basket in view of Crystal Pier (patio
seating available) alongside pancakes, eggs
and Kono potatoes. Burgers and sandwiches for
lunch. It's always crowded but well worth the wait.

🛏 **Crystal Pier
Hotel & Cottages**   Cottage **$$$**
(☑858-483-6983; www.crystalpier.com; 4500
Ocean Blvd, Pacific Beach; cottages $225-600;
🅿 ⊖ 🤶) Hear the waves crashing below
while you sleep in one of the charming 1930s
cottages on San Diego's wooden Crystal Pier

– in a fabulous location in the center of Pacific
Beach boardwalk. The dreamy ocean views and
sunsets from spacious decks don't get much
better than this. Most have small kitchens, and
newer, larger cottages sleep up to six.

La Jolla ❻

✕ **George's at the Cove**   Californian **$$$**
(☑858-454-4244; www.georgesatthecove.com;
1250 Prospect St; mains $20-56; ⊖11am-10pm
Sun-Thu, 11am-11pm Fri & Sat) The Euro-Cal
cooking is as dramatic as the oceanfront
location, thanks to the bottomless imagination of
chef Trey Foshee. George's has graced just about
every list of top restaurants in California – and,
indeed, the USA. Three venues allow you to enjoy
the food in different atmospheres and at different
price points: Ocean Terrace, George's California
Modern and the no-reservations Level 2.

Encinitas ❽

✕ **Swami's Café**   Cafe **$**
(☑760-944-0612; www.swamiscafe.com; 1163
S Coast Hwy 101; mains $6-15; ⊖7am-4pm
Mon-Fri, 7am-5pm Sat-Sun; 🖝 🖶) Across from
the Self-Realization Fellowship Retreat, this local
institution (now a local chain) can't be beaten for
breakfast burritos, multigrain pancakes, stir-fries,
salads, smoothies and three-egg omelets. Most
of the seating at this original Encinitas location is
out on an umbrella-covered patio.

Carlsbad ❾

🛏 **Legoland Hotel**   Hotel **$$$**
(☑760-918-5346, 760-786-0034; www.legoland.
com; 5885 The Crossings Dr; r from $396;
🅿 ⊖ ✳ @ 🤶 🥋) Lego designers were let
loose on this hotel, just outside Legoland's main
gate, and boy is it fun. Thousands of Lego models
(dragons to surfers) populate the property, and
the elevator turns into a disco between floors.
Each floor has its own theme (pirate, adventure,
kingdom), down to the rooms' wallpaper, props
(Lego cannonballs – cool!), even the shower
curtains.

SoCal Pop Culture

29

Star in your own reality show on this whirlwind tour of SoCal, sampling eye-popping filming locations, superstar hangouts and Hollywood's cult of celebrity.

TRIP HIGHLIGHTS

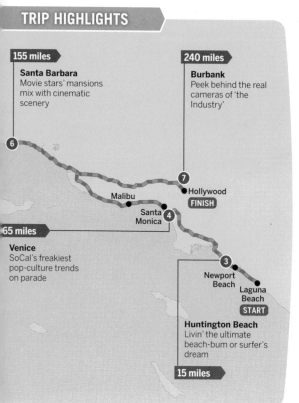

155 miles

Santa Barbara
Movie stars' mansions mix with cinematic scenery

6

65 miles

Venice
SoCal's freakiest pop-culture trends on parade

240 miles

Burbank
Peek behind the real cameras of 'the Industry'

7

Malibu

Hollywood
FINISH

Santa **4**
Monica

3

Newport
Beach   Laguna
Beach
START

Huntington Beach
Livin' the ultimate beach-bum or surfer's dream

15 miles

3 DAYS
245 MILES / 395KM

GREAT FOR...

BEST TIME TO GO
Year-round, although winter can be rainy.

ESSENTIAL PHOTO
Your favorite star on the Hollywood Walk of Fame.

 BEST FOR MOVIE FANS
Burbank's behind-the-scenes studio tours.

SoCal Pop Culture

Begin on the cinematic beaches of Orange County. Then zoom northwest along the Pacific past the skater punks of Venice Beach, Hollywood moguls' mansions in Malibu and celebrity haunts in Santa Barbara. Swing back to LA's San Fernando Valley for a TV and movie studio tour, then wind up in Hollywood with a cruise down the rockin' Sunset Strip.

1 Laguna Beach

Filled with cliffs and coves, Laguna may be the OC's most photogenic beach town, as seen in the 1954 Judy Garland classic *A Star is Born*, MTV's *Laguna Beach*, Bravo's *Real Housewives of Orange County*, and the Netflix series *Dead to Me*. The real Laguna is more bohemian bon-homie than Hollywood hype, but you can shop the chic boutiques in downtown's **village**, then strike your own pose on **Main Beach** in your

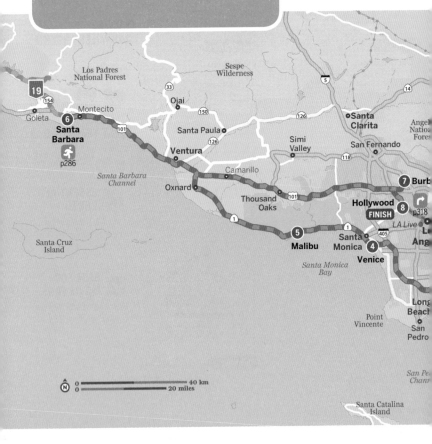

teeny-weeny bikini. Jealously guarded by locals, **Thousand Steps Beach** (off 9th Ave) is hidden off Hwy 1 just south of Mission Hospital, where a stairway leads down to a rocky beach, postcard-perfect for sunbathing.

✗ 🛏 p301

The Drive >> Join Hwy 1, aka Pacific Coast Hwy (PCH), for the quick 10-mile trip north to Newport Beach, passing oceanfront Crystal Cove State Park. Exit onto Newport Blvd, following it down onto the Balboa Peninsula.

② Newport Beach

Even if you've never visited Newport Beach, if you've seen *The OC, Arrested Development* or the *Real Housewives* series, the local culture of yachtsmen, trophy wives, their beautiful yet angsty teens, and, yes, frozen bananas on a stick will be oh-so-familiar. The **Newport Beach Film Festival** (www.newport beachfilmfest.com; ⏰Aug), headquartered in the chi-chi Lido Village shopping district, offers up-close-and-personal stargazing. The 2-mile, oceanfront **Balboa Peninsula** connects the **Balboa** and **Newport Piers**, teeming with surfers and glamazons, and more lifestyles of the rich and famous revolve around the posh **Fashion Island** (📞949-721-2000; www.shopfashionisland.com; 401 Newport Center Dr; ⏰10am-9pm Mon-Fri, to 7pm Sat, 11am-6pm Sun) mall.

✗ 🛏 p300, p319

The Drive >> Keep going north up Hwy 1, often crawling with bumper-to-bumper traffic on summer weekends when everyone's heading to the beach. Relax, it's only 4 miles to Huntington Beach, at the intersection of Main St and PCH.

TRIP HIGHLIGHT

③ Huntington Beach

Huntington Beach has been *the* SoCal surf hot spot since George Freeth first demonstrated the Hawaiian sport of wave-riding here a century ago. 'HB' has even trademarked its nickname 'Surf City USA'. Surf scenes for the reboot of *90210* were shot at Huntington State Beach, and James Corden and pals received lifeguard training here. Buyers for major retailers come to see what surfers are wearing and then market the look, while volleyballers blithely play on the golden sand and skaters whiz past the oceanfront pier.

✗ 🛏 p300

SOUTHERN CALIFORNIA **29** SOCAL POP CULTURE

LINK YOUR TRIP

19 Santa Barbara Wine Country

Follow Hwy 154 up into the mountains of the Santa Ynez Valley, where *Sideways* wine country is ready for its close-up.

27 Disneyland & Orange County Beaches

If you can't get enough of the OC's sunny sands, keep cruising south on coastal Hwy 1, then hit Disneyland.

The Drive >> Keep going north for 12 miles on Hwy 1 passing Sunset Beach. Then join I-405 north, driving past industrial areas of Los Angeles. Take the Hwy 90 westbound exit toward Marina del Rey, slingshot around the marina to Pacific Ave by the beach, turn right and roll north to Venice.

TRIP HIGHLIGHT

4 Venice

Venice Beach has been a lure for filmmakers since its founding in 1905, so you may experience déjà vu if you've seen *Speed, The Doors, White Men Can't Jump, I Love You Man, The Big Lebowski, Nightcrawler, LA Story,* or the opening of TV's *Three's Company.* Nowadays, new-age hippies, modern-day muscled Schwarzeneggers, cannabis seekers, goth punks and tribal drummers all share the must-see **Venice Boardwalk** (Ocean Front Walk; Venice Pier to Rose Ave). Venice is also the birthplace of SoCal skater-punk culture, as chronicled in the movies *Dogtown and Z Boys* and *Lords of Dogtown.* So board your board, strap on some in-line skates, or hop on a fluorescent beach cruiser and shake what yo' mama gave you.

✕ ⌂ p319

The Drive >> Drive north on Ocean Ave and rejoin PCH past I-10. Cruise past Santa Monica's carnival pier with its solar-powered Ferris wheel. Keep following PCH north as it curves alongside the ocean to Malibu, just over a dozen miles away.

5 Malibu

Mile for fabulous oceanfront mile, Malibu may have SoCal's densest celebrity quotient. Keep your eyes peeled for A-listers sipping iced lattes as they shop at the **Malibu Country Mart** (📞310-456-7300; www.malibu countrymart.com; 3835 Cross Creek Rd; ⊙10am-midnight Mon-Sat, to 10pm Sun; 🍴; 🚌Metro Line 534). Down the street, spot sushi-scarfing celebs at **Nobu Malibu** (📞310-317-9140; www.noburestaurants.com/malibu; 22706 Pacific Coast Hwy; dishes $18-78; ⊙noon-10pm Mon-Thu, 9am-11pm Fri & Sat, 9am-10pm Sun; 🅿; 🚌Metro Line 534). About 15 miles further west, the hidden coves of **Leo Carrillo State Park** (📞310-457-8143; www.parks.ca.gov; 35000 W Pacific Coast Hwy; per car $12; ⊙8am-10pm; 🅿🍴) made a romantic backdrop in *Pirates of the Caribbean* and *The Karate Kid.* Beware of rough surf: John Travolta and Olivia Newton-John almost got swept out to sea here in the opening scene of *Grease.*

✕ p60

The Drive >> Hug the coast by following Hwy 1 north, which turns inland to intersect Hwy 101, a multilane freeway that swings back to the coast at Ventura, then flows past ocean cliffs and beaches northwest to Santa Barbara, about a 90-minute trip from Malibu without traffic jams.

TRIP HIGHLIGHT

6 Santa Barbara

A Mediterranean vibe and red-roofed, white-stucco streetscape give credence to Santa Barbara's nickname, the 'American Riviera.' Spanish Colonial Revival buildings clustered along downtown's **State St** have made cameos in countless movies, including *The Graduate, It's Complicated* and *20th Century Women.* A 45-minute drive up into the mountains via

Skateboard park in Venice Beach

scenic Hwy 154, Santa Barbara's **wine country** sets the hilarious scene for the Oscar-winning 2004 film *Sideways*. Just east of Santa Barbara off Hwy 101, celeb-heavy **Montecito** is a leafy suburb tucked between the mountains and the Pacific. Heavy hitters like Oprah Winfrey, Steven Spielberg and Ellen Deeneres have homes here and occasionally venture out along downtown's boutique-and-patio-lined main drag, **Coast Village Road**.

p60, p72, p217, p319

The Drive » Take Hwy 101 south back to Ventura, then head up into the mountains via the steep Conjeo (Camarillo) Grade. Leveling off, Hwy 101 zooms east through the San Fernando Valley. Veer left onto Hwy 134 toward Burbank, almost 90 miles after leaving Santa Barbara.

TRIP HIGHLIGHT

7 Burbank

Long ago, the TV and movie biz (locals just call it 'the Industry') de-camped from Hollywood, and the San Fernando Valley has since been the origin of countless block-busters (and also, infa-mously, ground zero for

SoCal's porn industry). 'The Valley' also gave the world 1980s 'Valley Girl' speak and SoCal's ubiqui-tous mall-rat culture.

Go behind the scenes on the **Warner Bros Studio Tour** (☎818-972-8687; www.wbstudiotour.com; 3400 Warner Blvd; tours adult/child 8-12yr from $69/59; ⏰8:30am-3:30pm year-round, extended hours Jun-Aug; ☒155, 222, 501 stop about 400yd from tour center), or take your scream-ing tweens and teens to **Universal Studios Holly-lywood** (☎800-864-8377; www.universalstudiosholly wood.com; 100 Universal City Plaza, Universal City; 1-/2-day

DETOUR: LA LIVE

Start: ❽ Hollywood

Next to downtown's **Staples Center** (📞888-929-7849; www.staplescenter.com; 1111 S Figueroa St; 👪; Ⓜ A/E Lines to Pico), the saucer-shaped sports and entertainment arena, **LA Live** (📞213-763-5483; www.lalive.com; 800 W Olympic Blvd; Ⓟ👪; Ⓜ A/E Lines to Pico) is a shiny corporate entertainment hub. Glimpse larger-than-life statues of Magic Johnson and Wayne Gretzky. Visitors to the **Grammy Museum** (📞213-765-6800; www.grammymuseum.org; 800 W Olympic Blvd; adult/child $15/13; ⊙10:30am-6:30pm Sun, Mon, Wed & Thu, 10am-8pm Fri & Sat; Ⓟ👪; Ⓜ A/E Lines to Pico) can get lost in sound chambers; try mixing and remixing, singing and rapping; and view icons like GnR's bass drum, Yo-Yo Ma's cello and MJ's glove enshrined like holy relics (though exhibitions do rotate). It's about 8 miles southeast of Hollywood via Hwy 101 and I-110 south (exit at 8th St).

from $109/149, child under 3yr free; ⊙daily, hours vary; Ⓟ👪; Ⓜ B Line to Universal City) theme park, where you can escape into the Wizarding World of Harry Potter, ride a tram tour past working sound stages and pick up free tickets for a live TV show taping. To buy cast-off TV and movie star fashions, visit **It's a Wrap!** (📞818-567-7366; www.itsawraphollywood.com; 3315 W Magnolia Blvd; ⊙11am-8pm Mon-Fri, to 6pm Sat & Sun).

The Drive ›› It's a quick 3-mile trip south on Hwy 101 from Universal Studios to Hollywood. Take the Highland Ave exit and drive south on Highland Ave, which intersects Hollywood Blvd.

----

❽ Hollywood

Like an ageing starlet making a comeback, this LA neighborhood is undergoing a not-quite-ready-for-its-close-up renaissance of hip hotels, restored movie palaces and glitzy bars and nightclubs. Although you're unlikely to see any in-person celebrities, the pink-starred **Hollywood**

Walk of Fame (www.walkoffame.com; Hollywood Blvd; Ⓜ B Line to Hollywood/Highland) still attracts millions of wide-eyed visitors every year. Snap a souvenir photo amid the concrete handprints and footprints outside the **TCL Chinese Theatre** (Grauman's Chinese Theatre; 📞323-461-3331, guided tours 323-463-9576; www.tclchinesetheatres.com; 6925 Hollywood Blvd; 👪; Ⓜ B Line to Hollywood/Highland), and swing by the **Dolby Theatre** (📞323-308-6300; www.dolbytheatre.com; 6801 Hollywood Blvd; tours adult/child $25/19; ⊙10:30am-4pm; Ⓟ; Ⓜ B Line to Hollywood/Highland), home to the Academy Awards ceremony, before visiting the **Hollywood Museum** (📞323-464-7776; www.thehollywoodmuseum.com; 1660 N Highland Ave; adult/senior/student/child $15/12/12/5; ⊙10am-5pm Wed-Sun; 👪; Ⓜ B Line to Hollywood/Highland), a trove of costumes, props and memorabilia.

Cruise west along the **Sunset Strip**, packed with celeb-slumming bars and dog-eared rock venues where the Rolling Stones and the Doors once tore up the stages.

✕ 🛏 p319

Eating & Sleeping

Newport Beach ❷

✘ Malibu Farm Lido   Californian $$

(www.malibu-farm.com; 3420 Via Oporto,
Lido Marina Village; small plates $13-20, large
plates $20-31; [P]) Coastal chic rules at this
whitewashed, indoor-outdoor *boîte* facing the
yachts on the harbor. Cauliflower-crust pizzas,
Newport nachos, branzino fish tacos and
Swedish mini-pancakes just taste better with a
view this good.

Venice ❹

✘ Gjelina   American $$

([☎]310-450-1429; www.gjelina.com; 1429 Abbot
Kinney Blvd,; mains $10-35; [🕐]8am-midnight;
[🚍]Big Blue Bus line 18) If one restaurant defines
the new Venice, it's this. Carve out a spot on
the communal table between the hipsters and
yuppies, or get your own slab of wood on the
elegant stone terrace, and dine on imaginative
small plates (raw yellowtail spiced with chili and
mint and drenched in olive oil and blood orange)
and sensational thin-crust, wood-fired pizza.

🛏 Hotel Erwin   Boutique Hotel $$$

([☎]310-452-1111; www.hotelerwin.com; 1697
Pacific Ave; r from $269; [P][❄][@][🛜]; [🚍]Metro
Line 733, [🚍]Big Blue Bus Line 1) This one-time
motor inn has been dressed up, colored and
otherwise funkified in retro style. Think eye-
popping oranges, yellows and greens, framed
photos of graffiti art and ergo sofas in the
spacious rooms. Book online for the best deals.
Whether or not you stay here, the High rooftop
lounge is wonderful for a sundowner. Valet
parking is $42.

Santa Barbara ❻

✘ La Super-Rica Taquería   Mexican $

([☎]805-963-4940; 622 N Milpas St; dishes
$1.55-6.80; [🕐]11am-9pm Sun-Mon & Thu, to
9:30pm Fri & Sat; [👶]) Although there's plenty
of good Mexican food in town, La Super-Rica

is deluged daily by locals and visitors keen on
tasting the dishes once so loved by the late
culinary queen Julia Child. Join the line to tuck
into tacos, tamales and other Mexican staples,
and see for yourself what the fuss is about.

🛏 Belmond
El Encanto   Luxury Hotel $$$

([☎]805-845-5800; www.elencanto.com;
800 Alvarado Pl; r/ste from $575/811;
[P][❄][@][🛜][♿][🐕]) This 1918 icon of Santa
Barbara style is a hilltop hideaway for travelers
who demand the very best of everything. An
infinity pool gazes out at the Pacific, while
flower-filled gardens, fireplace lounges, a
full-service spa and private bungalows with
sun-drenched patios concoct the glamorous
atmosphere perfectly fitted to SoCal socialites.

Hollywood ❽

✘ Musso & Frank Grill   European $$$

([☎]323-467-7788; www.mussoandfrank.
com; 6667 Hollywood Blvd; mains $17-55;
[🕐]11am-11pm Tue-Sat, 4-9pm Sun; [P]; [Ⓜ]B
Line to Hollywood/Highland) At Tinseltown's
oldest eatery (1919) Charlie Chaplin knocked
back vodka gimlets, Raymond Chandler
penned scripts and, more recently, Quentin
Tarantino shot scenes from *Once Upon a Time
in Hollywood*. Appropriately, the menu favors
bistro classics, from shrimp cocktail and lobster
thermidor to steaks and a decent burger.

🛏 Hollywood
Roosevelt   Historic Hotel $$$

([☎]323-856-1970; www.thehollywoodroosevelt.
com; 7000 Hollywood Blvd; d from $318;
[P][❄][@][🛜][♿]; [Ⓜ]B Line to Hollywood/
Highland) At the heart of the action, the
Roosevelt heaves with Hollywood lore: Shirley
Temple learned to tap dance on the stairs off
the lobby, Marilyn Monroe shot her first print
ad by the pool (later decorated by artist David
Hockney) and it's said that the ghost of actor
Montgomery Clift can still be heard playing the
bugle.

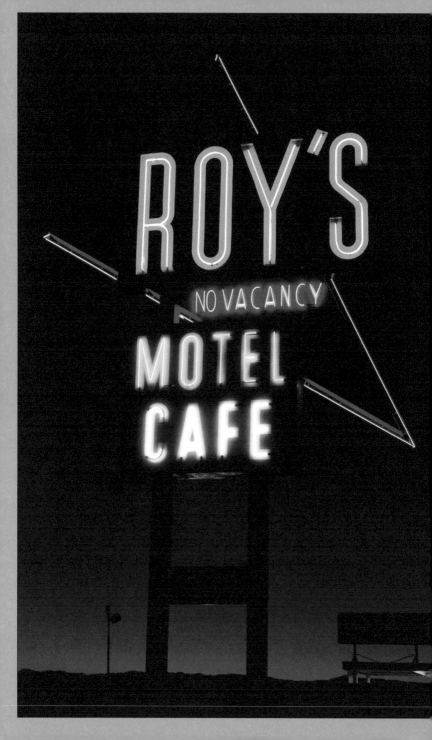

Classic Trip

Route 66

Search for the Californian dream on westernmost Route 66. This is a trip of retro roadside relics, desert vistas, sprawling LA, classic Hollywood and, finally, the beach.

30

TRIP HIGHLIGHTS

335 miles
Hollywood
Get your kicks in Tinseltown

30 miles
Goffs
Lonesome schoolhouse meets Route 66 vehicle relics

200 miles
Oro Grande
Wander through a forest of bottle trees

● 6
● Victorville
● San Bernardino
● 13 ● Los Angeles
● 14

● 2
● Needles
● 3

Santa Monica
End this epic trip on the Pacific shore
350 miles

Amboy
The big sky and empty byways are starkly photogenic
95 miles

3–4 DAYS
350 MILES / 565KM

GREAT FOR...

BEST TIME TO GO
Spring and fall, for cruising with the windows down, without summer heat.

ESSENTIAL PHOTO
Laying on faded asphalt by a Route 66 sign.

BEST ROAD
National Trails Hwy between Amboy and Ludlow is the quintessential middle-of-nowhere stretch.

30 Route 66

For generations of Americans, California, with its sparkling waters and sunny skies, was the promised land for road-trippers on Route 66. Follow their tracks through the gauntlet of Mojave Desert ghost towns, railway whistle-stops like Barstow and Victorville, and across the Cajon Pass. Finally, wind through the LA Basin and put your vehicle in park near the crashing ocean waves in Santa Monica.

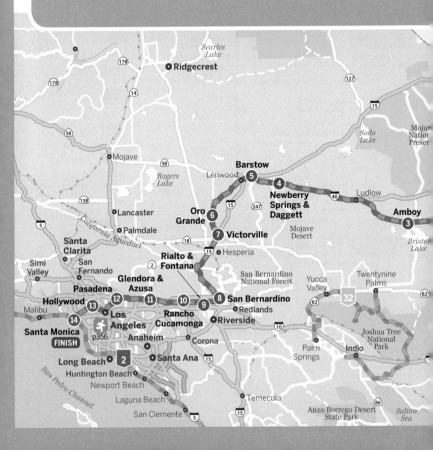

❶ Needles

At the Arizona border, the arched 1916 **Old Trails Bridge** (Needles-Topock; ⊘ no public access; **P**) marked the Mother Road's entrance to California until 1948. In the movie version of John Steinbeck's novel *The Grapes of Wrath*, the Depression-era Joad family used it to cross the Colorado River. For the best vantage point of the bridge, head to the Route 66 Welcome Sign off National Trails Hwy about a quarter mile south of I-40 (exit 153).

About 14 miles north, the jewel of the dusty railroad town of Needles is the restored **El Garces train depot.** It's one of only a few remaining 'Harvey Houses', a chain of early 20th-century railway hotels and restaurants managed by the Fred Harvey Company. They were famous for employing traveling waitresses as portrayed in the 1946 MGM musical *The Harvey Girls*.

The Drive ≫ Drive west on I-40 for about 15 miles, take exit 133 and follow Hwy 95 north for 6 miles. Turn left and follow Goffs Rd (Historic Route 66) for another 15 miles. You'll inevitably be running alongside a long train – this is a primary rail shipping route to the West Coast.

TRIP HIGHLIGHT

❷ Goffs

The 1914 Spanish Mission–style **schoolhouse** (☏760-733-4482; www.mdhca.org; 37198 Lanfair Rd, Essex; ⊘9am-4pm Sat-Mon Oct-Jun, outdoor 24hr; **P**) in Goffs (population 12) is a fun stop along this sun-drenched stretch of highway. In the old classroom – complete with wooden desks and a US flag sporting 48 stars – historic photographs illustrate the tough life on the edge of the Mojave. Outside you're free to wander around a graveyard of gracefully rusting vintage cars, gas pumps and even a bullet-riddled old yellow school bus.

The Drive ≫ Until the flood-damaged Route 66 stretch between Fenner and Amboy reopens, you need to detour 30 miles west on I-40 and cut 12 miles south on Kelbaker Rd before rejoining the National Trails Hwy. Just before reaching Amboy, keep an eye out for a pair of gleaming white, massive Chinese guardian lion sculptures incongruously perched in the sun-baked emptiness.

TRIP HIGHLIGHT

❸ Amboy

In the near-ghost town of Amboy, **Roy's Motel**

50 km
25 miles

NEVADA ARIZONA

Bullhead City

95

offs ❷

40 **START** ❶

Needles

Danby Lake

62

177

Sonoran Desert

10 Blythe

Colorado River

---

❺ LINK YOUR TRIP

32 Palm Springs & Joshua Tree Oases

Cut southwest on I-10 out of San Bernardino and head for a pastiche of palms, mountains, oases and whimsical Joshua Trees.

2 Pacific Coast Highways

This equally classic route takes you on a cruise along California's epic coastal ribbon: Hwy 1. When you finish Route 66, follow Hwy 1 north.

Classic Trip

& Cafe (www.visitamboy.
com; National Old Trails Hwy,
Amboy; ⏰7am-8pm, seasonal
variations; 🅿) has been a
popular pit stop since
1938. If you believe the
lore, Roy once cooked his
famous Route 66 double
cheeseburger on the hood
of a '63 Mercury. There's
no food or lodging today,
but at least Roy's iconic
neon sign kicked back
into glimmering glory
in 2019.

Two miles west,
Amboy Crater (📞760-
326-7000; www.blm.gov/
visit/amboy-crater; Crater
Rd; ⏰sunrise-sunset; 🅿)
is a 250ft-high, almost
perfectly symmetrical
volcanic cinder cone. It's
a 3-mile round-trip hike
to the top for great views
over the lava fields where
NASA engineers field-
tested the Mars Rover
(avoid in summer).

The Drive ›› Travel 28 miles
along National Trails Hwy to
Ludlow. Turn right onto Crucero
Rd and pass under I-40, then
follow the north frontage road
west for 8 miles before it makes
a sharp left and crosses under
I-40 on Lavic Rd. Take the first
right to get back on National
Trails Hwy and travel past Lavic
Lake volcanic field.

④ Newberry Springs & Daggett

Near Newberry Springs,
Route 66 passes by
the grizzled **Bagdad
Cafe**, the main filming
location of Percy Adlon's
eponymous 1987 cult flick
starring CCH Pounder
and Jack Palance. The
interior is chockablock
with posters, movie stills
and memorabilia, while
outside the old water
tower and Airstream
trailer are slowly rusting
away.

The highway passes
under I-40 and 12 miles
later reaches windswept
Daggett, site of the harsh
California inspection
station faced by Dust
Bowl refugees in *The
Grapes of Wrath*. Pay
your respects to such
early desert adventur-
ers as Sierra Nevada
naturalist John Muir at
the long-shuttered **Stone
Hotel** (35630 Santa Fe St,
Daggett; ⏰no public entry;
🅿). A fun 6-mile detour
north, **Calico Ghost Town**
(📞800-862-2542; www.
calicotown.com; 36600 Ghost
Town Rd, Yermo; adult/child
$8/5; ⏰9am-5pm; 🅿 🚻 👶)
is a park of reconstructed
pioneer-era buildings
amid vestiges of a late-
19th-century silver min-
ing operation.

The Drive ›› Return to
Daggett, then drive west to Nebo
Rd, turn left and rejoin I-40.
You'll drive about 4 miles before
exiting at E Main St, which runs
through workaday Barstow, a
railroad settlement and historic
crossroads, where murals adorn
empty buildings downtown. Turn
right on N 1st St.

⑤ Barstow

Exit I-40 onto Main St in
the Barstow, a railroad
settlement and historic
crossroads, where murals
adorn empty build-
ings downtown. Follow
N 1st St over a trestle
bridge across the Mojave
River to the beautifully
restored 1911 Harvey
House, nicknamed **Casa
del Desierto** and de-
signed by Western archi-
tect Mary Colter. Inside
is the **Route 66 Mother
Road Museum** (📞760-255-
1890; www.route66museum.
org; 681 N 1st St; ⏰10am-4pm
Fri & Sat, 11am-4pm Sun, or by
appointment; 🅿 🚻) with
B&W photographs, a 1915
Ford Motel T and odds
and ends from the hey-
day of Route 66 travel.
At the depot's other end
you'll find an outdoor
collection of historic
locomotives, a bright-
red caboose and other
railroad relics.

🍴 p329

The Drive ›› Leaving Barstow
via Main St, rejoin the National
Trails Hwy heading west as it
meanders alongside the Mojave
River through Lenwood. Loved
by Harley riders, this rural byway
is like a scavenger hunt for
Mother Road ruins, including
antique filling stations and
tumbledown motor courts. After
25 miles you'll arrive in Oro
Grande.

TRIP HIGHLIGHT

6 Oro Grande

Colorful as a box of crayons, **Elmer's Bottle Tree Ranch** (24266 National Trails Hwy; ⊙24hr; **P**) in Oro Grande is a quirky piece of roadside folk art with over 200 'bottle trees.' It's the work of Elmer Long, a cracked artistic genius and career man at the cement factory just outside of town. Elmer, who died in 2019, used bottles in all sorts of colors, shapes and sizes to build this offbeat sculpture garden, incorporating telephone poles, railroad signs and other bric-a-brac.

The Drive » Continue south on National Trails Hwy and cross over the Mojave River on a 1930s steel-truss bridge, then roll into downtown Victorville, a trip of 12 miles.

7 Victorville

Opposite the railroad tracks in Victorville, the **California Route 66 Museum** (📞760-951-0436; www.califrt66museum.org; 16825 South D St; donations welcome; ⊙10am-4pm Thu-Sat & Mon, 11am-3pm Sun; **P** 🚹) is an adorably cluttered kitchen sink's worth of yesteryear's treasures. Exhibits include old signs and roadside memorabilia as well as a selfie-worthy '50s diner and a flower-power VW 'Love Bus'.

🍴 p329

TOP TIP: NAVIGATING THE MOTHER ROAD

Because Route 66 is no longer an official road, it doesn't appear on many maps, although AAA state maps show portions. Consult these sources for additional info:

Historic Route 66 (www.historic66.com) Offers turn-by-turn directions.

National Historic Route 66 Federation (www.national66.org) Has links to myriad attractions and resources.

EZ66 Guide for Travelers Jerry McClanahan's intricately detailed book is a must.

The Drive » Get on I-15 south and travel over the legendary Cajon Pass, a haven for trainspotters. Descending into San Bernardino, follow I-215 and take exit 45 for Baseline St. Head east and turn left onto N 'E' St.

8 San Bernardino

Look for the Golden Arches outside the unofficial **First McDonald's Museum** (📞909-885-6324; www.facebook.com/firstoriginalmcdonaldsmuseum; 1398 N E St; by donation; ⊙10am-5pm; **P** 🚹). Though not technically in the original building created in 1948 by Dick and Mac McDonald, it was here that salesman Ray Kroc dropped by hoping to sell the brothers a mixer. Eventually Kroc used his moxie – as portrayed by Michael Keaton in *The Founder* (2016) – to buy the rights to the McDonald's name and build an empire. Half of the museum is devoted to Route 66, with some neat photographs and maps.

The Drive » Turn west on 5th St, leaving San Bernardino via Foothill Blvd, which continues straight into the urban sprawl of Greater Los Angeles. It's a long haul west to Pasadena (over 50 miles), with stop-and-go traffic most of the way, but there are some gems to uncover en route.

9 Rialto & Fontana

In Rialto, swing by the Wigwam Motel (p329), a cluster of 32ft-tall tipis that have welcomed travelers since 1950. Cruising through Fontana, birthplace of the Hells Angels biker club, pause for a photo by the **Giant Orange**, a 1930s juice stand of the kind that was once a fixture alongside SoCal's citrus groves. It used to offer weary Route 66 travelers 'all the juice you could drink' for a mere 10 cents. Find it in the parking lot

BARSTOW

ROUTE 66

WHY THIS IS A CLASSIC TRIP
ANDREA SCHULTE-PEEVERS, WRITER

The final stretch of America's most storied road trip adds a cinematic, sensory dimension to your SoCal adventure. Follow the dreams of generations of pioneers as you steer through open desert lidded by cornflower skies, past mysterious ghost towns and sunbaked mountains until the LA megalopolis and the shimmering Pacific salute you with sparkling promise and glamour.

Above: Sign for Barstow
Left: Elmer's Bottle Tree Ranch in Oro Grande
Right: Rancho Cucamonga

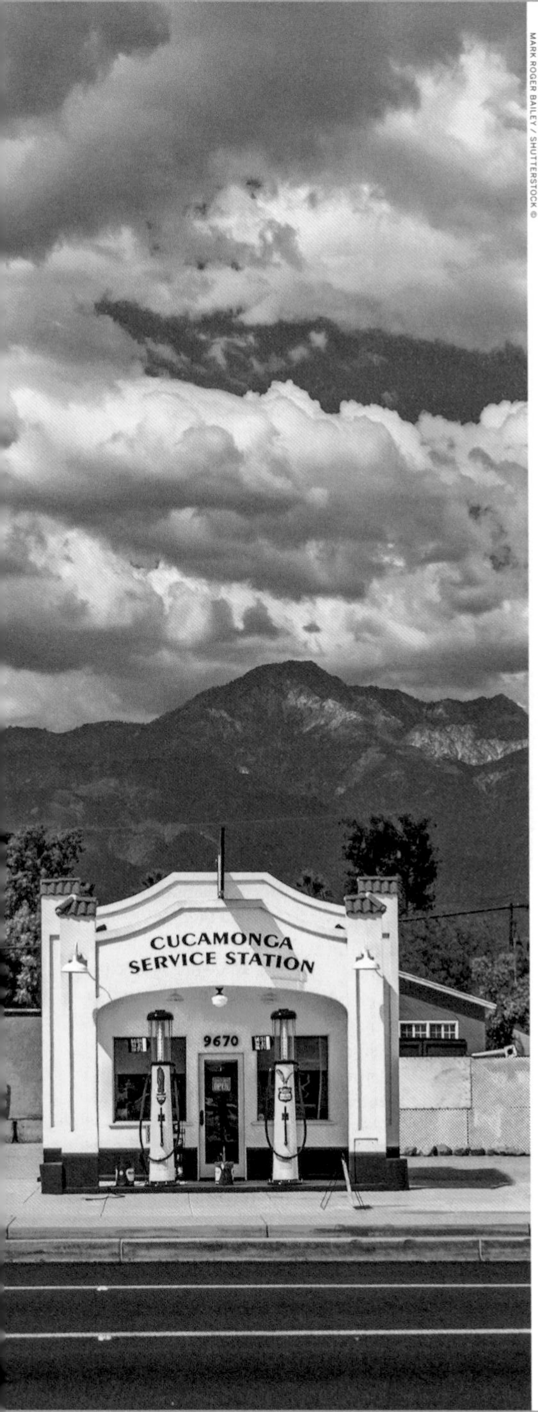

MARK ROGER BAILEY / SHUTTERSTOCK ©

of **Bono's Italian Restaurant** (☎909-441-4036; www.bonsitalia.com; 15395 E Foothill Blvd, Fontana; pizza & pasta $11-14; ⏰11am-10pm Wed-Sun; P ❄), a historic Route 66 diner that was reimagined as a pizza and pasta parlor in 2019.

🛏 p329

The Drive » Continue west on Foothill Blvd to Rancho Cucamonga.

⑩ Rancho Cucamonga

Rancho Cucamonga is home to two old-school steakhouses with a Route 66 pedigree. First up is the **Magic Lamp Inn** (p329), easily recognized by its fabulous neon Aladdin's lamp. Its interior sparkles with shiny dark woods and stained-glass windows. A bit further on, storied **Sycamore Inn** (☎909-982-1104; www.thesycamoreinn.com; 8318 Foothill Blvd; mains $28-59; ⏰5-9pm Mon-Thu, to 10pm Fri & Sat, 4-8:30pm Sun; P ❄) has fed its juicy steaks to generations of meat lovers, including Marilyn Monroe.

🍴 p329

The Drive » Continue driving west on Foothill Blvd.

⑪ Glendora & Azusa

A key stop in Glendora is **The Hat**, a small local chain that's been serving its famous hot pastrami

sandwiches since 1951. Route 66 continues as Huntington Dr in Duarte, where a boisterous Route 66 parade rolls through in September. Turn right on Magnolia Ave and rejoin Foothill Blvd in Azusa whose supposedly haunted 1925 **Aztec Hotel** (☑626-358-3231; 311 W Foothill Blvd, Monrovia) sports a striking Mayan Revival–style facade. Hollywood celebs knocked 'em back in this beloved landmark en route to the Santa Anita racetrack.

✕ p329

The Drive ≫ Continue west on Foothill Blvd, then turn left (south) on Santa Anita Ave, right (west) on Huntington Dr and right again on Colorado Pl past the 1930s Santa Anita Park horse-racing track. It's where the Marx Brothers filmed *A Day at the Races* (1937) and where legendary thoroughbred Seabiscuit once ran.

⑫ Pasadena

Colorado Blvd leads straight into bustling Old Pasadena, where boutiques and cafes are housed in handsomely restored historic Spanish Colonial Revival–style buildings. Follow Fair Oaks Ave south to the nostalgic 1915 **Fair Oaks Pharmacy** (☑626-799-

1414; www.fairoakspharmacy. net; 1526 Mission St, South Pasadena; sundaes $7-10; ⊙9am-9pm Mon-Sat, 10am-7pm Sun; P ✳ ♿) where so-called 'soda jerks' still dish out 'phosphates' (flavored syrup, soda water and 'secret potion'), giant banana splits and other sugary kicks.

The Drive ≫ Rejoin the modern world on the Pasadena Fwy (Hwy 110), which streams south into LA. One of the first freeways in the US, it's a truck-free state historic freeway. Take exit 24B and follow Sunset Blvd northwest to Santa Monica Blvd westbound.

TRIP HIGHLIGHT

⑬ Hollywood

The exact track that Route 66 ran through Tinseltown isn't possible to follow these days (it changed several times). Start exploring at the **Hollywood & Highland** (www.hollywoodandhighland. com; 6801 Hollywood Blvd; ⊙10am-10pm Mon-Sat, to 7pm Sun; 🛜 ♿; Ⓜ B Line to Hollywood/Highland) shopping, dining and entertainment complex in the center of the action. Travelers looking for a creepy-fun communion with stars of yesteryear should stroll the **Holly-wood Forever Cemetery** (☑323-894-9507; www.hollywoodforever. com; 6000 Santa Monica Blvd; ⊙8:30am-5pm Mon-Fri, to 4:30pm Sat & Sun; guided tours 10am most Sat; P ♿; 🚇Metro Line 4, DASH Hol-

lywood/Wilshire Route) next to Paramount Pictures, which is crowded with such famous 'immortals' as Rudolph Valentino, Jayne Mansfield and Cecil B DeMille. Buy a map at the flower shop near the entrance.

✕ p329

The Drive ≫ Follow Santa Monica Blvd west for 13 miles to reach the end of the road – it meets Ocean Ave at Palisades Park. Hwy 1 is downhill from Ocean Ave heading north. The pier is a few blocks to the south.

TRIP HIGHLIGHT

⑭ Santa Monica

This is the end of the line: Route 66 reaches its finish, over 2400 miles from its starting point in Chicago, on an ocean bluff in **Palisades Park** (☑800-544-5319; Ocean Ave btwn Colorado Ave & San Vicente Blvd; ⊙5am-midnight), where a Will Rogers Hwy memorial plaque marks the official end of the Mother Road. Celebrate on **Santa Monica Pier** (☑310-458-8901; www.santamonicapier. org; ♿), where you can ride a 1920s carousel featured in *The Sting* (1973) and enjoy other attractions and carnival rides. With the glittering Pacific as a backdrop, take a selfie with the 'Santa Monica 66 End of Trail' sign. Then hit the beach.

🛏 p329

Eating & Sleeping

Barstow ⑤

✖ Peggy Sue's 50's Diner — Diner $

(📞760-254-3370; www.peggysuesdiner.com; 35654 Yermo Rd, Yermo; mains $10-15; ⏰6am-10pm; 🅿 ❄ 👶) The original 1954 nine-stool, three-booth diner is still there, but Peggy Sue's has since grown into a rambling mini empire with an ice-cream shop, a pizza parlor and a 'diner-saur' sculpture park. Many meals are named after Hollywood stars and there's photogenic memorabilia throughout.

Victorville ⑦

✖ Emma Jean's Holland Burger Cafe — American $

(📞760-243-9938; www.hollandburger.com; 17143 N D St; breakfast $4-10, burgers & sandwiches $6-9; ⏰5am-2:45pm Mon-Fri, 6am-12:30pm Sat; 🅿 ❄) This famous outpost on Route 66 has plied weary travelers with gargantuan breakfasts and burgers since 1947. Still family-run, it's as warm and welcoming as a hug from an old friend.

Rialto ⑨

⌂ Wigwam Motel — Motel $

(📞909-875-3005; www.wigwammotel.com; 2728 W Foothill Blvd; d with bath $107-159; 🅿 ❄ 📶 👶 🐾) Get your kitsch on Route 66 by staying snug in a 32ft-tall tipi. Opened in 1950, these 19 conical units are equipped with contemporary furniture and motel-type mod-cons. A kidney-shaped pool sits out the back.

Rancho Cucamonga ⑩

✖ Magic Lamp Inn — Steak $$

(📞909-981-8659; www.themagiclampinn.com; 8189 Foothill Blvd; mains lunch $12-21, dinner $25-50; ⏰11am-11pm Mon-Thu, to 2am Fri, 4:30pm-1am Sat, 5-11pm Sun; 🅿 ❄) This classic 1955 steakhouse serves up damn-the-cholesterol sandwiches and choice cuts, including a mighty Chateaubriand for two carved tableside.

Glendora ⑪

✖ The Hat — Sandwiches $

(📞626-857-0017; www.thehat.com; 611 W Rte 66, ; mains $3-11; ⏰10am-11pm Sun-Wed, to 1am Thu-Sat; 🅿 ❄ 👶) The classic sign featuring a chef's toque and the words 'World Famous Pastrami' greets hungry diners at the original Hat in Glendora where they've been piling up hot pastrami sandwiches since 1951. Thinly sliced and generously salted, they're served on French rolls au jus or gravy for dipping.

Hollywood ⑬

✖ Musso & Frank Grill — European $$$

(📞323-467-7788; www.mussoandfrank.com; 6667 Hollywood Blvd; mains $17-55; ⏰11am-11pm Tue-Sat, 4-9pm Sun; 🅿; Ⓜ B Line to Hollywood/Highland) Hollywood history hangs in the thick air at Musso & Frank Grill, Tinseltown's oldest eatery (since 1919). Charlie Chaplin used to knock back vodka gimlets, Raymond Chandler penned scripts in the high-backed booths, and movie deals were made on the old phone at the back. The menu favors bistro classics, from shrimp cocktail and lobster thermidor, to steaks and a decent burger.

Santa Monica ⑭

⌂ Sea Shore Motel — Motel $$

(📞310-392-2787; www.seashoremotel.com; 2637 Main St; r $140-195, ste $240-300; 🅿 ❄ 📶; 🚌Metro Line 733, 🚌Big Blue Bus Lines 1, 8) The friendly, family-run lodgings at this comfy 25-unit motel put you just a Frisbee toss from the beach on happening Main St (quadruple-pane windows help cut street noise). The tiled, rattan-decorated rooms are basic, but 2nd-floor rooms have high ceilings and, a few doors down, families can stretch out in suites with kitchen and balcony.

Classic Trip

Life in Death Valley

Drive where California pioneers and gold miners once rolled their wagons in Death Valley National Park, where the magnum forces of natural and human history collide.

31

TRIP HIGHLIGHTS

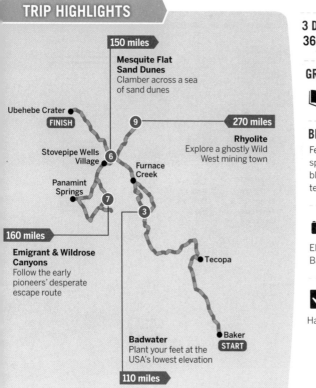

150 miles

Mesquite Flat Sand Dunes
Clamber across a sea of sand dunes

Ubehebe Crater ●
FINISH

⑨

270 miles

Rhyolite
Explore a ghostly Wild West mining town

Stovepipe Wells Village ⑥

Furnace Creek

Panamint Springs

⑦

③

160 miles

Emigrant & Wildrose Canyons
Follow the early pioneers' desperate escape route

● Tecopa

Badwater
Plant your feet at the USA's lowest elevation

● Baker
START

110 miles

3 DAYS
365 MILES / 585KM

GREAT FOR...

BEST TIME TO GO
February to April for spring wildflower blooms and cooler temperatures.

📷 ESSENTIAL PHOTO
Elevation sign at Badwater Basin.

✓ BEST FOR HISTORY
Harmony Borax Works.

dwater Elevation sign at Badwater Basin

Classic Trip

31 Life in Death Valley

The name itself evokes all that is harsh, hot and hellish – a punishing, barren and lifeless place of Old Testament severity. Ghost towns and abandoned mines are proof of the human struggle to survive here. Yet a scenic drive through the park reveals that nature is spectacularly alive in Death Valley: sensuous sand dunes, water-sculpted canyons, rocks moving across the desert floor, extinct volcanic craters, palm-shaded oases, soaring mountains and plenty of endemic wildlife.

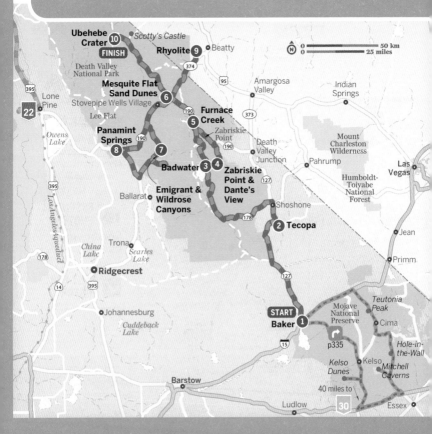

❶ Baker

Death Valley is a land of extremes – you'll find the lowest elevation in North America here, not far from Mt Whitney, the highest peak in the US outside Alaska. More infamously, Death Valley is the hottest place in the nation. Just take a look at the **World's Largest Thermometer** in Baker, right off I-15. An eye-catching tower of roadside kitsch, it stands exactly 134ft tall to commemorate the record-breaking temperature of 134°F (57°C) measured in Death Valley on July 10, 1913.

The Drive » From Baker, follow Hwy 127 (Death Valley Rd) north for 50 miles, crossing railroad tracks and zooming through a serene desert landscape. Turn right onto Old

LINK YOUR TRIP

22 Eastern Sierra Scenic Byway

From Panamint Springs, it's 50 miles northwest to Lone Pine, a gateway to lofty Sierra Nevada peaks, via Hwys 190, 136 and 395.

30 Route 66

From Baker, drive south through the Mojave National Preserve and across I-40 to meet California's original road trip.

Spanish Trail Hwy and drive 4 miles east toward Tecopa.

---

❷ Tecopa

Even when the desert looks bone-dry, you can still find oases such as the dusty outpost of Tecopa. Natural hot springs used by Native Americans for centuries bubble up at three basic resorts. The best of the bunch is **Delight's Hot Springs Resort** (☏760-852-4343; www.delightshotspringsresort. com; 368 Tecopa Hot Springs Rd; day pass $15-25; ⏲8am-10pm), which has four private soaking pools adorned with endearing desert-themed murals. A fun 5-mile detour south, **China Ranch Date Farm** (☏760-852-4415; www. chinaranch.com; China Ranch Rd; ⏲9am-5pm; P ✦) is a refreshingly green refuge where you can go hiking or bird-watching, then stock up on fresh dates or try their yummy date shakes. It's well signposted from Tecopa. The last stretch is unpaved, steep and winding, sometimes requiring 4WD (or park and walk in). At the junction of Old Spanish Trail Hwy and Tecopa Hot Springs road, you'll drive past an old railroad tie shack housing **Death Valley Brewing** (☏760-298-7014; www.deathvalley brewing.com; 59 Old Spanish Trail Hwy; ⏲noon-6pm Fri-Sun Nov-Apr), a teensy craft brewery where non-

---

drivers can quench their thirst with an ale or IPA.

 p339

The Drive » Continue north on Tecopa Hot Springs Rd to rejoin Hwy 127. Turn right and drive 4 miles north to Shoshone, your last chance for gas, drinks and snacks (p339) until Furnace Creek, some 70 miles away. Turn left onto Hwy 178 (Jubilee Pass Rd), which wrenches right at Ashford Junction, becoming Badwater Rd and curving lazily north along the valley floor.

TRIP HIGHLIGHT

❸ Badwater

Cresting Jubilee Pass (1290ft), the highway dips down into Death Valley itself. Despite its harsh name, the valley is actually a thriving wildlife habitat and has supported human life for millennia, from Shoshone tribespeople to Old West pioneers, gold seekers and borax miners. It's the silence and solemnity of the vast expanse that inspires today. That cracked, parched-looking salt pan extending across the valley floor, which suddenly sears your retinas with its dazzling white light, is Badwater. At 282ft below sea level, it's the lowest point in North America. A **boardwalk** hovers over the constantly evaporating bed of salty, mineralized water, almost alien in its beauty. Prehistoric **Lake Manly** covered the entire valley during the last ice age, and in 2005

it briefly reappeared for the first time in recorded human history when heavy rainfall could not be absorbed by the dry, compressed desert soil. This was followed by a spectacular superbloom of red poppies, yellow primroses, purple sand verbena and other desert flowers. The phenomenon reoccurred in 2015 and again in 2019.

The Drive ›› Eight miles north of Badwater, past the Natural Bridge turnoff on your right and the bizarre salt crystals of Devils Golf Course on your left, detour along Artists Drive, a one-way 9-mile scenic loop (no vehicles with trailers or over 25ft long). Rejoining Badwater Rd, drive 5 miles north, then go right on Hwy 190 for 3.5 miles to Zabriskie Point.

➍ Zabriskie Point & Dante's View

For spectacular valley views across Death Valley's golden badlands eroded into waves, pleats and gullies, **Zabriskie Point** (☎760-786-3200; www.nps.gov/deva; Hwy 190; P) can't be beat. The spot was named for a manager of the Pacific Coast Borax Company and also inspired the title of Michelangelo Antonio's 1970s movie. The cover of U2's *Joshua*

Tree album was also shot here.

To escape the valley's midday heat, or catch a memorable sunset, continue for 20 miles uphill from Zabriskie Point to breezy **Dante's View** (☎760-786-3200; www.nps.gov/deva; Dante's View Rd, off Hwy 190; P). From this lofty perch you can simultaneously view the highest (Mt Whitney) and lowest (Badwater) points in the contiguous USA. Budget at least half an hour (each way) for the winding drive.

The Drive ›› Backtrack downhill, then turn left on Hwy 190 and drive 7 miles, past the elegant Inn at Furnace Creek and the Badwater Rd turnoff, before rolling past the Ranch at Furnace Creek to the park's excellent visitor center.

➎ Furnace Creek

At the visitor center, don't miss the gorgeously shot 20-minute movie introducing you to the park's history, geology and natural attractions. A short drive south, on the grounds of the Ranch at Death Valley, the outdoor **Borax Museum** (Date Grove Rd; ⏱dawn-dusk; P ♿) lets you poke around a jumble of pioneer-era transportation equipment, including an original 'Twenty Mule Team' wagon and a steam tractor. To see where the mules kicked off their 165-mile slog to the nearest train station

in Mojave, drop by the **Harmony Borax Works**, just north of Furnace Creek.

✕ ⛺ p339

The Drive ›› If you didn't fill up outside the park, Furnace Creek has an expensive gas station with 24-hour credit-card pumps. Head north from Furnace Creek on Hwy 190. After about 20 miles, turn left to stay on Hwy 190 west toward Stovepipe Wells Village. Just over 5 miles later, pull into the Mesquite Flat parking lot on your right.

TRIP HIGHLIGHT

➏ Mesquite Flat Sand Dunes

It's time to take up a famous strand of history in Death Valley: the story of the lost forty-niners. When the California gold rush took off in 1849, a small group of pioneers chanced what they hoped would be a shortcut to the California goldfields, leaving behind the Old Spanish Trail. Exhausted, dangerously running out of food and water, and struggling with broken wagons and worn-out pack animals, the woeful group arrived near Furnace Creek on Christmas Eve. Failing to get their wagons across the Panamint Mountains, the survivors slaughtered their oxen and burned their wagons near what today is the Mesquite Flat. Get out of the car to hike up and down across the rolling field of sand dunes that look like a mini Sahara. They are at their most photogenic at sunrise or sunset when bathed in soft light and accented by long, deep shadows. Keep an eye out for animal tracks.

📛 p339

The Drive ≫ You can fill up the gas tank and buy food and drinks at Stovepipe Wells Village, 2 miles further west along Hwy 190. Heading west, you'll pass the side road to Mosaic Canyon on your left before reaching Emigrant Canyon Rd after 9 miles. Turn left and start winding uphill toward Emigrant Pass.

TRIP HIGHLIGHT

❼ Emigrant & Wildrose Canyons

Faced with no other choice, the forty-niner pioneers eventually walked out of torturous Death Valley over **Emigrant Pass**. As they left, one woman reputedly looked back and fatalistically uttered the words: good-bye, death valley. Later pioneers flooded back when gold was discovered in Death Valley, including at **Skidoo**, a boomtown that went bust in the early 20th century, and where the influential silent movie *Greed* was filmed in 1923. Nothing remains of the ghost-town site today. Further south, the ruined **Eureka Mine** is en route to vertigo-inducing **Aguereberry Point**, where you can see the

Funeral Mountains and the parched valley spread out below. Both of these side trips travel on rough, rutted dirt roads (high-clearance 4WD vehicles recommended). Turn left onto Wildrose Canyon Rd to reach the abandoned **Wildrose Charcoal Kilns**. Built in 1876, these bee-hive-shaped stone kilns produced the charcoal

needed by the miners for smelting Death Valley's silver and lead ore. The landscape is subalpine, with forests of piñon pine and juniper; it can be covered with snow, even in spring.

The Drive ≫ Backtrack downhill, turning left at the intersection with Emigrant Canyon Rd onto Wildrose Canyon Rd, which snakes through a flash-flood zone (don't

---

↱ DETOUR: MOJAVE NATIONAL PRESERVE

Start: ❶ Baker

For another dose of Wild West history, point the wheels toward the lonely **Mojave National Preserve** (📞760-252-6100; www.nps.gov/moja; btwn I-15 & I-40; 🅿), southeast of Baker off I-15. Make a beeline for the **Kelso Depot**, a gracefully restored 1920s Spanish Mission–style railway station rebooted as the preserve's main visitor center. Watch the 20-minute introductory movie and poke around the exhibits of local history and lore. Head south to the honey-colored **Kelso Dunes** that are among the tallest sand piles in the US. Hiking to the top will have you mopping your brow but also give you a chance to hear the dunes 'sing', ie emanate a low humming or booming sound caused by shifting sands. Head south to I-40, turn east and exit on Essex Rd, then drive north to the otherworldly **Mitchell Caverns** (book ahead for a tour). A bit further north, scramble around the hole-riddled cliffs of **Hole-in-the-Wall**, once used by Native Americans to escape Western ranchers. Drive north, then turn left on the old Mojave Rd blazed by Spanish missionaries, fur trappers and traders and, oddly enough, camels on an 1867 military expedition. Head right toward Cima, then veer left to reach the trailhead for **Teutonia Peak**, a 3-mile round-trip hike through the world's largest forest of Joshua trees, ending with panoramic desert views peppered with colorful cinder cones. From here it's another 38 miles back to Baker. The entire detour clocks in at 180 miles.

Classic Trip

FEEL4NATURE / SHUTTERSTOCK ©

WHY THIS IS A CLASSIC TRIP
ANDREA SCHULTE-PEEVERS, WRITER

Yes, it can get hotter than Satan's hoof, but most of the year Death Valley is a sensory immersion in nature at its most primal and soul-stirring. Feel your spirits soar and your mind clear as you steer through this pastiche of sun-blistered mountains, sensuous sand dunes, crackling salt flats and untamed canyons. Delight in the light playing otherworldly tricks on the landscape throughout the day, then look forward to being cradled by a starry canopy at night.

Above: Mesquite Flat Sand Dunes
Left: Wildrose Charcoal Kilns
Right: Zabriskie Point

attempt this road except during dry weather). After 14 miles, turn right on Panamint Valley Rd and drive north to Hwy 190, then turn left. The longer all-weather route is to backtrack down Emigrant Canyon Rd to Hwy 190, then turn left for the 22-mile drive to Panamint Springs.

⑧ Panamint Springs

At the far western edge of Death Valley National Park, Panamint Springs is an off-grid camp with incredible views back at the muscular Panamint Range. In spring, you can drive the 2.5-mile graded gravel road, followed by a mile-long cross-country scramble, to **Darwin Falls.** Here, a natural-spring cascade plunges into a gorge, embraced by willows that attract migratory birds in springtime. Continuing west on the highway for about 8 miles takes you to **Father Crowley Vista**, which peers deep into Rainbow Canyon, aka Star Wars Canyon, created by lava flows and scattered with multihued volcanic cinders. With any luck, you get to witness US Air Force and Navy fighter jets zooming through the canyon on training runs.

The Drive ❱❱ Turn around and drive back downhill east on Hwy 190. About 7 miles past Stovepipe Wells Village, turn left and then right onto Daylight Pass Rd for 16 miles, exiting the park and following Hwy 374 into Nevada for 9 miles to the signposted turnoff for Rhyolite on your left.

337

9 Rhyolite

Just 4 miles west of Beatty, NV, **Rhyolite** (off Hwy 374; P ♿) was the queen of Death Valley's mines during its heyday. It epitomizes the hurly-burly, boom-and-bust story of Western gold-rush mining towns. After the first nugget was discovered in 1904, the population soared to 8000 by 1908, only to plummet a couple of years later when the mines began petering out. The remaining ruins, including a school, store, bank and railway station, reflect the high standard of living created for such a short period. One much photographed curiosity is a house made of thousands of beer bottles.

En route, you'll pass the surreal **Goldwell Open Air Museum** (Rhyolite Rd, off Hwy 374; ⏱24hr; P ♿), a trippy sculpture installation rising up from the desert floor. It was conceived in 1984 by the late Belgian artist Albert Szukalski and added to over the years by fellow creatives. Standout pieces include a giant prospector incongruously accompanied by a penguin, and a ghostly plaster cast version of Da Vinci's *Last Supper*.

The Drive ❯❯ Backtrack down Daylight Pass Rd, turning right onto Scotty's Castle Rd, which winds for 33 miles through the valley, shadowed by the Grapevine Mountains. Turn left near the ranger station at Grapevine Junction onto the side road to arrive near Ubehebe Crater after about 5 miles.

10 Ubehebe Crater

One of the most impressive geological features in the northern valley, 600ft-deep Ubehebe Crater is believed to have formed some 2100 years ago in a single eruptive event by the meeting of fiery magma and cool groundwater. Its Martian beauty is easily appreciated from the parking lot, but for closer inspection and compelling views into its volcanic depth embark on the 1.5-mile trek along the rim (not recommended if vertigo-prone). For a longer walk, add a detour to **Little Hebe Crater**.

SCOTTY'S CASTLE

Walter E Scott, alias 'Death Valley Scotty,' was the quintessential tall-tale teller who captivated people with his stories of gold. His most lucrative friendship was with Albert and Bessie Johnson, a wealthy insurance magnate and his wife from Chicago. Despite knowing that Scotty was a freeloading liar, the Johnsons bankrolled a whimsical, elaborately constructed desert estate here in Death Valley during the 1920s. Nicknamed Scotty's Castle, the Johnson's historic home has been restored to its 1939 appearance, featuring sheepskin drapes, carved California redwood, handmade tiles, wrought iron, woven Shoshone baskets and a bellowing pipe organ upstairs.

In 2015, a massive flood in Grapevine Canyon significantly damaged the access road to Scotty's Castle and several historic structures. While repairs are ongoing, the castle remains closed to visitors until at least 2021. Check the official national park website (www.nps.gov/deva) for updates.

Eating & Sleeping

Tecopa ②

✕ Tecopa Brewing Company
Barbecue $

(☎760-852-4343; www.delightshotspringsresort.com; 420 Tecopa Springs Rd; breakfast $3-8, mains $7-21; ☺noon-10pm Thu-Sat, to 8pm Sun & Mon Oct-Apr; P ❄ 🛜) Yes, th operates a nanobrewery, but the main reason to pop by TBC is for the finger-lickin' barbecue. Choose from beef brisket, pulled pork or pork ribs and load up on sides of coleslaw, smoked beans or cornbread, all homemade. Also serves breakfast and a wicked Tecopa Mary.

Shoshone

✕ Crowbar Cafe & Saloon
American $$

(☎760-852-4224; www.shoshonevillage.com; 112 Old State Hwy 127; mains $13-31; ☺8am-9:30pm; P ❄ 🛜 ♿) Shoshone's only restaurant has fed locals and travelers since 1920. Its main stock-in-trade is burgers and sandwiches, but it also serves breakfast, Mexican dishes and something called 'rattlesnake' chili (sorry, there are no actual snakes in it). The attached saloon can get lively on weekend nights.

Furnace Creek ⑤

✕ Last Kind Words Saloon
American $$$

(☎760-786-3335; mains lunch $19-25, dinner $24-105; P ❄ 🛜) Despite the name, the aloon at the **Ranch at Death Valley** (☎760-786-2345; www.oasisatdeathvalley.com; Hwy 190; d from $180; P ❄ 🛜 ⛳) is actually more restaurant than drinking hole. The menu is meat-centric Americana, from chili and burgers to steaks and ribs. Devour it in the high-ceilinged Disney-esque dining den amid stuffed animals, vintage guns and signs, oil paintings and other Wild West trappings.

✕ Inn Dining Room
International $$$

(☎760-786-2345; www.oasisatdeathvalley.com; Inn at Furnace Creek, Hwy 190; breakfast $15-21, lunch $14-28, dinner $32-71; ☺7-10:30am & 11:30am-2:30pm year-round, 5-9pm Oct-Apr, 6-10pm May-Sept; P ❄ 🛜) This formal restaurant delivers continental cuisine with stellar views of the Panamint Mountains. Reservations are key for dinner when a 'no shorts or tank tops' policy kicks in. If you just want to sample the refined ambience without eviscerating your bank account, swing by the lounge for cocktails and nibbles ($11 to $16), preferably at sunset.

🛏 Death Valley National Park Campgrounds
Campground $

(www.nps.gov/deva; campsites free-$22) The National Park Service operates nine campgrounds on a first-come, first-served basis (exception: Furnace Creek between mid-October to mid-April). At peak times campsites often fill by midmorning.

🛏 Inn at Death Valley
Hotel $$$

(☎760-786-2345, reservations 800-236-7916; www.oasisatdeathvalley.com; Hwy 190; d from $390; P ☕ ❄ 🛜 ⛳) Pull back the curtains and count the colors of the desert at this 1927 Spanish Mission–style hotel brimming with all the expected 21st-century comforts. Languid valley views await as you relax by the spring-fed swimming pool with a spa and pool bar, in the warmly furnished lounge or in the library. A class act.

Mesquite Flat ⑥

🛏 Stovepipe Wells Village Hotel
Motel $$

(☎760-786-2387; www.deathvalleyhotels.com; 51880 Hwy 190, Stovepipe Wells; RV sites $40, d $144-226; P ❄ 🛜 ⛳) The 83 rooms at this private resort have beds draped in quality linens and accented with cheerful Native American–patterned blankets. The small pool is cool and the on-site cowboy-style restaurant serves breakfast and dinner daily, with lunch available in the next-door saloon.

Palm Springs & Joshua Tree Oases

Southern California's deserts can be brutally hot, barren places – escape to Palm Springs and Joshua Tree National Park, where shady fan-palm oases and date gardens await.

32

TRIP HIGHLIGHTS

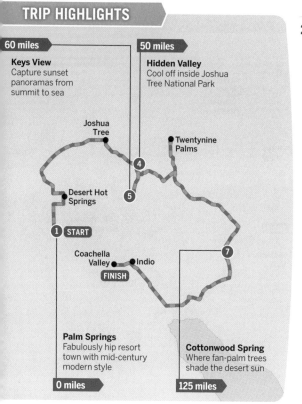

60 miles

Keys View
Capture sunset panoramas from summit to sea

50 miles

Hidden Valley
Cool off inside Joshua Tree National Park

Joshua Tree

Twentynine Palms

4

5

Desert Hot Springs

1 START

Coachella Valley • Indio

FINISH

7

Palm Springs
Fabulously hip resort town with mid-century modern style

0 miles

Cottonwood Spring
Where fan-palm trees shade the desert sun

125 miles

**2–3 DAYS
170 MILES / 274KM**

GREAT FOR...

BEST TIME TO GO

February to April for spring wildflower blooms and cooler temperatures.

 ESSENTIAL PHOTO

Sunset from Keys View.

 BEST FOR SOLITUDE

Hike to the Lost Palms Oasis.

tskirts of Palm Spring

32

Palm Springs & Joshua Tree Oases

Just a short drive from the chic resorts of Palm Springs, the vast Mojave and Sonoran Deserts are serenely spiritual places. You may find that what at first looked like desolate sands transform on foot into perfect beauty: shady palm tree and cactus gardens, tiny wildflowers pushing up from hard-baked soil in spring, natural hot-springs pools for soaking, and uncountable stars overhead in the inky dark.

TRIP HIGHLIGHT

❶ Palm Springs

Hollywood celebs have always counted on Palm Springs as a quick escape from LA. Today, this desert resort town is a showcase of retro-chic mid-century modern buildings. Stop at the **Palm Springs Visitors Center** (☏760-778-8418; www.visitpalmsprings.com; 2901 N Palm Canyon Dr; ☉9am-5pm), inside a 1965 gas station by Albert Frey, to pick up a self-guided architectural tour

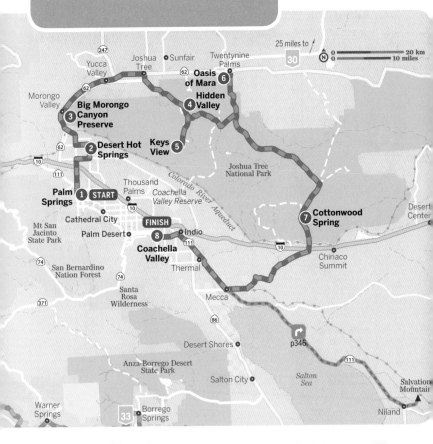

map. Then drive uphill to be whisked from desert floor to alpine forest on the rotating **Palm Springs Aerial Tramway** (📞760-325-1391; www. pstramway.com; 1 Tram Way; adult/child $27/17, parking $8; ⏰1st tram up 10am Mon-Fri, 8am Sat & Sun, last tram up 8pm, last tram down 9:45pm daily, varies seasonally; [P][♿]) in just 15 minutes. Back down, drive south on Palm Canyon Dr to get your culture kicks at the excellent **Palm Springs Art Museum** (📞760-322-4800; www.psmuseum. org; 101 Museum Dr; adult/student/under 18yr $14/6/free; ⏰10am-5pm Fri-Tue, noon-8pm Thu; [P]), followed by a hop between art galleries, cafes, cocktail bars, trendy restaurants and chic boutiques. Finally, head 10 miles downvalley

LINK YOUR TRIP

30 **Route 66**
Follow Hwy 62 east of Twentynine Palms, turn left onto Godwin Rd, then right onto Amboy Rd for a 50-mile journey to join America's 'Mother Road.'

33 **Temecula, Julian & Anza-Borrego**
From Mecca, drive along the Salton Sea's western shore, then head inland to Borrego Springs, a 50-mile trip.

for a saunter around the magnificent gardens of **Sunnylands** (📞760-202-2222; www.sunny lands.org; 37977 Bob Hope Dr, Rancho Mirage; visitor center & gardens free; ⏰house tours Wed-Sun, birding tours 8:45am Thu & Sat, visitor center & gardens 8:30am-4pm Wed-Sun mid-Sep–early Jun; [P]), the desert retreat where Walter and Leonore An-nenberg once welcomed US presidents, royalty and celebs.

🗼 🛏 p47, p347

The Drive » Drive north out of downtown Palm Springs along Indian Canyon Dr for 7 miles, passing over I-10. Turn right onto Dillon Rd, then after 2.5 miles cut a left onto Palm Dr, which heads north into central Desert Hot Springs.

- - - - - - - - - - - - - - - - - - -

② Desert Hot Springs

In 1774 Spanish explorer Juan Bautista de Anza was the first European to encounter the desert Ca-huilla tribe. Afterward, the Spanish name Agua Caliente came to refer to both the indigenous people and the natural hot springs that still bub-ble up restoratively from below the town of Desert Hot Springs (www.visit deserthotsprings.com). You can 'take the waters' in family-friendly resorts or stylish adult-only heal-ing hideaways like the **Two Bunch Palms Resort & Spa** (📞760-288-7801; www.twobunchpalms.com/spa;

67425 Two Bunch Palms Trail; day pass $125, treatments from $95; ⏰day pass valid 10am-6pm) that sits atop an actual oasis. Imitate Tim Robbins who enjoyed a mud bath here in the 1992 Robert Altman's film *The Player*, then bounce between pools and sunbathing areas or enjoy a massage all the while maintaining the code of silence (actually, whispers only).

🛏 p347

The Drive » Head west on Pierson Blvd back to Indian Canyon Dr. Turn right and drive northwest through the dusty outskirts of Desert Hot Springs. Turn right onto Hwy 62 eastbound toward Yucca Valley; after about 4 miles, turn right onto East Dr and look for signs for Big Morongo Canyon Preserve.

- - - - - - - - - - - - - - - - - - -

③ Big Morongo Canyon Preserve

An oasis hidden in the high desert, **Big Morongo Canyon Preserve** (📞760-363-7190; https://parks. sbcounty.gov; 11055 East Dr, Morongo Valley; ⏰7:30am-dusk; [P][♿]) is a riparian habitat flush with cotton-wood and willow trees. Attracted by the water, mule deer, bighorn sheep, coyotes and other critters pass through this wildlife corridor linking the San Gorgonio Mountains and Joshua Tree National Park. The preserve is also an internationally recognized bird-watching hot spot; around 250 bird species have been identified here, including at least 72 that use the area as breeding grounds, such as the coral-red summer tanager and the brown-crested flycatcher. Keep an eye out (better yet, bring binoculars) as you trek along several short trails meandering through this marshy land where hummingbirds flutter and woodpeckers attack trees.

The Drive » Rejoin Hwy 62 eastbound which soon passes through Yucca Valley where you'll find some cool roadside antiques, vintage shops, art galleries and cafes. Continue east for another 16 miles to the town of Joshua Tree, which makes a handy base for the night. If necessary, fill up your gas tank at the intersection with Park Blvd before turning right and driving 5 miles to Joshua Tree National Park's west entrance.

TRIP HIGHLIGHT

❹ Hidden Valley

It's time to jump into **Joshua Tree National Park** (📞760-367-5500; www.nps.gov/jotr; 7-day pass per car $30; P 🚻), a wonderland of bulbous boulders and jumbo rocks interspersed with sandy forests of Joshua trees. Related to agave plants, Joshua trees were named by Mormon settlers who thought the twisted, spiky arms resembled a prophet's arms stretching toward God. Revel in the scenery as you drive along the

winding park road for about 8 miles to Hidden Valley parking area. From here, an easy 1-mile loop trail meanders between whimsical rock clusters to a hidden valley where cattle rustlers once hid their hoard. If you enjoy history and Western lore, check with the national park office for ranger-led walking tours of nearby **Keys Ranch** (📞reservations 877-444-6777; www.nps.gov/jotr; tours adult/child 6-11yr $10/5, plus park admission; ☉tours Oct-May; 🚻) where pioneer homesteaders tried their hand at cattle ranching, mining and desert farming here in the 19th century.

🛏 p347

The Drive » Backtrack to Park Blvd, turn left and head south again past jumbled rock formations and fields of spiky Joshua trees. Take the well-signed right turn toward Keys View. You'll pass several trailheads and roadside interpretive exhibits over the next 5.5 miles leading up to the viewpoint.

TRIP HIGHLIGHT

❺ Keys View

Make sure you embark at least an hour before sunset for the drive up to Keys View (5185ft), where panoramic views look into the **Coachella Valley** and reach as far south as the shimmering Salton Sea or, on an unusually clear day, Mexico's Signal Mountain. Also looming in the distance are **Mt**

San Jacinto (10,834ft) and **Mt San Gorgonio** (11,500ft), Southern California's highest peaks that are often snow-dusted until late spring. Down below snakes a section of the **San Andreas Fault**.

🛏 p347

The Drive » Head back downhill to Park Blvd. Turn right and wind through the park's Wonderland of Rocks (where boulders call out to scampering kids and serious rock jocks alike), passing more campgrounds. After 10 miles, veer left to stay on Park Blvd and drive north for 8 miles toward the town of Twentynine Palms onto Utah Trail.

Keys View, looking at the Coachella Valley desert

6 Oasis of Mara

Drop by Joshua Tree National Park's **Oasis Visitor Center** (📞760-367-5500; www.nps.gov/jotr; 74485 National Park Dr, Twentynine Palms; ⏰8:30am-5pm) for its educational exhibits about Southern California's desert fan palms. These palms are often found growing along fault lines, where cracks in the earth's crust allow subterranean water to surface. Outside the visitor center, a gentle half-mile nature trail leads around the **Oasis of Mara** with the original 29 palm trees that gave Twentynine Palms its name. They were planted by native Serranos who named the area Mara, meaning 'the place of little springs and much grass'. Ask for directions to the trailhead off Hwy 62 for the 3-mile, round-trip hike to **49 Palms Oasis**, where a sun-exposed dirt trail marches you over a ridge, then drops you into a rocky gorge, doggedly heading down past barrel cacti toward a distant speck of green.

🛏 p347

The Drive >> Drive back south on Utah Trail and re-enter the park. Follow Park Blvd south, turning left at the first major junction onto Pinto Basin Rd for a winding 30-mile drive southeast to Cottonwood Spring.

TRIP HIGHLIGHT

7 Cottonwood Spring

On your drive to Cottonwood Spring, you'll pass from the high Mojave Desert into the lower Sonoran Desert. Stop at the **Cholla Cactus Garden**, where a quarter-mile loop winds through a dense grove of 'teddy bear' cholla cactus and ocotillo plants that look like green octopus tentacles and are adorned

DETOUR: SALTON SEA & SLAB CITY

Start: ❼ Cottonwood Spring

Driving along Hwy 111 southeast of Mecca, you soon hit a most unexpected sight: California's largest lake in the middle of its largest desert. The Salton Sea was created by accident in 1905 when spring flooding breached irrigation canals built to bring water from the Colorado River to the farmland in the Imperial Valley. As a long-time stopover along the Pacific Flyway, it's a prime birding spot. Alas, the winged creatures' survival is threatened by decreasing water levels and rising salinity from decades of agricultural runoff bloated with fertilizers.

About 10 miles east of the Salton Sea, near Niland, an even stranger sight is folk-art **Salvation Mountain** (☑760-624-8754; www.salvationmountaininc. org; 603 E Beal Rd; donations accepted; ☺dawn-dusk; **P**), an artificial hill slathered in paint and decorated with flowers, waterfalls, birds and religious messages. It's part of **Slab City**, an off-grid community set up atop the concrete remains of a former military base. It attracts society dropouts, drifters, retirees, snowbirds and just plain kooky folk – thousands in the winter, a few hardened souls year-round. Self-dubbed 'the last free place on earth', the Slabs is more organized than first meets the eye, with individual 'neighborhoods' and even a library and a hostel. While here, also check out the wacky installations at the **East Jesus** artist colony.

with flaming scarlet flowers in spring. Turn left at the **Cottonwood Visitor Center** (www.nps. gov/jotr; Cottonwood Spring Rd; ☺8:30am-4pm; 🚹) for a short drive east past the campground to **Cottonwood Spring** (☑760-367-5500; www.nps.gov/jotr;

P). Once used by the Cahuilla, who left behind archaeological evidence such as mortars and clay pots, the springs became a hotbed for gold mining in the late 19th century. The now-dry springs are the start of the moderately strenuous 7.5-mile

round-trip trek out to **Lost Palms Oasis**, a fan-palm oasis blessed with solitude and scenery.

🛏 p347

The Drive » Head south from Cottonwood Springs and drive across I-10 to pick up scenic Box Canyon Rd, which burrows a hole through the desert, twisting its way toward the Salton Sea. Take 66th Ave west to Mecca, then turn right onto Hwy 111 and drive northwest toward Indio.

❽ Coachella Valley

The hot but fertile Coachella Valley may be world-famous for its star-studded indie music and art festival held every April in Indio, but it's also the ideal place to find the date of your dreams – the kind that grows on trees, that is. Date farms let you sample exotic-sounding varieties like halawy, deglet noor and zahidi for free. The signature taste of the valley is a rich date shake from certified-organic **Oasis Date Gardens** (☑760-398-9354; www.oasisdate.com; 59-111 Grapefruit Blvd/Hwy 111; ☺9am-5pm; **P** 🚹) in Thermal or the 1920s pioneer **Shields Date Garden** (☑760-347-7768; www.shieldsdategarden.com; 80-225 Hwy 111; gardens $5; ☺9am-5pm; **P** 🚹) in Indio.

Eating & Sleeping

Palm Springs ❶

✖ Cheeky's   Californian $

(📞760-327-7595; www.cheekysps.com; 622
N Palm Canyon Dr; mains $9-15; ⏱8am-2pm;
❄ ✦ ⚙ 🐾) Waits can be long at this hip
breakfast and lunch spot, but the farm-to-table
dishes dazzle with witty inventiveness. The
offerings change on a weekly basis but faves
such as custardy scrambled eggs, grass-fed
burger with pesto fries, and bacon flights never
rotate off the list. No reservations.

✖ Farm   French $$

(📞760-322-2724; www.farmpalmsprings.
com; 6 La Plaza; breakfast & lunch mains $7-18,
dinner prix-fixe $56; ⏱8am-2pm daily, 6-9pm
Fri & Sat; ❄ 🛜 ✦ 🐾) Farm is so fantastically
Provençal, you expect to see lavender fields
pop up in the desert. Greet the day with fluffy
crêpes or omelets, tuck into a salad or sandwich
for lunch or book ahead for the three-course
prix-fixe surprise dinner. It's in the heart of Palm
Springs, yet secluded thanks to its country-
style courtyard.

🛏 Ace Hotel & Swim Club   Hotel $$

(📞760-325-9900; www.acehotel.com/
palmsprings; 701 E Palm Canyon Dr; d $160-210,
ste $280-660; 🅿 ❄ 🛜 🏊 🐾) Palm Springs
goes Hollywood – with all the sass, sans the
attitude – at this former Howard Johnson motel
turned hipster hangout. The 176 rooms (many
with patio) sport a sophisticated cabin look
and such mood-enhancers as a fireplace, a
vintage record player or an MP3 docking station.
Happening pool scene, low-key spa, and an on-
site restaurant and bar to boot.

Desert Hot Springs ❷

🛏 El Morocco Inn
& Spa   Boutique Hotel $$$

(📞760-288-2527; httpelmoroccoinn.com; 66810
4th St; d from $250; ⏱check-in 8:30am-7pm
or by arrangement; 🅿 ❄ 🛜 🏊) Heed the
call of the casbah at this drop-dead gorgeous
hideaway where the scene is set for romance.

Twelve exotically furnished rooms wrap around
a pool deck where your enthusiastic hosts
serve free 'Morocco-tinis' during happy hour.
The on-site spa offers tempting treatments; the
Moroccan Mystical Ritual includes a 'Moroccan
Rain' massage that uses seven detoxifying
essential oils.

Joshua Tree

✖ Crossroads Cafe   American $

(📞760-366-5414; www.crossroadscafejtree.
com; 61715 29 Palms Hwy/Hwy 62, Joshua Tree;
mains $8-17; ⏱7am-9pm; ❄ 🛜 ✦ 🐾) Before
hitting the trail, rocks or road, fuel up at this JT
institution with a carb-loaded breakfast, garden
salad or fresh sandwiches that make both
omnivores (burgers, Reuben) and vegans ('Fake
Philly' with seitan) happy. Also a chill spot to
unwind with a cold one at the end of the day.
Kids' menu available.

🛏 Kate's Lazy Desert   Cabin $$

(📞845-688-7200; www.lazymeadow.com;
58380 Botkin Rd, Landers; Airstreams Mon-Thu
$175, Fri & Sat $200; 🅿 ❄ 🛜 🏊 🐾) Owned
by Kate Pierson of the band B-52s, this desert
glamp-camp has a coin-sized pool (May to
October) and half-a-dozen artist-designed
Airstream trailers to sleep inside. Sporting
names such as 'Tinkerbell,' 'Planet Air' and 'Hot
Lava,' each is kitted out with matching fantasia-
pop design, a double bed and a kitchenette.

Joshua Tree
National Park ❹ ❺ ❻ ❼

🛏 Joshua Tree National
Park Campgrounds   Campground

(📞877-444-6777; www.recreation.gov) Of the
park's eight campgrounds, only Cottonwood
and Black Rock have potable water, flush
toilets and dump stations. The two also accept
reservations, as do Indian Cove and Jumbo
Rocks; the others are first-come, first-served.
None have showers. Backcountry camping is
allowed outside of day-use areas and at least 1
mile from any road or 500ft from any trailhead.

Temecula, Julian & Anza-Borrego

33

Embark on a multifaceted getaway with stops in Temecula's Wild West wine country; Julian, a gold-mining town cradled by fruit orchards; and the vast Anza-Borrego Desert State Park.

TRIP HIGHLIGHTS

0 miles

Temecula
Taste the grapes outside this Wild West town

1 START

Palomar Mountain

4

Santa Ysabel

3

5

FINISH

100 miles

Julian
Stop for historical gold mines and sweet apple pie

150 miles

Borrego Springs
Sleep under starry desert skies

Slot Canyon
Carve your way through a hideout canyon

165 miles

3 DAYS
300 MILES / 485KM

GREAT FOR...

BEST TIME TO GO

February to April for wildflowers and moderate temperatures.

ESSENTIAL PHOTO

Font's Point in Anza-Borrego Desert State Park.

BEST FOR FAMILIES

Julian's apple pie and gold mine tours.

rego Spring Font's Point at sunset

349

33

Temecula, Julian & Anza-Borrego

In just about any season, incredible scenery will roll past your windshield on this SoCal sojourn. In spring, the desert comes alive with a riot of wildflowers and ocotillo plants festooned with scarlet blooms. In autumn, you can pick apples in Julian's pastoral orchards and celebrate the grape harvest in Temecula's vineyards. For a winter warm-up, escape to Borrego Springs' desert resorts. In summer, cool off in the mountains outside Julian.

TRIP HIGHLIGHT

1 Temecula

Temecula means 'Place of the Sun' in the language of the native Luiseño people, who were present when the first Spanish missionaries arrived in 1797. It became a ranching outpost for Mission San Luis Rey in the 1820s, and later a stop along the Butterfield stagecoach line and California Southern Railroad. Today, Temecula is a popular short-break destination thanks to its Old

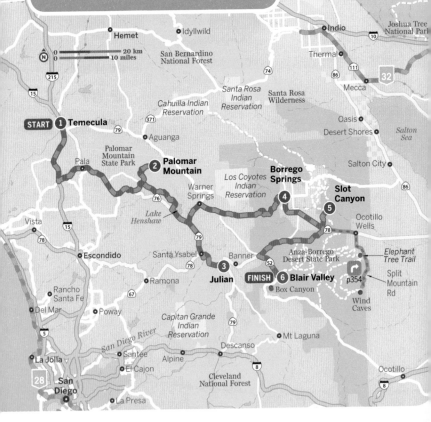

West Americana main street, over three dozen wineries and California's largest casino, Pechanga.

Although tourist-geared, a stroll along Front St in **Old Town** is a must. Pop into little boutiques, swill a craft beer, sample some jerky or stop for a free olive oil and vinegar tasting at the **Temecula Olive Oil Company** (☏951-693-4029; www.temeculaoliveoil.com; 28653 Old Town Front St; large bottles from $23; ☺9:30am-6pm Sun-Thu, to 7pm Fri & Sat). Some of its oils are pressed from the same types of olives that Spanish priests cultivated at 18th-century California missions.

But it's the wine that draws most visitors to Temecula. Many grape varietals, especially sun-seeking Mediterranean reds like Syrah, Tempranillo and Sangiovese, flourish throughout the valley because of its granite-based soil and a microclimate that sees coastal fog blowing inland overnight. Many wineries have public tasting rooms along with bistros or restaurants. Tasting fees vary but about $20 for six samples is average.

Get a winery map at the **visitor center** (☏888-363-2852; www.visittemecula valley.com; 28690 Mercedes St; ☺9am-5pm Mon-Sat), or download it from their website, and pick a designated driver for a self-guided tour. Guided tasting tours are offered by **Grapeline Temecula** (☏951-693-5755; www.gogrape.com; tours from $79). For more viticultural info, check out www.temeculawiners.org.

✖ p355

The Drive 》 From Temecula, head southeast on Hwy 76, which winds through wide green valleys bordered by citrus groves, protea farms and mountains. After about 25 miles, take the signposted left turn onto County Rd (CR) S6, aka 'Highway to the Stars', which climbs 11.5 miles up Palomar Mountain.

- - - - - - - - - - - - - - - -

➋ Palomar Mountain

High on Palomar Mountain, at an elevation of 5500ft to minimize light pollution, the **Palomar Observatory** (☏760-742-2119; www.astro.caltech.edu; 35899 Canfield Rd; tours adult/child 5-12yr $5/3; ☺9am-3pm Nov–early Mar, to 3:30pm mid-Mar–Oct, guided tours 10:30am, 12:30pm & 2pm Sat & Sun Apr-Oct; P 🚹) is simply spectacular – as large as Rome's Pantheon, with a classic design dating from the 1930s. Run by Pasadena's prestigious California Institute of Technology, it peers into space through five telescopes, including the 200in Hale Telescope, once the world's largest. Call ahead to check road conditions before making the long, winding drive up here and bring a warm jacket – temperatures inside the observatory hover around freezing. Guided one-hour tours are available on weekends from April to October, but it's just as rewarding to explore the grounds on your own. For a more in-depth experience, download the free audio-tour from the website before you arrive (cell phone reception is poor at the top). To stretch your legs, nearby **Palomar Mountain State Park** (☏760-742-3462; www.parks.ca.gov; 19952 State Park Dr; per car $10; ☺dawn-dusk; P 🚹 🐾) has forested hikes along panoramic-view trails where wildflowers bloom in early summer.

LINK YOUR TRIP

28 **Fun on the San Diego Coast**

San Diego's sunny and bodacious beach towns are only an hour's drive southwest of Temecula's vineyards.

32 **Palm Springs & Joshua Tree Oases**

From Borrego Springs, drive east toward the Salton Sea, then north to the Coachella Valley's date farms, a 60-mile trip.

The Drive » Drive 4.5 miles back down CR S6, then turn left onto CR S7, which winds southeast 11 miles downhill. Turn left on Hwy 76 and drive east past Lake Henshaw to Hwy 79. Turn right, heading south toward Santa Ysabel, where you could stop for a bite to eat (p355), then turn left and continue for 7 miles on Hwy 78/79 to Julian.

TRIP HIGHLIGHT

❸ Julian

Winding through pine-covered mountains and tree-shaded valleys, you'll arrive at the mountain hamlet of Julian. Settled by Confederate veterans after the Civil War, flecks of gold were found in the creek here in 1869, sparking a short-lived burst of speculation. Pan for gold and be regaled with tales of the hardscrabble life of early pioneers on an hour-long underground tour by the **Eagle Mining Co** (📞760-765-0036; www.theeaglemining.com; 2320 C St; adult/child $10/5; ⏱10am-4pm Mon-Fri, to 5pm Sat & Sun; 🅿 ♿).

The mines quickly petered out, but more lasting riches were found in its fertile soil. In modern times, apples are the new gold, with orchards blanketing the surrounding countryside. The apple harvest in late September brings lots of events, but crowds descend year-round on Julian's three-block **Main Street** with its galleries, antiques shops, craft stores and bakeries that each claim to make the very best apple pie – you'll have to be the judge of that.

❌ 🛏 p355

The Drive » Backtrack 7 miles west of Julian on Hwy 78. Turn right onto Hwy 79 northbound through Santa Ysabel toward Warner Springs. Turn right onto CR S2 (San Felipe Rd), then take a left some 5 miles later onto CR S22 (Montezuma Valley Rd), which twists and turns 17 miles down to Borrego Springs, revealing panoramic desert views along the way.

WATCHING STARS & WILDFLOWERS

A designated International Dark Sky Park, Anza-Borrego Desert State Park is a favorite spot for stargazing. In springtime, it's also prime wildflowers terrain. Depending on winter rains, wildflowers bloom brilliantly, albeit briefly, starting in late February, making a striking contrast to the desert's earth tones. Call the Wildflower Hotline (760-767-4684) or check the park website (www.parks.ca.gov) to find out what's blooming during your visit.

❹ Borrego Springs

With restaurants, lodging, ATMs and gas stations, Borrego Springs is the main settlement in **Anza-Borrego Desert State Park** (📞760-767-4205; www.parks.ca.gov; 🅿), California's largest state park. It's a majestic quilt of creased mountains rising from parched badlands, palm oases cocooning within narrow canyons, an abundance of wildlife and wildflowers as well as traces of thousands of years of Native American habitation.

Aerial view of Temecula

Drop by the park's visitor center to pick up information on hiking trails and road conditions. Just 1 mile from here, the popular 3-mile **Borrego Palm Canyon Nature Trail** travels through a rocky canyon to a grove of shaggy fan palms and little waterfalls.

For a dose of culture, check out the latest exhibit at the **Borrego Art Institute** (☎760-767-5152; www.borregoartinstitute.org; 665 Palm Canyon Dr; ☺10am-4pm Tue-Sun; P) or drive by quirky **metal sculptures** flanking Borrego Springs Rd just north and south of town. Find a free basic map at www.borrego springsartmap.com.

East of Borrego Springs, a signed 4-mile dirt road (sometimes passable without a 4WD) hooks south off CR S22 to **Font's Point** (1249ft) where you can take in a spectacular panorama of the otherworldly, wind-and-water-chiseled Borrego Valley to the west and the Borrego Badlands to the south. Best at sunset.

✗ 🛏 p355

The Drive » From Christmas Circle in Borrego Springs, follow Borrego Springs Rd south for 11.5 miles, then turn left on Hwy 78 and left again after 1.5 miles onto Buttes Pass Rd. Keep left at the Y junction and park at the mouth of Slot Canyon after another mile.

- - - - - - - - - - - - - - - -

TRIP HIGHLIGHT

⑤ Slot Canyon

One of the top hikes in Anza-Borrego, the short but memorable **Slot trail** threads through a siltstone canyon that, at one point, narrows so much that you have to squeeze through sideways. The winding trail ends just past a rock bridge wedged into the towering eroded walls above. Backtrack (recommended) or

ELEPHANT TREES & WIND CAVES

Start: ➎ **Slot Canyon**

Caveat: Check road conditions with the visitor center before setting out on this trip.

If you have a 4WD, you'll find stunning landscapes and solitude in the eastern reaches of Anza-Borrego Desert State Park. From Slot Canyon, backtrack to Hwy 78 and turn left. After 5 miles, turn right on Split Mountain Rd and drive 5.8 miles to the 1-mile **Elephant Trees Discovery Trail.** This species of large shrubs gets its name for its stubby trunks, but alas, only one living specimen remains among the barrel cactus, ocotillos and other desert plants you'll walk past.

Continue for another 2.5 miles until the pavement ends before turning right onto the rough Fish Creek dirt road for an adventurous 4-mile rumble to the start of the **Wind Caves Trail.** It's a steep 2-mile in-and-out trek to these holes carved into sculpted sandstone outcrops. Aside from playing hide-and-seek in this natural playground, you also get to savor the spirit-lifting expanse of undulating badlands stretching out toward the horizon.

climb up and return via the longer and less scenic dirt road.

The Drive » Return to Hwy 78, turn right and drive 17 miles, then turn left on CR S2 (Great Southern Overland Stage Route) and follow it for 5 or 6 miles before making a left for Blair Valley.

➏ Blair Valley

Blair Valley provides access to a trio of beautiful hiking trails leading off the dirt road that loops around the valley east of CR S2. The peaceful desert valley abounds with Native American pictographs and *morteros*

(hollows in rocks used for grinding seeds), best seen on the half-mile round-trip **Ehmuu-Morteros Trail** (pick up a self-guided brochure for background info).

For a bit of history, take the steep 1-mile scramble up **Ghost Mountain** to the sparse remains of a Depression-era adobe homestead where desert recluse Marshall South and his family eked out a living in the 1930s and '40s. Aside from exploring the ruins, you can feast your eyes on the sweeping Blair Valley with Granite

Mountain looming in the background.

Finally, the **Pictograph/Smuggler's Canyon Trail** delivers two big payoffs. About a mile in along a gently climbing sandy path, you'll reach a massive boulder with rust-colored pictographs painted by Native Americans many moons ago. Keep going for another half mile toward a seemingly impenetrable pile of raggedy rocks and follow narrow Smuggler's Canyon to the edge of a dry waterfall with the geologic wonderland of the Vallecito Valley unfolding below you.

While in this part of the park, also check out the **Foot and Walker Pass**, a roadside historical monument on the north side of Blair Valley. It marks a difficult spot on the Butterfield Overland Mail Route where stagecoach passengers had to disembark and walk – or even push the wagon – over the pass.

A few miles south on CR S2, at **Box Canyon**, you can still see the marks where the pioneers of the Mormon Battalion hacked through the rocks to widen the gorge sufficiently for wagons to pass through.

The Drive » Follow CR S2 south through the park, winding downhill past the Carrizo Badlands Overlook to I-8, which heads west to San Diego.

Eating & Sleeping

Temecula ●

✗ Restaurant at Ponte Californian $$$

(☑951-252-1770; www.pontewinery.com; Ponte Winery, 35053 Rancho California Rd; mains $24-41; ⊙11am-4pm Mon-Thu, to 8pm Fri & Sat, to 5pm Sun) New American cuisine melds with farm-fresh flavors at this busy winery bistro, with specialties like five-peppercorn-spiced lamb or seafood pasta. It's a local favorite for weekend lunch on the airy patio.

✗ EAT Marketplace Health Food $

(☑951-694-3663; www.eatmarketplace. com; 28410 Old Town Front St; mains $11-17; ⊙8am-3pm; P 🛜) Freshness is king at EAT (Extraordinary Artisan Table), a wholesome cafe just off Front St. The menu covers the gamut of food trends, from plant-based to paleo, using mostly local organic ingredients.

✗ The Bank – Plates & Pours Mexican $$

(☑951-676-6160; www.thebankoldtown.com; 28645 Old Town Front St; mains $9-23; ⊙11am-9pm Sun-Thu, to 10pm Fri & Sat; 🚼) This handsome former bank (c 1912) was robbed in 1930. In a truly Wild West story, the robber was caught by townspeople and the swag was returned in full. You can now try enchiladas, burritos and tacos in this fabled setting, while gazing at the historical photos on the walls. Alternatively, people-watch from a nice patio bar. Lunch specials $12 (11am to 3pm Monday to Friday).

Santa Ysabel

✗ Dudley's Famous Bakery Bakery $

(☑760-765-0488; www.dudleysbakery.com; 30218 Hwy 78; items $3-10; ⊙8am-3pm Mon-Thu, to 5pm Fri-Sun; P 🚼) Generations of travelers have stopped at Dudley's to pick up sandwiches, picnic lunches and fresh-baked loaves of bread in almost two dozen flavors.

Julian ❸

✗ Julian Pie Company Bakery $

(☑760-765-2449; www.julianpie.com; 2225 Main St; whole pies $21-25; ⊙9am-5pm; P 🚼) Many visitors are beholden to this family-run business. Its classic apple pies are indeed crave-worthy, but variations such as apple-berry crumb are just as tempting, especially when topped with a dollop of ice cream.

🛏 Julian Gold Rush Hotel Historic Hotel $

(☑760-765-0201; www.julianhotel.com; 2032 Main St; d $105-175; P ⊖ ❄ 🛜) At this 1897 antique-filled B&B, lace curtains, cast-iron fireplaces, claw-foot tubs and other relics painstakingly evoke a bygone era in all 16 rooms and the public areas.

Borrego Springs ❹

✗ Red Ocotillo American $$

(☑760-767-7400;www.redocotillo.com; 721 Avenida Sureste; breakfast $8-17, mains $13-21; ⊙7am-8:30pm; P ❄ 🛜 🚼 🐾) Empty tables are as rare as puddles in the desert at this artily painted charmer in a central Borrego Springs bungalow. Fuel up for a day on the trail with the smoked salmon eggs Benedict breakfast, tuck into fresh salads or sandwiches at lunch or wrap up the day with classics from burgers to short ribs.

🛏 La Casa del Zorro Resort & Spa Resort $$$

(☑760-767-0100; www.lacasadelzorro.com; 3845 Yaqui Pass Rd; d from $280 Oct-Apr, $110-153 May-Oct; P ⊖ ❄ 🛜 🏊 🐾) This venerable 1937 resort is the region's grandest stay. The ambience speaks of romance and relaxation in 63 elegantly rustic poolside rooms and family-sized casitas sporting vaulted ceilings and marble bathtubs. Two restaurants and a bar provide sustenance, while five pools, tennis courts, a fitness center and yoga studio help keep the love handles at bay.

STRETCH YOUR LEGS
LOS ANGELES

Start/Finish Union Station

Distance 3.5 miles

Duration four to six hours

Nobody walks in LA? That's just not true in Downtown's historic core. Sample the jumbled sights, sounds and tastes of the city's Mexican, Asian and European heritage, with iconic architecture and famous TV and film locations, on this half-day ramble.

Take this walk on Trips

2 3 30

Union Station

This iconic 1939 **edifice** (www.unionstation la.com; 800 N Alameda St; P; MB/D/L Lines to Union Station) was the last of the USA's grand railway stations to be built. It's a glamorous exercise in Mission Revival style with art-deco and Native American accents. The marble-floored main hall, with cathedral ceilings, original leather chairs and 3000lb chandeliers has been glimpsed in dozens of movies and hit TV shows from *Speed* to *24*.

The Walk ≫ Walk a block up N Alameda St, cross W Cesar E Chavez Ave and walk west a half block. Turn left down the passageway of Olvera St.

El Pueblo de Los Angeles

Compact and colorful, this **historical monument** (☏213-485-6855; www.elpueblo. lacity.org; Olvera St; ☼ tours 10am, 11am & noon Tue-Sat; ♿; MB/D/L Lines to Union Station) sits near the spot where LA's first Spanish colonists plunked down in 1781. Wander through narrow Olvera St, lined with Mexican-themed stalls, and explore **LA Plaza** (La Plaza de Cultura y Artes; ☏213-542-6200; www.lapca.org; 501 N Main St; ☼ noon-5pm Mon & Wed-Fri, 10am-5pm Sat & Sun; ♿), its exhibits offering snapshots of the Mexican-American experience in Los Angeles.

The Walk ≫ Continue southwest along Main St, crossing Hwy 101 toward LA's City Hall (1928). Turn left onto E Temple St, right onto S Los Angeles St and left onto E 1st St, entering Little Tokyo.

Little Tokyo

Walk past ramen shops and *izakaya* (Japanese pubs serving food) to the **Japanese American National Museum** (☏213-625-0414; www.janm.org; 100 N Central Ave; adult/senior/child $16/7/7, 5-8pm Thu & all day 3rd Thu of month free; ☼11am-5pm Tue, Wed & Fri-Sun, noon-8pm Thu; ♿; ML Line to Little Tokyo/Arts District). Exhibits include those on WWII internment camps. Beside it lies **MOCA Geffen** (☏213-625-4390; www.moca.org; 152 N Central Ave; special exhibitions adult/senior & student/child under 12yr $18/10/free, 5-8pm Thu free; ☼ daily,

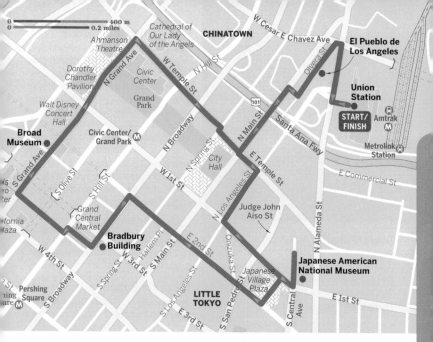

check website), dedicated to the Museum of Contemporary Art's larger and more conceptual works.

The Walk ›› West of Central Ave, turn left to walk through Japanese Village Plaza. Turn right onto E 2nd St, walk five blocks uphill to S Broadway, then turn left and walk a block to W 3rd St.

Bradbury Building

Featured in *Blade Runner*, the 1893 **Bradbury Building** (www.laconservancy. org/locations/bradbury-building; 304 S Broadway; ☺lobby 7am-6pm Mon-Fri, 9am-5pm Sat & Sun; Ⓜ B/D Lines to Pershing Sq) is one of LA's architectural treasures. Its red-brick facade conceals a glass-roofed atrium with inky filigree grillwork, birdcage elevators and yellow-brick walls that glisten gold in the afternoon light.

The Walk ›› Walk through Grand Central Market, with its artisanal food stalls. Catch the Angels

Flight cable car across the street to California Plaza, veering northwest to Grand Ave. Turn right and walk a block northeast.

Broad Museum

Designed by Diller Scofidio + Renfro (designers of Manhattan's High Line), the **Broad** (☎213-232-6200; www.thebroad. org; 221 S Grand Ave; ☺11am-5pm Tue & Wed, 11am-8pm Thu & Fri, 10am-8pm Sat, 10am-6pm Sun; ⓅⒶ; Ⓜ B/D Lines to Civic Center/Grand Park) houses postwar pieces by heavy hitters including Andy Warhol, Jeff Koons and Yayoi Kusama. Admission is free; advance ticket reservation recommended.

The Walk ›› Continue northeast up Grand Ave, passing Walt Disney Concert Hall. Turn right on Temple St and roll downhill past the Cathedral of Our Lady of the Angels back to City Hall, retracing your steps north through El Pueblo to Union Station.

STRETCH YOUR LEGS
SAN DIEGO

Start/Finish: California Quadrangle

Distance: 2 miles

Duration: one to six hours

The zoo, museums and gardens of sun-drenched Balboa Park, originally built for the 1915–16 Panama-California Exposition, make it a highlight of any San Diego stopover. Explore fantastical architecture along its curved walking paths.

Take this walk on Trips

2 3 28

California Quadrangle

East of Cabrillo Bridge, El Prado passes under an archway into the California Quadrangle. Just north, the anthropological **Museum of Man** (☏619-239-2001; www.museumofman.org; Plaza de California, 1350 El Prado; adult/child under 5yr $13/free; ☉10am-5pm; ♿) is one of the park's most ornate Spanish Colonial Revival creations, its landmark **California Tower** richly decorated with blue and yellow tiles. Inside, exhibits span Egypt, the Maya and the local indigenous Kumeyaay people.

The Walk >> Amble east under the white colonnades along the south side of El Prado. Duck into the formally hedged Alcazar Garden on your right, then continue east toward the spritzing fountain in Plaza de Panama.

Plaza de Panama

The exterior of the **San Diego Museum of Art** (SDMA; ☏619-232-7931; www.sdmart.org; 1450 El Prado; adult/student/child under 17yr $15/8/free; ☉10am-5pm Mon, Tue, Thu & Sat, 10am-8pm Fri, noon-5pm Sun) was designed in 16th-century Spanish Renaissance plateresque style. Nearby, the **Timken Museum of Art** (☏619-239-5548; www.timkenmuseum.org; 1500 El Prado; ☉10am-4:30pm Tue-Sat, from noon Sun) has an impressive collection of artworks by European masters, while the San Diego Museum of Art exhibits Spanish masterpieces.

The Walk >> Stroll north alongside the lily pond into the Botanical Building greenhouse. Back outside, cut east to Village Pl, then turn left and walk north past the giant Moreton Bay fig tree and the shops of the Spanish Village Art Center.

San Diego Zoo

Since its grand opening in 1916, the **San Diego Zoo** (☏619-231-1515; www..san diegozoo.org; 2920 Zoo Dr; adult/child 3-11yr day pass from $58/48; 2-visit pass zoo &/or safari park $92.80/82.80; ☉9am-9pm mid-Jun–early Sep, to 5pm or 6pm rest of year; 🅿 ♿) has pioneered ways to house animals that mimic their natural habitat, in the process also becoming one of the country's great

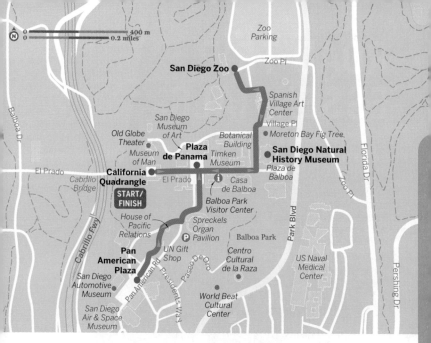

botanic gardens. A guided double-decker bus tour gives you a good overview of the zoo.

The Walk ≫ Retrace your steps south to El Prado, turning left and walking straight ahead to Bea Evenson Fountain. Then backtrack a short distance west to the natural history museum.

San Diego Natural History Museum

With its giant-screen cinema and mega traveling exhibitions, **'The Nat'** (☏619-232-3821; www.sdnhm.org; 1788 El Prado; adult/child 3-17yr/under 2yr $20/12/free; ⏱10am-5pm; 🚻) houses around 7.5 million specimens, including rocks, fossils, taxidermy animals and skulls, as well as an educational and eco-conscious exhibit on SoCal's water resources.

The Walk ≫ Backtrack west along El Prado, passing the Casa de Balboa, which houses photography, city history and a Model Railroad Museum, on your left. Turn left at Plaza de Panama, heading south past the Japanese Friendship Garden and Spreckels Organ Pavilion.

Pan American Plaza

Fast-food stands and ice-cream vendors set up shop on Balboa Park's central plaza. The **UN Gift Shop** (☏619-233-5044; www.ungiftshop.org; 2171 Pan American Plaza; ⏱10am-4:30pm) sells globally minded crafts, jewelry and souvenirs, donating profits to worldwide children's charities. Nearby, the **House of Pacific Relations** (☏619-234-0739; www.sdhpr.org; 2191 W Pan American Rd; ⏱ cottages 11am-3pm 4th Tue each month; 🚻) actually comprises 15 cottages, inside which you can view furnishings, artworks and museum-like displays from an Olympian mix of countries. Further south is the famous and superb **San Diego Air & Space Museum** (☏619-234-8291; www.sandiegoairandspace. org; 2001 Pan American Plaza; adult/child 3-11yr/ under 2yr $20/11/free; ⏱10am-5pm, last entry 4:30pm; 🚻).

The Walk ≫ Make a U-turn and walk back up Pan American Rd all the way northeast to Plaza de Panama. Turn left onto El Prado and head west back to California Quadrangle, where your walk began.

ROAD TRIP ESSENTIALS

California Driving Guide

With jaw-dropping scenery and one of the USA's most comprehensive highway networks, California is an all-star destination for a road trip any time of year.

DRIVER'S LICENSE & DOCUMENTS

Out-of-state and international visitors may legally drive a car in California with their home driver's license. If you're driving into the USA from Canada or Mexico, bring your vehicle's registration papers, liability insurance and home driver's license; an International Driving Permit (IDP) is a good supplement but isn't currently recognized as a valid driver's license in California.

If you're from overseas, an IDP will have more credibility with traffic police and simplify the car-rental process, especially if your license doesn't have a photo or isn't written in English. International automobile associations can issue IDPs, valid for one year, for a fee. Always carry your home license together with the IDP.

The American Automobile Association (AAA) has reciprocal agreements with some international auto clubs (the CAA in Canada and the AAA in Australia), so bring your membership card from home.

INSURANCE

California law requires liability insurance for all vehicles. When renting a car, check your home auto-insurance policy or your travel-insurance policy to see if rental cars are already covered. If not, expect to pay about $11 to $20 per day for liability insurance when renting a car.

Insurance against damage to the car itself, called Collision Damage Waiver (CDW) or Loss Damage Waiver (LDW),

costs another $14 to $32 or more per day for rental cars. The deductible may require you to pay up to the first $500 for any repairs. If you decline CDW, you will be held liable for all damages up to the full value of the car.

Some credit cards cover CDW/LDW, provided you charge the entire cost of the car rental to that card. If you have an accident, you may have to pay the rental-car company first, then seek reimbursement. Most credit-card coverage isn't valid for rentals over one month or for 'exotic' models (eg convertibles, RVs).

RENTAL VEHICLES

To rent your own wheels, you'll typically need to be at least 25 years old, hold a valid driver's license and have a major credit card, *not* a check or debit card.

Rates generally include unlimited mileage, but expect surcharges for additional drivers and one-way rentals. Airport locations may have cheaper rates but higher fees; if you get a fly-drive package, local taxes may be extra when you pick up the car. Child or infant safety seats are compulsory; reserve them (from $12 per day) when booking your car.

Major car-rental companies:

Alamo (844-354-6962; www.alamo.com)

Budget (800-218-7992; www.budget.com)

Dollar (800-800-5252; www.dollar.com)

Enterprise (855-266-9289; www.enterprise.com)

Fox (855-571-8413; www.foxrentacar.com)

Driving Fast Facts

Right or left? Drive on the right

Legal driving age 16

Top speed limit 70mph (some interstate and state highways)

Best bumper sticker Keep Tahoe Blue, Lake Tahoe

Hertz (☑800-654-3131; www.hertz.com)

National (☑844-382-6875; www.national-car.com)

Payless (☑800-729-5377; www.paylesscar.com)

Thrifty (☑800-847-4389; www.thrifty.com)

Some major car-rental companies offer 'green' hybrid or biofueled rental cars, but they're in short supply; make reservations far in advance and expect to pay significantly more for these models. Many companies rent hand-controlled vehicles and vans with wheelchair lifts at no extra charge, but you must also reserve these well in advance.

For independent car rentals, check the following:

Mobility Works (☑877-275-4915; www.mobilityworks.com) Rents wheelchair-accessible vans in Los Angeles (multiple locations), San Diego, the San Francisco Bay Area, Sacramento and a few other locations.

Rent-a-Wreck (☑877-877-0700; www.rentawreck.com) Minimum rental age and under-25 driver surcharges vary at six locations, including in LA and the San Francisco Bay Area.

Simply Rent-a-Car (☑323-653-0022; www.simplyrac.com) Rents SUVs, luxury and classic vehicles in LA.

Sixt (☑888-749-8227; www.sixt.com) Economy and luxury car and SUV rentals around LA, San Diego and the San Francisco Bay Area.

Super Cheap! Car Rental (☑in Los Angeles 310-645-3993, in San Francisco 650-777-9993; www.supercheapcar.com) Near international airports LAX and SFO. No surcharge for drivers under 25, but they are responsible for the first $400 in damages.

Wheelchair Getaways (☑888-432-9339; www.wheelchairgetaways.com) Rents wheelchair-accessible vans in Sacramento, San Diego, San Francisco and Los Angeles.

Motorcycles

Motorcycle rentals and insurance are very expensive.

Bartels' (☑310-593-9767; www.eaglerider.com/bartels-harley-davidson; 4141 Lincoln Blvd; ⊙9am-6pm Tue-Sat, 10am-5pm Sun) Harley-Davidson motorcycle rentals in Marina del Rey, between Venice Beach and LAX.

Eagle Rider (☑310-321-3180; www.eaglerider.com) Nationwide company with 15 locations in California, as well as locations in Las Vegas, NV.

Recreational Vehicles & Campervans

Book recreational vehicle (RV) and campervan rentals as far in advance as possible. Rental costs vary by size and model; rates often don't include mileage, bedding or kitchen kits, vehicle prep or taxes.

Cruise America (☑480-464-7300; www.cruiseamerica.com) Nationwide RV-rental company with two dozen locations in California.

El Monte (☑888-337-2214; www.elmonterv.com) With 11 locations in California, this national RV-rental agency offers AAA discounts.

Escape Campervans (☑310-672-9909; www.escapecampervans.com) Awesomely painted campervans at economical rates in the San Francisco Bay Area, LA and Las Vegas, NV.

Jucy Rentals (☑800-650-4180; www.jucyusa.com) Campervan rentals in the San Francisco Bay Area, LA and Las Vegas, NV.

Road Bear (☑818-865-2925; www.roadbearrv.com) RV rentals in LA, the San Francisco Bay Area and Las Vegas, NV.

Vintage Surfari Wagons (☑714-585-7565; www.vwsurfari.com) VW campervan rentals in Orange County.

BORDER CROSSINGS

California is an important agricultural state. To prevent the spread of pests and diseases, certain food items (including meats, fresh fruit and vegetables) may not be brought into the state. Firewood will also be inspected and you are discouraged from bringing it into the state. If you drive across the border from Mexico or the neighboring states of Oregon, Nevada or Arizona, you may have to stop for a quick agricultural inspection. For a list of banned fruits and vegetables, check out the chart provided online by the California Department of Food & Agriculture (www.cdfa.ca.gov/plant/factsheets/BringingFruits-Veggies_to_CA.pdf).

If you're driving across the Mexican border, check the ever-changing passport and visa requirements with the **US Department of State** (www.travel.state.gov) beforehand. **US Customs and Border Protection** (https://bwt.cbp.gov) tracks current wait times at every border crossing. Between San Diego and Tijuana, Mexico, San Ysidro is the busiest border crossing in the western hemisphere. US citizens do not require a visa for stays in Mexico of 72 hours or less in a border zone, but they do need a passport.

Unless you're planning an extended stay in Tijuana, taking a car across the Mexican border is more trouble than it's worth. Instead, leave your car on the US side of the border and walk. If you drive across, you must buy Mexican car insurance either beforehand or at the border crossing.

MAPS

Visitor centers and tourist information offices distribute free (but often very basic) maps. GPS navigation cannot be entirely relied upon, especially in remote desert or mountain areas. If you are planning on doing a lot of driving, you'll need a more detailed road map or atlas. DeLorme's comprehensive *California Atlas & Gazetteer* ($25) shows campgrounds, recreational areas and topographical land features, although it's less useful for navigating urban areas. The American Automobile Association (AAA) offers maps online, by mail order and in its offices.

ROAD CONDITIONS

For highway conditions, including road closures and construction updates, dial ☑800-427-7623 or visit www.dot.ca.gov.

In places where winter driving is an issue, snow tires or tire chains may be required, especially on mountain highways. Ideally, carry your own chains and learn how to use them before you hit the road. Otherwise, chains can usually be bought (but not cheaply) on the highway, at gas stations or in nearby towns. Before driving to ski resorts in Lake Tahoe in winter, check the California State Highway

Road Trip Websites

AUTOMOBILE CLUBS

American Automobile Association (AAA; ☑800-922-8228; www.aaa.com) Emergency roadside assistance (24 hour), free maps and travel discounts for members.

Better World Club (☑866-238-1137; www.betterworldclub.com) Ecofriendly auto-club alternative to AAA.

DRIVING CONDITIONS & TRAFFIC

California Department of Transportation (Caltrans; ☑800-427-7623; www.dot.ca.gov) Highway conditions, construction updates and road closures.

511 SF Bay (www.511.org) San Francisco Bay Area traffic updates.

Go511 (www.go511.com) LA and Southern California traffic updates.

MAPS

Google Maps (http://maps.google.com) Free online maps and driving directions.

National Park Service (www.nps.gov) Links to individual park sites for road condition updates and free downloadable maps.

ROAD RULES

California Department of Motor Vehicles (www.dmv.ca.gov) Statewide driving laws, driver's licenses and vehicle registration.

Patrol's Truckee Facebook page (www.facebook.com/chp.truckee) for the latest road conditions and tire or chain requirements.

Most car-rental companies don't permit the use of tire chains. Driving off-road, or on unpaved roads, is also prohibited by most car-rental companies.

ROAD RULES

Driving laws change with some frequency, and there are many rules not included here. For general requirements and the latest information, check out the California Driver Handbook online at www.dmv.ca.gov. It is published by the California Department of Motor Vehicles.

➡ Drive on the right-hand side of the road.

➡ Talking or texting on a cell (mobile) phone without a hands-free device while driving is illegal.

➡ The use of seat belts is required for drivers, front-seat passengers and children under 16.

➡ Infant and child safety seats are required for children under eight years old unless they are at least 4ft 9in tall.

➡ High-occupancy vehicle (HOV) lanes marked with a diamond symbol are reserved for cars with multiple occupants, sometimes only during rush hours.

➡ Unless otherwise posted, the speed limit is 65mph on freeways, 55mph on two-lane undivided highways, 35mph on major city streets and 25mph in business and residential districts.

➡ At intersections, U-turns are permitted unless otherwise posted.

➡ Except where indicated, turning right at red lights after coming to a full stop is permitted, although intersecting traffic still has the right of way.

➡ At four-way stop signs, cars proceed in the order in which they arrived. If two cars arrive simultaneously, the one on the right has the right of way. When in doubt, wave the other driver ahead.

➡ When emergency vehicles (ie police, fire or ambulance) approach from either direction, carefully pull over to the side of the road.

➡ If a police car, Caltrans (California Department of Transportation) or emergency vehicle, or a tow truck is pulled off on the shoulder of the road, drivers in the right-hand lane are legally required to merge left, as long as it's safe to do so.

➡ It's illegal to carry open containers of alcohol or marijuana inside a moving vehicle, even empty ones. Unless containers are full and still sealed, store them in the trunk away from the passenger area and outside your possession. Carrying a proper medical ID or physician's recommendation may provide an exception for the marijuana.

PARKING

Parking is plentiful and free in small towns and rural areas, but scarce and/or expensive in cities. You can pay municipal parking meters and centralized pay stations with coins (usually quarters) or sometimes credit or debit cards. When parking on the street, read all posted regulations and restrictions (eg street-cleaning hours, permit-only residential areas) and pay attention to colored curbs, or you may be ticketed and towed. Expect to pay at least $2.50 per hour or $30 overnight at a city parking garage. Flat-fee valet parking at hotels and restaurants is common in cities; tip the valet attendant at least $2 when they hand your keys back.

Warning!

As of early 2020, the US State Department (www.travel.state.gov) has issued a Level Two: Exercise Extreme Caution travel warning about violence and crime along the US–Mexico border. Travelers should exercise caution in the northern Mexican state of Baja California, including the city of Tijuana.

For the latest news and statistics about the Covid-19 pandemic in California, visit www.covid19.ca.gov. The website also shares specifics about Covid-related entry restrictions into California for domestic and international travelers.

Driving Problem-Buster

What should I do if my car breaks down? Call the roadside emergency assistance number of your car-rental company or, if you're driving your own car, your automobile association.

What if I have an accident? If it's safe to do so, pull over to the side of the road. For minor fender benders with no injuries or significant property damage, exchange insurance information with the other driver and file a report with your insurance provider as soon as possible. For major accidents, call ☑911 and wait for the police and emergency services to arrive.

What should I do if I am stopped by the police? Be courteous. Don't get out of the car unless asked. Keep your hands where the officer can see them (eg on the steering wheel). For traffic violations, there is usually a 30-day period to pay a fine; most matters can be handled by mail. Police can legally give roadside sobriety checks to assess if you've been drinking or using drugs.

What should I do if my car gets towed? Immediately call the police nonemergency number for the town or city that you're in and ask where to pick up your car. Towing and hourly or daily storage fees can quickly total hundreds of dollars.

What if I can't find anywhere to stay? If you're stuck and it's getting late, it's best not to keep driving on aimlessly – just pull into the next roadside chain motel or hotel with the 'Vacancy' light lit up. Some Walmart stores allow RVs to park in their lots overnight. Check with the individual store before parking and settling in.

FUEL

➡ Gas stations in California, nearly all of which are self-service, are everywhere, except in national parks and sparsely populated desert and mountain areas.

➡ Gas is sold in gallons (one US gallon equals 3.78L). In early 2020, the cost for regular fuel in California averaged $3 per gallon.

SAFETY

In rural areas, livestock sometimes graze next to unfenced roads. These areas are typically signed as 'Open Range,' with the silhouette of a steer. Where deer or other wild animals frequently appear roadside, you'll see signs with the silhouette of a leaping deer. Take these signs seriously, particularly at night or in the fog.

In coastal areas, thick fog may impede driving – slow down and if it's too soupy, get off the road. Along coastal cliffs and on twisting mountain roads, watch out for falling rocks, mudslides and snow avalanches that could damage or disable your car if struck.

California Travel Guide

GETTING THERE & AWAY

AIR

California's major international airports are in Los Angeles (www.lawa.org) and San Francisco (www.flysfo.com). Smaller regional airports are served primarily by domestic US carriers, including low-cost and discount airlines.

Major car-rental agencies operate out of all of California's biggest airports, including international and domestic hubs.

BUS

Greyhound (www.greyhound.com) is the major long-distance bus company, with routes throughout the USA, including to/from California. Greyhound has ended service to many small towns; routes trace major highways and may only stop at larger population centers.

Car rentals are seldom available at bus terminals, though agency branch offices may be located nearby in some cities.

CAR & MOTORCYCLE

If you're driving into the USA from Canada or Mexico, bring your vehicle's registration papers and proof of liability insurance. If you're renting a car or a motorcycle, ask beforehand if the agency allows its vehicles to be taken across international borders. Expect long border-crossing waits, especially on weekends and holidays and during weekday commuter rush hours.

TRAIN

Amtrak (www.amtrak.com) operates a fairly extensive rail system throughout the USA. Trains are comfortable, if a bit slow, and are equipped with dining and lounge cars on long-distance routes. Fares vary according to the type of train and seating (eg coach or business class, sleeping compartments).

A few agencies make rental cars available at some train stations, usually by advance reservation only.

Practicalities

Electricity 110/120V AC, 50/60Hz

Radio National Public Radio (NPR), lower end of FM dial

Smoking Illegal indoors in all public buildings, including restaurants, bars and casinos/gaming establishments. Some lodgings offer smoking rooms upon request. The minimum age for buying tobacco products, which includes cigarettes, e-cigarettes and vaping pens, is now 21.

Time California is on Pacific Standard Time (UTC-8). Clocks are set one hour ahead during Daylight Saving Time (DST), from the second Sunday in March until the first Sunday in November.

Weights and measures Imperial (except 1 US gallon = 0.83 gallons)

DIRECTORY A–Z

ACCOMMODATIONS

➡ Budget-conscious accommodations include campgrounds, hostels and motels.

➡ At midrange motels and hotels, expect clean, comfortable and decent-sized rooms with at least a private bathroom, and standard amenities such as cable TV, direct-dial telephone, a coffeemaker, and perhaps a microwave and mini fridge.

➡ At top-end hotels and resorts, swimming pools, fitness rooms, business centers, full-service restaurants and bars are all standard.

➡ In Southern California nearly all lodgings have air-conditioning, but in Northern California, where it rarely gets hot, the opposite is true. In coastal areas as far south as Santa Barbara, only fans may be provided.

➡ There may be a fee for wireless internet, especially for in-room access. Look for free wi-fi hot spots in hotel public areas (eg lobby, poolside).

➡ Many accommodations in California are exclusively nonsmoking. Where they still exist, smoking rooms are often left unrenovated and in less desirable locations. Expect a hefty 'cleaning fee' ($100 or more) if you light up in a designated nonsmoking room.

Hotels & Motels

Rooms are often priced by the size and number of beds, rather than the number of occupants. A room with one double or queen-size bed usually costs the same for one or two people, while a room with a king-size bed or two double beds costs more.

There is often a small surcharge for the third and fourth person, but children under a certain age (this varies) may stay free. Cribs or rollaway cots usually incur an additional fee. Be aware that suites or 'junior suites' may simply be oversized rooms; ask about the layout when booking.

Recently renovated or larger rooms, or those with a view, are likely to cost more. Descriptors like 'oceanfront' and 'ocean view' are often too liberally used, and you may require a telescope to spot the surf.

You can make reservations at chains by calling their central reservation lines, but to learn about specific amenities and local promotions, call the property directly. If you arrive without reservations, ask to see

> ## Book Your Stay Online
>
> For more accommodations reviews by Lonely Planet authors, check out http://hotels.lonelyplanet.com. You'll find independent reviews, as well as recommendations on the best places to stay. Best of all, you can book online.

a room before paying for it, especially at motels.

Rates may include breakfast, which could be just a stale donut and wimpy coffee, an all-you-can-eat hot and cold buffet, or anything in between.

B&Bs

For an atmospheric or even romantic alternative to impersonal motels and hotels, bed-and-breakfasts traditionally inhabit fine Victorian houses or other heritage buildings, bedecked with floral wallpaper and antique furnishings. More modern inns do exist, especially near the coast. Travelers who prefer privacy may find B&Bs too intimate.

Rates often include breakfast, but occasionally do not (never mind what the name 'B&B' suggests). Amenities vary widely, but rooms with TV and telephone are the exception; the cheapest units share bathrooms. Standards are high at places certified by the **California Association of Boutique & Breakfast Inns** (www.cabbi.com).

Most B&Bs require advance reservations; only a few will accommodate drop-in guests. Smoking is generally prohibited and children are often not welcome. Multi-night minimum stays may be required, especially on weekends and in high season.

Camping

➡ On public lands, primitive campsites usually have fire pits, picnic tables and vault toilets. Developed campgrounds, such as those in state and national parks, usually offer more amenities, including flush toilets, BBQ grills and occasionally hot showers.

➡ Private campgrounds often cater to RVs (recreational vehicles) with full electricity and water hookups and dump stations; tent sites may be sparse and uninviting. Hot showers and coin-op laundry are often available, and possibly a pool, wi-fi and camping cabins.

➡ Many public campgrounds, especially in the mountains, are closed from late fall through early spring or summer. Opening and closing dates vary each year, depending on weather and snow conditions. Private campgrounds closer to cities, beaches and major highways are often open year-round.

➡ Many public and private campgrounds accept reservations for all or some of their sites, while a few are strictly first-come, first-served. Overnight rates range from free for the most primitive campsites to $60 or more for pull-through RV sites with full hookups.

➡ If you can't get a campsite reservation, plan to show up at the campground between 10am and noon, when last night's campers may be leaving. Otherwise, ask about overflow camping and dispersed camping nearby.

➡ If you didn't bring your own tent, you can buy (and occasionally rent) camping gear at outdoor outfitters and sporting-goods shops in most cities and some towns, especially near national parks.

Rates & Reservations

➡ Lodgings in national parks including Yosemite, Sequoia and Kings Canyon generally sell out months in advance for the summer, as do backcountry lodgings that operate on a lottery system.

➡ Generally midweek rates are lower, except at urban hotels geared toward business travelers. Hotels in Silicon Valley, downtown San Francisco, LA and San Diego may lure leisure travelers with weekend deals.

Sleeping Price Ranges

The following price ranges refer to a private room with bath during high season, unless otherwise specified. Taxes and breakfast are not normally included in the price.

➡ **$** less than $150 (less than $200 in San Francisco)

➡ **$$** $150 to $250 ($200 to $350 in San Francisco)

➡ **$$$** more than $250 (more than $350 in San Francisco)

➡ Discount membership cards (such as AAA and AARP) may get you about 10% off standard rates at participating hotels and motels.

➡ Look for freebie-ad magazines packed with hotel and motel discount coupons at gas stations, highway rest areas, tourist offices and online.

➡ High season is from June to August everywhere, except the deserts and mountain ski areas, where December through April are the busiest months.

➡ Demand and prices spike around major holidays and for festivals, when some properties may impose multiday minimum stays.

➡ Reservations are recommended for weekend and holiday travel year-round, and every day of the week during high season.

➡ Bargaining may be possible for walk-in guests without reservations, especially at off-peak times.

ELECTRICITY

Type A
120V/60Hz

FOOD

➡ Lunch is generally served between 11:30am and 2:30pm, and dinner between 5pm and 9pm daily, though some restaurants stay open later, especially on Friday and Saturday nights. A few roadside diners are open 24 hours.

➡ If breakfast is served, it's usually between 7:30am and 10:30am. Some diners and cafes keep serving breakfast into the afternoon, or all day. Weekend brunch is a laid-back affair, usually available from 11am until 3pm on Saturdays and Sundays.

➡ Like all things Californian, restaurant etiquette tends to be informal. Only a handful of restaurants require more than a dressy shirt, slacks and a decent pair of shoes; most places require far less, especially near the beaches.

➡ Tipping 18% to 20% is expected anywhere you receive table service, unless the menu or your bill specifically states that tipping and/or a service charge is already included (common for groups of six or more).

➡ Smoking is illegal indoors. Some restaurants have patios or sidewalk tables where smoking is tolerated (ask first, or look around for ashtrays), but don't expect your neighbors to be happy about secondhand smoke.

➡ You can bring your own wine to most restaurants; a 'corkage' fee of $15 to $30 usually applies. At lunch, a glass of wine or beer is socially acceptable at most places.

➡ If you ask the kitchen to divide a plate between two (or more) people, there may be a small split-plate surcharge.

➡ Vegetarians, vegans and travelers with food allergies or restrictions are in luck – many restaurants are used to catering to specific dietary needs.

LGBT+ TRAVELERS

California is a magnet for LGBT+ travelers. Hot spots include the Castro in San Francisco, West Hollywood (WeHo), Silver Lake, Long Beach and Downtown in LA, San Diego's Hillcrest neighborhood, the desert resort of Palm Springs, Guerneville in the Russian River Valley and Calistoga in Napa Valley.

Same-sex marriage is legal in California. Despite widespread tolerance, homophobic bigotry still exists. In small towns, especially away from the coast, tolerance often comes down to a 'don't ask, don't tell' policy.

Advocate (www.advocate.com/travel) Online news, gay travel features and destination guides.

Eating Price Ranges

The following price ranges refer to an average main course at dinner, unless otherwise stated. These prices don't include taxes or tip. Note the same dishes at lunch will usually be cheaper, even half-price.

➡ **$** less than $15

➡ **$$** $15 to $25

➡ **$$$** more than $25

Damron (www.damron.com) Classic, advertiser-driven gay travel guides and 'Gay Scout' mobile app.

Gay & Lesbian National Hotline (☎888-843-4564) For counseling and referrals of any kind.

GayCities (www.gaycities.com) Activities, tours, lodging, shopping, restaurants and nightlife in a dozen California cities.

misterb&b (www.misterbandb.com) Like Airbnb, but for gay (mostly male) travelers.

Out Traveler (www.outtraveler.com) Free online magazine with travel tips, destination guides and hotel reviews.

Purple Roofs (www.purpleroofs.com) Online directory of LGBTQ accommodations.

INTERNET ACCESS

➡ With branches in most cities and towns, **FedEx Office** (☎800-463-3339; www.fedex.com) offers internet access at self-service computer workstations (around 30¢ per minute) and sometimes free wi-fi, plus digital-photo printing, scanning and faxing.

➡ Free or fee-based wi-fi hot spots can be found at major airports; many hotels, motels and coffee shops (eg Starbucks); and some tourist information centers, campgrounds (eg KOA), stores (eg Apple), bars and restaurants (including fast-food chains like McDonald's).

➡ Public libraries have internet terminals (online time may be limited, advance sign-up required and a nominal fee charged for out-of-network visitors) and free wi-fi.

MONEY

ATMs

➡ ATMs are available 24/7 at most banks, shopping malls, airports and grocery and convenience stores.

➡ Expect a minimum surcharge of around $3 per transaction, in addition to any fees charged by your home bank.

➡ Most ATMs are connected to international networks and offer decent foreign-exchange rates.

➡ Withdrawing cash from an ATM using a credit card usually incurs a hefty fee and high interest rates; contact your credit-card company for details and a PIN number.

Credit Cards

➡ Major credit cards are almost universally accepted. In fact, it's almost impossible to rent a car, book a hotel room or buy tickets over the phone without one. A credit card may also be vital in emergencies.

➡ Visa, MasterCard and American Express are the most widely accepted credit cards.

Money Changers

➡ You can exchange money at major airports, bigger banks and currency-exchange offices such as **American Express** (www.americanexpress.com) or **Travelex** (www.travelex.com). Always enquire about rates and fees.

➡ Outside big cities, exchanging money may be a problem, so make sure you have a credit card and sufficient cash on hand.

Taxes

➡ California state sales tax (7.25%) is added to the retail price of most goods and services (gasoline and groceries are exceptions). Local and city sales taxes may tack on up to 3%.

➡ Tourist lodging taxes vary statewide, but average 10.5% to 15.5% in major cities.

➡ No refunds of sales or lodging taxes are available for visitors.

OPENING HOURS

Businesses, restaurants and shops may close earlier and on additional days during the off-season (usually winter, except summer in the deserts). Otherwise, standard opening hours are as follows:

Banks 9am to 5pm Monday to Thursday, to 6pm Friday, some 9am to 1:30pm Saturday

Bars 5pm to 2am daily

Business hours (general) 9am to 5pm Monday to Friday

Pharmacies 8am to 9pm Monday to Friday, 9am to 5pm Saturday and Sunday, some 24 hours

Post offices 8:30am to 4:30pm Monday to Friday, some 9am to noon Saturday

Restaurants 7:30am to 10:30am, 11:30am to 2:30pm and 5pm to 9pm daily, some later Friday and Saturday

Shops 10am to 6pm Monday to Saturday, noon to 5pm Sunday (malls open later)

Supermarkets 8am to 9pm or 10pm daily, some 24 hours

Tipping Guide

Tipping is not optional. Only withhold tips in cases of outrageously bad service.

Airport skycaps and hotel bellhops $2 per bag, minimum $5 per cart

Bartenders 15% to 20% per round, minimum $1 per drink

Concierges Nothing for simple information, up to $20 for securing last-minute restaurant reservations, sold-out show tickets etc

Housekeeping staff $2 to $4 daily, left under the card provided; more if you're messy

Parking valets At least $2 when handed back your car keys

Restaurant servers and room service 18% to 20%, unless a gratuity is already charged (common for groups of six or more)

Taxi drivers 10% to 15% of metered fare, rounded up to the next dollar

HOLIDAYS

Public Holidays

On the following national holidays, banks, schools and government offices (including post offices) are closed, and transportation, museums and other services operate on a Sunday schedule. Holidays falling on a weekend are usually observed the following Monday.

New Year's Day January 1

Martin Luther King Jr Day Third Monday in January

Presidents' Day Third Monday in February

Good Friday Friday before Easter in March/April

Memorial Day Last Monday in May

Independence Day July 4

Labor Day First Monday in September

Indigenous Peoples' Day Second Monday in October

Veterans Day November 11

Thanksgiving Day Fourth Thursday in November

Christmas Day December 25

School Holidays

➡ High schools and colleges take a one- or two-week 'spring break' around Easter, sometime in March or April. Some hotels and resorts, especially along the coast, near SoCal's theme parks and in the deserts, raise their rates during this time.

➡ School summer vacations run from mid-June until mid-August, making July and August the busiest travel months almost everywhere except the deserts.

SAFE TRAVEL

Despite its seemingly apocalyptic list of dangers – guns, violent crime, riots, earthquakes – California is a reasonably safe place to visit. The greatest danger is posed by car accidents (buckle up – it's the law), while the biggest annoyances are metro-area traffic and crowds. When hiking or swimming in wilderness areas, be sure to understand the route, bring proper equipment and water, and read up on dangers such as rock slides, flash floods or riptides. Wildlife can also pose a threat.

Fire season in California has become significantly more severe in recent years, affecting travel in many areas of the state. Active fires can limit access to roads and destinations, including parks, and poor air quality can also become an issue.

Tourist areas most affected by fires and hazardous air in 2020 included the Santa Cruz Mountains, Napa and Sonoma Wine Country, Big Sur, Yosemite National Park, Point Reyes National Seashore, San Francisco, Los Angeles, Mojave National Preserve, Sequoia & Kings Canyon National Parks, Lake Tahoe and all of the state's national forests. For updated information about how wildfires may affect your trip, check the website of **Visit California** (www.visitcalifornia.com/experience/california-wildfire-travel-update). For more information about road closures, air-quality readings and wildfires, visit www.fire.ca.gov/incidents.

Earthquakes happen all the time, but most are so tiny they are detectable only by sensitive seismological instruments. Here's what to do if you're caught in a serious shaker:

➡ If indoors, get under a desk or table or stand in a doorway. Protect your head and stay clear of windows, mirrors or anything that might fall. Don't head for elevators or go running into the street. If you're in a shopping mall or large public building, expect the alarm and/or sprinkler systems to come on.

➡ If outdoors, get away from buildings, trees and power lines. If you're on a sidewalk near buildings, duck into a doorway to protect yourself from falling bricks, glass and debris. If you're driving, pull over to the side of the road away from bridges, overpasses and power lines. Stay inside the car until the shaking stops.

➡ Prepare for aftershocks. Turn on the radio and listen for bulletins. Use the telephone only if absolutely necessary.

TELEPHONE

➡ US phone numbers consist of a three-digit area code followed by a seven-digit local number.

➡ When dialing a number within the same area code, use the seven-digit number (if that doesn't work, try all 10 digits).

➡ For long-distance calls, dial 1 plus the area code plus the local number.

➡ Toll-free numbers begin with 800, 844, 855, 866, 877 or 888 and must be preceded by 1.

Important Numbers

Country code ☏ 1

International dialing code ☏ 011

Operator ☏ 0

Emergency (ambulance, fire, police) ☏ 911

Directory assistance (local) ☏ 411

→ For direct international calls, dial 011 plus the country code plus the area code (usually without the initial '0') plus the local phone number.

→ If you're calling Canada, the country code is 1 (the same as for the US, but beware international rates apply between the two countries).

Cell Phones

→ You'll need a multiband GSM phone to make calls in the USA. Popping in a US prepaid rechargeable SIM card is usually cheaper than using your own network.

→ SIM cards are sold at telecommunications and electronics stores. These stores also sell inexpensive prepaid phones, including some airtime.

Payphones & Phonecards

→ Where payphones still exist, they're usually coin-operated, although some may only accept credit cards (eg in national parks). Local calls usually cost 50¢ minimum.

→ For long-distance calls, you're usually better off buying a prepaid phonecard, sold at supermarkets, pharmacies, newsstands and electronics and convenience stores.

TOURIST INFORMATION

→ For pre-trip planning, peruse the information-packed website **Visit California** (www.visitcalifornia.com).

→ The same government agency operates more than a dozen statewide **California Welcome Centers** (www.visitcwc.com), where staff dispense maps and brochures and may be able to help find accommodations.

→ Almost every city and town has a local visitor center or a chamber of commerce where you can pick up maps, brochures and information.

TRAVELERS WITH DISABILITIES

More-populated areas of coastal California are reasonably well equipped for travelers with disabilities, but facilities in smaller towns and rural areas may be limited.

Download Lonely Planet's free Accessible Travel guide from https://shop.lonelyplanet.com/products/accessible-travel-online-resources-2019.

Accessibility

→ Most traffic intersections have dropped curbs and sometimes have audible crossing signals.

→ The Americans with Disabilities Act (ADA) requires public buildings built after 1993 to be wheelchair-accessible, including restrooms.

→ Motels and hotels built after 1993 must have at least one ADA–compliant accessible room; state your specific needs when making reservations.

→ For nonpublic buildings built prior to 1993, including hotels, restaurants, museums and theaters, there are no accessibility guarantees; call ahead to find out what to expect.

→ Most national and many state parks and some other outdoor recreation areas offer paved or boardwalk-style nature trails accessible by wheelchairs.

→ Many theme parks go out of their way to be accessible to wheelchairs and guests with mobility limitations and other disabilities.

Communications

→ Telephone companies provide relay operators (dial 711) for the hearing-impaired.

→ Many banks provide ATM instructions in braille.

Discount Passes

→ US citizens and permanent residents with a permanent disability qualify for a free lifetime **'America the Beautiful' Access Pass** (https://store.usgs.gov/access-pass), which waives entry fees to all national parks and federal recreational lands and offers 50% discounts on some recreation fees (eg camping). If you order a pass online, there is a $10 processing fee.

→ California State Parks' lifetime disabled discount pass ($3.50) entitles those with permanent disabilities to 50% off day-use parking and camping fees; for an application, go to www.parks.ca.gov.

Helpful Resources

A Wheelchair Rider's Guide to the California Coast (www.wheelingcalscoast.org) Free accessibility information covering beaches, parks and trails, plus downloadable PDF guides to the San Francisco Bay Area and Los Angeles and Orange County coasts.

Access Northern California (http://accessnca.org) Links to accessible-travel resources, publications, tours and transportation, including outdoor recreation opportunities.

Visit San Diego (http://access-sandiego.org) Tourism office's list of resources for disabled visitors.

Achieve Tahoe (http://achievetahoe.org) Organizes summer and winter sports and 4WD adventures around Lake Tahoe in the Sierra Nevada.

Disabled Sports Eastern Sierra (http://disabledsportseasternsierra.org) Offers summer and winter outdoor activity programs around Mammoth Lakes.

Los Angeles for Disabled Visitors (www.discoverlosangeles.com/travel/the-guide-to-disability-access-in-los-angeles) Tips for accessible sightseeing, entertainment and transportation.

Tapooz Travel (www.tapooztravel.com) Travel agency organizing personalized itineraries, including accessible road trips, for travelers with disabilities, mobility issues and other special needs.

Wheelchair Traveling (www.wheelchair-traveling.com) Travel tips, lodging and helpful California destination info.

Yosemite National Park Accessibility (www.nps.gov/yose/planyourvisit/accessibility.htm) Detailed, downloadable accessibility information for Yosemite National Park, including sign-language interpretation services (usually available by advance request).

Transportation

➡ All major airlines, Greyhound buses and Amtrak trains can accommodate people with disabilities, usually with 48 hours of advance notice required.

➡ Major car-rental agencies offer hand-controlled vehicles, but you must reserve these well in advance. Vans with wheelchair lifts are not typically available in the US from the major car-rental agencies.

➡ For wheelchair-accessible van rentals, also try **Wheelchair Getaways** (☎888-432-9339; www.wheelchairgetaways.com) in Sacramento, San Diego, San Francisco and Los Angeles or **Mobility Works** (☎877-275-4915; www.mobilityworks.com) in Los Angeles (multiple locations), San Diego, San Francisco, Oakland, San Jose and Sacramento.

➡ Local buses, trains and subway lines usually have wheelchair lifts. Service dogs are permitted to accompany passengers on public transportation.

➡ Taxi companies have at least one wheelchair-accessible van, but you'll usually need to call and then wait for one.

VISAS

➡ Visa information is highly subject to change. Depending on your country of origin, the rules for entering the USA keep changing. Double-check current visa requirements *before* coming to the USA.

➡ As of 2020, under the US Visa Waiver Program (VWP), visas are not required for citizens of 39 countries for stays up to 90 days (no extensions) as long as you have a machine-readable passport that meets current US standards and is valid for six months beyond your intended stay.

➡ Citizens of VWP countries must still register with the **Electronic System for Travel Authorization** (ESTA; https://esta.cbp.dhs.gov) at least 72 hours before travel. Once approved, ESTA registration ($14) is valid for up to two years or until your passport expires, whichever comes first.

➡ For most Canadian citizens traveling with Canadian passports that meet current US standards, a visa for short-term visits (usually up to six months) and ESTA registration aren't required.

➡ Citizens from all other countries, or whose passports don't meet US standards, need to apply for a visa in their home country. The process has a nonrefundable fee (minimum $160), involves a personal interview and can take several weeks, so apply as early as possible.

➡ For up-to-date information about entry requirements and eligibility, check the visa section of the **US Department of State website** (http://travel.state.gov), or contact the nearest USA embassy or consulate in your home country (for a complete list, visit www.usembassy.gov).

BEHIND THE SCENES

SEND US YOUR FEEDBACK

We love to hear from travelers – your comments help make our books better. We read every word, and we guarantee that your feedback goes straight to the authors. Visit **lonelyplanet. com/contact** to submit your updates and suggestions.

Note: We may edit, reproduce and incorporate your comments in Lonely Planet products such as guidebooks, websites and digital products, so let us know if you don't want your comments reproduced or your name acknowledged. For a copy of our privacy policy visit lonelyplanet.com/privacy.

WRITER THANKS

AMY BALFOUR

Big thanks to the following locals, former locals and ski fans who shared their favorite places in Tahoe, Reno and the Gold Country: Chris Crossen, Kerrie Tonking, Roy Pillay, Todd Frick, Lacy Davidson, Julee Messerich, Blakely Atherton and Tom Phillips. Special thanks to Amy & Chris Rose for your friendship, hospitality and recs for Reno and the outdoors. Thanks also to Brandon Dekema, Mike Roe and Lucy Anderson for the great local leads and contacts.

ACKNOWLEDGEMENTS

Climate map data adapted from Peel MC, Finlayson BL & McMahon TA (2007) 'Updated World Map of the Köppen-Geiger Climate Classification', *Hydrology and Earth System Sciences*, 11, 1633–44.

Front cover photographs (clockwise from top): Sunrise over Emerald Bay, Lake Tahoe, Dennis Frates/Alamy Stock Photo©; Mailboxes in Sausalito, Susanne Kremer/4Corners Images©; Chevrolet Bel Air in Joshua Tree National Park, Susanne Kremer/4Corners Images©

Back cover photograph: Golden Gate Bridge framed by old cypress trees at Presidio Parkk, San Francisco, Scott Wilson/Alamy Stock Photo©

THIS BOOK

This 4th edition of Lonely Planet's *California's Best Trips* guidebook was researched and written by Amy Balfour, Brett Atkinson, Andrew Bender, Alison Bing, Cristian Bonetto, Celeste Brash, Jade Bremner, Bailey Freeman, Michael Grosberg, Ashley Harrell, Mark Johanson, Andrea Schulte-Peevers, Wendy Yanagihara. The previous two editions were written by Sara Benson, Nate Cavalieri and Beth Kohn. This guidebook was produced by the following:

Senior Product Editors Grace Dobell, Daniel Bolger

Regional Senior Cartographer Alison Lyall

Cartographer Mark Griffiths

Product Editor Amy Lynch

Book Designer Fergal Condon

Coordinating Editors Brana Vladisavljevic

Assisting Editors Sarah Bailey, Monique Perrin, Mani Ramaswamy, Kirsten Rawlings, Tamara Sheward, Gabrielle Stefanos, Simon Williamson

Cover Researcher Brendan Dempsey-Spencer

Thanks to Sasha Drew, Sandie Kestell, Genna Patterson, Angela Tinson

INDEX

T